Writing to Clients and Referring Professionals About Psychological Assessment Results

Writing to Clients and Referring Professionals About Psychological Assessment Results

A HANDBOOK OF STYLE AND GRAMMAR

J. B. Allyn

FOREWORDS BY STEPHEN E. FINN AND CONSTANCE T. FISCHER

Routledge
Taylor & Francis Group
New York   London

Routledge
Taylor & Francis Group
711 Third Avenue
New York, NY 10017

Routledge
Taylor & Francis Group
27 Church Road
Hove, East Sussex BN3 2FA

Printed in the United States of America on acid-free paper
Version Date: 2011902

International Standard Book Number: 978-0-415-89123-3 (Hardback) 978-0-415-89124-0 (Paperback)

Library of Congress Cataloging-in-Publication Data

Allyn, J. B. (Janet B.)
    Writing to clients and referring professionals about psychological assessment results : a handbook of style and grammar / Janet B. Allyn.
        p. cm.
    Includes bibliographical references and index.
    ISBN 978-0-415-89123-3 (hardback) -- ISBN 978-0-415-89124-0 (paperback)
    1. Psychology--Methodology. 2. Behavioral assessment. 3. Psychodiagnostics.
    4. Report writing. 5. English language--Writing. I. Title.

BF38.5.A458 2012
808.06'615--dc23   2011033325

Visit the Taylor & Francis Web site at
http://www.taylorandfrancis.com

and the Routledge Web site at
http://www.routledgementalhealth.com

Contents

Foreword   xi
Stephen E. Finn, PhD

Foreword   xiii
Constance T. Fischer, PhD, ABPP

Acknowledgments   xv
Introduction   xvii

PART I   Building Blocks of the Report: Attitude, Tone, Style, and Voice

Chapter 1   Attitude: The Writer's View   5

What Is Attitude in Writing?   6
    Attitude Toward Your Own Writing   7
    Attitude Toward Your Subject and Audience   9
What Influences Attitude?   10
Attitude and Your Reader   12

Chapter 2   Tone: Words and More   17

Formality in Tone   19
Formality and Contractions   22
Word Choice   22
    Accuracy and Clarity   23
    Clarity Versus Variety   25
    Denotation and Connotation   26
Selecting Material and Subtext   27
Juxtaposition and Finn's Levels 1, 2, 3   28

Chapter 3   Style: Content Plus Structure   31

Beginning, Middle, and End   33
Communication Qualities: Clarity and Accuracy   34
Communication Qualities: Specificity   35
    Concrete Versus Abstract Terms   37
    Abstraction and Hayakawa's Ladder   38

Communication Qualities: Sensitivity, Compassion,
Respect for Your Subject and Reader 40
Jettison Unnecessary Jargon 42
Clear Away Clutter 43
Energize Text 44
   Dynamic Versus Linking Verbs 45
   "Smothered" Verbs 47
   Active Versus Passive Structure 48

Chapter 4   Voice: What Is It and How Do I Find It? 49

Active Versus Passive Voice in Sentence Structure 49
Using Active and Passive Voice 52
Narrative Voice/Point of View 53
   Third Person 54
   First Person and Second Person 55
Stylistic Voice 55
   Narrative Stance 58
   Neutral Voice and Objectivity in Writing 59

PART II Mortar to Fortify the Building Blocks: Grammar and Editing

Chapter 5   Big Picture, Small Details: Format, Write, Edit, Proof 67

Formatting 68
   Choosing Font: Style and Size 68
   Ordering Sections and Content 69
   Possible Formats 72
   Using an Outline 74
   An Alternative Approach to Outlining 76
Writing 77
Evaluating and Editing 78
Proofing 79

Chapter 6   Content that Communicates: Sentences and Paragraphs 81

Sentence: What Is It and How Is It Structured? 81
   Initial Decisions 82

Sentence Structure	83
Basic Sentence	83
Sentence Order	84
Varying Your Sentences	86
Paragraph: How Do Sentences Build Into Paragraphs?	87
Building the Paragraph	88
Standard Phrases for Reports	89
Parallel Structure	90
Fillers, Redundancies, and Unnecessary Phrases	92
Assessing Readability	93
Readability Tools: Various Formulas	94

Chapter 7 Reaching Agreement: Subject–Verb, Pronoun, and Gender 99

Verb Tenses	100
"Mood" in Grammar	101
Verb Pairs: Which to Use?	101
Used To Versus *Use To*	102
Can Versus *May*	103
Fewer Versus *Less*	103
Lay Versus *Lie*	104
Raise Versus *Rise*	104
Set Versus *Sit*	104
Subject–Verb Agreement	105
Intervening Words	106
Compound Subjects	107
Collective Nouns	107
Additional Subject–Verb Agreement Challenges	108
Pronouns	109
Selecting Pronouns	110
Indefinite Pronouns	111
Gender Neutrality in Pronouns	111
Pronoun as Subject or Object	114
Prepositions	116

Chapter 8 Modifying the Main Idea: Adjectives and Adverbs 119

Adjectives	120
Articles = Adjectives	120
Using Adjectives of Quantity	120
Compound Adjectives	122

Placing Adjectives 122
Adverbs 124
Splitting Verbs With Adverbs 124
Adjectives, Adverbs, and Linking Verbs 125
Degrees of Comparison in Adjectives and Adverbs 126
Avoiding Ambiguity and Awkwardness 127
Separating Related Words 129
Misplacing Modifiers 129
Constructing Awkward Adverbs 129
Adding Too Many Adjectives or Adverbs 129
Modifying Absolutes 129
Using *Hope*fully and *How*ever 130
To + Base Verb: To Split or Not to Split 131

Chapter 9   Precision: Right Word, Right Spelling   133

Spelling in the Body of a Word 135
Prefixes and Suffixes 135
Spelling Plural Nouns 136
Numbers: Digits or Words? 137
Spelling Words That Sound Alike 138
Effect Versus *Affect* 138
Other Words Easily Confused 142
Abbreviations and Acronyms 142
Capital Letters 144
When Not to Capitalize 147
Spelling Variations and Modern Usage 147

**Chapter 10 Guiding the Reader: Punctuate and Connect for
Clarity   149**

Independent and Dependent Clauses 150
Connecting for Clarity 150
Punctuation Marks: How and Why We Use Them 151
Periods and Semicolons 152
Commas 153
Recognizing Fragments and Run-on Sentences 154
Colons 157
Hyphens and Dashes 159
Apostrophes 161
Quotation Marks 162
Ellipsis 165

Connecting Words Revisited: Special Challenges 165
Although, Though, While 166
Since 166
Like Versus *Such as* 166
That Versus *Which* 167
Beginning a Sentence With a Conjunction 168

PART III Beyond the Report: Extending Clear and Effective Communication

Chapter 11 Continuing the Therapeutic Goals: Writing Letters and Stories 173

Letter to the Individual Assessed: An Overview 174
Tone in Letters Written as Feedback 175
Can a Letter of Written Feedback Be "Therapeutic"? 175
A Clinician's Approach: Assessing Personal Warmth in Letters to the Person Assessed 177
Metaphor: A Bridge Between Fact and Truth 178
Conceptual Metaphor: Everyday Life 180
Metaphor and the Brain 183
Therapeutic Stories 184
Children's Stories: Fables 185
Adult and Adolescent Stories: Allegories 187
Narrative and Dialogue 188

Chapter 12 Richness, Texture, Safety, and Risk: Communicating Verbally 191

Written Versus Spoken Communication 193
Richness and Texture in Communication 194
"Voice" in Speech 195
Pacing and Pauses 196
Loudness and Pitch 196
Interruptions and Overlap 197
Report-Talk Versus Rapport-Talk 198
Nonverbal Cues 198
Active Listening 200
Communicating When Fear Equals Risk 202

Glossary of Terms: Grammar, Style, and Communication   205

References   213

Index   221

Foreword

"This book aims to make effective writing and clear communication a bit less hard, if not outright easy." So begins J.B. Allyn's helpful and inspiring book, *Writing to Clients and Referring Professionals about Psychological Assessment Results: A Handbook of Style and Grammar*, and Allyn achieves this goal with lucidity and grace. It may seem hyperbole to call a text on such topics as writing style, grammar, and sentence structure inspiring. But I challenge even experienced psychological assessors to read this book and not come away with a renewed commitment to clearer communication in their assessment reports. Also, those of us who teach psychological assessment have been waiting for a book like this to give to our graduate students. For Allyn not only deals with practical issues such as subject–verb agreement, punctuation, and spelling, but also with advanced topics such as attitude, tone, and voice—aspects of report writing that are not touched upon in any assessment text I know. Her chapter on writing letters and stories to clients in Collaborative/Therapeutic Assessment is novel and contemporary. I greatly appreciated Allyn's down-to-earth, non-preachy tone. For example, instead of just repeating the age-old admonition against using passive voice, she intelligently discusses instances when passive voice makes sense. Allyn even talks about times when it may be better to split an infinitive! This book is an invaluable resource for any psychological assessor who writes in English, and I hope it becomes widely known and used. In these 12 highly readable chapters, J.B. Allyn may single-handedly raise the standard-of-practice in psychological assessment for generations to come.

Stephen E. Finn, PhD
Center for Therapeutic Assessment
Austin, Texas

Foreword

This is a stand-out volume, far exceeding the standard manuals on grammar and style (writing conventions). It is written specifically for psychologists, but is useful and even inspiring for all writers. The goal throughout is to encourage clear, powerful, and memorable writing, both to other professionals and to clients. Allyn herself writes in just that way. Her expertise and creativity reflects her experience in theater, writing, and in coauthoring psychological reports in the form of fables for clients.

I imagine that while consulting this book, most of us often will find ourselves thinking, "Right, I knew that, but I'd forgotten, and never understood the principle so clearly." Allyn cites sources and history, but always in an interesting, conversational manner. Her tone is never dictatorial or authoritarian. Her suggestions invite one to craft, not just write, documents, and to do so with multiple readers in mind.

The many tables are concrete, clear, and helpful. I anticipate using them not just for my own writing, but also when penning notes to graduate students on papers and dissertations—naming the principle and/or table instead of having to spell out what should be done.

Writing to Clients and Referring Professionals is a keeper. I anticipate seeing it in colleagues' and students' offices for years to come.

Constance T. Fischer, PhD, ABPP
Psychology Department
Duquesne University

Acknowledgments

Creating a book takes the efforts of a small community, with each member offering different skills and perspectives. Stephen Finn founded that community when he heard a talk I gave and said, "This should be published." At Routledge, editor George Zimmar saw value in the topic and expanded its approach. Marta Moldvai organized endless details with grace and patience, and Prudence Board efficiently steered the book on its final journey through production.

Constance Fischer encouraged the book's creation by her enthusiasm for the English language. Irving Weiner gave helpful suggestions early in the writing process, and Hale Martin shared thoughtful ideas at various stages. The Society for Personality Assessment provided a welcoming home for a series of panels on effective writing and communicating in psychological assessment. This book evolved from those panels and the contributions of their participants: Cynthia Austin, Diane Engelman, Erin Jacklin, Lauren Krumholtz, Melissa Lehmann, Noriko Nakamura, Caroline Purves, and Deborah Tharinger.

Diane Engelman reviewed every chapter—some more than once—with the same specificity she brings to assessment work. She also supported me with friendship, laughter, and encouragement during the many months of writing. Steven Frankel provided quiet moral support throughout. Skye Davis supplied sanity breaks and advice on the book's visual aspects. My brother and niece, Dave Balding and Juli Balding, contributed humor, great meals, and unqualified understanding during the months I lived at my computer. Dave also shared stories of communication challenges on the front lines of corporate America and in the military.

Over time, writing can become as spontaneous as speaking or breathing. I don't remember exactly where and how I learned the basic tenets of written and spoken communication, but I thank a lifetime of teachers who guided me. I also thank the students who helped me to learn more as I taught them. Finally, I dedicate this book to my parents, who by example taught me to love reading, and to Daryl D. Allen, who encouraged me to write.

Introduction

A psychological assessor and colleague asked me, a writer, "How does a person decide what voice to have in her writing?"

Writer: It isn't so much that we decide on a voice. It's made up of other things—attitude, tone, style. They build on each other and create voice in our writing.

Assessor: I can see tone or style in fiction. But do they really show up in professional and technical writing? In psychological assessment reports?

Writer: They do, whether we recognize them or not. For instance …

Assessor: Wait. *This* is what you should present at the next conference. Other assessors probably have the same questions. We can really use this information.

The audience of psychological assessors responded positively to that conference presentation and this book grew out of it.

Why a Writing Handbook for Psychological Assessors?

As well as giving a verbal report of their findings, assessors create written reports. The books that are available in the psychological field suggest structure and give examples of assessment reports. Most also include diagnostic terms and methods of phrasing information. All of this information is valuable for the assessor. But few of these books give even brief attention to writing itself. Little is said about how to solve grammatical concerns or how to write in a way that communicates information clearly to the reader. Written reports carry the assessor's name out into the larger world. Writing those reports according to standard usage of the English language provides that larger world a clearer picture of the assessor's abilities.

Countless books and online sources give tips on grammar. Many touch on tone and style, and a few mention attitude. Some embrace varying perspectives on voice. But none of those books on the skill and craft of writing specifically addresses the concerns of psychological assessors and graduate students training in assessment. The books use examples from mainstream business and personal writing, not from psychological reports. While useful, those standard references do not directly address the assessor-writer's needs.

"Writing is hard, even for authors who do it all the time," writes American essayist Roger Angell in his foreword to Strunk and White's classic *The Elements of Style* (2000, p. ix). But how much harder for the writer when the ins-and-outs of grammar are understandably a secondary focus to the ins and outs of the human mind. Graduation from a four-year college or university can carry with it an unrealistic assumption: that the graduate has learned all the English grammar and writing skill needed and will retain it indefinitely. This impression remains, even if she majored in a science or he took no English course beyond 101. Plunging directly into graduate studies in psychology, the student has all s/he can handle learning the technicalities of the field, including how to administer, score, and interpret assessment measures. Building and maintaining a clear writing style is the last thing s/he is likely to worry about. And even if s/he does, little help with writing may be available.

After achieving that hard-earned advanced degree, the new psychological assessor must write reports for a range of audiences: referring professionals, schools, agencies, courts, adult clients, and parents. Even after being in practice for some time, the challenge of writing well remains a factor; each report for each client must be readable and understandable. Psychologist and assessor Constance Fischer (1994) writes of the importance of indexing testing situations to the client's other life events when writing reports. In doing this, either verbally or in writing, the assessor puts words not only to the assessment results, but also to essential aspects of the person's life and history. Communicating all of the important components of an assessment requires confidence and skill. When an assessor communicates effectively, the report's recipient is more likely to hear and understand—whether that person be the person assessed or a third party. Effective writing is a tool toward that end.

How Can a Nonassessor Writer Give Advice on Writing Psychological Assessment Reports?

For the psychological assessor, the assessment process is the area in which s/he is trained; writing is merely the mechanism for communicating results. For the writer, however, writing *is* the specialty area. Words, sentences, structure, grammar, and style are subjects in which the writer has training and experience. And if that writer's experience includes technical writing—that is, translating specialty concepts and words into plain English—and editing psychological reports, we begin to see how assessment reports and writing might meet in a nonassessor. Assume, too, that this writer has a background in teaching written and spoken communications and in tutoring both English and writing. Finally, assume that the writer has worked for several years with a neuropsychologist, collaborating on many writing projects and conference presentations. The neuropsychologist provides the writer thoughtful answers to questions about psychology and assessment and generously shares her library. Though this writer has a "foot in two worlds," so to speak, she would not presume to write a book about the psychological content of assessment reports. Her topic would be her own specialty area—effective written and spoken communications and how to apply those in the assessment arena. All of these descriptors apply to me, this book's author, and to my approach in creating this handbook.

How to Use This Book

This book is both a reference and a tutorial on writing style and grammar. I geared it toward the individual practitioner who writes reports to the person assessed or to third parties. Some students may decide individually that the book will be useful in learning to write more effectively and/or as a grammar reference. For others, a teacher or supervisor may recommend the book to strengthen writing skills. The practicing psychological assessor with periodic questions on grammar or style may also use the book as reference. Not everyone needs all chapters or points within chapters. Feel free to move around to different sections and look up specific writing challenges as they occur.

Only Part I (Chapters 1–4) benefits from being read in sequence, since the components discussed in its four chapters—attitude, tone, style, and voice—build on each other. Part II (Chapters 5–10) is a grammar handbook, with each topic standing alone. Part III (Chapters 11 and 12) expands the topic of effective writing into wider effective communication. It covers personal letters written in place of a report, therapeutic stories, and aspects of verbal and nonverbal communication.

What This Book Attempts to Do—and What It Does Not

For assessor-writers, writing is likely a tool, not a calling. This book intends to give guidelines that clarify rather than confuse. The respected *Publication Manual of the American Psychological Association* guides those who write for publication in the world of psychology, and psychology students have been schooled in its conventions. More than a dozen other style manuals exist, however, and among them, some details conflict—for example, information on capitalization. In writer Jefferson D. Bates's *Writing with Precision* (2000), he discusses the variation in rules among different manuals, and then says, "My editorial philosophy is to make clear communication easier" (p. 179). That philosophy is also the goal of this writing handbook for assessors. Its guidance on English grammar presents composite information from different sources in as straightforward a manner as possible. It also points out the abundance of gray areas in English grammar where individual judgment is called for. Being sensitive to your audience—and in some cases that will be a teacher or editor with his or her own requirements for writing—will help you to make those choices thoughtfully.

In writing, the word *style* can be used in two ways: (a) to reflect the individual writer's way of writing and (b) to refer to the conventions of writing according to a certain set of guidelines (e.g., *Chicago Manual of Style*). This book primarily addresses the first meaning as it relates to well-written standard English. It does not attempt to give a thorough overview of all style manuals encompassed by the second meaning. In deference, however, to the APA *Publication Manual* as the standard in psychological writing, this book refers to APA's conventions in many situations.

What the Book Contains

Information in the book divides into three parts. Each chapter provides tables or bullet lists of examples based on that chapter's topics. Part I contains four chapters. They present attitude, tone, style, and voice as "building blocks" that lead to clear communication between the assessor-writer and the reader of an assessment report, be they referring professionals or the person assessed.

Chapter 1 discusses attitude as the starting point in a report. It illustrates the benefit of the assessor-writer's being conscious of his or her attitude in three areas before writing a report: (a) toward the assessor's own writing ability, (b) toward the person assessed, and (c) toward the report's intended reader. The chapter also examines the downside of being unaware of attitude and how it can derail communication. Chapter 2 moves on to talk about tone, the quality that demonstrates the writer's attitude in word choice, phrasing, and arrangement of data. It examines how juxtaposition can magnify nuance in the context of rank-ordering assessment results. Chapter 3 presents style as the point where attitude and tone meet grammar and structure. It describes (a) a defined beginning, middle, and end as essential in a written document and (b) the importance of clear sentences that reflect the assessor-writer's sensitivity to the reader. It discusses jargon, cluttered writing, and linking (static) verbs. Chapter 4 reaches the last building block of Part I, that of voice. It discusses the difference between active and passive sentences, between tentative and definite phrasing. The chapter then moves into voice as depicted in first-, second-, and third-person narration. Finally, it explores the conscious or unconscious steps that contribute to stylistic voice, how it can be discerned, and the role of neutral voice. It also talks about the process by which research and data, questions asked and answered, and the assessor-writer's narrative stance contribute to voice.

Part II forms the longest section of the book; it is a grammar reference section of issues frequently encountered by the assessor-writer. These chapters envision grammar as the mortar that binds the writer's building blocks from Part I.

Chapter 5 sets a context for the beginning, middle, and end of a report. It discusses the importance of knowing who your reader is and techniques for planning the flow of material, either using a checklist or a standard outline. It gives steps for expanding the content, discusses when to edit, and gives suggestions for proofreading. Chapter 6 explores how to craft sentences that clearly express ideas and how to grow them into paragraphs. It also covers topic and transitional sentences, sentence and paragraph length, parallel structure, filler phrases, and how to assess readability. Chapter 7 delves further into the sentence. It discusses challenges with subject–verb agreement, compound subjects, and reconciling pronouns with the words they refer to. It also examines past and present verb tenses in writing assessment reports, since different sections of a report require different tenses. Chapter 8 covers adjectives and adverbs: what they modify, how to place them accurately in the sentence, how to use them judiciously, and when to hyphenate compound forms. It also explains degrees of comparison for both regular and irregular words and gives examples of the most challenging. Chapter 9 discusses the importance of choosing the right word and spelling it correctly. It gives examples of words that sound alike but are spelled differently and mean different things. It addresses prefixes, suffixes, and plural forms as well as the use of abbreviations, acronyms, and capital letters. The chapter also illustrates when to write numbers as numerals and when to spell them out. Chapter 10 covers punctuation, which can stymie even full-time writers. It discusses when and how to use hyphens, colons, semicolons, apostrophes, quotation marks, and periods, with special attention paid to commas. It illustrates how to recognize fragments and run-on sentences and discusses the words *that* and *which* in relation to comma use.

Part III extends the concept and techniques of clear communication beyond the standard assessment report. It explores approaches used in the subset of assessment known as Collaborative/Therapeutic Assessment (C/TA), which emphasizes the importance of language and clear communication in the practice of psychological assessment.

Chapter 11 expands and refines the process of report writing into two documents that can be used as therapeutic interventions with the person assessed. First, it discusses writing a more informal letter in place of a standard report, and second, it explores creating a therapeutic, metaphorical story as an extension of the letter or as individual intervention. Chapter 12 explores tenets of clear yet sensitive verbal communication and nonverbal cues. This area provides a critical foundation for C/TA and is important within the larger field of assessment. As in earlier chapters on written communication, this chapter discusses the value and strength of clarity, precision, accuracy, and compassion. It also examines the unique challenges of verbal and nonverbal communication in the assessment context, incorporating both linguistic and sociological perspectives.

Throughout these chapters, this book aims to make effective writing and clear communication a bit less hard, if not outright easy.

PART **I**

BUILDING BLOCKS
OF THE REPORT

Attitude, Tone, Style, and Voice

Although symbols existed in various cultures in antiquity, the Sumerians are generally attributed with creating written text in approximately 3200 BCE (Wilford, 1999). Writing about medical and scientific topics in the English language began over 1,000 years ago. During those centuries, scientific writing shifted back and forth between a more detached style and a more involved one. It also moved from extensive use of Latin vocabulary to simpler words and style (Taavitsainen & Pahta, 2004). Nevertheless, even simpler scientific style can be difficult to follow for anyone not accustomed to it. When the assessor-writer begins to write reports, s/he may rely on scientific writing. But the intended reader of these reports may not be trained in psychological assessment or even in a scientific field. For that reason, the assessor-writer needs to find a way of writing that is professional and clear for anyone who reads the report.

To reach that point, we move back toward the writing we learned in school, so-called literary writing. The word *literary,* however, can conjure visions of fiction writing, so we will refer to it simply as effective writing. Types of writing encompassed under that heading are

1. *Descriptive*: describes a person, place, or thing
2. *Informative*: gives information or explains
3. *Narrative*: relates a series of events
4. *Persuasive*: attempts to convince the reader (Warriner, 1988, p. 64)

Of these types, persuasive may be used less often and more judiciously in the assessment report: Attempting to persuade your reader may not be the intent of your report or the requirement of your client. Various sections and paragraphs of your report, though, will rely on descriptive, informative, and narrative types of writing.

In the four chapters on effective writing style, most especially in Chapter 4, "Voice," you encounter the concept of *narrative*. Narrative is a term often applied to fictional storytelling, but it has a larger meaning. Narrative is the way that we connect events over time and make sense of the whole. In writing, as well as speech, humans tend to "link events narratively" (Richardson, 1990, p. 21). Some of you will be familiar with the term from the field of narrative therapy that focuses on "the stories of people's lives" (Narrative therapy, n.d.). In writing assessment reports, too, you will be employing narrative to tie together the parts of your assessment. One of the basic qualities of effective narrative is clarity, without needless embellishment.

Psychologist and assessor Gary Groth-Marnat writes of four types of assessment reports—literary, clinical, scientific, and professional (2009a). He believes that few reports fall 100% into the first three categories, suggesting that the assessor-writer may need to use aspects of all three. He describes professional style as including "short words in common usage and that have precise meanings" (p. 561) and cites R. L. Ownby in stressing that approach to writing the overall report. That approach parallels this book's perspective on effective writing.

Whether writing a report for a third-party referring professional or directly to the person assessed, clear communication is essential. As one assessor put it, "Effective writing is critical for effective assessment" (D. H. Engelman, personal communication, May 2010). Even when writing to a third party, the assessor

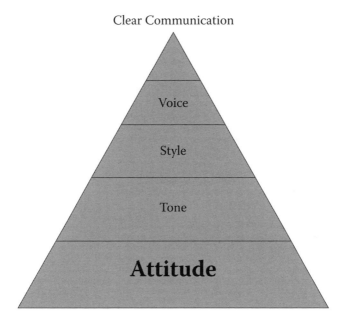

Clear Communication

Voice

Style

Tone

Attitude

FIGURE P1.1 Building blocks of the assessment report.

can assume that the person assessed may read the report at some point. With that in mind, effective communication must also include awareness of and sensitivity to all potential readers.

The chapters in Part I build a pyramid of effective writing style, as shown in Figure P1.1. Clear communication sits as the capstone on that pyramid. Topics in these chapters are interrelated and yet build on each other. Starting with attitude, the chapters proceed through tone, style, and voice in writing. And since writing style is not detachable from content and grammar (Strunk & White, 2000), they, too, weave through these four chapters. In turn, some issues that are more stylistic show up in Part II's chapters on grammar. Style and grammar work together to create impact in the content of your report.

CHAPTER 1

Attitude
The Writer's View

You must not come lightly to the blank page.

Stephen King, American writer

"I never take this lightly. I worry every step of the way—about my writing and about how I phrase facts and inferences in my report," commented a psychological assessor after reading the King quote that opens the chapter (D. H. Engelman, personal communication, September 2010). Attitude marks the assessor's starting place for crafting the report; attitude is often values-driven and subliminal, though simple words or phrases can reveal it. Consciously recognizing attitude gives the writer greater control over the impact of written material, strengthening his or her ability to communicate essential data. Who is the intended reader of your report? Is the relationship between assessor and reader direct or implied? What is the purpose in communicating with that person? Is there a secondary audience? Who? And not least important, what is the assessor-writer's attitude toward his or her own writing abilities? These questions and their answers guide awareness of attitude in writing (see Figure 1.1).

This chapter discusses how written material can convey the assessor-writer's view of the subject of a report. This material can also demonstrate his or her stance toward the intended audience, whether that be the person assessed, a judge, an educator, or a clinician. Attitude and tone—the latter discussed in the chapter that follows—are less about the basic steps in effective

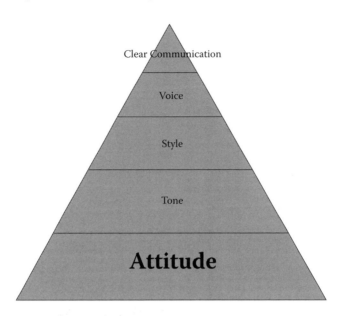

FIGURE 1.1 Building blocks of the assessment report: Attitude.

writing and more about your motivation for communicating in the first place.

What Is Attitude in Writing?

The word *attitude* in popular usage refers to a person who appears haughty, cocky, or "full of himself." While that may, indeed, apply in some cases, we will discuss attitude here in its larger definition: "A manner of acting, feeling, or thinking that *shows* one's disposition or opinion [italics added]" (Webster's, 2001).

Regardless how objective a writer intends to be, attitude will be the grounding for what becomes the written word. Even factual material conveys the writer's attitude toward a subject through the choice to include or not include facts as well as by the words used to describe those facts (Gerard, 2000). Attitude can remain unconscious. Yet, when left unconscious, it complicates the writer's task. It can selectively influence which facts are given and the words used to express them. The writer might easily be unaware that attitude is driving the bus. By bringing attitude to consciousness, we can carefully choose our facts and words. This conscious choice gives greater control over our material and our ability to communicate important information. (For more on care in choosing words, see Chapter 2.)

Two forms of attitude can affect your writing:

- Attitude toward yourself and your abilities (in both writing and assessment)
- Attitude toward the subject of the assessment as well as the audience who will read the report

We will examine both through the lens of cognitive psychology of the past 30 years, focusing on development in children's writing. We all began as children. We then went through varying lengths and depths of training in writing and English, so we can readily apply the findings to our writing as adults.

Attitude Toward Your Own Writing

Studies indicate that those with a more positive attitude toward their ability to write are likely to be more productive with the written word than those whose attitude is negative. In addition, negative writing attitudes may demand more effort cognitively than do positive attitudes (Zumbrunn, 2010). By extension, the more a person knows about writing and has confidence in that skill, the more likely s/he will meet professional writing requirements with ease and accomplishment. Skill level can also affect the writer's ability to write with depth and breadth. Two models from Bereiter and Scardamalia (1987) differentiate the writing processes of novice and expert writers into *knowledge telling* and *knowledge transforming* approaches.

Knowledge telling represents a straightforward, less complex approach that involves the following steps:

1. Mentally define the topic and purpose of writing.
2. Store both knowledge of topic and knowledge of writing process in long-term memory.
3. Put the two together into the process of creating text in a linear fashion, that is, into knowledge telling.

While adequate, this model delivers shorter, less complete, and lower-quality writing (Graham & Harris, 2000).

Knowledge transforming embeds knowledge telling into a more cognitively complex process:

1. Mentally define the topic and purpose of writing.
2. Plan and set goals, using both knowledge of content (e.g., assessment process and resulting data) and knowledge of the writing process.
3. Create text while continuously analyzing content and reframing goals, text, or both.

This last step allows the writing process itself to provide feedback that develops and changes the writer's thinking as the writing progresses.

Steps two and three of the latter approach provide the greatest distinction between knowledge telling and knowledge transforming: Planning and setting goals upfront and then allowing those to shift based on feedback from the writing itself "serve to change goals, text, or the relationship between the two" (Cameron & Moshenko, 1996). Skilled writers use more upfront time in planning before plunging into writing. They may also spend more time actually writing, since they allow feedback to occur and refine the document. Table 1.1 shows differences between the two processes. Notice that knowledge transforming takes more specific and carefully chosen words than does knowledge telling.

You, the assessor-writer, are the expert at knowing what your client expects and needs in an assessment report. Knowledge telling may suffice in certain reports and may even be preferable in some. But the more confident you are about your writing as well as your assessment skills, the more likely you can deliver reports that are knowledge transforming when you so choose. This knowledge-transforming quality may benefit you as well as your reader. A reference book such as this one can help build confidence in your writing so that you have that choice.

Another model of the relationship between cognitive processing and writing explores how the writer's goals, beliefs, and attitudes motivate and affect the progress and success of the writing process (Flower & Hayes, 1981). These aspects may include and reflect the assessor-writer's attitude toward his or her writing ability as well as toward the intended audience. Discussing how he finally managed to write clearly on a topic, American writer and English professor Peter Elbow (1998) wrote the following: "[T]he difference was a *decision* I made about my stance toward the reader.... [R]eadjusting

TABLE 1.1 Writing Process: Knowledge Telling Versus Knowledge Transforming

	Steps in Process	Written End Result
Knowledge telling	1. Mentally define topic/ purpose 2. Store knowledge (topic and writing) in long-term memory 3. Combine content and writing in linear fashion to form text	Tommy would benefit from being placed with a teacher who is structured in his classroom and approach.
Knowledge transforming	1. Mentally define topic/ purpose 2. Plan and set goals for both content and writing 3. Create text; continuously analyze content and adjust goals/text	Being seated in the front of the classroom or in a location that limits distractions will likely benefit Tommy's learning: • Give him instructions concretely and briefly. • Break down multiple-part instructions into smaller components. • Give Tommy clear information about upcoming expectations to help him prepare for the next steps and anticipate changes.

Note: Steps are adapted from *The Psychology of Written Composition*, by C. Bereiter and M. Scardamalia, 1987, Hillsdale, NJ: Erlbaum. Copyright 1987 by Lawrence Erlbaum Associates.

my transaction with readers *caused* the words and ideas to finally come out in a different and better order" (p. 211).

Attitude Toward Your Subject and Audience

Among other qualities, the Writing Cognitive Processes Model (Flower & Hayes, 1981) discusses the following:

■ The specific audience you are writing to influences the direction of what you write. The collaborators you work with also affect its direction.

■ The writer's knowledge of the audience resides in his or her long-term memory and affects the written text. If secondary readers are likely, you will be holding that information in memory along with what you know of the primary audience.

We perceive others through our understanding, our body's various senses (sight, hearing, etc.), and our intuition (Webster's, 2001). We may meet a person whose manner or appearance reminds us of a relative we fought with as kids and still do not like now that we are adults. Or perhaps we come upon someone with a drinking problem whose behavior mirrors our alcoholic parent's and makes us feel out of control. Maybe you were once involved in a lawsuit and now have an aversion to attorneys or judges. Understandably, these deep-seated responses can influence your attitude toward the person in question. Now assume for a moment that that person is a client or a referring professional, either of whom might be the intended audience for an assessment report. Being aware of the individual's personal impact on you enables you to monitor your attitude as you write and to reframe it as necessary.

But how do you deal with attitude when writing for a reader you never meet, such as educators or representatives of a court? Or what about when the report is written for one audience, but you know that one or more secondary audiences will read it? In these diffuse situations, attitude can become even harder to recognize because your audience is not clear in your mind. In the first case, when your relationship with the unknown reader is implied rather than direct, simply envisioning the recipient as a living person can help. How would you speak to that person if s/he were in front of you? What is your purpose in communicating with him/her? What information does this person need in order to take a next step in the situation? You, as the expert, may be expected to present all sides of the situation assessed but may also be called on for opinion or recommendations. In the second situation—that of multiple audiences—the primary reader will likely define your attitude. Be sensitive, however, to those secondary audiences, and avoid unknowingly displaying an unproductive or negative attitude toward them.

What Influences Attitude?

Attitude represents the writer's view of her or his subject and reflects feelings as well as thoughts. The writer's beliefs, values, doubts, and fears participate strongly in the process, even when s/he intends neutrality (more on neutrality in Chapter 4). If you remain unaware of the subliminal influences on attitude, you can reach conclusions based on little or no data and believe they are correct. The careful writer reaches his or her attitude toward a subject after intentional research and data gathering. That process enables the writer to create the most effective narrative and to ground it in fact rather than assumption. The mere presence of extensive data and facts, however, does not preclude attitude from presenting itself, knowingly or not. Gerard (2000) gives the example of coauthors writing a well-researched book on the U.S. Supreme Court. Although leaving out personal opinion and backing all quotes with sources, the reader has no doubt of the writers' perspective on the story due to very specific word usage. In describing a group's perspective on a situation, the writers said that this group *realized* and *knew* certain things. Both verbs indicate that the group's perceptions were "true." A more objective account might have replaced those words with *thought* and *believed*.

We also encounter the issue of "propositions" in writing (Landon, 2008, citing Chomsky). This concept refers to our ability to embed unspoken assumptions and ideas into sentences that convey those unspoken ideas to the reader. For example, your underlying premises in writing an assessment report (a) for a child seeking school assistance will be different from a report (b) to an adult who has struggled with attention issues and wants to understand how to better cope with them. In the first case, based on testing data and your own attitude, just a few of the underlying premises influencing your report might include

- The child is smart enough or is not smart enough to be helped.
- The school will or will not make teaching concessions.
- The parents support or do not support the needed adjustments for their child.

In the second case, premises could include

- The adult is or is not able to hear and make sense of the information you give.
- S/he is or is not willing to make changes to improve life.
- Important people in his or her world will or will not be a resource.

Table 1.2 lists the components of attitude in an assessment report. Cumulative information from the assessment process—history,

TABLE 1.2   Components of Attitude in Writing an Assessment Report

Component	How Is It Formed?
Assessor-writer's view of topic or person	Personal beliefs, values, judgments, doubts, fears
Data gathering	Interviews, tests, tasks, questionnaires, education, experience, reading, research
Communication qualities:	
• Sensitivity, compassion, respect for the subject and/or reader	Empathy toward others Awareness of the impact of how information is phrased
• Clarity	Care with the written word
• Accuracy	Understanding that accurate need not mean blunt

interviews, tests, tasks, and questionnaires—comprises extensive data gathering. Add in the substantive background of training in psychology and assessment, and the assessor-writer has a strong base for developing his or her attitude about a person or topic. S/he also has an equally strong base for consciously managing that attitude.

Communication qualities could easily be included under the component "Assessor-writer's view of topic or person." But because attitude is most clearly manifest in the way a person communicates, in either the spoken or written word, communication qualities deserve a separate category in this discussion. A report—or a sentence or paragraph within a report—may be accurate and clear, but still lack the third, joint communication quality: sensitivity, compassion, and respect for the subject. One approach to showing this quality has been attributed to countless sources from Socrates and Voltaire to Buddha and other spiritual figures: that is, to ask oneself, before speaking or writing, whether a fact is true, kind, and useful. We can also keep in mind another take on the same idea, this one attributed to Viennese-born psychologist Rose N. Franzblau in her *New York Post* (1966) advice column: "Honesty without compassion and understanding is not honesty, but subtle hostility."

Attitude and Your Reader

In general, a reader expects a writer to convey an attitude toward his or her subject (Gerard, 2000). Perhaps this idea applies even more when the writer is trained and practicing in a scientific and technical field like psychological or neuropsychological assessment. Those outside the field see you as the expert and may seek both facts and opinion from you. Especially in the subset of Collaborative/Therapeutic Assessment (C/TA), with its personalized approach, an entirely neutral stance in the writer's attitude could be considered counterproductive. (See the preface to Part III for more on C/TA.) Although attitude may be expected by the reader, no one wants to read bluntly judgmental interpretations of his or her behavior or performance—or that of their child. Even in documents where we expect an objective perspective, the writer's view of the subject can creep through. For example, words and phrases such as "no doubt," "obviously," or "by no means" can betray attitude toward the subject, the reader, or both. If the person writing a report remains unaware of his or her own attitude toward the subject, the situation becomes complex and potentially damaging. Though certain words may be accurate and clear, they can also betray insensitivity to the person described and be a form of editorializing—of presenting opinion as if it were an objective report. The example in the indented text—a composite from actual sanitized reports—illustrates editorializing in this way.

If the assessor-writer feels secretly contemptuous of the person assessed, at some point that attitude will likely emerge, often betrayed by tone as shown in word choice. Use of telltale words can be a special challenge if writing about a difficult person, due to the risk of attitude bleed-through. For example, assume a client was loudly vocal and behaved unpredictably before, during, and after assessment sessions. The frustrated assessor carefully retained a neutral stance in writing his traditional report—except in one paragraph. In that single paragraph, the assessor's contempt for the client came through in excessive use of evocative and judgmental descriptors. None was present in the remainder of the report. Through word choice, that series of sentences betrayed the writer's dismissive, even contemptuous attitude toward the subject:

Mr. M. had an *unfortunate tendency* to arrive late for appointments. Another *personality quirk* was that he was *erratically* emotional and hostile one time and more calm the next. *Unhappily,* he even showed these behaviors in the waiting room. After an

TABLE 1.3 Attitude: Revise to Eliminate Judgmental Quality

Original Sentence	Problem	Revision
Mr. M. had an *unfortunate tendency* to arrive late for appointments.	Judgmental; editorializing	Mr. M. frequently arrived late for appointments.
Another *personality quirk* was that he was *erratically* emotional and hostile one time and more calm the next.	Judgmental; editorializing	From one visit to the next, his calm demeanor would alternate with agitation.
Unhappily, he even showed these behaviors in the waiting room.	Editorializing	Others in the waiting room noticed the times he was agitated.
After an *overabundance* of these swings, the office's clerical assistant made *derisive* private comments about the client's *emotional instability.*	Judgmental; insensitive; editorializing	Sentence unnecessary; no revision—eliminate.
Mr. M. used *excessively ornate* and detailed words and phrases to describe his *perceived* problems.	Judgmental; editorializing	Mr. M. described his problems in specific and detailed words and phrases.
His *exasperated* insistence on the severity of his problems seemed *excessive.*	Judgmental; editorializing	Several times he mentioned how severely he experienced the problems.

overabundance of these swings, the office's clerical assistant made *derisive* private comments about the client's *emotional instability.* Mr. M. used *excessively ornate* and detailed words and phrases to describe his presenting problems. His *exasperated* insistence on the severity of his problems seemed *excessive.*

The reader might not be able to pinpoint adjectives and nouns as the offenders. The assessor-writer may not even know what s/he did, but the attitude would still reach the reader on some level. And imagine if the intended reader was the person assessed; unease and feelings of being harshly judged or dehumanized are possible responses. Table 1.3 shows these sentences revised to eliminate the negative attitude. Although we will examine word choice in more detail in Chapter 2, you can readily see the impact of the italicized words in the examples.

In essence, attitude in a document reflects what you, the assessor-writer, value most in communicating. Your views on the world

TABLE 1.4 What Is My Attitude in Writing This Report?

- What is my attitude toward my writing ability?
- What is my attitude toward my psychological assessment ability?
- Is my approach to this report knowledge telling or knowledge transforming? Why?
- Who is the intended reader of my report?
- Is the relationship between assessor and primary reader direct or implied?
- What is the purpose in communicating with that reader?
- Is there a secondary audience? Who?
- What is my attitude toward my reader(s)?
- What is my attitude toward the subject of the assessment?
- Have I done thorough research or data gathering that backs up this attitude?
- How does my attitude show through in word choice?
- Is my writing clear, accurate, sensitive, compassionate, and respectful?

set a context for deciding what to communicate and how you do that. Data provides the information you need to come to reasoned conclusions. The joint communication quality of sensitivity, compassion, and respect for your reader then plays the largest part in feeding your words. The additional communication qualities of clarity and accuracy also show up in attitude, though they actually expand and deepen in the area of written style (more about them in Chapter 3).

Finally, Table 1.4 lists a series of questions to ask yourself before and while you write a report. These may help you navigate among the icebergs of attitude in all its many forms.

CHAPTER **2**

Tone
Words and More

> Say all you have to say in the fewest possible words, or your reader will be sure to skip them; and in the plainest possible words or he will certainly misunderstand them.
>
> **John Ruskin, English artist and critic (1819–1900)**

"Don't you take that tone with me, young lady!" How many of us heard some version of that while growing up? Sometimes we could hear the offending tone in our own voices but could not stop it. It seemed to pop unbidden from deep inside as we spoke to a parent. The teenager's response to her parent likely expressed an attitude of annoyance. She could have felt annoyed by having to do something she did not want to do, or with the person making the demand, or perhaps both.

Attitude represents a speaker or writer's internalized, often unconscious, perception of a subject or person. Tone then grows out of attitude and becomes the manner in which attitude expresses itself (see Figure 2.1). "If writing has a morality, it is expressed in tone" (Gerard, 2000, p. 68). Morality is that quality of being tuned in to what a person knows to be right in action or word, written as well as spoken. If each person was consistently conscious of what s/he felt to be right in every situation, tone would seldom be a problem. But as with attitude, tone often finds itself adrift in the sea of the unconscious, often left to tread water before sinking and taking us down with it.

Tone reflects the assessor-writer's attitude toward the subject of a report, the reader of it, or both. Working consciously, first with

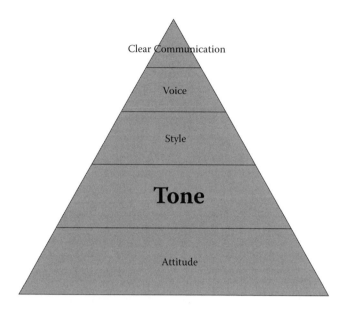

FIGURE 2.1 Building blocks of the assessment report: Tone.

attitude and then with tone, can strengthen your writing and your control over how your assessment report is received.

Conceptually, tone shows up in many lines of endeavor:

- In *music*, tone has a distinct and constant pitch, quality, and duration. It is different from mere noise in that it can be harmonized with other sounds.
- In *painting*, tone is the general effect produced by combining light, shade, and color. Tone also refers to the quality of color in this combining.
- In *linguistics*, tone is the relative height of pitch used in pronouncing a word, phrase, or sentence. The vocal intonation or modulation expresses the speaker's particular meaning or feeling. (See Chapter 12 for more on vocal pitch.)*

Writing may borrow components from each of these areas in its use of tone. You might say, for example, that a written document "hit the right tone," drawing a metaphorical comparison with music. Or it may be described as "dark" in tone, paralleling it with

---

* *Note*: All definitions from Webster's (2001).

TABLE 2.1 Components of Tone: Derived From Assessor-Writer's Attitude

Component	What Defines It?
Degree of formality	Contractions: when and when not to use them Sentence structure: appropriate to audience

Choice of words:
  Accuracy
  Clarity
	Difference in similar or similar-sounding words
	Repeating words as necessary
	Using synonyms carefully

Arrangement of material	Tightly organized and written = strong linkages Strong linkages = increased perception of nuance
Juxtaposition	Rank-ordering for impact: easiest to hardest Aids both subject and reader

painting. "His tone was flat" evokes all three—music, painting, and linguistics.

Tone is a "manner of speaking or writing that shows a certain attitude on the part of the speaker or writer" (Webster's, 2001). To convey attitude through tone, a speaker uses an expanded range of skills not available to the writer. The speaker not only can use the vocal quality of tone, as in the linguistic definition, but also can use facial expressions and other body language. In the example of the young person talking to her parent, she could display displeasure by rolling her eyes or slouching, arms crossed, in an "I don't care" position, with one hip shifted sideways. The parent might stand upright, hands on hips with head and torso slightly forward, when chastising the girl. All of these would support the tone used in speaking. A writer, however, must rely solely on words. And since we cannot directly convey in writing the pitch of a word in speech, we look for tone to manifest in other ways. These contributors to tone include formality in phrasing, accuracy and clarity in choice of words, selecting and arranging material, and juxtaposition of ideas. Table 2.1 lists these components of tone and what defines them. The following sections explore them and give examples.

Formality in Tone

Building on attitude, as discussed in Chapter 1, tone needs to match your knowledge of the reader and the material you are discussing. After you clarify for yourself your attitude toward the subject of your assessment and the recipient(s) of your report, you can more readily recognize the tone you wish to take in writing to them. Formality is a straightforward place to begin. We can divide degree of formality in writing into three categories: popular or casual, conversational, and formal.

1. *Popular or casual* writing aims to get a message across quickly—no muss, no fuss. It usually takes place between friends or people with some degree of personal connection. This category would include texting style that uses no caps or punctuation but adds acronyms (LOL). The cues that would normally be present in body language (when speaking) or in punctuation and careful wording (in writing) are given as explicit prompts such as LOL for "laughing out loud." This way of writing would not be used in professional documents, including e-mails.

2. *Conversational* writing attempts to give the impression of conversation, often through use of contractions (*I'm* rather than *I am*) and everyday expressions (*kids* instead of *children*). Conversational writing seems deceptively simple: Relax the rules of formality and speak directly to the recipient. Conversational writing, however, can lead us off on tangents in subject matter and can result in what Strunk and White (2000) caution against as a "breezy" manner (p. 73). In this approach, attempting to sound spontaneous can too easily come across as trying too hard in a gratingly overpersonal way. The same attempt at spontaneity can lead us to use three long sentences when one short one would do. The best conversational writing avoids this problem by paying attention to organization and flow in the same way as in formal writing.

3. *Formal* writing does not mean that the writer must use an overabundance of multisyllabic terminology (i.e., lots of big words). It means that s/he relies on effective organization, structure, and phrasing, as well as on correct grammar and punctuation. In most cases, s/he does not use contractions and usually relies on third person (he, she, they) as opposed to first or second (I, we, you). *Formal* is not synonymous with *academic* and *dense*, nor does it mean that writing must be in obscure passive voice (see Chapters 3 and 4 for discussions of passive voice). Passive voice too often relies on complex, hard-to-follow sentences and complicated words. Such words are called for only if they are the correct and

TABLE 2.2   Degrees of Formality in Writing

Quality	Popular/Casual	Conversational	Formal
Organization and planning	None to little	Some to much	Extensive
Effective grammar and punctuation	None to little	Some to much	Extensive
Seriousness	None to little	Some to much	Extensive
Spontaneity and/ or humor	extensive	Some to much; managed carefully	None to little; managed carefully
Straightforward words/phrases	Extensive, though often abbreviated	Some to extensive	None to extensive

most effective ones to describe the subject and if the reader will understand them. If the need for obscurity and density was ever an actual rule in formal writing, it no longer is. Table 2.2 shows differences in the three levels of formality.

Understanding the basic differences in the three approaches described here can help us decide what form a written document should take, hence what tone will likely emerge. In practice, however, gradations exist, giving more than three possibilities:

■ A journal article would be written in formal though not stilted English. Depending on the publication and subject matter, you may choose to strike a somewhat conversational tone, though never veering into popular language except when quoting someone.

■ In writing assessment reports, your choice will likely be formal, since that covers the largest number of potential audiences for your report. But again, formal need not mean stilted or awkward. You might, on occasion, take a somewhat conversational tone if your report is in the form of a personal letter directly to the person assessed (more on this type of letter in Chapter 11). Even then, effective organization and correct grammar and punctuation will underscore your information as reliable and professional.

■ Suppose you choose to send a thank-you note or e-mail to a referral source even though the referral did not work out.

You would not choose words that create an angry or bitter tone, nor would you force humor. Depending on how well you know the person, your tone would aim between popular and conversational.

- In an e-mail to a good friend, offering to provide additional information, a person might joke in the dialect of his youth, "Well, darlin', if you're game, I'm fixin' to cut the light on for ya." But in writing to a stranger, even when writing conversationally, the message would be no more informal than, "If you'd like to know more about that, I'll be glad to discuss it when we meet."

In the last example, informality would be suggested by the contractions *you'd* and *I'll* that are not used in more formal writing.

Formality and Contractions

In grammar, a contraction refers to shortening a word or phrase by omitting one or more sounds or letters (Webster's, 2001). Though in casual usage a contraction may be categorized as an abbreviation, they are not the same (see Chapter 9 for more on abbreviations). When words are contracted in popular or conversational usage, an apostrophe takes the place of the omitted letter(s). Using contractions lends a decidedly more casual and conversational tone to writing. While some style manuals and other writing authorities say that contractions in formal writing are acceptable (Chicago Manual, 2010a), others do not. And still others say to rely on your inner ear and use contractions only when the full words sound stiff. Table 2.3 shows examples of contrasting tone, with and without contractions. (Also see Chapters 9 and 10 for use of apostrophes with contractions.)

Word Choice

Tone manifests in nearly endless variations, obvious as well as subtle. Word choice provides much of this variation through nouns, verbs, and descriptors that may be understated or excitable, sad or witty, matter-of-fact or melodramatic, kind or sarcastic, and so on.

TABLE 2.3 Contrasting Tone: With and Without Contractions

Informal Tone	Informal Example	Formal Example	Formal Tone
Subjective	I'd like to know what you think.	I would appreciate your perspective.	Objective
Relaxed	Don't hesitate to call if you've got any questions.	Please call if you have questions.	Crisp
Personal	I can't tell you how great it's been getting to know you.	Working with you has been a pleasure.	Professional

Accuracy and Clarity

For clear tone that leads to clear communication, accuracy matters. American writer Mark Twain said, "Choose the right word, not its second cousin" (1918, p. 63). A precise count of the words in the English language would be difficult if not impossible, but we can make an estimate. Based on active and obsolete words included in the second edition of the 20-volume *Oxford English Dictionary*—as well as on technical, regional, and evolving terms not included—we are likely dealing with between 250,000 and 750,000 words (Oxford Dictionaries, 2011). Somehow, speakers and writers of the English language must keep track of the accurate meaning of every word used. A speaker stands at a lectern, not a podium. A podium is the platform on which a lectern might be placed to raise it higher. To write that a client appeared *un*interested says he was bored. To say that she was *dis*interested means she was neutral. Table 2.4 lists some words that are easily confused. See also Table 9.8 for words that sound alike but mean different things.

Depending on the audience for your report, the right word need not be the most complex. People educated or trained in an area such as psychology know that certain words are the most precise. Yet those words can easily confuse a lay reader. If the more accurate and technical word is the absolute right one and your reader(s) will easily know what you mean, then use it. If not, find a clear way of saying it that will not confuse the reader. Paraphrasing may actually take more words to give an accurate picture of your meaning, but the result will provide a tone that shows you have considered your audience.

TABLE 2.4 Accuracy: Using the Right Word

Word	Part of Speech	Meaning	Example in Sentence
Careen	Verb	Swerve while in motion	William *careened* from one side of the hall to the other.
Career	Verb	Move at full speed	Earlier, his truck had *careered* into the parking lot.
Faint	Adjective	Feeling weak and dizzy	He told the assessor he was feeling *faint*.
Feint	Noun	Deceptive action to divert attention	The assessor wondered if William's behavior was a *feint* to avoid testing that day.
Flout	Verb	Openly disregard or show contempt for	William said he had *flouted* many rules when younger.
Flaunt	Verb	Exhibit ostentatiously	His family's money had allowed him to *flaunt* his status.
Founder	Verb	Fail or collapse	His father's business finally *foundered*.
Flounder	Verb	Struggle awkwardly to move or speak	William *floundered* when he tried to describe that period in his life.
Imply	Verb	Indicate indirectly	He *implied* that his father left.
Infer	Verb	Conclude from something known	The assessor *inferred* that the family never recovered.
Loath	Adjective	Unwilling or reluctant	William had been *loath* to contact his father after he left the family.
Loathe	Verb	Feel intense dislike or hatred for	He said that he *loathes* his father.

Note: Definitions from *American Heritage Dictionary* (2000) and *Webster's Dictionary* (2001).

- *For a knowledgeable reader*: "This assessment tool provides information regarding a child's linguistic strategies and competencies. It measures the child's ability to use semantic, syntactic, and pragmatic language."
- *Paraphrased for a lay reader*: "This assessment tool gives us information about children's abilities with language. It measures their understanding of words, the rules of language, and how they use them in everyday speaking or writing."

Clarity Versus Variety

Somewhere during our schooling in English, many of us picked up the idea that a rule existed about when we could repeat a word in writing. This presumed rule said that we should never repeat the same word in a sentence, paragraph, or within so many words of its original use. English grammarian H. W. Fowler referred to this practice of substituting one word for another simply for the sake of variety as "elegant variation" (1906, pp. 175–180)— and he was not complimenting the practice. Effective variety in word choice is one tool to retain your reader's attention. Variety for the sake of variety, however, can seem awkward and strained as well as sometimes being inaccurate. It is more important to use the right word than to avoid repeating. Do not hesitate to repeat a word if it is the most accurate and will increase the clarity of your sentence (Bates, 2000). When the substitute does not mean precisely the same as the word you first used, the sentence meaning becomes diffuse. But if the replacement word means the same thing—and especially if the new word or phrase adds to our understanding—then you can be confident in adding variety by word choice. You might also add variety by revising the sentence so that the repetition need not occur. For example, start with a sentence that repeats words: "*Testing* a child who is 4 years old has different challenges than *testing* a child who is 10 or *testing* a teenager." (Assume that testing refers specifically to administering measures, not to the overall assessment process.)

- **Inaccurate variety**: "*Testing* a child who is 4 has different challenges than *evaluating* a child who is 12 or *assessing* a teenager." (Inaccurate because it converts the concept from testing to the overall evaluation or assessment.)
- **Selective repetition and varying the sentence**: "*Testing* a child who is 4 has different challenges than *testing* a 12- or 16-year-old."
- **Revising sentence and generalizing the concept**: "The assessment process may vary depending on the age of the person. The testing portion presents different challenges with children of different ages."

Another consideration regarding variety is that of clarity for the reader. In a report where you are giving extensive data, a reader can easily become confused if you vary the way you give that data from sentence to sentence. Assume that you start by saying, "She scores better than or equal to 98 out of 100 of her peers." Then, in the next sentence, you switch to "Compared to her age mates, her score exceeds that of approximately 56 out of 100." With that back-to-back change in structure, your reader will have to shift thinking, and his or her comprehension will likely slow. If you find an effective template per section and stick with it, your reader will not have to work so hard. And if you don't want to keep repeating a phrase, such as "of her peers," write it once and then add, "All scores to follow compare her to her peers."

Denotation and Connotation

Denotation refers to the direct meaning of a word, as from the dictionary. *Connotation* is an idea or meaning attributed to the word. Connotation often has an emotional component, since it reflects attitude and can conjure imagery, either positive or negative. A single word heavy with connotation affects the tone of a sentence or paragraph. Change that word, change the tone. The words "skinny" and "gaunt" could accurately describe a very thin person, but each carries connotations that "slender" does not. Although we have a general sense of positive, negative, and neutral connotations in words, we also must take into account personal attitudes in the recipient as well as the writer. People may have individual and strong reactions for and against certain words or phrases. After you have interviewed and spent considerable time with the client during an assessment, you will likely have a good sense of which words might be loaded with connotation for them. You can then choose to use or avoid those in your report. If the report is for a third party, you might never have met that person. In that case, you will rely on general knowledge of words that might carry unexpected connotation. Table 2.5 lists some words that can carry negative connotations in general usage, along with their neutral and positive counterparts.

In some cases, depending on individual perception, the neutral or positive connotations could change places, but that's hardly ever the case with the negative. As with all other choices you make in writing your report, select the clearest and most accurate word, but take into account the impact on the reader. The more problematic the subject matter or message, the more nuance becomes

TABLE 2.5   Connotations

Positive	Neutral	Negative
Carefree	Relaxed	Irresponsible
Clever	Skilled	Scheming
Delayed	Late	Tardy
Expert	Knowledgeable	Elitist
Friendly	Outgoing	Talkative
Frugal	Careful	Cheap
Strong-willed	Confident	Arrogant
Thorough	Detailed	Picky

magnified (Gerard, 2000). Nuance is akin to connotation; it evokes a "shade of difference" in meaning or tone (Webster's, 2001). That shade of difference can lend power to your report but requires careful attention to avoid unintended effects. As French philosopher and writer Jean-Paul Sartre expressed it, "Words are loaded pistols" (1947/1988). Handle them carefully.

Selecting Material and Subtext

Accuracy, clarity, and sensitive word choice create tone by giving texture, depth, and applicability to writing. But careful attention to arrangement of material is also essential. Tone also expresses itself in the selection of information to include in your report and the ultimate arrangement of that information. In music and art, sounds and colors influence each other; they coordinate or contrast, leaving the listener or viewer with synchronized or discordant impressions. The work is not just its individual parts or the sum of its parts, but the way that those parts influence each other. So it is with the arrangement of written material.

Arranging material also affects connotation and implicit versus explicit meaning. By placing information in a certain order, you draw attention toward or away from it. Subtext in literature refers to what is not said—content that lies beneath the surface of the obvious subject matter. Omitted material can say as much as what's included, and the more tightly a written form is constructed, the more likely that a reader will see clearly what is *not* being said. A skilled fiction writer carefully constructs descriptions of behavior and actions so that a subtext is apparent to the reader—not murder simply for the sake of murder.

The same can be true of a factual piece such as an assessment report. Being conscious of your reader's ability to read between the lines is essential. In writing about real people in a report, the assessor-writer has an even greater responsibility to be aware of subtext. Assume that including that description of childhood abuse is essential for the history in a report: Can it be framed so that important facts are communicated without bluntness or too much detail doing damage to the subject? Can you trust the reader to understand the nuance if you touch on something without extensive detail?

In the case of a young woman referred for assessment by her therapist, measures showed extreme attachment problems (Engelman & Allyn, projected publication February/March 2012). She had suffered early childhood abuse from one parent, and the other had not done enough to protect her. In spite of this, the young woman was ultraprotective of both parents. The young woman, her parents, and her therapist would all see the finished report, and all were fully aware of the early family dynamic. The assessor chose to address these loaded facts only tangentially in the report and a therapeutic story, focusing instead on the issues that had brought the young woman for assessment. By doing this—and not hitting the family history head-on—the assessor avoided using labels that would cause one party or another to raise protective walls. During writing, the assessor carefully evaluated the report for impact through word choice and arrangement of material. Table 2.6 in the next section gives examples from this report, which took the form of a letter to the young woman.

Juxtaposition and Finn's Levels 1, 2, 3

In selecting and organizing material, juxtaposition contributes to tone. *Juxtapose* means, "to put material side by side or close together especially for comparison or contrast" (Webster's, 2001; American Heritage, 2000). When you thoughtfully align items of information near each other, they gain power by that alignment, and tone is influenced in the document as a whole.

Assessment reports may confirm or explain information the person tested had feared. When you write a report to the person assessed—or assume that they will read it at some point—each subtlety in your explanation takes on added weight. With difficult material, subtleties become enlarged and influence tone. In

TABLE 2.6 Juxtaposing Material: Based on Finn's Levels 1, 2, and 3

	Response to Information	Example of Juxtaposing Material
Level 1	Easily heard and accepted	You have been aware of cognitive inconsistencies that have been confusing for you. You have obvious intellectual talents, yet you can feel overwhelmed and stressed with new challenges.
	Juxtaposition moves toward Level 2 material	Please remember that emotional stress and childhood trauma affect one's cognitive capacities, especially memory and learning.
Level 2	Mostly accepted, after consideration	Findings based on this assessment suggest that you conceptually understand what happened to you in childhood.
	Juxtaposition moves toward Level 3 material	The fault appears to lie with both parents— one who raged at you and the other who didn't protect you from those rages. You do not seem to have worked through the trauma to the point that you *know* that the child's trauma was not your fault.
Level 3	Not easily accepted	The suicidal incident encompassed all the hopelessness and helplessness you felt as a child, an awareness you probably were not in touch with. You believed you were totally hopeless—an awful, messed up, "bad" person. When your defenses were low, it was only a few short steps to try to kill yourself.

many cases, building to the more-difficult findings may be war-ranted, whether addressing the person assessed or a referring pro-fessional. Psychologist and assessor Stephen Finn suggests levels to rank-order assessment findings (2007, pp. 8–9). These levels move from the information most easily accepted by a client to the hardest for the person to hear. Finn's approach also applies in considering juxtaposition of material in the report. In each case, information gains strength from the material that precedes it and affects tone. In Finn's model,

■ *Level 1* material fits with a person's ways of perceiving him or herself and so is easily accepted. This material is not always the most positive; sometimes a negative self-image keeps the client from easily hearing positive things about himself or herself. In this case, first addressing the negative information eases acceptance of the material that follows for Levels 2 and 3.

- *Level 2* information modifies the client's self-perception or expands it in some way. For the most part, this material does not threaten self-perception and so is mostly accepted by the client after some thought and discussion.
- *Level 3* material goes counter to the client's usual ways of perceiving herself in the world. This material is hardest to hear and not easily accepted.

When structuring material by levels, you create tone by carefully aligning information of like impact—that is, juxtaposing Level 1 findings with each other, leading into Level 2, and so forth. In this way, the assessor-writer builds toward the information that is most troubling. By use of word choice and juxtaposition, s/he creates a tone that both informs and reassures. Finn (2007) mentions including the referring therapist in making these decisions: Together, assessor and therapist identify information as Level 1, 2, and 3 and choose specific words that can best be heard by the person tested (p. 112). Table 2.6 gives examples of this approach, using examples from the letter mentioned earlier in this chapter.

Perhaps this sensitivity to impact may seem less directly applicable when writing reports for removed third parties, such as courts or schools. In those cases, the assessment could be viewed as a simple blood test that provides black-and-white information. Even a blood test, however, presumes a level of help offered to the person tested: If her electrolyte levels are low or his blood sugar is high, action can be taken to correct it. The same idea can apply to assessment reports. Assume that the report will be used for decision making and will ultimately have an impact on the person assessed. Finn's levels can provide a way to present findings so that third parties can more easily track the potential impact of their actions or decisions on the person assessed.

CHAPTER **3**

Style
Content Plus Structure

The hardest thing in the world to do is to write straight, honest prose on human beings. First, you have to know the subject, then you have to know how to write.

Ernest Hemingway, American writer (1899–1961)

Some say that knowledge is power. In psychological assessment reports, words convey knowledge and are powerful. In using those words, style is the point where attitude and tone meet grammar and structure. Style is "a way of using words to express thoughts" (Webster's, 2001). In the writing world, style may also apply to the conventions of writing according to a certain set of guidelines (e.g., *APA Publication Manual* or *Chicago Manual of Style*). This chapter's discussion focuses more on style as reflecting the individual assessor-writer's approach. Too often, people assume that style must jump up and shout for attention, that to be compelling a written style must be ornate or obvious or both. But style can also show itself in simplicity and directness. The most effective style weaves itself out of attitude and tone (see Figure 3.1). In the previous two chapters, we saw how attitude toward our own writing, our subject, and our reader influences what and how we write. We recognized that our attitude influences tone when we choose an appropriate level of formality, select words carefully, and arrange material with thought.

Allowing style to evolve out of attitude and tone requires expansion of the communication qualities first encountered in Chapter 1. To clarity, accuracy, and respect for the reader, we now

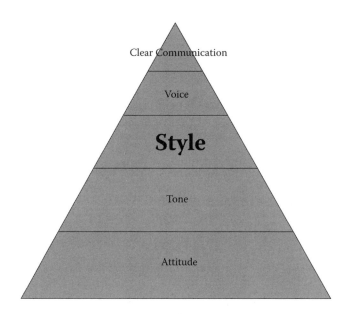

FIGURE 3.1   Building blocks of the assessment report: Style.

add specificity—the ability to move beyond general statements into precise details. Style also demands a clear beginning, middle, and end to the document as a whole. And since style grounds itself in the sentence (Gerard, 2000), by extension it requires a beginning, middle, and end to each sentence, paragraph, and section of the report. Other areas, too, affect style, such as jargon, clutter, and energy in writing. All aspects of style interact with the basics of grammar covered in Part II.

To build sentences into paragraphs that have both meaning and sensitivity, the assessor-writer must develop writing awareness. Making conscious choices about what you say and how you say it will increase that awareness. This discussion addresses a number of questions about style in writing psychological assessment reports:

- How is concrete writing different from abstract? What role does each play in clear and effective writing?
- What is jargon? When is it appropriate? When should the assessor-writer reduce jargon in favor of simpler terms?
- Do certain phrases clutter writing? How do we recognize and replace them with more meaningful information?

TABLE 3.1   Components of Style

Component	Expansion
Sentence-based writing	Sentences anchor the document
Beginning, middle, end	• To report
	• To report's sections
	• To individual sentences and paragraphs
Communications qualities:	
Same as in attitude plus specificity	• Clarity
	• Accuracy
	• Specificity
	• Sensitivity/compassion/respect for reader
Jettison jargon Clear clutter Energize text	All enable clarity in writing and contribute to voice (see Chapter 4).

- How does writing convey energy that propels a reader through the document?
- What are linking (static) verbs? When do we use them? When should they and adjectives be replaced by more active verbs and adverbs?

Table 3.1 lists components of style. Taken together, they help create the assessor-writer's unique voice, as Chapter 4 explores.

Beginning, Middle, and End

In narrative writing, either nonfiction or fiction, information can be given clearly and compellingly by remembering that a story has a beginning, a middle, and an end. A story is "the telling of a happening or connected series of happenings, either true or fictitious" (Webster's, 2001). In that definition, an assessment report can be viewed as a story. You will write about a series of happenings: referral questions, history, interviews with concerned parties, prior assessments, current testing, results, and recommendations. Your reader will expect clear information, logically structured so they can follow the story told in your report. Whatever format you choose (as discussed in Chapter 5), clarity can be enhanced by knowing how and where your report begins, what you wish to cover in the middle, and how you will tie it off at the end. Say all that needs to be said—no more, no less. The same is true for each section of your report and, more specifically, for each paragraph and sentence. No extraneous words. Use only what is necessary to convey information clearly. Style begins in the sentence and grows out of the snowball effect by which sentences become paragraphs. No sentence can hitch along just for the ride in order to fill space; each must contribute to the overall sense and impact of the whole.

Many beginning or unaware writers use the cooked spaghetti approach: the idea that throwing enough at the wall will cause some of it to stick and they will know it is "done." Regardless of the type of document, these writers write around a topic rather than figuring out precisely what they need to say. Good ideas become buried in imprecise verbiage. Eventually, however, if they stick with it, they can learn to work with sentences at the most basic level—that of the word—choosing them carefully and stringing them together with focus and presence of mind. By both narrowing sentences down to words and expanding them to paragraphs, the muscle of writing style strengthens. Awareness is key. If not aware, a writer can easily and absent-mindedly lapse back into imprecise writing. On days when s/he battles to stay present, style again becomes nonspecific and ideas unclear. Reclaiming awareness and making the effort to clear up ideas and words also reclaims effective style. In the words of writer William Zinsser, "A clear sentence is no accident" (1980, p. 13).

Communication Qualities: Clarity and Accuracy

Clarity and accuracy help create style. Chapter 2 discussed accuracy and clarity in individual word choice. Clarity and accuracy also apply when structuring those words into sentences and paragraphs. (See Chapter 6 for more on crafting sentences and paragraphs.) The most complex material can be explained clearly, accurately, and simply if we give it thought. Most of us have heard the phrase, "I asked him what time it was, and he told me how to build a clock." If building one is your goal, the minute technical details are useful, but they matter little if you simply want to know the time. Knowing how much detail your audience needs and expects can help you to be both clear and accurate in your written report.

When choosing your words and structuring sentences and paragraphs, keep in mind that English grammar is complex but not arbitrary. It has specific rules, though interpretations may vary, depending on which source explains those rules. English changes slowly, but it does evolve, over time. Even the best writers refer to one source or another to remind themselves of the rules, to check for subtle changes, and to be sure they are making the right choices. This book aims to help in two ways:

1. Part II is a grammar handbook that synthesizes the rules an assessor-writer may need most often and gives examples of use.
2. The reference list at the end of this book includes books and other sources that also may be useful.

Whichever source you use, when it comes to writing your sentences, fiercely insist on clarity and accuracy in word and sentence structure. Your reader will thank you.

Psychologist and assessor Gary Groth-Marnat (2009b, p. 303), citing V. S. Harvey, listed five practices that would enhance the readability of a psychological report:

- Shorten sentences
- Minimize number of difficult words
- Reduce jargon
- Reduce use of acronyms
- Increase use of subheadings

The category "increase use of subheadings" might include using bullets and numbered lists. These not only give the reader easy-to-locate points, but also increase white space in your page layout. The eye scans more easily down the page when the sea of letters is broken up by islands of white, is pinpointed by bullets, or is strung together by numbers. Lists interspersed within your report narrative enable you to get to the point. They can be clearer and more accurate for the reader, since lists require specificity, as discussed in the following section.

Communication Qualities: Specificity

Words, phrases, even whole sentences we write may fall anywhere on a continuum from specific to general. A general word or phrase will apply to broader areas or groups. Moving along the

TABLE 3.2   From General to Specific for Three General Terms

General→	→	→	→Specific
Neuropsychological assessment	Assessment of personality domain	Personality measures	MMPI-2
Assessment process	Information gathering	Interviews; tests	Interview mother; Give BASC-2 to son
Assessment report	Format/write/edit	Analyze data and choose essentials	Score tests

continuum, words and phrases become more specific until they reach the level of individual subsets of the original broader group. Table 3.2 shows increasing specificity for three general terms.

Leading off a sentence with a general observation will let your reader know the larger context that your paragraph will address. If you write only in general terms, however, the reader finds it harder to grasp essentials because s/he is forced to read between the lines. Suppose you started with the general statement,

Joseph worked harder on the written expression essay than he had on other subtests.

To help your reader to understand what you mean by "worked harder," follow up with specific detail:

He sat with his head down, focused on the task. He first made an outline on a piece of scratch paper and then wrote rapidly until time was up.

In most cases, the more general your writing, the more vague and less compelling your end product will be. Style relies on your ability to help your reader accurately understand your message. Giving the reader only general observations makes it harder to do that.

On the other end of the spectrum, if you write only details, the reader can easily be overwhelmed by "all those trees." With no general context for your writing, the reader has no sense for the larger forest in which the trees of detail grow. But when you balance just enough of a general frame with salient details in each sentence and paragraph, your style unfolds and communicates with your reader.

You might ask how you know when you have reached that balance point. Chapter 5 discusses the value of having a second pair of eyes proof your written work. That same person can help you to see where you have made leaps into detail or generality that might lose the reader of your report. But if no second person is available to review your report, the assessor-writer then must walk awhile in the shoes of the intended reader. Examine what you have written, section by section, as if you are that reader. Does your written report assume more knowledge than the reader has available? Your reader likely will not know all that you know after completing an assessment in which you tie together many disparate pieces. You are the integrator. Do you give them too much detail with no context or, perhaps, all general frame and no specifics? By reviewing your reports from this perspective, you will begin to see a pattern to how you use detail and generality, and the balance will become more evident.

Concrete Versus Abstract Terms

Concrete words or phrases describe qualities we perceive through our senses. We can taste, touch, see, and smell a sandwich, so we can probably agree in our shared understanding of that term, *sandwich*. Questionnaire, scoring manual, pencil, desk, door—all are items we perceive with our senses, hence concrete terms. *Abstract* terms refer to intangible ideas or concepts with no physical shape; we know these through thought process, not through our senses. We cannot taste, touch, see, or smell hope, kindness, love, honor, or freedom. Each of those abstract terms filters through individual life experiences. They may have as many definitions as people who write them and may shift depending on what stage of life a person is in.

Studies have shown that our brains process concrete words more quickly and efficiently than they do abstract ones (Kiehl et al., 1999; West & Holcomb, 2000). This idea becomes especially important when writing psychological assessment reports. To the extent possible, the assessment process quantifies abstractions, such as intelligence. We cannot touch, taste, or smell intelligence. You can see it—or think you see it—only in the numbers that testing delivers or in the person's behavior and ways of functioning in the world. And because those observations are even less concrete

TABLE 3.3 Abstract vs. Concrete Sentences

Abstract	Concrete
The child is *smart*.	The child scored in the 99th percentile on this measure. She has a straight *A* average in all courses, and she tutors younger students in several subjects.
An assessment takes *a long time* to complete.	A full neuropsychological battery may take as much as 10–12 hours of direct testing, using more than one measure for each of nine brain areas.

than the numbers from testing, your assumption of intelligence becomes ever more abstract. In writing about these abstractions, the more concrete and specific you can be, the more your reader will understand the value and importance of the abstraction. Table 3.3 provides some examples.

Metaphor is a specialized category of abstraction. Many metaphors have filtered into our everyday language in the form of "conceptual metaphors" that are discussed in Chapter 11. Because of this common usage, those metaphors have shifted away from pure abstraction and closer to concrete. But if uncertain that a reader will understand a metaphor, better to rely on more concrete descriptions.

Abstraction and Hayakawa's Ladder

Linguist S. I. Hayakawa created an Abstraction Ladder, a progression of related words or phrases ranging upward from most concrete to most abstract (Hayakawa & Hayakawa, 1990, pp. 84–85). Since all words we deal with in language represent a thing or idea but are *not* the thing itself, all words can be viewed as abstractions. The question is how high up the ladder a word or phrase resides and how hard it is for the reader to understand that term at that level. If we decide that we are speaking or writing at a higher level of abstraction and wish to make it more concrete, we ask what is the next step down the ladder for that word or concept. Or if we have been dealing in concrete details, we might ask, "What is the next level up the ladder?" Moving up a level might help synthesize the detail into a higher abstraction. See Table 3.4 for an example.

Abstraction may be viewed as the process through which you gather details (concrete facts) into generalizations. In the world of psychological assessment, abstraction would mean

TABLE 3.4 Levels of Abstraction

Level	Word or Phrase	What it Encompasses
6 (most abstract)	Knowledge	Highest level of abstraction; no longer refers to specific characteristics of lower levels
5	Written feedback (also verbal feedback)	Essential information from levels 1, 2, 3, and 4
4	Assessment	Tests, questionnaires, interviews, history, report
3	Tests	All tests used in an assessment
2	WIAT-III	All subtests of WIAT-III
1 (most concrete)	Written expression	One subtest of WIAT-III

accumulating and sifting information, reaching recognition of how they fit together, and communicating that synthesis to the recipient of your report. When you move up the levels of abstraction, the detail that defines the bottom, concrete level becomes more diffuse. Each higher level abstracts similarities—that is, it shares only certain traits with the levels below it. In moving up to the second level of Table 3.4, Written Expression begins to lose the specifics of sentence building and essay composition and becomes more about the overall measurements provided by WIAT-III. Moving to the third level, WIAT-III's specifics are abstracted to the more general category of Tests. And so on through the levels until you reach the highest level of abstraction, Knowledge. At that level, writing an assessment report for any reader would likely be so abstract as to be unusable. Recognizing when you reach that level of abstraction in your writing enables you to drop down a level or two and make your report more understandable.

Effective writing demands a balance between lower- and higher-level abstractions (Hayakawa & Hayakawa, 1990). If you give only concrete facts without pulling them together into meaning, the reader simply wanders through a maze of details. On the other hand, if all you give are abstractions, a person has no way of applying it to real life or to the questions addressed by the report. Guiding your reader through the concrete facts can better allow the reader to understand your higher levels of abstraction. *Specific* words and phrases will often be concrete and *general* ones more abstract. When something you write seems vague to you, look to whether your writing tends toward generality and abstraction. If so, move down the levels toward concreteness and specificity in your words or examples. Your writing style will grow as you balance specific and concrete with general and abstract in a way that is unique to you and your understanding of the material.

Communication Qualities: Sensitivity, Compassion, Respect for Your Subject and Reader

The final subset of communication qualities addresses the degree to which your writing shows sensitivity to your subject and reader. The audience for an assessment report may be a referring professional, an educator, a court, the person assessed, his or her family, or any combination of these. Keeping in mind the potential reader(s) reminds you to choose ways of writing your report that show respect for any who might read it. Once the assessor-writer has submitted a report to its intended recipient, s/he has no control over when it may be passed on. As Chapter 5 also mentions, even with a third-party report not intended for the person assessed, that individual may see it at some point.

Chapter 1 on attitude mentions this same joint communication quality of sensitivity, compassion, and respect for subject/reader. We revisit it here because attitude directly flows into tone and continues through to style, where it can be more fully felt. Sensitivity and compassion do not refer to sentiment. Rather, they suggest awareness that the subject of the assessment is a complex human being—with strengths as well as challenges—who may be deeply affected by seeing in print what is "wrong" with her or him. That recognition requires portraying a person with care as well as with honesty. True compassion summons humility, not irony or superiority in descriptions. Chapter 1 also touches on the ways that attitude can unknowingly seep into written material and betray insensitivity toward the subject or reader of the report. The attentive assessor-writer remains alert to stylistic choices that could betray such insensitivity. Table 3.5 gives examples of sentences we might find in reports, lists communication qualities they do or do not have, and suggests their potential impact on a reader. Based on the qualities shown in the

TABLE 3.5 Sensitivity, Compassion, and Respect for Subject/Reader

Sentences from Reports	Qualities and Impact
1. He does not have the cognitive capacity for any job in the national economy at this time or in the immediate future.	Accurate, using specific and concrete terms Clear for lay or professional reader Insensitive to impact on person assessed should s/he read report
2a. Results indicate that her current intellectual function is psychometrically within the mentally defective range. 2b. Follow-up test results continue to demonstrate extreme cognitive deficits.	Accurate, though higher on abstraction ladder Clear and specific for professional reader Insensitive to impact on person assessed should s/he read report
3. His overall response time variability was significantly impaired. Response-time variability indicated borderline impairment in quarter 3 and significant impairment in 2 and 4.	Assume accuracy, though only another in the same field would know for certain Unclear—very high on abstraction ladder Obscure language shows lack of respect for all readers other than fellow professionals

right-hand column of Table 3.5, the writing style of each might be described as follows:

1. Accessible but blunt
2. Professional, moderately readable, and blunt
3. Professional, difficult to understand, and laden with jargon

Groth-Marnat wrote in the 2009 article mentioned earlier—again, citing Harvey—that the three primary reasons psychologists create overly technical reports are (2009b, p. 304)

■ They feel they are writing for other professionals.
■ They want to impress their supervisors.
■ They want to bolster their prestige.

These overly technical reports would rely on language specific to the field of psychological or neuropsychological assessment, that is, on jargon.

Jettison Unnecessary Jargon

Jargon is one form of communicating, with distinct advantages but also many disadvantages. Jargon refers to "specialized vocabulary and idioms used by those in the same profession or work" (Webster's, 2001). It is a genuine tool that conveys precise meaning to colleagues. Its drawback, though, is that those words may not be understood by people outside the profession.

Jargon can reflect anxiety, intentional or not, and a desire to keep information safe from those who do not hold a "badge of membership" in a profession. The Three Mile Island nuclear plant accident at Middletown, Pennsylvania, in March 1979, provides illustrations of both.

- Officials worried that an explosion and meltdown of the nuclear core might occur. In public statements, however, they couched that fear in words so complex that listeners thought they were saying the exact opposite.
- Transcripts of phone calls between nuclear engineers were simpler and easier to understand than transcripts of engineers giving the same information to laypersons at news conferences (Sandman, 2004, topic 4, para. 8–10).

The badge-of-membership explanation parallels Groth-Marnat's list in the previous section and could easily apply to an assessment report. Some level of anxiety may also apply for the assessor-writer. S/he might be dealing with a complex case and fear that the recipient could blame the messenger delivering negative information. Either reason can result in an assessment report laden with terminology not easily understood outside the profession.

Suppose you walked through a theater with someone who worked in that profession. If she used the term "follow spot," you would probably understand that the term referred to the lighting. But if she mentioned leko and Fresnel, grid, fly, drop, business, and tag line, you might be hard-pressed to decide whether those words referred to lighting, stage, business management, or acting. (The first two are lighting; the third, fourth, and fifth involve the stage; and the last two refer to acting.) The terms represent two aspects of jargon: (a) words unique to a profession, expressing a thing or idea specific to that field, or (b) a word in common usage that is used somewhat differently within a professional field. A couple of simple examples in psychology:

- *Dysthymia* is a word unique to psychology, describing a mood disorder within the depression spectrum.
- *Affect*, a word in common usage, is somewhat redefined in the field of psychology. In general use, it is a verb meaning "to influence," as in "The story *affected* him deeply." But in psychology, it becomes a noun, is pronounced differently, and means emotion or emotional response.

With others in your profession, you can be easily understood when you use terms such as *dysthymia* or *affect* in its psychological meaning. But use those words with clients who are teachers, lawyers, or businesspeople, and they may get lost. As discussed in Chapter 2, accurate and accessible word choice provides a bridge from your world to theirs.

Clear Away Clutter

Even experienced writers find "clutter" in their writing if they pay attention (Zinsser, 1980). Clutter is made up of those words and phrases that provide no information and no energy to writing. Sugar, with its so-called empty calories, provides a short-lived boost to a body. But cluttered writing merely saps energy from your words and the meaning you want to convey. Why write "It is interesting to note..."? The phrase adds nothing. It telegraphs to the reader that s/he should stop reading on automatic, sit up, and take notice. But if you write with clarity and specificity, the reader will not be on automatic and you can trust that s/he will get the point. Chapter 6 discusses unnecessary phrases (i.e., clutter), and Table 6.7 lists common phrases and their simpler counterparts.

Clutter also appears when quoting or paraphrasing many comments from the same source. In assessment reports, you may be quoting extensively from interviews, other sources of history, questionnaires, and comments during testing. You will, of course, need to be specific about the source of all information (Groth-Marnat, 2009a). But continually repeating expressions such as "she said," "she stated," "noted the mother," or "she commented" within a paragraph clutters the writing. Instead, indicate clearly, once, that you are quoting that person, then simply give the

TABLE 3.6 Jargon and Clutter: Before and After

Sentence	Problem	Revision
At this point in time, assessment results suggest dysthymia.	Clutter and jargon	Assessment results show that he now struggles with chronic depression less severe than a major depression.
His lack of affect regulation is also problematic.	Jargon	He also manages his emotions erratically.
It should be noted that he shows indications of commitment to treatment.	Clutter	He said he is committed to extended treatment.

quotes (Strunk & White, 2000). They can be bulleted, numbered, or listed within a paragraph and separated by semicolons.

Table 3.6 provides examples of sentences that rely on clutter, jargon, or both and of how they might be reframed. As with so much else in writing, remaining present and aware will help filter out clutter as it pops up and will allow you to consciously choose whether or not to use jargon. Attending to both will strengthen your style.

Energize Text

We speak of a person "moving with energy" or "speaking with energy." Energy in those uses need not mean speed, but it does mean that the individual moves or speaks with purpose and conviction. Energy in writing demands the reader's attention and insists that s/he stay with you. Energy comes from concrete, specific words and active verbs. American professor of English Peter Elbow describes verbs as "pure energy" and nouns or adjectives as "pieces of used up energy" (1998, p. 137). Compare the different meanings of energy put forth by different forms of the word *energy* used in Table 3.7. Each of the examples is correct, but use of the verb in the last example draws a more precise picture and invites the reader to move to the next sentence. Obviously, we cannot write with verbs alone, as also discussed in Chapter 8. We can recognize that energy and movement in our writing increase, however, if we select strong verb forms whenever possible. We also see that effective use of verbs helps us avoid abstraction. Too many abstractions and clutter deflate energy. As discussed earlier in this chapter, however, a writer can clear away clutter and choose

TABLE 3.7 Energy in Noun, Adjective, and Verb

Word	Part of Speech	What it Does	Example
Energy	Noun	Describes a static, abstract concept	The child's *energy* filled the room.
Energetic	Adjective	Less abstract, but describes a quality that is not energy itself	The child used *energetic* gestures.
Energize	Verb	Most concrete; creates movement in the sentence	The child's gestures and stories *energized* his observers and himself.

appropriate levels of abstractions. Precision and energy will give your writing both strength and effectiveness (Elbow, 1998).

Dynamic Versus Linking Verbs

Energy also leaks away when sentences rely too heavily on linking verbs and not dynamic ones.

■ A *dynamic* or *active verb* shows movement. The subject of the sentence does something—for example, s/he writes, sits, speaks, or walks:
  "The assessor *signed* the report" or "The client *parked* his car" both show the subject taking clear action.
■ A *linking verb*, on the other hand, has no such movement. Instead, it merely shows a state or condition (Warriner, 1988):
  "The child *is* happy" or "His parents *were* waiting."

Linking verbs describe the subject of the sentence rather than the action the subject takes. Although not passive alone, when any form of *to be* joins with certain verb forms, together they create passive voice (Garner, 2009). Too many linking verbs and your writing becomes static and lifeless. Table 3.8 lists common linking verbs and shows how they become passive.

In the latter six examples in Table 3.8, you can usually figure out if the verb is being used as a linking verb one of two ways:

■ Notice in the table that *seem* has no active form; it is always a linking verb. So, try replacing the other five latter verbs with some form of *seem*. If it makes sense with that change, then it is linking. In the example "The child

TABLE 3.8 Common Linking Verbs

Verb	When Passive	Examples
To be (all forms): be, being, been; also I am, he is, they are, she was (were, has been, had been, will be, will have been, etc.)	Paired with verb form usually ending in -ed Also may end in -en or -t	She *was asked* to sit down. She *is being given* the test.
Appear	Passive: Paired with word that describes the subject of sentence	He *appeared* anxious.
	Active: Paired with word that does not describe the subject	He *appeared* at the door.
Feel	Passive	She *felt* nervous.
	Active	She *felt* the earthquake.
Look	Passive	The child *looked* sad.
	Active	The child *looked* at the assessor.
Seem	Passive	He *seemed* eager to start.
	Active	No active form.
Sound	Passive	She *sounds* angry.
	Active	She *sounded* the alarm.
Taste	Passive	The grilled fish *tastes* good.
	Active	The fish *tasted* the algae.

looked sad," replacing *looked* with *seemed* yields "The child *seemed* sad"; it makes sense, so *looked* is a linking verb in this case.

■ Or substitute *am, is, are* for the verb, and if the sentence makes sense, it is a linking verb (e.g., in the sentence, "The child *looked* sad," replacing *looked* with *is* yields "The child *is* sad," hence *looked* is linking).

(See also Chapter 8 for a discussion of adjectives and adverbs used with linking verbs.)

Psychological assessment reports and other professional writing often rely extensively on linking verbs. This use may stem from two dynamics:

1. Writers who feel the need to protect themselves from criticism
2. The assumption that objectivity in writing requires that the writer be invisible

Linking verbs, especially in the passive forms listed in Table 3.8, can give a feeling of protection from criticism. By using "seems" or "appears," writers avoid an active verb that commits them to a position in black and white. Those same words can contribute to a perception of objectivity in the writing. Unfortunately, overreliance on static verbs also reduces the power of a sentence in a way similar to the reduction caused by passive voice. (See the end of this chapter and the beginning of Chapter 4 for more on passive voice.) Examine these sentences:

1. John *seemed* uneasy and agitated.
2. Several times, John *leapt* from his chair and *paced* about the room.

The first example relies on the linking verb *seemed*. As shown in Table 3.8, that verb has no active form, and so the sentence has no movement. The second example, however, creates a specific, strong image because of its two active verbs: leapt and paced. The reader does not have to guess what the writer means by "uneasy and agitated" because it specifies John's behavior.

Writing gains power if we avoid using linking verbs as a matter of course. Rather, we can choose them consciously, either for effect or to express an idea with care.

"Smothered" Verbs

The forms of *to be* listed in Table 3.8 also help to "smother" verbs. When you convert a strong clear verb into a noun, it often requires pairing with some form of *to be* and leads to passive sentence structure (Bates, 2000).

- Clear: The client *authorized* release of the report.
- Smothered: *Authorization* to release the report *was given* by the client.

The first sentence clearly states who did what, using the verb *authorized*. The second smothers the verb by converting it to the noun *authorization* and pairing it with a form of *to be* (*was + given*). This change creates a passive structure and obscures the meaning. When you see too many nouns showing up paired with a form of *to be* in the same sentence, examine them. If you reclaim the stronger verb and describe its action, you move your sentence to active structure and shift back to clear style.

Active Versus Passive Structure

Psychologist and assessor Constance Fischer has emphasized the need for action in the language of assessment. Toward that end, she has used "languaging" as a verb, saying, "We are not just finding words to express states of affair. We are creating visions of reality" (Fischer, 2011). Active sentence structure will aid in creating those visions. Active structure compels the reader in a way that passive structure does not. Active structure shows clearly who performs what action:

Active: The *assessor wrote* her report.

Passive structure slows things down by shifting the focus:

Passive: The report *was written* by the *assessor*.

If a writer writes actively, while sometimes consciously choosing passive structure for effect, her overall writing gains power. Understanding the impact of passive structure is the final step toward energizing your writing style. Knowing when and how to use active and passive voice also contributes to your unique voice. Chapter 4 expands on active and passive voice and also discusses narrative and stylistic voice.

CHAPTER 4

Voice
What Is It and How Do I Find It?

Yet the concept of voice...keeps not going away.

Peter Elbow, American professor of English

H aving travelled through attitude, tone, and style, we finally reach voice (see Figure 4.1). Voice is a slippery term—it means different things to different people. The previous chapter's discussion of linking verbs touches on the concept of passive versus active voice. That fairly well-defined usage is, for many, the most easily understood frame for voice. Most people are also acquainted with the idea of first-, second-, or third-person narrative voice (or point of view). This chapter expands on the idea of active versus passive voice, as reflected in sentence structure. It then explores narrative voice and, finally, moves on to stylistic voice.

Active Versus Passive Voice in Sentence Structure

Many fields of work and study in our society struggle with passive voice in written communication. Government agencies have a reputation for turning out bureaucratic writing that relies heavily on passive voice. Corporations, too, often use this indirect writing structure. The scientific world, including psychology, has relied on passive voice in writing, likely an attempt to reflect objectivity. Nevertheless, individuals in a range of areas, including the sciences, increasingly support what English teachers have long

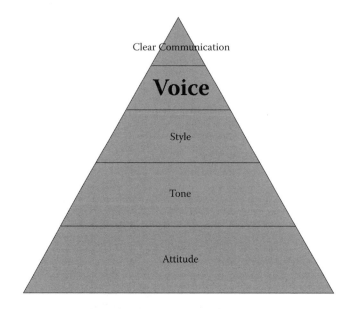

FIGURE 4.1 Building blocks of the assessment report: Voice.

stressed: Write in active voice. Use passive voice infrequently and for conscious effect.

> *Active sentence*
>> Structurally, a sentence is in active voice when the subject of the sentence carries out the action:
>> Active voice: I recommend therapy.
>> The subject *I* performs the action *recommend*, with *therapy* as the object of the action.
>
> *Passive sentence*
>> A sentence turns passive when the object of the original sentence moves to the subject position in the sentence:
>> Passive voice: Therapy is recommended by this assessor.
>> *Therapy*, the object of the first sentence, becomes the subject in passive voice.
>
> *Passive verb*
>> Any verb that acts on an object can be stated in passive voice by adding to it a form of the verb *to be*: *is, are, am, was, were, has been, had been, will be, will have been, being*, etc. In the active sentence, "I recommend therapy," the verb *recommend* acts on the object *therapy*. The verb

becomes passive by combining *is* + *recommend* + *-ed* = *is recommended*, i.e., "Therapy is recommended."

Active voice gives both clarity and action to a sentence; the reader has no doubt about who did what. Passive voice, on the other hand, puts information in reverse order, so the reader's brain has to take an extra step in deciphering who did what (Garner, 2009, p. 613). Reading comprehension slows, and the action present in the active sentence dissipates in the passive one. A second example of a sentence, first in active and then in passive:

Active voice: The judge ordered a psychological evaluation.
   The subject *judge* performs the action *ordered*, with *psychological evaluation* as the object of the action.
Passive voice: A psychological evaluation was ordered by the judge.
   The object of the first sentence, *psychological evaluation*, becomes the subject in passive voice.

Both active and passive forms are technically correct. Using passive voice does not mean that the writer's grammar is faulty. But the meaning of a sentence easily becomes buried in passive voice, so using active or passive voice relates mainly to clarity for the reader. A second important impact is one of retaining the reader's interest: Active writing compels attention in ways that passive does not. So why doesn't everyone write actively? Why the long history of passive voice in writing? One issue may be one of accountability. In the sample sentences given here, the final phrases could be dropped, and the reader would have to work to figure out who was responsible for the action described:

Therapy is recommended.
A psychological evaluation was ordered.

Who recommended the therapy? Who ordered the evaluation? In some cases that might have legal components, the assessor-writer may believe that lack of directness (e.g., using passive voice) will in some way protect himself or herself or the person assessed. In reality, it merely slows the reader's understanding. Since the assessor-writer signs the report, the reader can rightly assume the assessor's active role when anything seems vague. And since vagueness can also be resolved by directly asking for clarification, why not just be clear to begin with?

Using Active and Passive Voice

One assessor referred to the difference in active/passive phrasing as "definite" versus "tentative" and asked whether tentative phrasing is ever called for. The more tentative your writing, the less effective it is. Nevertheless, passive structure (i.e., tentative phrasing) might be chosen when the message is likely to unsettle the report's reader. In that case, the person assessed may either receive the report directly or is highly likely to read it. The delay needed to process the passive sentence, "Any job in the national economy is precluded by his cognitive capacity," might give the client time and space to accept the message with less distress. The active sentence, "His cognitive capacity precludes any job in the national economy at this time or in the immediate future," would give less distance from the topic and less time to assimilate it. Tentative or passive phrasing may also surface in writing when the assessor-writer is dealing with legal issues and feeling anxious about it. Either anxiety or fear can have an effect on communication, as discussed in Chapters 3 and 12. Whatever the anxiety about speaking too plainly, being conscious of your feelings will help you decide whether tentative phrasing or passive voice is truly called for.

An assessor-writer might *choose* to use passive voice in a report in three other situations:

1. When s/he wants to emphasize the object (person or thing receiving the action) rather than the subject/person who took action.

   Passive: Several more measures are required to complete testing.

   ■ Passive structure emphasizes *several more measures* as the important component.

   ■ The active structure, "Testing requires several more measures before completion," places emphasis on testing. The assessor-writer would choose the passive version to stress the important point that several more measures remain undone.

2. When s/he does not know who the subject/actor is or was.
   Passive: The child was placed for adoption at age 6 months.
   - Passive structure emphasizes *the child* as most important.
   - Active structure, "One or more of the birth parents placed the child for adoption at age 6 months," is accurate but vague due to lack of information about the birth parents. And since the child is the focal point, passive structure is likely best in this case.
3. When it is not important for the reader to know who the actor is.
   Passive: James was evaluated for learning disabilities.
   - Passive structure emphasizes *James* as the essential role.
   - Active structure, "Dr. Jones evaluated James for learning disabilities," emphasizes the role of Dr. Jones. Depending on the intended reader, either is accurate. If the reader is a court and Dr. Jones might be called on to testify, use of his name in the active version might be essential. If the report is for the person assessed, however, he already knows who evaluated him, and so passive voice could be acceptable.

Table 4.1 compares the pros and cons of using active and passive voice and when to use either. For the most part, passive voice has less power and less clarity than active and so is more likely to get the writer into problems with style. If you recognize when your writing lapses into passive voice, then you can make conscious choices about its use for any of the reasons listed in Table 4.1. But for the majority of your writing, think subject + verb + object. It is clear, clean, and least confusing for writer and reader.

Narrative Voice/Point of View

Narrative voice reflects the point of view the assessor-writer takes in writing the report. Pronouns are the keys to defining that point of view:

- First person: I, we
- Second person: You
- Third person: He, she, they, it

TABLE 4.1 Active Versus Passive Voice: Pros, Cons and How and When to Use Each

	Active Voice	Passive Voice
How to form	Subject/noun + verb + object [a] Example: The *judge* + *ordered* + a *psychological evaluation*.	Object becomes subject Add form of *to be* [b] to main verb Example: A *psychological evaluation* + *was ordered* + by the *judge*.
When to use	In most writing, most of the time	By choice, when: • Object is more important than subject • Subject is not known • Reader does not need to know subject • Message requires softening • Responsible party seeks concealment
Pros	Clear and concise Connects most directly with reader Conveys action	Emphasizes object Softens difficult message Conceals responsible party to some extent
Cons	Direct message may upset or offend reader Specifies responsible party when s/he seeks concealment	Indirect and vague Reader's brain must process harder to figure out who does what Holds reader at arm's length More wordy

[a] *Subject/noun*: In a sentence, the person or thing that acts. *Verb*: The action taken by the subject. *Object*: The person or thing that receives the action of the verb.

[b] Forms of *to be*: *I am, she is, they are* (also *was, were, has been, had been, will be, will have been, be, being, been,* etc.). (See also "Dynamic Versus Linking Verbs" in Chapter 3 and Table 3.8.)

Third Person

Reports to third-party referring professionals will likeliest be written in third-person narrative voice. *He*, *she*, and *they* are the pronouns that provide the most emotional distance from both subject and reader of a report. Two variations on third person play a part in these reports.

■ Third-person *objective* strives for an unbiased view and intends to report only facts and observable actions without interpretation. This is the third-person technique that scientific writing and newspaper articles usually intend and is likely the narrative voice most assessor-writers aim for in a standard report.

- Third-person *subjective* most often occurs in fiction narrative. It tells a story through the thoughts, feelings, and opinions of a specific character. Some qualities of third-person subjective voice may find their way into assessment reports. In writing a report, the assessor-writer does not merely report facts. S/he also interprets observed behavior and testing data, draws conclusions, and makes recommendations. Those subjective aspects intentionally draw on the assessor-writer's training and expertise; due to them, an assessment report may combine third-person *subjective* and third-person *objective*.

First Person and Second Person

Assessor-writers may hesitate to use the word *I* in a report, due to their training in academic and/or scientific writing that emphasizes objectivity. As discussed in the preceding section, however, an assessment report carries some degree of subjectivity. For that reason, first-person voice/point-of-view can clarify the subjective, interpretive portions and make narrative sense in even a standard report.

A variation on the standard report specifically calls for use of both first person (I) and second person (you): a letter directly to the person assessed (more on this type of letter in Chapter 11). This letter can be somewhat more informal than a standard report and many degrees more personal. In this case, using *I* and *you* will aid the reader's sense of being in direct communication with the assessor-writer through the written document. You will also use third person in portions of the letter that describe factual information and data. Second person (you) as the only point of view will likely not occur in your letter. For the most part, only instructional manuals and self-help books use second-person narrative voice exclusively. Table 4.2 provides an overview of narrative voice/point-of-view and its impact on your reader.

Stylistic Voice

Stylistic voice reflects the assessor-writer's unique perspective on the material and how s/he chooses to communicate that material.

TABLE 4.2 Narrative Voice: 1st-, 2nd-, and 3rd-Person Point of View

Point-of-View Pronoun	When to Use	Impact on Reader
3rd: he, she, they, it Objective 3rd Subjective 3rd	Standard report for referring professional	Distance Varying levels of objectivity
2nd: you	Letter to person assessed; in combination with 1st and 3rd person	Brings reader into the communication process
1st: I, we	Letter to person assessed; often in combination with 2nd and 3rd person	Directly connects assessor-writer with reader

It encompasses all the aspects of attitude, tone, and style covered in previous chapters:

- Base your attitude on data gathered, questions asked and answered.
- Understand your attitude toward your subject and audience.
- Choose the right words to express your ideas.
- Select and arrange material carefully.
- Juxtapose material with sensitivity to nuance.
- Build words into sentences and sentences into paragraphs.
- Structure sentences, paragraphs, and report with a clear beginning, middle, and end.
- Be clear, specific, and accurate.
- Say what is necessary—no more, no less.
- Maintain communication values of sensitivity, compassion, and respect for your subject and reader.

Stylistic voice includes the components listed in Table 4.3.

Some say that you hear voice in your head rather than reading it on the page (Gerard, 2000). Think of the times when you read

TABLE 4.3 Components of Stylistic Voice

Assessor-writer's unique perspective

Attitude + tone + style

Research and questions answered + structure

Narrative stance

Instinctive

Unfolds naturally, not fabricated

TABLE 4.4   Some Pros and Cons of Voice: The Both/And Approach

Reasons for Attending to Voice	Reasons Against Attending to Voice
Makes written words easier to understand	Distracts readers from meaning of words
Contributes to more effective writing by lending subliminal power to words	Avoiding voice can be a powerful tool in objective (scientific) writing
Helps people enjoy writing more	"Voice" is too vague a metaphor for use
Helps people with reading	"No voice" enlarges possibility of meaning and interpretation

Note: Adapted from "Voice in Writing Again: Embracing Contraries," by P. Elbow, 2007, in *College English,* 70.2, pp. 168–188. Copyright 2007 by P. Elbow.

words automatically but do not get the meaning of the words until you slow down and read them again. When you silently reread them, with attention, you "hear" the voice of the writer.

Others have denied the existence of voice or its value in writing. American professor of English Peter Elbow traces the periodic argument about voice back to the Ancient Greeks' "conflict about the self in language" (2007, p. 1). The Greeks disagreed whether a writer's words reflected true self-disclosure or the act of crafting a self. Elbow argues for a both/and approach to the value of voice. For example, on the one hand, he observes that voice is useful as metaphor—that it can help writers improve by recognizing that "writing is a transaction between humans" (p. 8). On the other hand, he stresses that exclusive focus on voice can lead the writer astray. S/he might assume that "good writing requires *only* voice [emphasis added]" (p. 11), while ignoring the need for intellectual rigor. See Table 4.4 for additional pros and cons of voice.

This discussion will not try to decide a debate that has spanned centuries. We will take the both/and approach and accept that writing is not *just* about voice, but that voice plays a part in how the writer connects with the reader.

Voice grows as you work through your research—through the questions asked and answered during the assessment—and as you choose your structure to communicate that information. Part II of this book addresses structure, wording, and punctuation that the assessor-writer might choose for a document. These are not mere window-dressing. Rather, they are essential components, representing aspects of attitude, tone, style, and voice in the completed report. Voice also deepens as you allow it to unfold through your narrative stance.

Narrative Stance

Voice grows from your "narrative stance," the perspective you take in communicating with your reader. What works in one case for a writer may not work in another case or for another writer. Choice of narrative stance will depend on the assessor-writer's skills, preferences, and goals in writing the report (Richardson, 1990).

Not the least important consideration is that of the comfort level of the primary reader. If you are writing for a court, for example, the intended reader might be a judge. If you are writing about a school-age child, your reader could be a parent. The substantive information would be the same for either reader; both would appreciate clear, understandable English, rather than dense, jargon-laden writing. The judge, however, would likely expect and feel more comfortable with a formal report in near-neutral voice. The parent, on the other hand, might well respond better to a less formal letter. While still giving all the important information, the assessor-writer's voice could be more personal in this letter format.

Narrative stance defines itself in two related subsets: first, whether the writer speaks in first or third person (as discussed earlier in this section), and second, what level of emotional distance s/he maintains from the subject of the report (Gerard, 2000). Clear-cut distinction in narrative stance appears when contrasting the standard, formal assessment report, as written for the judge, with a report in the form of the personal letter to the parents of a child:

- *The standard formal report* is written in third person (he, she, they). It likely uses passive voice in its sentence structure and many linking verbs (as discussed in Chapter 3). Any clear indication of attitude that breaks through is a discordant exception. The assessor-writer's attitude may be suggested through tone (word choice and juxtaposition of material) but is otherwise imperceptible. Personality is erased from the written document, and voice is faint, at best, reflecting extensive emotional distance between writer and subject and/or reader. This approach results in a neutral or nearly neutral voice and lends the report a quality of objectivity.

- *A report as a personal letter* combines first, second, and third person (I, you, s/he, or they) and strives for active sentence structure and active verbs. The assessor-writer's attitude clearly reveals itself in tone (words and material) and style (clarity, accuracy, compassion, respect). Strong voice grows out of this specificity and reaches out to bridge the distance between writer and reader.

Neutral Voice and Objectivity in Writing

Do these exist? Yes—and no. Certainly, the intent toward objectivity can be real in a writer's mind, as can the intent to erase voice from a document. The real questions, however, are whether it is desirable and possible to accomplish this intent.

In scientific writing for publication, the researcher must make a careful case for the objectivity of the research and its results. Reputation and standing can well depend on it. Avoiding personal pronouns (I, we) to encourage neutral voice appears one way to accomplish the perception of objectivity. Yet, some scientists question whether even scientific writing must be 100% devoid of first-person voice. Granted, the use of "I" throughout a scientific paper would be discordant and could leave the perception of non-objectivity. But as psychologist Martin Seligman (1991) observes, the occasional use of "I" is less clumsy than a convoluted sentence using passive voice. And the APA *Publication Manual* (2010, p. 69) specifically permits personal pronouns to avoid ambiguity. The total absence of voice need not be the only way of achieving objectivity in scientific writing.

By extension, we can see that this is even more the case in writing psychological assessment reports. Though a professional relationship demanding a professional report, this process is also one of personal interaction—and in Elbow's phrase quoted earlier in this chapter, writing is a transaction between humans (2007, p. 8). While the assessor-writer may wish to communicate a sense of objectivity in the testing process, s/he is, after all, dealing with fellow humans—in the person tested, referring professional, parents, etc. The report's intended audience knows who the writer is, at least by name, and in many cases actually sought the assessor-writer's expertise. Since the parties are clearly identified, the need for neutral voice declines in importance.

As for the possibility of accomplishing a 100% neutral voice, achieving 100% of anything can be a challenge. But in theory, complete neutrality could be accomplished by conscious choices throughout the report-writing process. Through the components explored in this and previous chapters, we see how a report conveys different qualities depending on the assessor-writer's choices as s/he writes. Voice begins with all the earlier decisions that contribute to attitude, tone, and style; the aspects discussed previously in this chapter then complete its formation. As an outgrowth of all steps in the process, voice can appear in our writing, consciously or unconsciously. Voice may show up unplanned in the same way that attitude can become apparent by bleed-through in choice of words. The more unaware we are of choices, the more likely that voice can surprise us and the less likely that we can truly accomplish neutral voice if that is our wish. How much better to make a conscious choice to allow, encourage, or minimize it. The goal or forum for the assessment report determines that decision. In a formal third-party report, with emphasis on the data, the assessor-writer may intend a neutral voice. In a more conversational letter format, s/he may feel freer to allow opinion or personal connection to show through. In either case, the writer encourages the desired, specific voice by careful, conscious attention to attitude, tone, and style.

Being conscious of voice does not mean forcing a voice, nor does it mean becoming self-conscious about it. Either can lead to awkwardness or artificiality. The essence of voice is instinctive—we uncover it, rather than fabricating it (Gerard, 2000). Returning to the music metaphor from Chapter 2's discussion of tone, a singer seldom begins with the depth and breadth in singing that s/he achieves after years of extensive work. During those years, s/he may need to experiment—to imitate the phrasing and style of other singers before finding the voice truest to him/herself. And so with voice in writing. It might be natural to take on another's style, for awhile, as a way to work toward the voice that is yours alone (Lamott, 1994). Paying attention to the details within attitude, tone, and style helps to grow your own voice. Ultimately, that voice will enable you to "sing"—that is, to clearly communicate as shown in Figure 4.2.

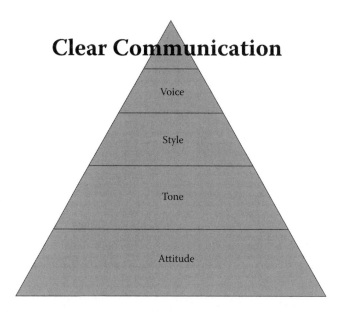

FIGURE 4.2   Building blocks of the assessment report: Clear communication.

MORTAR TO FORTIFY THE BUILDING BLOCKS

Grammar and Editing

Unless you find intriguing the twists and turns of English grammar, you may well consider Part II to be "the boring bit," as our British cousins might express it. Part II provides a handbook of common grammar problems encountered in writing psychological assessment reports. The chapters in this part will discuss grammar in its broadest usage, including spelling and punctuation as well as sentence structure. Third-party reports benefit from correct grammar, as do letters written directly to the person assessed. The chapters in Part II will use examples that apply to both.

Figure P2.1 shows the relationship among the building blocks of style in Part I and the mortar of grammar in Part II. Grammar binds the content and style of your writing. American professor of English Peter Elbow (1998) points out that the word *glamour* began as a regional pronunciation of the word *grammar*. In the Middle Ages, if you knew grammar, you had glamour because you "understood a mystery" (p. 167) that most did not—the system of rules that governed language. Knowing this system opened doors to a better life. Today, most people would not describe English grammar as glamorous, but it still provides a door—this time into

FIGURE P2.1 Wheel of connection: Grammar + style.

clear communication with others. And without some standardized grounding, written communication would descend into a metaphorical Tower of Babel.

Many people view grammar with dread, and they fear getting it wrong. Meaning can get lost in worry about sentence structure or irregular verbs. English grammar begins with a high level of complexity; many parts of it then spiral upward into more complex and hard-to-remember alternatives. Add to that the differences among the conventions of more than a dozen different style manuals—not to mention the requirements of the American Psychological Association's *Publication Manual* (2010)—and any writer might feel understandably overwhelmed. But English grammar relies on certain basic rules that we can learn or look up, as required. This part of the book aims to cut through as much chaff as possible in those rules to uncover the basic grain underneath. Tables throughout these chapters give reminders of those basics and provide examples of usage. As a handbook and reference, the chapters are thorough. They do not, however, give all intricacies of English grammar, nor do they give comprehensive alternatives among the many style manual interpretations. For anyone interested in those details, sources in the reference list

TABLE P2.1   Parts of Speech and What They Do

Part of Speech	What It Does	Examples
Adjective	Qualifies or alters meaning of a *noun* or *pronoun*	Tall, short, big, green, happy, sad
Adverb	Qualifies or alters meaning of a *verb*, an *adjective*, or another *adverb*	Slowly, quickly, late, everywhere, frequently
Conjunction	Connects words or groups of words	And, but, although, before, until
Noun	Names a person, place, thing, action, quality, etc.	Test, assessment, office, client
Preposition	Connects a *noun* or *pronoun* to another word	Over, under, around, through
Pronoun	Replaces *noun*(s)	He, she, they, who, all, few, this
Verb	Shows action or states existence	Write, score, drive, is, seems

Note: Adapted from *English Composition and Grammar: Complete Course,* by J. E. Warriner, 1988, Orlando, FL: Harcourt Brace Jovanovich. Copyright 1988 by Harcourt Brace Jovanovich.

will provide a place to start. And since assessor-writers are familiar with APA format, when basic or standard usage differs from APA's, those differences are mentioned.

As discussed in Chapter 3, those in a specialized field such as psychology often communicate via jargon, using words that laypeople may not know. Grammar, too, has its share of jargon, such as in the area of verb tenses. Chapters throughout the book—most notably these in Part II—avoid those specialized grammatical words or phrases as much as possible. Rather than use jargon to label a concept, discussions rely on descriptions of what a concept does and how it is used. Some use of grammar jargon, however, is unavoidable; when labels must be used, they are defined in the text and also listed in the book's glossary. To start, Table P2.1 lists the most common grammatical terms and what they do.

CHAPTER **5**

Big Picture, Small Details
Format, Write, Edit, Proof

Bird by bird, buddy. Just take it bird by bird [father's advice to son, about writing a long report].

Anne Lamott, American writer

On the desk of Ms./Mr./Dr. Assessor-Writer sits a very thick, brown accordion folder. It is filled with testing results, questionnaires, interview data, former reports, letters, and supervision notes. S/he knows how to organize and sift data. With the help of education, training, and experience, s/he can set up worksheets, spreadsheets, and lists of testing results, analyze and integrate the data, and figure out important findings. But when it comes time to sit at the computer and write a report, s/he finds any excuse not to begin. S/he dreads the struggle to make the data hang together in the writing process. S/he wonders how to structure the report—how to find the right words to speak to the intended audience and still keep it a reasonable length. How will s/he craft a well-realized assessment report that has a beginning, a middle, and an end?

Some assessor-writers may have already chosen standardized report formats that work. Experience, sanitized report samples, or examples from books will have provided your template. Others may feel that a customized approach may better serve the client. For you who wish to consciously create one or more formats, the ideas in this chapter will help you to do that. In addition to steps in establishing format, we will also discuss general approaches to

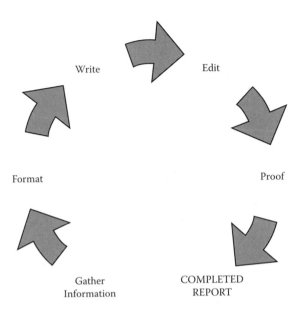

Write

Edit

Format

Proof

Gather
Information

COMPLETED
REPORT

FIGURE 5.1 Writing process flow.

the writing process as well as how to evaluate, edit, and proof the report. Figure 5.1 shows the steps and flow in this process.

Formatting

As important as clear writing is to the reader's understanding, equally so is the structural logic of the document and the flow of its content. Planning the format before writing enables both to unfold. You, the assessor-writer, are the expert on psychological or neuropsychological assessment. You must not only provide individual pieces of information, but also tie disparate pieces together for your readers. You will lead them through the complicated maze of assessment data and bring them out at the end with a real understanding of how and why you came to the conclusions you did. Thinking through the flow of material will better enable you to do this.

Choosing Font: Style and Size

The APA *Publication Manual* (2010) calls for Times New Roman font at 12-point size for manuscript submission. That same font and size has also become the standard for use in business documents. This font derives from typeface considered more readable than others because of the way that the ends of the letters are formed. You may, of course, choose to use any font you wish, but since an assessment report represents both a profession (psychology) and a business (yours), adhering to the standards of APA and the larger business world makes sense.

Ordering Sections and Content

To figure out which sections you need and what content will fill them out, start by answering two questions:

1. Who is my audience, the intended reader?
   If writing a third-party report to the referral source, do they expect a certain format, or is the assessor-writer free to design what s/he feels will work? If the report goes to the person assessed, might a letter format be acceptable, even desirable?
2. What is my specific objective in writing the report?
   Make suggestions for treatment? Get learning accommodations for a student? Convey information and recommendations to an attorney or court? Provide suggestions for situation management to a client? Or some combination of these?

The more clear and specific you can be in defining your intended audience and answering the referral question(s), the stronger will be your report. Bear in mind, however, that a report ultimately may have additional audiences downstream. As psychologist and assessor Irving Weiner wrote, "Psychologists doing these evaluations are well advised to keep in mind that their written report, although not addressed to the client, may be shown to him or her" (personal communication, June 2010). A report intended primarily for the parents of a teenager, for example, may also be shared with his or her high school, therapist, and eventually, college. When older, the teen may read the report. Neuropsychologist and assessor Diane Engelman described her approach: "Though the report will be addressed to the primary audience, I know it may be read by others—may be called on to serve more than one purpose—and so I must keep that in mind when I write" (personal communication, October 2010).

Factoring in multiple audiences, however, can create a diffuse and possibly less useful report. To counteract that diffusion, the

TABLE 5.1 Writing Reports for Primary and Secondary Audiences

	Exclusive Focus on Primary Audience	Simultaneous Inclusion of Multiple Audiences	Sequential Integration of Multiple Audiences
Writing method	Information directed to primary audience only	Information included for all audiences, section by section, as report is written	In first draft, information directed to primary reader; in editing, add detail for other audiences
Pros	Simplicity and clarity	Ability to integrate primary and secondary details in first draft of report	Clear-cut distinction in writing process between primary and secondary audiences
Cons	Excludes impact on potential secondary audiences	Time consuming, possibly confusing, to go back and forth between audiences	Takes time to add detail for additional audiences after first draft

assessor-writer can choose to (a) write exclusively to the primary audience; (b) consciously include specific information for secondary audiences as s/he writes; or (c) draft the report for the primary audience, then integrate details for the secondary audiences during the editing process. Table 5.1 lists pros and cons of each of these approaches.

Even when taking into account secondary, downstream readers, the report should be crafted with the principal audience clearly in mind. Designate sections based on what you believe the reader needs and wants to know. Set up section headings of the report first, so that you have a place to put the various pieces of information you'll be writing about. Order the sections logically. The audience and the use you believe they will make of the information will define the structural logic of the report. Its flow of content will include all necessary information—but nothing extraneous.

Typical ways of ordering written material include (Bates, 2000; Warriner, 1988)

- Inductively (specific to general)
- Deductively (general to specific)
- Chronologically (to describe steps in a process)
- Spatially (shows where items are in relation to each other)

- In order of importance (usually with most important coming either first or last)
- Showing comparison or contrast
- As an analogy

In this list, the last five could be used to structure entire documents. For our purposes, though, they are probably most valuable within sections or paragraphs. (See Chapter 6 for more on that subject.) In the present discussion, we'll touch on only the roles that inductive versus deductive approaches play in writing the report.

The nature of an assessment may be called inductive: The assessor gathers a wealth of specific details that lead to general conclusions. It might seem, then, that the most logical format for a report would likewise be inductive, taking the reader through each detail before putting them together into a general conclusion. While valuable for analysis, however, induction is not necessarily the best approach for developing a readable report.

The opposite approach, deduction, works from general-to-specific and provides the clearest method of communicating why and how details are important. The reader, who may be a layperson, can easily get lost if you do not establish a larger context for the facts you spell out in your report. Simply put, describe the "forest" within which the assessment took place before spelling out the "trees" that point toward your findings. The fields of psychological and neuropsychological assessment are rich in detail. The more specific detail a writer must incorporate, the more important it is to define the general structure of the forest before bringing in the detail of the trees. (See Chapter 3 for more on specific versus general terms.)

In general, material read first and last will stick with the reader longest (Emmons, 1975). Think of it as a sort of upside-down normal distribution, with the peaks on either end representing the sections the reader will most easily remember. The first section stays with the reader because s/he brings a clear mind to the document and its subject. The last section lingers because it is the last thing read and so is freshest in memory. The bulk of the material in the middle can become vague and thereby less useful, unless the assessor-writer takes steps to accent it. One way of doing this is to craft each individual section in the report as having a beginning, middle, and end, as does the report as a whole.

This structure allows you to emphasize important material at the beginning and end of each section, with the transitional material in the middle. This middle material may bridge or weave together the more important pieces at the start and finish of a section. Set up the report with attention to structure—overall and within individual sections. In doing so, the choices of which information to include become more conscious and their impact greater.

Possible Formats

A number of publications give examples of sections to include in an assessment report (Braaten, 2007; Goldfinger & Pomerantz, 2010; Groth-Marnat, 2009a; Zuckerman, 2005). Many discuss which types of reports call for which sections, and some also list standard terms and statements to use. Ultimately, each assessor-writer will develop his or her own formats to meet the needs of various principal audiences—clinical, educational, forensic, or the person assessed. While specifics may vary depending on style of report, sections will likely include some variation and combination of those listed in Table 5.2. Certain sections may remain constant from one audience to the next, though the weight placed on any section in a given report may vary (Groth-Marnat, 2009a).

Little wonder that Ms./Mr./Dr. Assessor-Writer might feel overwhelmed with so much information to integrate into a wide variety of segments. S/he might ponder whether a simpler approach is possible. "Simple" can be a confusing premise: Does it mean shorter, or less complex, or less rigorous? Those who understand all the complications of a subject may believe that simple

TABLE 5.2 Assessment Reports to Third Parties: Possible Sections to Include

Personal information

Reasons for referral

Dates of evaluation and testing

Pertinent history

Assessment procedures

Behavioral observations

Test results

Discussion of findings

Diagnostic impressions

Summary and recommendations

indicates a sacrifice of rigor, whereas the opposite is often more accurate. Two meanings of the word simple are "unembellished" and "easy to understand" (Webster's, 2001). If we can take a complex idea and state it simply—that is, clearly and concisely—we have a far better chance of being understood.

Donders (1999) makes a compelling case for shorter pediatric neuropsychological reports. The author proposes a straightforward structure that focuses not so much on the data itself as on its meaning to the intended reader. He suggests writing succinctly and specifically, breaking down the information into just what the reader needs to know and conveying it in a manner easily understood. While this approach will likely be shorter, it does not follow that it will be less complex or less rigorous. The assessor-writer will have sifted the complexity and rigor of the work until what remains is its clear essence. That clarity is what s/he then shares with the person receiving the report.

When writing a report for the person being assessed or the parents of a child or adolescent, the report might be formatted as a personal letter, with necessary data incorporated into the discussion. Sections might be similar to those in third-party reports but adjusted to speak to the individual and his or her needs. Throughout, the information would be presented conversationally, directly to the client, with special attention to the impact of word choice on the person assessed or on the parents of a child. (For more on the topic of sensitivity in word choice, see Chapter 2.) Although a letter might use a more conversational writing approach, ordering material for clarity and flow is still important. Table 5.3 lists possible sections in a neuropsychological report in letter format to the parents of a child or adolescent.

Additionally, findings in a letter may be presented in a variation of the order-of-importance method listed earlier in this chapter. That is, the information may be rank-ordered, as discussed in Chapter 2, according to Finn's levels 1, 2, and 3 of easiest-to-hardest material for the client to assimilate and accept (Finn, 2007). Table 5.4 contrasts ordering and phrasing material in a standard report versus a rank-ordered letter. The letter examples illustrate a personal letter format that is often used in the area of Collaborative/Therapeutic Assessment. In this form of assessment, questions that the client and assessor have jointly agreed to answer may drive the discussion of findings, the letter, and,

TABLE 5.3 Assessment Report to the Person Assessed: Possible Sections to Include in Letter

Personal information (in letter's subject block)
Dates of evaluation (in letter's subject block)
Referral information (incorporated into opening of letter)
Pertinent background
Overview of findings
Cognitive abilities
Academic abilities
Neuropsychological findings
Personality findings
Suggestions or recommendations

indeed, the assessment itself. In that case, the assessor-writer structures sections of the letter around those questions. (See Chapter 11 for more on this type of letter.)

Using an Outline

Mainstream writing and grammar books recommend outlining as a process for the writer to order thoughts and to figure out the shape of the document s/he plans to write (Strunk & White, 2000). The APA *Publication Manual* (2010) likewise recommends an outline as a way to both focus the writing and to notice omissions. Few people have fond memories of the requirement in school to outline a paper before writing it. Indeed, when required to turn in an outline and a paper together, students have been known to write the paper and then create the outline. Belatedly, a writer can come to recognize the value of outlining in order to get material firmly in hand. The standard outline, in which sections are divided into roman numerals, capital letters, numbers, and lowercase letters, may work for some. Others find it too rigid. This discussion will touch briefly on standard outlining as well as a less formal approach.

A standard outline can be one of either topics or sentences (Warriner, 1988). The *topic outline* will list words or phrases. A *sentence outline* can convey fuller meaning of the same headings through complete sentences. See Table 5.5 for examples of each. Whether the assessor-writer uses topics/phrases or sentences in standard outlining depends on the individual's working style and need for prompts when expanding the outline.

TABLE 5.4 Methods of Presenting Findings: Sample Order and Phrasing

	Standard Report: Ordered by Assessor's Impression of Most Important	Question from teen: "I seem to think differently from other people. I have trouble paying attention and focusing. Is my attention problem related to my variable moods?"	Letter to Teen/Parents: Answering Question Based on Finn's Levels 1, 2, 3
Reasons for referral: • Attention issues • Lower grades than previously • Depression	Client functions within the superior psychometric range of intelligence. In various elements of attention, initial registration of information is variable. Results reveal difficulties with various dimensions of attention. Tests imply frontal system involvement as may be observed in those with ADHD. Demonstrates the comorbidity of depressive-like symptoms.		Level 1: You are very smart; your overall intelligence was in the superior range. But you seem to have problems with thinking logically and perceiving events realistically, especially when you are anxious or overloaded. Level 2: Yes, unhappy moods can affect your ability to attend or focus. They may interfere with doing your schoolwork in a way that reflects your intelligence. Level 3: But you also have an attention problem that is separate from your emotions, as shown by other lower scores. These indicate that your problems are a result of ADHD.
Presentation of data:	Often presents data in tables, secondarily as descriptions in text.		Presents data mainly as descriptions in text; some short tables

TABLE 5.5 Example of Standard Outline: Topics Versus Sentences

Type of Outline	Advantage
Topic outline	
I. Pertinent background	Brevity
A. Childhood	Simplicity
B. Medical history	
Sentence outline	
I. Certain aspects of the client's background are pertinent to this assessment.	Thoroughness
A. His early childhood included family separation and problems in school.	Head start on writing process
B. A review of family medical history showed attentional difficulties in both maternal and paternal relatives.	

An Alternative Approach to Outlining

A less formal way of outlining might be called the "plumping" approach. It lends itself to smooth transition from topics and ideas through sentences to the first draft of an assessment report. The steps of this approach are listed as follows:

1. *List sections*: In a new document, list the sections you will include based on who you know to be your primary reader.
2. *Number/bold*: Number or highlight these major headings to help you keep track of them and easily find them on the page.
3. *List topics*: Under each main heading, list topics or phrases that identify what you'll be covering, each on a separate line.
4. *Dash/bullet*: Use dashes or bullets to precede each topic if you want a visual marker for each separate idea.
5. *Plump*: Add and expand each section/topic/phrase as your ideas develop. The more you add, the more the words and phrases begin developing into full thoughts and sentences. Don't worry at this point about the length or clarity of sentences—just get the important ideas and information down in writing.
6. *Reorder*: Cut and paste to change the sequence of information as you refine and work with each topic/phrase/sentence.
7. *A bit of self-deception*: Sometimes we can hold off anxiety about writing by the name we give it. Consider this an "outline" as long as you wish. But keep adding ideas to your

outline just as if you were writing your first draft. Finally, you will know when it's time to shift and change its name.

8. *Draft 1*: Save the outline into a new document as draft one and begin to write, section by section. If you have added and plumped content sufficiently, you will at this point have a rough first draft, or very nearly so.

9. *Number the pages*: Insert numbers at the top right of each page. A number at the top will guide the reader's eye, since s/he begins at the top. A staple or paper clip may obscure the left side, so place numbers on the right.

Writing

When you have all the information outlined in some way—whether a standard outline or a comprehensive list under each section heading—it's time to begin the actual writing. If your outline has retained its phrase/topic quality, and you have not "plumped" your ideas, now is the time to expand them into sentences. Neither the outline nor the first draft is the time for finessing your writing. Editing comes later. For now, write down your comprehensive thoughts and interpretations in sentence form, even if long and meandering. Just get them down. Later, you can smooth words, ideas, and transitions as you edit for length and clarity.

Good writing is good writing, whether it is explanatory nonfiction writing, such as that found in articles or reports, or so-called creative writing in stories. People often assume that the creative process can only apply to fiction writing and that clear thought and organization must apply only to nonfiction writing. In reality, both benefit from clarity and specificity in organization, sentence structure, and word choice. Both also gain from creative and intuitive ways of framing information for the reader. Creativity and critical thinking strengthen each other (Elbow, 1998).

While the psychological assessor interviews and tests a client, then scores, analyzes, and integrates findings, s/he relies on personal insight as well as on the numbers. This insight might be considered a sibling to creativity or intellectual inventiveness. Finding the right words for the meeting of data and insight demands a creative skill that goes well beyond mere recitation of facts. Dividing your writing into two stages enables both creativity and clear ideas:

1. *Creative, intuitive draft*: Work with the sections you have set up in the formatting step. Starting with the ideas you have plumped from phrases to more complex thoughts or sentences, allow words and ideas to flow in each section. Don't self-censor. American writer Anne Lamott writes, "Almost all good writing begins with terrible first efforts" (1994, p. 25). Let this creative step be your "terrible first effort," if necessary.

2. *Critical, evaluative revision*: Evaluate and refine your ideas, as discussed in the section to follow. Be critical of your material and how you frame the information.

Some writers with experience and self-knowledge are able to do both steps at once. And with practice and trusting our insight, the rest of us may find that more sections come out refined on our first pass through them. Counting on the two-step process, however, is probably wisest.

Evaluating and Editing

Read through what you have written. Evaluating critically and then editing provide your key to crispness and clarity. If you have written the first draft freely, some parts of your style may feel too loose or casual. Revise those during editing to better suit your intended style and voice (Elbow, 1998). Sometimes printing out your first draft allows you to see more clearly what you have or have not done. Evaluate your writing for

- *Content*: Do your details give all necessary information but nothing extraneous?
- *Structure*: Does your order and flow of material make sense? Do you have clear transitions between ideas? Is information that shares a common thread grouped together?
- *Attitude/tone/style/voice*: Is it appropriate for your intended audience(s)? Is the writing clear, accurate, kind, vivid, and crisp? Does it sound like you, in your unique voice?

When you have answered these questions, save the document again as your next draft and begin to revise, revise, revise. One excellent English grammar book suggests the following as useful techniques for revision:

1. Add
2. Cut
3. Replace
4. Reorder

Each of these can apply to information, sentences, or words/phrases (Warriner, 1988, p. 25). You plumped your material in the beginning to expand the detail; now you prune it to increase clarity and conciseness. Think of yourself as a gardener, accenting the lines, shape, and even individual branches of an overgrown bush by judicious pruning.

Also during the revising process you might decide to use one or more lists of bullet points. If your points are ranked, then numbering is the better choice, but if they could be rearranged and not lose impact, use bullets. These lists not only guide the reader's eye down a series of words, phrases, sentences, or paragraphs; they also allow additional white space in your formatting. White space, too, guides the reader by breaking up the unending text on a page.

You may also choose to add highlighting (bold, underscore, italics) to guide the reader's eye. Be judicious in highlighting, however—too much is as bad as too little. Too much underlining or italics can seem as if the writer does not trust the reader to interpret her or his words. And too much bolding or all CAPS can read as if the writer is shouting at the reader.

When you think you are done, bring in another person if possible. Ask him or her to read your report and tell you if what you wrote is easily understandable, especially if it is intended for a lay audience. Ask that they read it for clarity only; don't have them proof or correct copy at this stage. Change or elaborate any section your reader finds confusing. After you have created and refined your own template for reports, you may find this second eye less necessary, though always an advantage when possible.

Proofing

When you have made any changes and are satisfied that you have said what you intended, proofread your report. Before computer spell-checkers became commonplace, one experienced legal secretary spotted a small error in a finished document: Instead of the simple phrase "does not," the finished document read "doe snot." That error would be automatically corrected by today's spell-check feature, so by all means, start with both a spell and grammar check. These features are useful, though not infallible. For example, when writing this chapter, the spell-checker continued to find "attentional" a misspelling, a situation that often occurs with medical or psychological terms. Grammar checks, the green underlines, are useful for pointing out passive voice. But as discussed in Chapter 4, you may sometimes choose to use passive voice. So, check all those red and green underlines—perhaps against the information in this book or another writing handbook—but then use your own judgment.

After that, a second eye does the best proofing. If you have a colleague or committed friend who is willing to help, you will come closer to catching mistakes than if you rely on your eye alone. You will have worked extensively with the written material and could easily miss errors. The second person may read through the report alone and mark changes on a final copy. Or best of all, s/he may work in tandem with you: One of you reads aloud, including punctuation marks, and the other notes changes on a final, printed copy (Bates, 2000). Though that process is time-consuming, you are most likely to catch all mistakes.

Whether proofing copy solo or together, printing out the copy and reading it aloud will give both visual and auditory input. In order to focus on the sentence in front of you and not the rest of the document, you might

- Start at the beginning of the report, read sentence by sentence, blanking out the lines above and below; or
- Read backwards, starting with the last sentence of the report and progressing upward, so the flow of content does not hijack your attention.

Proofing is a thankless task. After spending time writing and editing, you may be tempted to skip this step. But your report represents you and your abilities to the reader. Misspellings or wrong punctuation can appear inattentive and leave a negative impression, so better to proof your work.

CHAPTER **6**

Content that Communicates

Sentences and Paragraphs

> Most readers are busy.... Help these readers by using short
> sentences and plain words.

Martin Seligman, American psychologist

With the template from the previous chapter, you have developed and formatted your report and have created an outline. Now we will look at how to craft sentences that clearly express ideas and how to grow them into paragraphs. After years of education and experience in writing our language, most of us construct sentences and paragraphs automatically. We give little thought to structure, specific word choice, or our underlying attitude toward the material. Many writers, inside and outside the field of psychology, agree with Seligman's statement quoted at the beginning of this chapter (1991). Different writers contribute individual perspectives on that issue, though few make a case for more words rather than fewer. And none argues for obscure writing. Chapters 2 and 3 discuss careful word choice and writing with clarity, specificity, accuracy, and compassion. Attention to these areas will benefit all documents, including your assessment report. With that grounding, we will look at creating readable sentences and paragraphs.

Sentence: What Is It and How Is It Structured?

Begin at the beginning—with a sentence that clearly expresses your idea. Craft it as simply as possible and then build on it. Any dictionary, writing guide, or grammar book will include some version of the following: A sentence is a group of words that contains a subject and a verb and expresses a complete thought. It states, asks, or commands something and concludes with some sort of ending mark—period, exclamation or question mark, etc. (Webster's, 2001).

The strongest sentences anchor their meaning with nouns and verbs: The nouns give the "what" or "who" in your report, and the verbs tell the reader "how." Adjectives and adverbs can provide more detail, allowing you to paint with subtler colors, but if the nouns and verbs are not strong to begin with, no adjective or adverb can improve the sentence. Think of a house with chipped and peeling paint covering much of its outside surface. Its overall appearance is not likely to improve if we paint only the trim, however meticulous the job. Nouns and verbs are the house; adjectives and adverbs are the trim.

Initial Decisions

Before reaching the point of putting sentences together, you first must make an initial series of decisions. These will likely be decided as you go through the outline process from Chapter 5:

1. What will you write about?
2. What are you trying to accomplish with that writing?
3. What are your underlying attitudes and premises?

In addition to the facts of your assessment, your sentences will reflect the underlying attitudes or premises you put forth, word by word, sentence by sentence. The facts you intend to communicate make up only the most obvious part of your report. The underlying "propositions" or premises of written material form an often unspoken and unspecified base for the sentences you create (Landon, 2008). As Chapter 1 discusses, your underlying premises in writing an assessment report will vary depending on the client and his or her needs.

In addition, one major, underlying premise never spelled out forms the broad basis for each report: You—and the client—believe you have the knowledge and understanding to help him or her. You have had the education represented by the initials that now—or will soon—follow your name. You likely have some experience to back up that education. The client and you rely on those to meet your joint unspoken assumption.

In all cases, countless additional attitudes and premises can affect each sentence and each paragraph. Bringing those to consciousness allows you to better control how you express what you wish to communicate with the intended reader(s).

Sentence Structure

Once you work with and answer that first set of questions, then you move into the structural creation of your sentences. While you work, you come up against two more choices that unfold as you write:

- What words do you use to give action to both the facts and underlying attitudes and premises?
- In what order do you place them?

The words you choose and the way you unfold your sentences determine how the material affects the reader. Being specific in word choice aids his or her understanding. The more abstract your terms, the harder your reader must work to grasp the texture, depth, and implications of your statement. (See Chapter 3 for a discussion of Hayakawa's Ladder of Abstraction.) A description that the person assessed "was dressed casually and not well-groomed" could apply to many people and scenarios. But if you say that "he wore blue jeans with a hole in the knee, he had not shaved, and his hair appeared uncombed," another picture emerges. Both descriptions are factual, but the second choice of words and word order evokes a living person who made choices that may have larger implications.

Basic Sentence

Two parts make up the basic sentence, the subject and the predicate:

- *Subject* (noun or pronoun): the person, place, idea, or thing that is taking action or being
- *Predicate* (verb): the words that tell what the subject is doing or being

In the basic sentence "Jane finished"

- "Jane" is the subject (proper noun, the person who took action).
- "Finished" is the predicate (verb describing the action Jane took).

Both subject and predicate may include additional words that modify or complement the noun/pronoun and verb. If we expand the sentence above to include an *object*, it becomes

"Jane finished the *test*."

"The test" is the object of the action she took because it receives the action. Further building the sentence by adding words that modify both subject and verb could give us, "An irritated Jane finished the boring, endless test." These modifications now make clear that the sentence is written from Jane's perspective and shows her mood.

When sentences become more complex, additional components can obscure the subject and object. Look again at the sentence, "Jane finished the test":

- *To find the subject*, first find the verb, then ask, "Who or what took the action described by the verb?" (Jane)
- *To find the object*, ask, "What or whom received the action?" (the test that Jane finished)

A sentence may also be a one-word statement that omits material. Assume that you ask a person, "Did you bring the forms I asked you to fill out?" The person's full-sentence answer would restate your original question as, "Yes, I brought the forms," although the one-word answer, "Yes," can still qualify as a complete sentence.

Sentence Order

The standard sentence pattern of subject + verb + object provides the most direct route for your reader to follow your thinking. Varying sentence arrangement, however, can lend interest and variety to your report and can also allow you to emphasize different aspects of a sentence. Adding a single word or phrase as a modifier also provides variety and allows for shifts in emphasis. Table 6.1 shows varying arrangements of the basic sentence and indicates the likely emphasis in each case, though the sentences before and after could also affect emphasis.

Sentences can have different purposes—to declare, exclaim, ask a question, or make a demand—and are built from clauses. Each clause contains a subject and a verb, but not every clause stands on its own. Those that stand alone are called *independent*; those

TABLE 6.1 Varying Sentence Order

Sentence	Order	Emphasis
An irritated Jane finished the boring, endless test.	Subject > verb > object	Equal: Jane and test
The boring, endless test was finished by an irritated Jane.	Object > verb > subject (passive voice[a])	Test
Irritated, Jane finished the boring endless test.	Subject > verb > object (preceded by single-word modifier of Jane)	Jane

[a] See discussion of passive voice in Chapters 3 and 4.

requiring support from the rest of the sentence are called *dependent.* (See Chapter 10 for more on independent versus dependent clauses.) Varying structures of a sentence—simple, compound, complex, and compound-complex—are shown in Table 6.2.

Knowing the names of the types of sentence structure is not important in itself, but punctuation varies depending on the type of clause. Recognizing the difference enables you to punctuate the sentence correctly. Anyone who has scored Written Expression in the WIAT-III has run into the range of rules governing commas—and many of those are determined by whether the clause is an independent or dependent clause (Wechsler, 2009). For instance, it is easy to confuse a simple sentence that has one subject and two verbs ("Jane finished the test *and* handed it to me"—no comma) with a compound sentence that has two separate subjects and two

TABLE 6.2 Sentence Structure

Type of Sentence	Definition	Example
Simple	1 independent clause + no dependent clause	1 subject, 1 verb: *Jane finished* the test. 1 subject, 2 verbs: *Jane finished* the test and *handed* it to me.
Compound	2 or more independent clauses + no dependent clause	2 subjects, 2 verbs: *Jane finished* the test, and *she handed* it to me.
Complex	1 independent clause + 1 or more dependent clauses	Jane, who had finished the test, handed it to me.
Compound-complex	2 or more independent clauses + 1 or more dependent clauses	Jane, who had finished the test, handed it to me, but she seemed irritated.

separate verbs ("Jane finished the test, *and she* handed it to me"—comma after first independent clause). Chapter 10 discusses more on clauses and their punctuation, including commas.

Varying Your Sentences

To keep your reader moving steadily through your report, use a bit of variety. If your writing uses a lot of long sentences, consciously choose to divide some of them into shorter ones. If the reverse is true, insert a few longer, more complex sentences among your short ones—provided, of course, that your long sentences will not lose your reader among its clauses. You can also vary sentences by mixing *loose* sentences with *periodic* ones (Bates, 2000).

- A *loose* sentence states the facts upfront and then gives any elaborations or modifiers. This type of sentence is also called cumulative, since clauses that follow the basic sentence build on it.
- A *periodic* sentence, on the other hand, shifts emphasis to the very end of the sentence. It sets the context for the facts first and becomes a mini-narrative, "telling the story" of the sentence as you go through it.

Table 6.3 gives examples and information about when to use each. Both examples would accurately report the interaction with the client, but the emphasis shifts. Your underlying premise and

TABLE 6.3   Loose (Cumulative) and Periodic Sentences

	Loose Sentence	Periodic Sentence
Example	The client stood and said he needed to leave early, after repeatedly sighing as he did the sentence-building task.	After repeatedly sighing as he did the sentence-building task, the client stood and said he needed to leave early.
What it does	States facts first Adds details in clauses that follow	Sets context before facts Creates a mini-narrative, with details before facts
When to use	In most sentences The structure that most readers view as "normal"	In shorter sentences To create suspense To leave reader with main idea

Note: Adapted from *Building Great Sentences: Exploring the Writer's Craft*, by B. Landon, 2008, Chantilly, VA: The Teaching Company. Copyright 2008 by The Teaching Company.

assumptions, as discussed earlier in this chapter, would affect which you use. Consciously choosing to write the occasional periodic sentence can create impact where you wish it, although most sentences in a report will likely be loose.

Paragraph: How Do Sentences Build Into Paragraphs?

A paragraph may be as basic as a single sentence, though it is more usually a series of related sentences. Structurally, each paragraph begins on a new line of your report. The paragraph presents a particular idea or makes a specific point and then develops it. A topic sentence provides the clearest way of establishing the main point. Sentences that follow expand on the main point and give additional details. The paragraph may conclude with a sentence that summarizes the paragraph's points or gives some overall insight. You may also include a transition into the next paragraph, either as a part of the summary, in place of it, or in addition to it (Warriner, 1988). Table 6.4 includes sentences from a short paragraph that illustrate these sentence types.

TABLE 6.4   Types of Sentences in a Paragraph

Type	Function	Example
Topic	Presents main idea	This evaluation did not reveal overt signs of learning disabilities, although David showed numerous signs and symptoms of Attention Deficit Hyperactivity Disorder, Predominantly Inattentive Type (ADHD).
Expansion	Develops and adds details	Recent studies have shown that young people with ADHD (a) often exhibit unexpected challenges in learning, even without the diagnosis of a formal learning disability, and (b) are frequently less efficient learners.
Summary	Summarizes points or gives insight	As we discussed in the feedback-discussion session, the finding of ADHD is supported by numerous pieces of assessment data that are listed below.
Transition	Ties to next paragraph	Same as summary.

As is the case with many paragraphs, the categories that sentences fall into are not necessarily black and white. In the Table 6.4 examples, the second part of the topic sentence beginning with "although" could also be considered a part of the expansion; the expansion sentence provides some insight, as might be included in a summary sentence; and the summary sentence also provides transition into the next paragraph.

Building the Paragraph

Although every paragraph is unique, the same general thought process can be used for each:

1. *Create the topic sentence*: Think of the topic sentence as the manager of the paragraph. It focuses the other sentences and the reader's attention on your main idea and so will usually be at the beginning, to set your context. It also may be placed later in the paragraph; in that case, it would provide a summary, after leading the reader through a series of facts or steps. Finally, the main idea may be only implied and not spelled out. In the case of assessment reports, however, where clarity is important and you want all readers to follow your thinking, spelling out your main idea is likely the better choice.

2. *Expand and support the main idea*: Your expansion sentence(s) will support your topic and expand on it. It will give details and may guide your reader by explaining how or what to think about your main premise. It may also answer these questions:
   - Why is this idea or these facts true?
   - Why are they useful?

3. *Summarize or give insight*: A summary sentence is not always called for. Sometimes the topic and details speak for themselves. When used, it may simply restate the topic idea or may summarize the details from the expansion sentences. Or, as a summary, you may also choose to mention a particular insight gained from the details mentioned in the paragraph.

4. *Make transitions*: Within the paragraph, transitional expressions, such as those examples in Table 6.5, help sentences flow from one to the other.

TABLE 6.5 Transitional Words or Phrases

Sample Transitions	What They Do
Also, likewise, similarly	Add information
Indeed, of course, in fact	Emphasize
Namely, for instance, specifically	Give example
Accordingly, hence, therefore	Show cause and effect
Nonetheless, on the contrary, yet	Show contrast
First, second, next, then	Show sequence
Additionally, equally important, moreover	Show similarity
Afterward, before, meanwhile	Show time
Above, adjacent, beyond	or place
Finally, thus, in conclusion, in summary	Summarize

In moving between paragraphs, those same transitional expressions help establish the relationship between two paragraphs and enable the reader to follow your logic. The sentences or phrases containing these expressions may end a paragraph, begin the next one, or bridge both. You might also dedicate an entire paragraph to making the transition from one complex topic to another.

As you will recall from Chapter 5, the material read first and last will likely stick with the reader longest. This first-and-last phenomenon can also apply within a section or a paragraph as well as in the report as a whole. Likewise, material may be ordered within paragraphs by using one or more approaches also mentioned in Chapter 5: chronological (steps in a process); spatial (where items are in relation to each other); showing comparison or contrast; or as an analogy.

Standard Phrases for Reports

Some publications on writing psychological assessment reports give lists of standard terms and statements for wording (Braaten, 2007; Zuckerman, 2005). In using these as reference or template for your report, simplify and clarify any wording that would likely lose your reader.

Parallel Structure

Just as parallel rails keep a train balanced and moving along, parallel construction can do the same for your report. In words, phrases, clauses, or paragraphs, you can show similar ideas or thoughts by similar use and arrangement of those elements. At its most basic, parallel means that you pair like with like. When speaking of adults, they are *men and women* not *men and girls* or *men and females*. *Female* and *male* can be either adjectives or nouns; if appropriate to use either, be sure you use them correctly and, when using them together, that they are parallel.

If you are describing a client's traits by a series of words, choose words from the same type. That is, give a list of adjectives, for example, instead of mixing adjectives with adverbs, nouns, or verb forms. Write that the client was "alert, reserved, and cooperative" (all adjectives = parallel) rather than that s/he was "alert, showed self-restraint, and cooperative" (adjective, verb phrase, adjective = nonparallel). And if one or more of those descriptors in the second sentence is closer to what you mean, then restructure the sentence so the other descriptions parallel it: "Mr. B. appeared alert, showed self-restraint, and seemed cooperative" (all verb phrases = parallel).

The most basic use of parallel form is a simple bullet list, provided the key words are from the same family (verb, noun, adverb, or adjective) and, if a phrase, that each entry is structured similarly. For example, assume you are listing some qualities important in executive functioning:

Starting actions or projects
Planning and organizing actions or projects
Organizing environment or materials
Accomplishing tasks
Monitoring tasks or social behavior

This list reflects use of parallel construction because (a) it is made up of a series of phrases describing an action and (b) each of the phrases begins with a verb form ending in *-ing*. The same applies if the list is made up of single words or full sentences—be sure you use the same parts of speech (noun, verb, adjective, or adverb) in each. The very symmetry of the list can reassure your readers that they are in good hands when reading your document.

TABLE 6.6   Parallel Structure

Action	Conjunctions Often Used	Parallel Examples: Yes and No
Coordinating equal ideas	And, or; but, nor	**No**: Testing revealed John's high *intelligence* but *that sometimes he makes careless errors.* (Noun paired with a clause) **Yes**: Testing revealed *that John has high intelligence* but *that sometimes he makes careless errors.* (Clause paired with a clause)
Comparing/contrasting differing ideas	As much as as well as	**No**: Testing revealed John's high *intelligence* as well as *that sometimes he makes careless errors.* (Noun paired with a clause) **Yes**: Testing revealed *that John was highly intelligent* as well as *that sometimes he makes careless errors.* (Clause paired with a clause)
Correlating two ideas/actions	Both…and either…or not only…but between…and	**No**: Testing revealed not only John's *intelligence* but also *that he is sometimes careless.* (Noun paired with clause) **Yes**: Testing revealed that John was not only *intelligent* but also sometimes *careless.* (Adjective paired with adjective)

Note: Adapted from *English Composition and Grammar: Complete Course*, by J. E. Warriner, 1988, Orlando, FL: Harcourt Brace Jovanovich. Copyright 1988 by Harcourt Brace Jovanovich.

Table 6.6 shows three actions in sentences that need parallel construction.

Somehow, many of us pick up the idea that building variety into our writing means constantly shifting words and structure even within the same sentence. A certain amount of variety can be important in keeping a reader's interest. Constantly shifting forms, however, can keep the reader from recognizing the connection between thoughts and ideas expressed in your report. Better to give the reader the stability of parallel construction and save the variety for ideas that need pointed emphasis (Strunk &

White, 2000). Once we know and have used a rule, we can better choose when to break it for effect.

Fillers, Redundancies, and Unnecessary Phrases

Your sentences and paragraphs will be stronger when you omit three qualities that weaken them.

- *Fillers* ("there is," "there are," "here is," "here are," "it is"): Some foods are said to contain "empty calories" because they add nothing nutritionally. These filler words are the equivalent in writing—they are empty because they add nothing to the sentence or paragraph and drain your report of life and action. In speech, we frequently rely on these phrases to get sentences started; it is not unexpected that we would also use them in writing. The second clause of the preceding sentence ("it is not unexpected that we would also use them in writing") contains both a filler phrase and a confusing negative. It can be rearranged and shortened to eliminate both. The reworked clause then reads, "understandably, we also use them in writing." Examine all sentences that begin with a filler phrase to see if they can be rearranged. Most can.
- *Redundancies*: Dozens of redundant phrases infiltrate our speech and writing: "2 p.m. in the afternoon," "circle around," or "revert back," for example. In each case, the second word or phrase merely restates the meaning of the single word. Those phrases are cleaner and clearer when shortened to "2 p.m.," "circle," and "revert." As with fillers, examine sentences for words or phrases that immediately restate a word or idea and prune them out.
- *Unnecessary phrases*: Unnecessary phrases also appear in speech to soften or moderate a statement. Instead of launching right into report feedback, an assessor-writer might say, "I'm writing to tell you..." While not incorrect, the statement is also not necessary. The bridge into the content can be straightforward, as in, "This letter summarizes, etc." Direct phrases are easier for the reader to follow; more complex ones add words but not meaning. Table 6.7 gives a few examples.

Is less direct, less clear writing ever preferable? As discussed in Chapter 4, the assessor-writer may choose to use passive voice

TABLE 6.7 Unnecessary Phrases

Long Version	Straightforward Version
At this point in time At the present time	Now or today (avoid *presently* except in that word's first meaning of "soon")
Due to the fact that	Because
Has a tendency to	Tends to
In a (serious, hasty, sharp) manner	Seriously; hastily; sharply
In my opinion	Drop this phrase. (You are signing the report; it will reflect your opinion unless you state otherwise.)
In the event that	if
It should be noted that	Drop this phrase. (If you frame the point clearly and compellingly, you need not "shake the readers by the shoulders" to get them to pay attention.)
Used for purposes of (example, illustration)	Used as an example Used for illustration

when s/he believes a direct, active sentence might be too blunt for the reader. Fillers and unnecessary phrases may, on occasion, fall into that same category. The assessor-writer might be tempted to use them when the politics or sensitivity of a case seems to require less directness or when trying for the tone used in spoken communication. As when using passive voice, though, make your use of filler words or phrases a conscious choice rather than a fallback. They easily muddy your writing and the reader's understanding. And redundancies are never called for; they can make the writer look inattentive to detail.

Assessing Readability

Some technical details can contribute to readability, including word count and sentence or paragraph length. Over time, you may begin to notice these as you work through your reports. The editing phase, however, is the time to focus on revising them to increase readability.

The word count tool in Microsoft Word can be applied to any selected text, so it is easy to get an idea of the length of a sentence. No rigid rule exists about sentence length. For most writing, various sources recommend an average of 14–22 words per sentence. Sentences that reach 25, 30, 40, or more words are often candidates for revision. The fewer the words and ideas a reader has to assimilate in a sentence, the easier it will be to understand it. But repeated short sentences can bore the reader (eight words in this one). On the other hand, a very long, very involved sentence, using many adjectives and requiring extensive punctuation, may lose the perplexed reader in the twists and turns of the many words and complicated sentence structure; hence, it will likely require that the reader reread the long sentence just to follow the ideas presented (54 words). The solution is to combine long, short, and average-length sentences. Varying sentence length—as well as type, as mentioned earlier in this chapter—helps the reader to stay focused and follow what you are saying (APA, 2010). Balancing long, short, and average sentences contributes to style in your writing as well as to its clarity (Bates, 2000).

Paragraphs break your ideas and information into logical sections. The breaks, as first-line indentations or blank white lines between flush-left paragraphs, give the reader visual clues of shifting subject matter. On occasion, paragraphs may be a single sentence. But these can seem brusque and awkward; it would also need to be nearly monumental in its implication to warrant being singled-out in that way. A paragraph that runs ½ page or less— and more often ¼ to ⅓ page—will better hold onto your reader (APA, 2010). Within paragraphs, break up your text by using bulleted or numbered lists; these devices vary the mass of letters and words on the page and also help keep the reader's focus.

Readability Tools: Various Formulas

Several tools are available to gauge overall readability of your reports. This discussion will look at three of them, pointing out their strengths and drawbacks and the best uses of them. All three were originally calculated manually but now have computerized versions available, both online and built into popular software.

- *Flesch–Kincaid Grade Level*: This tool is built into the spell check feature of Microsoft Word and may also be found online. It calculates the number of years in the United States educational system generally required to understand your written text. Since the grade level usually recommended for readability is 8th to 9th grade or lower, knowing the level of your report can be especially valuable when the formula results in a level higher than Grade 12. Aiming for 8th- or 9th-grade levels ensures that most anyone who picks up your report will understand it. Nevertheless, when dealing with the technical details of a specialty area such as psychology, you will likely be doing well to keep it within the 10th to 12th-grade range on this scale. It calculates readability from average sentence length and average number of syllables per word. Since psychology employs many multisyllabic words, the grade level will automatically be higher (Readability/Flesch-Kincaid Grade Level, 2011a).

■ *Flesch Reading Ease*: This tool, too, is a part of MS Word and other word-processing programs and is also online. It uses the same components as that of the Flesch-Kincaid Grade Level—average sentence length and average number of syllables per word—but a different formula. The premise of this formula is that shorter sentences and words lead to better reading ease. Its scale ranges from 0 to 100, with a higher score being better. A score of 0–29 is "very difficult," 90–100 is "very easy," and 60–70 is generally considered in the most readable range. The Flesch Reading Ease Formula seems simple but has several ambiguities in the way it operates (Readability/Flesch Reading Ease, 2011b).

Both the Grade Level formula and the Reading Ease formula may best be used for general feedback on your readability rather than a black-and-white judgment. Table 6.8 shows rough parallels between the ratings of the two formulas.

■ *Gunning's Fog Index*: The Gunning fog index also estimates the years of schooling in the U.S educational system needed to understand material on first reading. It calculates readability from the average sentence length and the percent of words with three or more syllables. The resulting score assesses "fog" or clutter in writing. A text intended for wide reading needs a score of less than 12; those meant for near-universal understanding need a score of 8 or less (Readability/Gunning, 2011c; Wikipedia, 2011e). One drawback to this index is that it rates all words of three or more syllables as being equally difficult. For example, a common word such as "watermelon" would be rated as difficult as a psychologi-

TABLE 6.8 Flesch-Kincaid Grade Level and Flesch Reading Ease

Flesch Reading Ease		Flesch-Kincaid Grade Level
Score	Ease	(approximate)
90–100	Very easy	Below 6th grade
80–89	Easy	6th
70–79	Fairly easy	7th
60–69	Standard	8th and 9th
50–59	Fairly difficult	10th to 12th
30–49	Difficult	Some college
0–29	Very difficult	College graduate

cal word such as "posttraumatic." Although not included in word-processing software, the fog index is widely available online.

Table 6.9 shows sample report paragraphs used in Chapter 5 (Table 5.4) and gives readability information as analyzed by the three tools described here. The selected passages give approximately the same information, but the readability varies widely. Recall that for Flesch-Kincaid Grade Level and Gunning's Fog

TABLE 6.9 Readability Comparisons

	Text	Flesch-Kincaid Grade Level	Flesch Reading Ease	Gunning's Fog Index
Standard report	Client functions within the superior psychometric range of intelligence.	14.1	9.7	16.93
	Client demonstrates the comorbidity of depressive-like symptoms.	20.1	0	22.40
Report as a therapeutic letter	You are very smart. Your overall intelligence was in the superior range.	7.4	52.6	12.40
	Yes, unhappy moods can affect your ability to attend or focus. They may interfere with doing your schoolwork in a way that reflects your intelligence.	8.1	58.7	11.40

Index, a *lower* grade level is likely more readable. For Flesch Reading Ease, a *higher* number is preferable.

While no readability formula can teach someone to write better, if used during the editing process, such tools can point out areas of potential problems. For example, if you have a higher grade-level score on the Flesch-Kincaid or Gunning than you would like, reframing passive sentences into active voice will help give you a lower grade level score. You can also ask yourself if all the longer words in your report are necessary. Might some be replaced by shorter or simpler ones? Might some of your sentences be shortened from 30 words to 20 or less?

This chapter began with a quote on brevity by a psychologist. To close, here is another by a nonpsychologist, writer William Zinsser: "Four basic premises of writing: clarity, brevity, simplicity, and humanity" (2009, p. 4).

CHAPTER 7

Reaching Agreement
Subject–Verb, Pronoun, and Gender

Reading maketh a full man, conference a ready man, and writing an exact man.

Sir Francis Bacon, English writer
and philosopher (1561–1626)

The word *agreement* means both "a contract" and "being in harmony or accord" (Webster's, 2001). In doing an assessment, the assessor-writer reaches an agreement with the client to perform certain actions and deliver a product, including a written report. In writing that report, "agreement" also plays a grammatical role.

In Standard English grammar, the general concept of agreement between words in a sentence means that number and person (first, second, third person—I, you, he/she/it, respectively) correspond. For example, subject and verbs must match. Throughout the development of the English language, agreement between subject and verb has become steadily *less* complicated. Older varieties of English used a system that gave all verbs person and number endings for both present and past tense. Today's standard pattern is far simpler and more regular than that. For instance, between subject and verb, agreement in the standard pattern of English (American Heritage, 2000) calls for

- *an -s ending*: on verbs in present tense that have singular, third-person subjects (such as "the client" and "he, she, or it" ("The client *arrives* on time")

■ *no ending*: on verbs paired with any other kind of subject ("The clients *arrive* on time")

Speakers of various dialects of English may sometimes use verb endings that do not conform to the standard pattern of subject–verb agreement. While valuing the diversity of various populations' standards of speech, your written assessment report will most often adhere to Standard English grammar. In that way, it will be both professional and understandable to a range of potential readers. The question of agreement is an important one, having to do with credibility and the perception of knowledge. Even if the reader does not know what is wrong with a sentence, if agreement is missing, the writing may "feel" wrong to the reader, and your message can get lost. This chapter's discussion about agreement begins with the action part of the sentence, the verb, and then moves on to include subjects, pronouns, and prepositions.

Verb Tenses

The verbs you use in writing your report may change their form to show the time of the action or state of being that you describe. Stating that the person you are assessing "is" suicidal carries different impact than saying that the person "was" or "has been" or "could be" suicidal. Describing a person's action as "he broke down in tears" (past tense—one action) is different from "he breaks down in tears" (present tense—perhaps more than once, so time could be repeated and ongoing). According to writer William Zinsser, "[T]he whole purpose of tenses is to enable a writer to deal with time…from the past to the hypothetical future" (1980, p. 54). Table 7.1 shows the basic verb tenses and when and how to use them.

To avoid switching tense so often that the reader gets lost, Zinsser stresses that a writer should choose a primary tense in which to address the reader (1980). For reports, the assessor-writer will likely use a mixture of present and past verb tense, with present tense used more often. As shown in Table 7.2, the area that the report covers will affect the tense used, as will the facts of the individual case.

TABLE 7.1   Basic Verb Tenses

Tense	When	How formed	Example
Present	Now	Basic verb form	I *score* the tests.
Past	Past; not continuing to present	Add *-d* or *-ed* to the verb	I *scored* the tests.
Future	Will occur at some time in future	Add *will* or *shall* to the verb	I *will score* the tests.
Present perfect	Occurred at no definite time in the past	Add *have* or *has* to the past tense of the verb	I *have scored* the tests.
Past perfect	Was completed in the past before some past action/event	Add *had* to the past tense of the verb	I *had scored* the tests before the client arrived.
Future perfect	Will be completed in the future before some other future action/event	Add *will have* or *shall have* to the past tense of the verb	I *will have scored* the tests before the client arrives.

Note: Adapted from *English Composition and Grammar: Complete Course,* by J. E. Warriner, 1988, Orlando, FL: Harcourt Brace Jovanovich. Copyright 1988 by Harcourt Brace Jovanovich.

"Mood" in Grammar

In psychology, mood represents an emotional state. In grammar, however, mood is a verb form or inflection that indicates the speaker's attitude. This attitude reflects whether the speaker believes the action (or condition) expressed by the verb is true or even likely (American Heritage, 2000). Recognizing mood and its most common names in grammar is not essential in everyday writing, but it does help the writer to choose correct verb forms in one case especially—the subjunctive. Subjunctive mood expresses a wish, a doubt, or anything nonfactual. Too often in the subjunctive mood, a writer incorrectly uses *was* instead of *were.* Table 7.3 compares subjunctive to two other common grammatical moods.

Verb Pairs: Which to Use?

The report you send out into the world is the public face of your practice. It represents you, your training, and your experience. If uncertainty in using some verbs, for example, crops up repeatedly, it can undermine the effectiveness of your written report. Some

TABLE 7.2   Verb Tense in Report Writing

Area of Report	Tense	Example
Current circumstances (e.g., age, grade, occupation) of person assessed	Present	Lee *is* 35 years old. He *manages* a small business.
Personal qualities (e.g., physical description, ethnicity, gender)	Present	He *reports* being 5′4″ tall and *appears* slight in build.
History/background	Past or mixed with present	He *says* that he *was born* in China but *moved* here at 2 years old.
Behavior during testing	Past (most often)	Lee *worked* diligently on most tasks; however, he *hurried* through the Tower of London.
Results of testing	Present	Results from the Tower of London and the Gordon Diagnostic System suggest that he has challenges with sustained attention.
Recommendations	Present (most often)	Consider computer programs aimed at aiding attention and working memory. Continue therapy.

Note: Adapted from *Psychological Assessment and Report Writing*, by K. Goldfinger and A. M. Pomerantz, 2010, Los Angeles, CA: Sage. Copyright 2010 by Sage.
Adapted from *Essentials of Assessment Report Writing*, by E. O. Lichtenberger, N. Mather, N. L. Kaufman, and A. L. Kaufman, 2004, *Hoboken, NJ:* Wiley. Copyright 2004 by Wiley.

of the forms discussed below can be a bit variable, but preference generally leans one way or the other. And in some cases, simply memorizing the required form is necessary.

Used To Versus Use To

These phrases refer to repeated actions or events in the past. Should you write "Lee *used to* attend college, but quit to manage the family business"? Or is it, "Lee *use to* attend college"? And what about in the negative? Would it be, "Lee didn't *use to* manage the family business" or "Lee didn't *used to* manage"? Generally speaking, in written American English, retain the *-d* on the end in both positive and negative formations of the sentence (Garner, 2009). Some

TABLE 7.3   Moods and How to Use Them

Mood	What it Does	Example
Indicative	Used in most writing: Makes statement of fact or asks a question.	Statement of fact: He finished the test. Asks a question: Have you finished the test?
Imperative	Issues a command.	Finish the test and leave it on the table.
Subjunctive	Expresses a wish, a doubt, or anything nonfactual. Uses *if* or *as though* before the subject and verb. Uses verb form *were*, not *was*.	Wish: I *wish* Lee *were* finished with testing. Nonfactual: 1. *If* I *were* Lee, I'd try to finish tomorrow. (I am not Lee.) 2. He spoke freely to me *as though* I *were* his therapist. (I am not his therapist.)

Note: Adapted from *English Composition and Grammar: Complete Course*, by J. E. Warriner, 1988, Orlando, FL: Harcourt Brace Jovanovich. Copyright 1988 by Harcourt Brace Jovanovich.

grammatical sources draw a distinction. They suggest including the ending *-d* when the sentence is a positive statement but dropping the *-d* when expressing the negative with *did not*. To be more correct, however, retain the *-d* on the end even with a negative sentence. And if "didn't used to" looks or sounds wrong to you, change it to the clearer standard phrase "never used to."

Can Versus May

Can indicates that you are able to do something, for example, "Lee *can* be here at 10 a.m. on Tuesday." *May* means that you have permission to do it ("You *may* take a break before the next test") or to show possibility that you might do it ("I *may* be late tomorrow") (Bates, 2000). Informally, especially in speech, *can* is often used interchangeably with *may*. But knowing the difference and deciding to use these words appropriately in writing will lend accuracy, clarity, and crispness to your assessment report.

Fewer Versus Less

Fewer refers to things you can count (tests, pages, cars, etc.). *Less* shows a decrease in something that cannot be counted numerically (effort, happiness, laughter, etc.) (Strunk & White, 2000). "The assessor administered *fewer* tests than he had planned" reflects tests that can be counted. "Lee had *less* trouble with Tuesday's testing than he had with Monday's" shows a lessening of something uncountable—trouble.

Lay Versus Lie

Lay means to put or place something, as in, "*Lay* the test on my desk." In addition, *lay* will have an object in the sentence, something that is or was placed. In the example sentence, *test* is the object. *Lie* means to recline: "The test *lies* on the desk." Notice that *lie* takes no object. When deciding which of these to use, ask yourself your meaning: Are you writing about placing something or reclining? (Bates, 2000). The other challenge with these two verbs is that their past forms are irregular. In order to use them correctly, the forms must be memorized:

■ *Lay, laid, have/had laid*:
"He *laid* the test on the desk"; "He *had laid* the test on the desk."

■ *Lie, lay, have/had lain*:
"The test *lay* on the desk for an hour" (past); "The test *had lain* on the desk for an hour."

Raise Versus Rise

Raise shows that someone is taking action to move something upward. As with *lay* in the previous example, *raise* will have an object (Warriner, 1988): "*Raise* the window (object) if you need some air." *Rise* means that the subject is moving upward on its own and takes no object in the sentence: "Lee *rises* from the chair." *Rise* has irregular past forms: *rose* and *have/had risen*.

Set Versus Sit

In most cases, *set* means to put or place an object, such as "He *set* his briefcase on the floor." *Sit* usually has no object and most often indicates that a person or animal takes a seated position: "He *sits* quietly in the waiting room." A couple of exceptions: We say that "the sun *sets*" or "cement *sets*" instead of *sits*. Past forms of *set* are *set* and *have/had set*; past forms of *sit* are *sat* and *have/had sat*. Table 7.4 summarizes when to use the preceding verb forms and gives examples.

TABLE 7.4 Verb Pairs

Verb Pair	When to Use	Example
Used to or use to	*Used to*: to make a positive or negative statement using *did* or *didn't*	*Did/didn't* Lee *used to* manage the family business?
	Use to: avoid this usage	No example
	Better revision in negative statement: Use *never* instead of *didn't*	Lee *never used to* manage the family business.
Can or may	*Can*: to show ability	Lee *can* be here at 10 a.m. on Tuesday.
	May: to show permission	You *may* take a break before the next test.
	May: to show possibility	I *may* be late tomorrow.
Fewer or less	*Fewer*: to indicate things you can count (e.g., tests)	The assessor administered *fewer* tests than he had planned
	Less: to show decrease that cannot be counted numerically (e.g., trouble)	Lee had *less* trouble with Tuesday's testing than he had with Monday's.
Lay or lie	*Lay*: to show placement of something	*Lay* the test on my desk.
	Lie: to indicate a reclining position	The test *lies* on the desk.
Raise or rise	*Raise*: to show that someone takes action to move something upward	*Raise* the window shade if you need more light.
	Rise: to show that the subject is moving upward on its own	Lee *rises* from the chair.
Set or sit	*Set*: to indicate placing an object	He *sets* his briefcase on the floor.
	Sit: to show that a person or animal takes a seated position	He *sits* quietly in the waiting room.

Note: Adapted from *English Composition and Grammar: Complete Course*, by J. E. Warriner, 1988, Orlando, FL: Harcourt Brace Jovanovich. Copyright 1988 by Harcourt Brace Jovanovich.

Subject–Verb Agreement

Singular subject takes a singular verb. Plural subject takes a plural verb. These guidelines are simple enough when the sentence is a direct one, with the verb immediately following the subject, as in

- "The *client works* silently on the test." (singular)
- "*Lee and his wife arrive* late for many appointments." (plural)

Most times, a verb that ends in an *-s* is in present tense and singular (*works*). When in past tense, a verb will be the same whether singular or plural: "Lee *arrived...*" (singular); "Lee and his wife *arrived...*" (plural). To figure out if you have used singular or plural in your sentences, remember these steps:

1. Find your verb (action word) and subject (who or what takes the action described by the verb).
2. Figure out the singular and the plural of the verb you used. Do this by pairing it with "she" (singular) and "they" (plural) in present tense. For example, with the verb *write*, you would have "she writes" (singular) and "they write" (plural).
3. By comparing what you wrote with the correct forms of singular or plural, you will likely find the correct verb form.

When sentences are more complicated, however, figuring out agreement between subject and verb can be harder. If you feel the subject and verb in your sentence still do not agree, one of the complications listed in the following subsections could be the culprit.

Intervening Words

When words come between the subject and the verb, make sure that subject and verb still agree—singular with singular, plural with plural. If the subject is singular but an intervening word is plural or vice versa, we can inadvertently switch to the wrong verb form (Strunk & White, 2000).

- "After I place an order, a new *packet* of scoring sheets *arrives* via UPS" (not *sheets arrive*).
- "*Responses* to my request for information *have* not come in" (not *request...has*).

Phrases such as *together with*, *as well as*, or *along with* may come between the subject and verb. If the subject is singular, these phrases do not change it to plural, so a singular verb is still used, as in, "The new *test* as well as a packet of scoring sheets *arrives* today."

TABLE 7.5   Using *and, or, nor* With Compound Subjects

Joining Word(s)	Subject	Verb	Example
And	Two or more singular or plural terms	Plural	Singular subjects: The PAI *and* the MMPI-2 *are* personality tests. Plural subjects: Tests *and* questionnaires *provide* data for an assessment.
Or/nor	Singular	Singular	The PAI *or* the MMPI-2 *provides* data.
Either/or Neither/nor	Singular	Singular[a]	*Either* Lee *or* his wife *answers* the phone. *Either* my colleague *or* I *administer* the MMPI-2.[a]
Or/nor Either/or Neither/nor	Singular plus plural	Agrees with nearest subject word[b]	*Either* a questionnaire *or* tests *provide* data in an assessment.[b]

Note: Adapted from *English Composition and Grammar: Complete Course*, by J. E. Warriner, 1988, Orlando, FL: Harcourt Brace Jovanovich. Copyright 1988 by Harcourt Brace Jovanovich.
[a] If "I" is one of the subjects, place it last, followed by a singular verb that matches "I."
[b] When combining singular plus plural, place the plural subject last, followed by a plural verb.

Compound Subjects

Two words may be joined by such words as *or, nor,* or *and* to create a compound subject. They may take either singular or plural verbs depending on which word joins them and whether the subject word is singular or plural. Table 7.5 lists these joining words and in which situations they take plural or singular verbs.

The combined phrase *and/or* can confuse the verb that follows, and hence, confuse the reader. Better to phrase simply what you mean without using that term. Instead of struggling with "Nonmedical treatments and/or medication provide (provides?) some relief for the client," revise it. The sentence would then read, "The client receives some relief from nonmedical treatments, medication, or both."

Collective Nouns

A collective noun names a group of persons or things that are viewed as a unit. This category includes the words listed in Table 7.6.

TABLE 7.6 A Few Common Collective Nouns

Army	Crowd	Panel
Audience	Family	Public
Committee	Jury	Team

Because the collective noun describes a unit made up of individuals, it can be used with either the singular or plural of a verb (Warriner, 1988). In American grammar, the collective noun takes a *singular* verb when referring to the unit as a single entity. It takes a *plural* verb when referring to the individuals who make up the group.

- *Single entity = singular verb*:
  "The *jury has* rendered a verdict."
  "The *family has* supported Lee."
- *Individuals of the group = plural verb*:
  "The *jury have* not spoken about the verdict."
  "The *family have* been supportive of each other."

In British usage, the collective noun more often refers to the individuals who make up the group and so uses the plural verb. Whichever way you use a collective noun, be certain that you don't mix singular and plural in the same sentence. For example, if treating a panel as a collective entity, the verb must match: "Saturday, the panel [as an entity] speaks on its topic." (Treating the panel members as individuals yields "Saturday, the panel speak on their topics.")

Additional Subject–Verb Agreement Challenges

1. Use a *singular* verb most often when any of the following are the subject of a sentence:
   - The word *every* or the phrase *many a* before a noun or noun phrase. Examples are
     "*Every* testing manual and scoring sheet *is organized* in the bookcase."
     "*Many a* client *seems* nervous before testing begins."
   - Titles of books, movies, or organizations, even if they are in plural form. Examples are

> "*Subcortical Structures and Cognition,* a recent publication, *presents* a context for assessing brain-based issues in testing."
>
> "The *Centers for Disease Control provides* general information and updates on diseases."

- Certain plural nouns, such as *mumps* or *measles*

2. Use a *plural* verb with words such as *scissors*.
3. *Plural* or *singular* verbs might be used in the following cases, depending on the noun:

- With nouns ending in *-ics,*

  Mathematics, physics, and *economics* take a *singular* verb.

  Tactics, gymnastics, and *athletics* most often take a plural verb.

  Politics can take either a *singular* or *plural* verb.

- With nouns showing *amount* (time, money, fractions) as a combined unit, use *singular*:

  "*Three days* [as a unit] of testing sessions *remains* to be completed."

- With nouns showing *amount* (time, money, fractions) as individual units, use *plural*:

  "*Three days* [individually] *remain* open in my calendar."

- With the phrase ***the*** *number of,* use *singular*:

  "*The number of* referrals I receive from him *has* increased."

- With the phrase ***a*** *number of,* use *plural*:

  "*A number of* referrals *have* come through."

Table 7.7 lists the preceding situations and summarizes when to use singular or plural.

Pronouns

A pronoun is a word that we use in place of a noun or a group of nouns (e.g., *he* in place of *Tom; they* in place of *the brother and sister*). A pronoun may also refer to another pronoun. In the sentences, "*One* of the tests took longer. *It* took two hours to administer," *it* refers to *one* in the previous sentence. Pronouns lend variety to our writing: By using them, we avoid repeating the same subject nouns over and over.

TABLE 7.7 Additional Challenges: Subject/Verb Agreement

Subject/Noun	Use Singular	Use Plural	Singular or Plural
Every + noun	X	...	...
Many a + noun	X	...	...
Title (book, movie, organization) even if plural	X	...	...
Certain plural nouns:			
measles, mumps	X	...	...
scissors	X	...	...
Nouns ending in *–ics*	E.g., mathematics, physics, economics	E.g., tactics, gymnastics, athletics	E.g., politics
Amount (time, money, fractions)	Considered as a combined unit	Considered as individual units	...
The number of	X	...	...
A number of	...	X	...

Note: Adapted from *English Composition and Grammar: Complete Course*, by J. E. Warriner, 1988, Orlando, FL: Harcourt Brace Jovanovich. Copyright 1988 by Harcourt Brace Jovanovich.

Selecting Pronouns

The antecedent of a pronoun is the word that the pronoun refers to (Warriner, 1988). In the examples from the previous paragraph, *Tom* is the antecedent of *he*, and *the brother and sister* are the antecedents of *they*. Use singular pronouns (*he*, *she*, *it*) with singular antecedents (e.g., *Tom*) and plural pronouns (*we*, *they*) with plural antecedents (e.g., *the brother and sister*). If the word *and* connects two or more antecedents, use a *plural* pronoun. But if either the word *or* or *nor* joins them, the pronoun should be singular. When the antecedent is masculine, the pronoun will be masculine (*he*, *him*, *his*). When the antecedent is feminine, use the pronouns *she*, *her*, *hers*, and when neuter, use *it* and *its*. Table 7.8 lists uses and examples.

Sometimes a pronoun could refer to more than one antecedent, as in the sentence, "*Jane* asked *her mother* if *she* left her laptop in the car." Does *she* refer to Jane or her mother? Reframe any sentence with confusing pronouns: "Jane asked her mother, 'Did *you* leave *your* laptop in the car?'"

TABLE 7.8 Selecting Pronouns

Antecedent	Singular Pronouns	Plural Pronouns	Examples
Feminine noun	She, her, hers	We, they, them, their, ours	Singular: *Jane* finished *her* test. Plural: The *clients* finished *their* tests.
Masculine noun	He, him, his	We, they, them, their, ours	Singular: *Tom* completed *his* questionnaire. Plural: The *clients* completed *their* questionnaires.
Neuter noun	It, its	They, them, their	Singular: The *company* sends *its* products by UPS. Plural: The *companies* send *their* products by UPS.
And connecting two or more antecedents		Use plural pronouns	Jane *and* Juli finished *their* tests.
Or/nor connecting two or more antecedents	Use singular pronouns		Neither Jane *nor* Juli finished *her* test.

Indefinite Pronouns

Indefinite pronouns do not refer to a specific antecedent and often express the idea of quantity, as in *all*, *few*, or *many*. Some of them are singular, some plural, and others can be either, depending on the sentence. Table 7.9 lists indefinite pronouns and indicates whether they take the singular or plural form of verbs and other pronouns.

Gender Neutrality in Pronouns

Since the 1700s, English speakers have been concerned about gender bias in pronoun usage (Williams, 2004). The masculine form has for centuries been the default in referring to both men and women. This usage may occur either when referring to a mixed group of men and women (as in using the term *brotherhood* to mean both) or when the gender of a person is unknown ("If *anyone* asks, tell *him* where I am"). Despite efforts beginning in the mid-1800s to coin new, gender-neutral pronouns, mainstream

TABLE 7.9 Indefinite Pronouns

	Singular	Singular or Plural	Plural
Word	Anyone, anybody, each, either, everyone (or every one), everybody, neither, one, no one, nobody, someone, somebody	Any, all, most, some, none[a]	Both, few, many, several
Verb form	Singular	Singular or plural, depending on sentence	Plural
Pronoun form	Singular	Singular or plural, depending on sentence	Plural
Example	*Each fills* out *his* own questionnaire.	Singular: *Some* of *his test is* difficult. Plural: *Some* of *their tests are* difficult.	*Both* of *them speak* clearly.

[a] The word *none* is most generally used to mean "no one" and in that usage takes a singular verb and pronoun. Nevertheless, for many centuries *none* has been used in both singular and plural form (American Heritage, 2000). In the sentence "*None* of the *test was* easy," *none* takes a singular verb, since it treats all the parts of the test as a single entity. But in "*None* of the tests *were* easy," the sentence refers to more than one test and takes the plural. *None* can also stand in place of *not one* or *not any* (Garner, 2009). Using these examples yields: "*None was* easy" (meaning *not one*) and "*None were* easy" (meaning *not any*).

written English still uses the ones we have had all along. We must work with them as best we can.

Especially in conversation, one solution has been the use of *they* or *their* as singular to avoid using *his* or *her* ("*Each* attorney asked *their* own questions of the expert witness"). As this chapter discusses, however, Standard English requires that the subject and verb agree—singular with singular and plural with plural. The best option is to recast the sentence or "write around" the problem to eliminate conflict in number (Chicago Manual, 2010b; Garner, 2009).

Other solutions to mentioning gender have paired both masculine and feminine in forms such as "he or she," "she or he," "s/he," "his/her," "him/her," etc. The APA *Publication Manual* (2010) suggests using these terms sparingly, as they can seem awkward. Some writers alternate between he and she, either by paragraph or by chapter, but this, too, can be distracting if not handled well. In this book, I have

TABLE 7.10   Reducing Gender Bias in Pronouns

Problem Sentence	Possible Solution	Revised Sentence
The client may find that the assessment process frustrates *him.*	Use plural subject	*Clients* may find that the assessment process frustrates *them.*
	Drop the pronoun and write around it	*The client* may find the assessment process *frustrating.*
	Use *or* or a slash between gender pronouns	*The client* may find that the assessment process frustrates *him or her* (or *him/her*).
The assessor and client work together to frame *his* questions.	Repeat a noun or use a related one, if necessary	The assessor and client work together to frame the client's (or the person's) questions.
The client brings *his* completed questionnaire to the first testing session.	Replace the pronoun with an article (*a, an,* or *the*)	*The client* brings *the* completed questionnaire to the first testing session.

chosen to use "s/he" in order to be as inclusive as possible in as small a space as possible. When faced with the need to include both genders in a written report, the assessor-writer may consider the approaches mentioned above as well as others listed in Table 7.10. The problem sentences in the table are written as if all clients are men.

Nouns, too, can be problematic in avoiding gender bias. The term *man* has a long history of standing in for all words referring to the human race (*mankind, manpower, workman*). Be conscious of how you use those terms to avoid bias. Replace them with clear nouns such as *people, personnel,* or *worker.* Also be careful of general assumptions that can inadvertently lead to biased phrasing. For example, if you assume that all physicians are men, you may write about a *woman* physician when that distinction is not called for or relevant. The phrase *woman physician* could reflect the assumption that the "standard" physician is a man and, therefore, the woman is an anomaly. In all descriptions of gender, race, sexual orientation, or disabilities, make conscious choices about their relevance to your report. If relevant, choose the simplest and most sensitive way to state those facts (APA, 2010, 2011).

Pronoun as Subject or Object

Choosing a pronoun to use in a sentence depends on whether it is the subject or object of the sentence. As covered in Chapter 6, the subject is the person, place, idea, or thing that is (a) taking action or (b) being. An object receives the action taken by the subject (e.g., "Jane finished the test," where *Jane* is the subject and *test* is the object). When a pronoun is the subject of a sentence, the forms are *I, you, he/she/it, we, you,* or *they.* When used as the object, however, those forms are, respectively, *me, you, him/her/it, us, you,* or *them. You* and *it* are the only ones that do not change form.

In a simple sentence, most of us choose the correct pronoun with little trouble. But when the sentence has a double subject, we can easily become confused. The simplest way to test which to use is by trying each individual subject with the verb. Look at the sentence, "*Her mother* and *her* arrived late." If we divide the subjects, we have "*Her mother* arrived late" and "*Her* arrived late." Clearly, the second phrase should be "*She* arrived late." Recombining the two subjects, the correct sentence is "Her mother and she arrived late."

Who and *whom* also can confuse a writer. *Who* is the subject form (equating to *he* or *she*), and *whom* is the object (*him* or *her*). A simple technique for choosing which to use is to ask a question or make a statement using *she* or *her.*

- In the sentence, "*Who/whom* will fill out the required forms?" the answer would be "*She* will fill out the forms," so the correct form is *who.*
- In "For *who/whom* are we waiting?" the answer would be "We are waiting for *her,*" so the correct form is *whom.*
- In "I met with the child's mother, for *who/whom* I had many questions," we could say, "I have questions to ask *her,*" so the correct form would be *whom.*

Table 7.11 lists subject and object forms of pronouns with examples of how to use them.

Pronouns also take the subject form (*I, you, he/she/it,* etc.) if they (a) follow a form of the verb *to be* (*am, is, are, was, were, will be, has/had/have been*) and (b) refer to the subject:

TABLE 7.11   Pronoun as Subject or Object

Subject	Example	Object	Example
I	*I* administered a test to the client.	Me	The client gave *me* the questionnaire.
You	*You* handed me the test.	You (no change)	I handed *you* the test.
He	*He* arrived late.	Him	I spoke to *him* about his lateness.
She	*She* brought the child for testing.	Her	I asked *her* to wait outside.
It	*It* was a short session.	It (no change)	We quickly completed *it*.
We	*We* said goodbye at the door.	Us	She waved goodbye to *us*.
You	*You* left together.	You (no change)	I waved goodbye to *you*.
They	*They* made an appointment for next week.	Them	I will meet *them* at 9 a.m.
Who	*Who* will arrive first? (*She* will arrive first; she = who)	Whom	To *whom* were you referring? (I was referring to *her*; her = whom)

- "*It* is *she* who will make the decision about testing her child," not "It is *her*..."
- "Could *it* be *he* who left the message?" not "Could it be *him*..."

In both of these examples, *it* is the subject, and *she* or *he* refers to that subject. In spoken, informal English, many of us use the object form ("It is *her*," "Could it be *him*?"). But knowing and using the correct subject form in writing will improve the quality of your reports.

If the pronoun ends a sentence and follows the words *than* or *as*, figure out the correct pronoun by finishing the sentence. For example, in the sentence, "Her mother was as late as *she/her*," finishing it could yield either pronoun: "Her mother was as late as *she* was" or "Her mother was as late as *her* daughter." Deciding which to use requires that you be clear about what you are saying in the sentence.

Prepositions

Prepositions are common words, such as *for, in, of, on, to,* and *with* (see Table 7.12 for a few more examples). They are literally in *pre* positions; most often, they lead off a phrase and connect nouns and pronouns to other words in a sentence. In administering a psychological assessment, you can ask the person being tested to sit *before* [in front of] the table or *beside* the table. *Before* [earlier than] testing, you can place the testing booklet *on* the table and when complete, lift it *off* the table. You can hand a pencil *to* the person, who may place her feet *under* [or *underneath*] the table as she sits *in* the chair. She may take a break *between* measures and, perhaps, bump *into* the table as she stands. When completed, you can speak *to* her or *with* her; the two *of* you can discuss her questions. As she leaves, she will walk *past* the table and will pass *through* the door.

Prepositions can show the location of the sentence's subject in time or space or in its relation to other words. Some years ago, the children's show *Sesame Street* educated its young viewers on the concept of the common prepositions *over, under, around, and through* with a Muppet and a freestanding swinging door. In turn, the Muppet demonstrated what each of those prepositions meant by enacting each in relation to the door. With so many prepositions in the English language—over 100 by some counts—most of us learned them by hearing others use them. Now we use them instinctively and sometimes incorrectly. Be sensitive to prepositions and correct use—*on* is not the same as *in,* and *of* means a different thing than *to.* In common usage, specific prepositions go with certain phrases. If two or more of those phrases join in the same sentence, all the correct prepositions should be included. For example, "The teenager's comments and demeanor indicated frustration *with* and anger *toward* the testing."

TABLE 7.12 Common Prepositions: An Incomplete List

About	Behind	During	Since	Up
Above	Below	Except	Throughout	Upon
Across	Between	Into	Toward	Within
Against	Beyond	Past	Until	Without

Is it ever OK to end a sentence with a preposition? Many of us were taught that doing so was an absolute no-no; a sentence such as, "Which test did she finish *with*?" would be corrected to read "*With* which test did she finish?" As many grammar experts have long pointed out, however, that rule originally came from Latin grammar and should not restrict English usage (Garner, 2009).

For guidance in deciding when and how to use prepositions, ask yourself

1. *Is the preposition necessary in the sentence?* If you write, "I asked her to choose a chair to sit *in*," dropping the preposition would leave you with, "I asked her to choose a chair to sit," and would make no sense. The preposition here is necessary to the meaning.
2. *Am I using two or more prepositions when one would do?* In the sentence, "The pencil rolled *off of* the table," the word *of* is unnecessary. The sentence is clear and proper as "The pencil rolled off the table."

Some writers still choose to avoid an ending preposition whenever possible, provided the sentence sounds natural. As Strunk and White write in *The Elements of Style* (2000), "The question of ear is vital" (p. 77). Read the sentence aloud; if the sentence sounds natural and has the impact you intend, then it is likely correct.

CHAPTER 8

Modifying the Main Idea
Adjectives and Adverbs

If the noun is good and the verb is strong, you almost never need an adjective.

J. Anthony Lukas, American journalist and writer (1933–1997)

The strongest writing relies on nouns and verbs for power. If the noun is inaccurate or the verb is weak, even a string of adjectives or adverbs will not improve the impact of a sentence (Strunk & White, 2000). Once the base sentence is strong and clear, however, adjectives and adverbs can lend variety and texture. Understanding what they do, where to place them, and how to use them can aid the assessor-writer in creating assessment reports that communicate with clarity and specificity.

Psychologist and assessor Constance Fischer (1994) makes a strong case for relying on verbs and adverbs in the assessment report, since those forms of speech provide concrete imagery of a person's behavior. Nouns and adjectives, on the other hand, can classify and categorize in a way that evokes judgment of the person's behavior; this apparent judgment is most noticeable when using a passive or linking verb: "Dave *was* anxious when he arrived." While factual, that sentence is nonspecific about how his anxiety showed and could be read as making a subtle judgment of his behavior. To write it actively, as an observation and without judgment, you might say, "Dave's voice shook when he greeted me."

Structurally, a sentence cannot stand on verbs and adverbs alone, of course, but the point is a valid one. Establish your base sentence with clear nouns and active verbs and then include adverbs for power. Adjectives are, perhaps, the last choice to add to an assessment report. But you will need to use some of them, so we will look at them first.

Adjectives

An adjective modifies a noun or pronoun. That is, it describes or limits the meaning of that word by specifying number, quality, size, age, shape, color, or other classification. If the noun were *assessment,* then the adjective used to limit its meaning could vary depending on the area it referred to. In the field of psychology, adjectives used with *assessment* might include *personality, psychological, academic, neuropsychological, comprehensive,* or *targeted.* (*Targeted* describes a simpler, shorter procedure where the client has chosen to focus only on specific questions and issues [Engelman, 2011a].) In other professional areas, one might write of a "financial assessment" or a "hearing assessment."

Articles = Adjectives

Articles are three words used as adjectives that indicate (a) one of a general group (*a, an*) or (b) a specific person or thing (*the*).

- *A* precedes words that start with a consonant sound: "Daryl worked on *a* test."
- *An* precedes words that start with a vowel sound: "Daryl worked for *an* hour." (In this case, the *h* in *hour* is not pronounced in speech, so it is treated as a vowel.)
- *The* indicates a specific test: "Daryl worked on *the* test."

Using Adjectives of Quantity

In most cases, we can use the same adjectives with any noun to which it applies. At other times, however, adjectives apply differently depending on whether a noun is *countable* or *uncountable*. (See Table 8.1 for examples.)

TABLE 8.1 Adjectives of Quantity: Using With Countable and Uncountable Nouns

Adjective	Use with Countable	Use with Uncountable	Example
Any	Yes	Yes	Countable: Do you have *any* scoring sheets? Uncountable: Is there *any* water in the pitcher?
Enough	Yes	Yes	Countable: Do you have *enough* pencils? Uncountable: Does the pot have *enough* coffee in it?
Few	Yes	No	Carol gave *few* reasons for her quietness.
Little	No	Yes	Carol had *little* cause for concern.
Many	Yes	No	*Many* assessors write reports.
Much	No	Yes	The client's physician sent so *much* information.
No	Yes	Yes	Countable: The assessor had *no* pencils. Uncountable: Bob had *no* time to finish.
Plenty of	Yes	Yes	Countable: The assessor had *plenty of* pencils. Uncountable: Bob had *plenty of* time to finish.
Some	Yes	Yes	Countable: She placed *some* stimulus cards before the client. Uncountable: She left *some* coffee in the pot.
A little bit of (informal)	No	Yes	She left *a little bit of* coffee in the pot.
A lot of; lots of (informal for *many*)	Yes	No	*A lot of* assessors write reports. *Lots of* attorneys request reports.
Lots of (informal for *much*)	No	Yes	The client's physician sent *lots of* information.

- A *countable* noun is one that can be described by a number (*two* tests, *six* clients) and that takes both singular and plural forms, usually by adding an -*s* on the end (test*s*, client*s*).
- *Uncountable* nouns usually cannot be plural; *water*, *air*, *attitude*, *perception*, for example, are not usually expressed in plural forms.

Some adjectives of quantity (e.g., *some*, *any*, *much*, *many*) can be used with both countable and uncountable nouns, but others apply only to one. Table 8.1 lists adjectives of quantity and their different uses with countable and uncountable nouns. Notice that countable nouns show they are plural by an -*s* added to the noun.

Compound Adjectives

Two or more adjectives that describe a noun can form a compound adjective. The first listed adjective changes or limits the adjective that follows, and many of these compounds will take a hyphen. In "the client was a small-business consultant," *small* limits the type of *business*. In American English, if the phrase is clear without a hyphen, it may be omitted. But without the hyphen in the example given, the reader does not know which is *small*, the client or the *business* she consults to. Over time, many hyphenated adjectives have become joined in American English, as in *downtown*. In British usage, though, hyphens may often remain. Use a hyphen in a compound adjective when placing the adjective in front of the noun ("The *well-known* Rorschach projective") but not after it ("The Rorschach projective is *well known*"). Chapter 10 discusses more on the use of hyphens.

Placing Adjectives

Most often, adjectives come before the noun or pronoun: "The *new* tests arrived yesterday." In some cases, adjectives will follow the word they describe:

- After a form of the verb *to be* or a linking verb (e.g., *feel*, *taste*, *look*): "The tests were *long*." (Even though separated by the verb, *long* still describes "tests.")
- To emphasize the adjective: "The people *present* included the teenager and her parents."

Adjectives either (a) have equal weight in describing the noun in a sentence (coordinate) or (b) build on each other (cumulative). To decide if two adjectives in a row build on each other or not, do the following:

- Put *and* between the two adjectives. Does the sentence sound right?
- Reverse the order of the adjectives. Does the sentence still sound right?

If the sentence works in both these cases, the adjectives do not build on each other. Since each can stand alone, separate the adjectives with commas:

"The teenager's parents are an *older, professional* couple."

If the sentence does not work, then the adjectives build on each other; they do not stand alone and so should be written with no commas between them:

"The teenager came to the appointment wearing *several bangle* bracelets."

As in other areas of grammar, the decision will not always be black and white. If the sentence seems to work either way, make a choice of which you feel sounds best. Table 8.2 compares the qualities and placement of adjectives and adverbs.

TABLE 8.2 Adjectives and Adverbs: Comparison of Qualities and Placement

	Adjective	Adverb
What it modifies	Noun or pronoun	Verb, adjective, another adverb
How it is formed	By adding to noun or verb various endings, e.g., *-able, -ful, -ish, -less, -y*)	Many by adding *-ly* on the end of an adjective
What it specifies or answers	Number, quality, size/ age/shape/color, or other classification	Answers the questions how, where, how often, when, or how much
Where it is placed in the sentence	Usually *before* noun or pronoun; sometimes *after* to emphasize or if following a form of *to be* or a linking verb	Variable; best placed next to verb, adjective or other adverb it describes; can be placed at beginning, middle, or end

Adverbs

Most often, an adverb describes or limits a verb. It also can modify an adjective or another adverb. Adverbs answer the question how, when, where, or how much (to what extent). Words that end in *-ly* are frequently adverbs, but not always. Some adjectives, too, end in *-ly*, such as *lively* or *elderly* (Warriner, 1988). Adverbs may also be phrases of more than one word describing the verb, adjective, or other adverb. Placing adverbs can vary. Depending on the word or phrase, it may be placed at the beginning or end of the sentence or in the middle. For example, all three of these sentences are correct:

> *Usually* (adverb), his interview session *lasts* (verb) one hour.
> His interview session *lasts* one hour *usually.*
> His interview session *usually lasts* one hour.

In the context of a whole paragraph, sometimes the adverb will sound better in one place than another. Wherever you place it, keep it close to the word it describes when possible, and be specific in your phrasing. Since adverbs can appear anywhere in the sentence, your reader can be confused by adverbs that could apply to more than one word. For instance, "He *nearly* finished the test in record time" says something different than "He finished the test in *nearly* record time."

Splitting Verbs With Adverbs

When the verb has two parts, as in *will finish,* we must decide where to place the adverb—before, after, or in the middle? The rigid rule had long been "Never split the verb." This rule apparently was an attempt to parallel English grammar with Latin. That rule still stands according to some experts, along with its sister rule, "Never split an infinitive" (more on splitting infinitives later in this chapter). Yet grammarians from 1906 (Fowler) and 2009 (Garner) agree that the rule against splitting verbs is unsupported. As with other facets of effective writing, perhaps the key lies in conscious choice. Decide for yourself what to use based on what sounds right to you. But be aware that some—such as journal editors, technical editors, or teachers—may take issue with split verbs. Others, however, will see nothing amiss.

Some possibilities for placing the adverb in relation to the verb are

1. Tracy will *gladly* finish writing the report.
2. Tracy *gladly* will finish writing the report.
3. Tracy will finish *gladly* writing the report.

In these three examples, numbers two and three do not split the verb. Number two, however, sounds a bit awkward and formal, and number three changes the meaning of the sentence. (Is Tracy glad to be writing the report or glad to be finishing it?) Number one splits the verb, but it probably sounds the most natural.

Adjectives, Adverbs, and Linking Verbs

Chapter 3 introduces linking verbs (i.e., forms of *to be* as well as verbs such as *taste, smell, feel, look*). How you use the verb determines whether the sentence will take an adjective or adverb. True linking verbs are static in that they describe the subject of the sentence rather than its action; those sentences usually require adjectives. By recasting a sentence, though, some linking verbs can also show action and then can take an adverb.

- *Linking verb takes an adjective*: "Hilary *looked thoughtful* after the test" describes Hilary's state rather than an action she is taking; in this use, *thoughtful* is an adjective. You might put a mental equal sign in place of the verb to remind yourself that the verb is not acting on anything—it simply describes Hilary.
- *Linking recast as action verb takes an adverb*: "Hilary *looked thoughtfully* out the window" shows Hilary taking action, *looking*, with the adverb *thoughtfully* showing how she is taking action.

See Table 8.3 for further examples of adjectives with linking verb and adverbs with action verbs.

One quick test of whether a verb of sense (such as those in Table 8.3) is used as a linking verb or an action verb is to replace it with a form of the word *to be* (*is, am*, etc.). Because forms of *to be* are always linking verbs, if this test makes sense, then your verb is one of linking, not action.

TABLE 8.3 Adjectives and Adverbs With Linking Versus Action Verbs

Verb	Example	Takes Adjective	Takes Adverb
Look	As linking verb: Hilary *looked sad.*	Yes (*sad*)	No
	As action verb: Hilary *looked sadly* at the puppy's hurt paw.	No	Yes (*sadly*)
Smell	As linking verb: The rose *smelled fragrant.*	Yes (*fragrant*)	No
	As action verb: Hilary *happily smelled* the rose.	No	Yes (*happily*)
Taste	As linking verb: The pie *tasted sweet.*	Yes (*sweet*)	No
	As action verb: Hilary *quickly tasted* the pie.	No	Yes (*quickly*)

- In the sentence "Hilary looked sad," testing it with a form of *to be* gives the sentence "Hilary *is* sad." This version makes sense, so the verb in the original sentence is one of linking, not action, and takes an adjective.
- On the other hand, "Hilary *looked* sadly at the puppy's hurt paw," when tested in this way, makes no sense: It yields "Hilary *is* sadly the puppy's hurt paw." Because it fails this test, the verb is an action verb here and takes an adverb.

Uncertainty over whether to use the adjective or adverb form of some words easily causes problems in writing. The answer can often be found by the previous test of linking versus action verb. Table 8.4 lists three common word pairings that are easy to mix up unless you know whether or not the verb is active. Of these, *good* versus *well* might cause special difficulty, since (a) *well* can be used as either an adjective (with a linking verb) or an adverb (with an action verb), and (b) though *good* is always an adjective, it can be used with either a linking or an action verb.

Degrees of Comparison in Adjectives and Adverbs

Adjectives and adverbs often convert to different forms when comparing the qualities of two or more items ("The Grooved Pegboard is a not a *long* test to administer; the Wisconsin Card Sort Test takes *longer*; and the NEPSY-II takes *longest* of the three"). The process of forming regular comparisons can vary

TABLE 8.4   Adjective or Adverb Form? Start With the Verb

Form	Type of Verb	Adjective	Adverb	Example
Bad	Linking	Yes	No	Linda *felt bad* about missing the session.
Badly	Action	No	Yes	Linda *performed badly* on the test.
Slow	Linking	Yes	No	Linda's performance on the test *was* slow.
Slowly	Action	No	Yes	Linda *wrote slowly* on the essay section of Written Expression.
Well	Linking	Yes	No	Linda *is well.* (Refers to health)
	Action	No	Yes	Linda *wrote well.* (Describes how she wrote)
Good	Linking	Yes	No	*Linda is good* at completing tasks. (Refers back to the subject, Linda)
	Action	Yes	No	Linda wrote a *good essay* on the test. (Describes the noun, essay)

Note: Adapted from *English Composition and Grammar: Complete Course,* by J. E. Warriner, 1988, Orlando, FL: Harcourt Brace Jovanovich. Copyright 1988 by Harcourt Brace Jovanovich.

depending on the original word ending or the number of syllables in the word. The basic process for adjectives is shown in Table 8.5 and for adverbs in Table 8.6.

Be careful, however, not to use both *-er/-est* and *more/most* with the same word. Write "The briefcase is *heavier* than the stack of books" but not "The briefcase is *more heavier* than the stack of books." And when the forms are irregular, we simply must memorize them, as in

- Good, better, best
- Bad, worse, worst
- Little, less, least

Avoiding Ambiguity and Awkwardness

If we have planned a document well, as we write we usually know what we are trying to say. But sometimes the words do not fall into place so that the reader can understand. The following short sections cover a number of problems we can stumble over.

TABLE 8.5 Adjectives: Regular Forms of Comparison

	Which Adjective			
	Most of One Syllable	Some of Two Syllables	Others of Two Syllables	All of Three or More Syllables
How it changes:	+ -er or -est	+ -er or -est	+ *more* or *most*	+ *more* or *most*
Examples:				
Base form	*Thick*: The test manual is *thick*.	*Lively*: The *lively* child kept fidgeting.	*Agile*: The child seemed to have an *agile* mind.	*Creative*: The child had a *creative* imagination.
Comparing two things	*Thicker*: The second manual is *thicker* than the first.	*Livelier*: The *livelier* of the two children was the boy.	*More agile*: Her speech was *more agile* than her brother's.	*More creative*: His drawing was more *creative* than the other child's.
Comparing three or more things	*Thickest*: Of the three manuals, the blue one is *thickest*.	*Liveliest*: The boy was *liveliest* of the five children.	*Most agile*: She was the *most agile* child on the playground.	*Most creative*: His drawing was the *most creative* among the four.

TABLE 8.6 Adverbs: Regular Forms of Comparison

	Which Adverb	
	Most of One Syllable	All Ending in *-ly*
How it changes:	+ -er or -est	+ *more* or *most*
Examples:		
Base form	*Fast*: He spoke *fast*.	*Slowly*: She wrote *slowly*.
Comparing two things	*Faster*: He spoke *faster* than the judge.	*More slowly*: She wrote more slowly than the other attorney.
Comparing three or more things	*Fastest*: He spoke *fastest* of the three attorneys.	*Most slowly*: Of the three attorneys, she wrote *most slowly*.

Separating Related Words

Logic in a sentence comes from the way in which words interact. Words placed together indicate their interrelationship. If we divide them, the thought gets muddled. For example, in the sentence, "She pointed out a mistake in his sentence that was at the end," the reader has to work to figure out what, exactly, was at the end—the sentence or the mistake. Better to write, "She pointed out a mistake at the end of his sentence."

Misplacing Modifiers

Akin to the problem of separating related words is that of placing phrases so they are both confusing and humorous (Bates, 2000). For example, "She suddenly recalled an error in the boy's Written Expression essay hurrying to her car." Of course, neither the error nor the essay was hurrying to her car, but that is the way it reads. Clear it up by writing, "While she hurried to her car, she suddenly recalled an error in the boy's Written Expression essay."

Constructing Awkward Adverbs

The English language contains many useful adverbs. More can be created by adding *-ly* to an adjective, but those creations often sound awkward ("He frowned *frustratedly* at the assessor"). In good written English, it is better to stick with the adjective forms ("With a *frustrated* expression, he frowned at the assessor"). "Do not dress up words by adding *-ly* to them, as though putting a hat on a horse," in the words of Strunk & White (2000, p. 75).

Adding Too Many Adjectives or Adverbs

This chapter led off with the idea that strong writing grounds itself in nouns and verbs and only secondarily in the judicious use of adjectives and adverbs. Avoid too many of them. They can make your document seem overwritten and overexplained. Be aware of using words such as *very*, *extremely*, and *really*; these words are called "intensifiers" and are intended to emphasize degree (Bates, 2000). But when overused, they make the writing go limp and the content meander.

Modifying Absolutes

Some adjectives are considered "absolute." An absolute describes a quality that a thing or person either does or does not have, with no gradations. Among them are terms such as *unique, perfect, infinite,* or *complete.* A finished painting may be *complete* but not *absolutely complete.* A person may be *unique* but not *very unique.* But this strict, logical perspective does not take into account what one source refers to as the metaphorical use of absolutes (American Heritage dictionary, 2000). In this usage, when describing something outside a strictly scientific realm, one might use a continuum that reflects degrees. If that painting mentioned previously was not finished but showed a degree of completeness, it could be described as *almost complete.* Or suppose a person wants to indicate that s/he knows of many job options but also recognizes that many more might be out there. Informally, s/he might say that the options are *nearly infinite.* In formal written English, however, modifying absolutes can bring criticism from a knowledgeable reader. If you choose to modify absolutes in your written reports, be conscious of the choice and know that some will view it as an error.

Using *Hopefully* and *However*

The word *hopefully* can also cause disagreement. In its original meaning, it is an adverb describing a hopeful attitude in the person who is the subject of the sentence, as in "Daryl *hopefully* completed the test." Yet, as far back as the 1800s, people began using *hopefully* in a different manner, one that became widespread by the 1930s and created objection beginning in the 1960s (Merriam-Webster, 2011). This different usage reflects the speaker or writer's attitude instead of that of the person described. "*Hopefully,* Daryl completed the test" indicates that the writer is hoping Daryl took action and not that Daryl is hopeful about the test. But a reader can be easily confused about which of the two meanings you intend. If you choose to use the word *hopefully,* examine your sentence for two things: (a) Who do you mean is hopeful, you or the subject of the sentence? and (b) Will the reader be able to make that distinction? If not, and you mean that you are the hopeful one, consider changing the sentence to something simpler like, "I hope that Daryl completed the test."

Using the adverb *however* within a sentence will draw attention to whatever precedes it (Garner, 2009). "Daryl, *however,* was late for his appointment" suggests comparison with someone who was not late. "Daryl was late, *however,* for his appointment" focuses on Daryl by himself. Placing *however* in that way points out that something else to follow was influenced by his lateness (e.g., "...

so we were not able to finish testing"). No grammar rule exists against starting a sentence with *however.* Nevertheless, many people still believe it incorrect. So, if you are writing for a critical audience—teacher, editor—you may choose to use caution in doing so. You might better use *but, yet, nevertheless,* or *in spite of that* to suggest contrast. The most correct use of *however* to begin a sentence is when you mean "in whatever way" (Garner, p. 428)—for example, "However you choose to view it, Daryl was late for his appointment."

To + Base Verb: To Split or Not to Split

A base verb is the form of a verb that you would see in an English dictionary (*write, test, finish*). Preceded by "to," the base verb becomes an infinitive: *to write, to test, to finish.* Most infinitives are used as nouns in a sentence ("Today, I want *to write*") but may also be used as adjectives ("She is the person *to test*"—adjective modifying the noun *person*) or adverbs ("I need *to finish*"—adverb modifying the verb *need*). One important issue with infinitives is that of splitting them. Is it ever all right to divide *to* from the word that follows by inserting a word or phrase between them? (e.g., "I need to *quickly* finish.") The question of splitting infinitives goes back centuries, with varying ideas of how the ban on doing so evolved. In contemporary times, grammar books and style manuals no longer stress the ban as unilateral. Some say that a split infinitive can be clearer than an unsplit one:

> "I decided *to gradually administer* the tests." (Split)
> "I decided *to administer* the tests *gradually.*" (Unsplit)
> "*Gradually,* I decided *to administer* the tests." (Unsplit, but changes the meaning)

As with the question of whether or not to end a sentence with a preposition (see Chapter 7), some sources say it is a matter of ear, and if the split infinitive sounds better, use it (Bates, 2000; Strunk & White, 2000). The ban remains alive, however, in the minds of many. If you choose to use split infinitives in your written reports, know that some readers will have strong opinions about them. If writing to a teacher or editor's guidelines, take those requirements into account.

CHAPTER **9**

Precision
Right Word, Right Spelling

> My spelling is Wobbly. It's good spelling but it Wobbles, and letters get in the wrong places.
>
> **A. A. Milne, English author of the *Winnie the Pooh* books**

The word *googol* is used in mathematics to represent the number 1 followed by 100 zeros. When naming their company, the creators of Google searched for an Internet domain name that would remind people of a huge amount of data such as the Internet provides. They meant to search on "googol" but keyed it incorrectly as "google." That domain name was open, and the founders decided to stick with the misspelling (Koller, 2004). Not all misspellings are as serendipitous.

While the assessor-writer composes a report, s/he carefully chooses words that will most effectively communicate with the intended reader. A crisp, clear, professional report depends on using the correct spelling of those chosen words in written Standard English. For the most part, we spell by eye, not by ear, in English. The ear can easily get confused in a language where one letter or combination may represent several sounds (*ch* in *ch*emistry vs. in ma*ch*ine) or where several letters or combinations may represent one sound (the "o" sound in *go*, *oath*, *sew* or the "k" sound in *c*all, *k*een, *ch*aos (Changes in Language, n.d.). When we learn to read and pronounce those sounds, many people initially do so through one of three methods:

- Phonics, by learning and sounding out the phonetic values of letters and syllables
- Whole-word recognition
- Combination of these two

Both phonetic and whole-word approaches can contribute useful tools to help us with correct spelling, though neither provides the complete kit. Whole-word recognition might give the visual memory of the entire word, while sounding out can provide an idea of the number of syllables and sounds the word contains. Correct pronunciation can play a part in helping us spell. If we don't pronounce the first *r* in *February*, for example, we may leave it out when we write it.

The APA *Publication Manual* (2010) recommends relying on *Merriam-Webster's Collegiate Dictionary*, 2005, for correct spelling of everyday words and on the APA *Dictionary of Psychology* for psychological terms. For many writers, the spell-checker in their word-processing program takes the place of a dictionary. Even though this computer feature is a good place to start, it is not 100% reliable, as discussed in Chapter 5's section on proofing the report. Spell-checkers do not always recognize technical, professional, or foreign words and so may indicate a misspelling where none exists. In addition, be attentive to the replacement choices offered by the program and which change you select. Replacement words can range from useful to laughable or worse.

One executive in a large organization had little confidence in his own spelling and relied heavily on spell-check. In one document, a person's name showed as misspelled, and he hastily clicked on the first highlighted replacement the program offered. Unfortunately, the word that replaced the proper name (which had actually been correct) was that of a body part—one found in some medical documents but certainly not in business correspondence. And he had sent the document to a long list of people. The mortified executive quickly apologized in person for the public mangling of the individual's name, and the offending word disappeared from spell-check, company-wide. Ultimately, the best way to guarantee correct spelling in your assessment reports is to learn a few rules and their exceptions and to consult a good dictionary, as needed.

TABLE 9.1 Some Exceptions to the *I*-Before-*E* Rule

Exception	Examples
Sounded as *A* ("ay")	Beige, eight, freight, sleigh, veil
Sounded as *I* ("eye")	Height, feisty, sleight
When -c sounds like -sh	Ancient, conscience, efficient, sufficient
Other words with C-I-E-N	Science, scientific
Other exceptions	Caffeine, counterfeit, either, forfeit, foreign, height, leisure, protein, neither, seized, weird

Spelling in the Body of a Word

The following rhyme has been around since the late 1800s (Wikipedia, 2011d): "*I* before *E* except after *C*." This memory device is useful as far as it goes, covering words such as

- believe, brief, friend (*I* before *E*)
- perceive, receive, ceiling (except after *C*)

But we rapidly reach the territory of exceptions to the rule, and those must simply be memorized. Table 9.1 lists some of these exceptions and a few examples.

Prefixes and Suffixes

A *prefix* is added to the beginning of a word to change its meaning. The prefix may be a single letter or a group of letters or syllables. Though the word's meaning changes, the spelling of its root word does not (Warriner, 1988). Table 9.2 provides some examples, and Chapter 10, Table 10.7, shows when to use hyphens with prefixes.

TABLE 9.2 Common Prefixes and Their Meanings

Prefix	Meaning	Examples
A-, de-, il-, im-, in-, ir-, mis-, un-	Indicates opposite or absence of the root word's quality	Amoral, desensitize, illegal, immoral, incorrect, irrelevant, misapply, unavailable
Pre-, post-	Indicates time, before or after	Pretest, postoperative
Super-, co-, in-	Indicates spatial relation—above, with, into	Supervisor, collaborate, inform

A *suffix* may be added to the end of a word to change its meaning. The suffix is a single letter or a group of letters or syllables. How to spell words with suffixes is governed by (a) the word's ending, (b) whether or not the ending is preceded by a consonant, or (c) both. As with so many rules in English grammar, however, exceptions are ever-present and sometimes inconsistent. For example, American English differs from British English in whether or not to drop a silent -*e* when adding a suffix to some words: judgment or judgement; aging or ageing; and acknowledgment or acknowledgement. British English more often retains the silent -*e* and American English drops it. Any one of these words is correct either way, though dictionaries and style manuals usually indicate a preferred variant. Tables 9.3 and 9.4 show rules, exceptions, and examples.

After many years of speaking and writing English, correct use of prefixes and suffixes becomes instinctive. Still, we can easily slip into using incorrect ones if we are not aware. Using an incorrect prefix is at best awkward sounding and at worst could cause your reader to question your ability to accurately express assessment results. If you were to use the term *un*relevant in place of the correct *ir*relevant, for example, it is merely awkward. But misuse *im*moral for *a*moral and the explicit meaning changes: *Immoral* describes breaking moral codes, while *amoral* is having no moral code at all. Though they may be small, prefixes and suffixes require careful attention so that your writing is clean, clear, and accurate.

Spelling Plural Nouns

Most nouns become plural simply by adding an -*s* at the end, such as test*s* or book*s*. But other words end in a sound that makes a single -*s* ending unpronounceable without an additional vowel; these words take an -*es*: prefix*es*, suffix*es*. A number of nouns with irregular plural forms must be memorized, such as *child, children; woman, women*. Compound nouns, which are made up of more than one word, have rules and exceptions, as do other special cases. In those situations, either memorize them or look them up in a dictionary as needed. Table 9.5 illustrates rules, exceptions, and examples for forming regular, irregular, and compound plural nouns.

Table 9.6 illustrates rules, exceptions, and examples for a number of special situations, such as words ending in -*y*, -*o*, -*f*, or -*fe*;

TABLE 9.3 Adding Suffixes, Part I: Final -*e* and Final -*y*

Word Ending	Rule and Exceptions	Examples
Final -*e*:		
silent	1. Drop the -*e* when the suffix starts with a *vowel*.	Complete + -*ed* = complet*ed*
	2. Keep the -*e* when the suffix starts with a *consonant*.	Complete + -*ly* = complete*ly*
	Exceptions:	
	3. Drop the -*e* before *any ending* if another *vowel* comes before the silent -*e*.	Argue + -*ment* = arg*ument* Argue + -*ed* = arg*ued*
	4. Keep the -*e* if the word could be mispronounced without it.	Change + -*able* = chang*eable* (not "changable")
	5. Certain words vary in whether they drop the silent -*e* before an ending, depending on whether American or British usage.	Judgment vs. judgement Aging vs. ageing
Final -*e*: sounded	Do not drop an -*e* from words with sounded double *vowels* when adding -*ing*.	See + -*ing* = seeing Agree + -*ing* = agreeing
Final -*y*	1. Keep the -*y* after a *vowel*.	Obey + -*ed* = obe*yed*
	2. Change -*y* to -*i* after a *consonant*.	Hurry = hurr*ied*
	Exception:	
	3. Keep the -*y* after a *consonant* if the ending is -*ing*.	Hurry = hurr*ying*

Note: Adapted from *English Composition and Grammar: Complete Course,* by J. E. Warriner, 1988, Orlando, FL: Harcourt Brace Jovanovich. Copyright 1988 by Harcourt Brace Jovanovich.

nouns that remain the same whether singular or plural; foreign words; and numbers, letters, and symbols.

Numbers: Digits or Words?

Knowing when to use numerals and when to spell out the number can confuse most of us. Rules regarding usage vary among style manuals and academic disciplines. Because users of this book are governed by the APA *Publication Manual* when preparing a publication, we will use that as the authority on dealing with numbers. Table 9.7 summarizes basic information on when to use figures and when to spell them out as words.

TABLE 9.4   Adding Suffixes, Part II: Doubling Final Consonants and When to Use -*sede*, -*ceed*, or -*cede*

Word Ending	Rule	Examples
Final consonant: doubled	Adding an ending that begins with a *vowel*, **double the final** *consonant* when	-*ing*, -*ed*
	1. Word is only 1 syllable **Or**	Plan + n
	2. Accent is on **last** syllable **And**	For**get** + t
	3. Word ends with single *vowel* followed by single *consonant*	Plan + n + -ed = planned Forget + t + -ing = forgetting
Final consonant: not doubled	Adding an ending that begins with a *vowel*, **do not double final** *consonant* when	-*ing*, -*ed*
	1. Accent is on **first** syllable **Or**	**Can**cel + -ed = canceled
	2. Word ends with two *consonants*	End + -ing = ending
-*sede*, -*ceed*, or -*cede*	1. Only one word in English ends in -*sede*.	Supersede
	2. Only three words end in -*ceed*.	Exceed, proceed, succeed
	3. All other words ending with a "seed" sound are spelled with -*cede* ending.	Concede, intercede, precede

Note: Adapted from *English Composition and Grammar: Complete Course*, by J. E. Warriner, 1988, Orlando, FL: Harcourt Brace Jovanovich. Copyright 1988 by Harcourt Brace Jovanovich.

Spelling Words That Sound Alike

A number of words in English sound alike but are spelled differently and mean different things, such as *to*, *too*, and *two*. Computer spell-checkers do not always flag these as errors because it recognizes them as real words. Since even words that are pronounced a bit differently can be confused with each other, stay alert to how you use similar words. That awareness will improve the clarity and accuracy of your report.

Effect Versus *Affect*

The words *effect* and *affect* have different meanings and are not pronounced exactly alike, yet they are easily confused. And in

TABLE 9.5   Plural Noun Endings, Part I: Regular, Irregular, and Compound

Nouns	Rules and Exceptions	Examples
Most nouns	Add -s to end of word	Assessments, results
Nouns ending in -s, -sh, -ch, -x, -z or with the soft *g* sound, as at end of "judge"	Add -es to end of word	-s: passes, bosses -sh: ashes, clashes -ch: speeches, benches -x: prefixes, suffixes -z: waltzes, topazes Soft *g* sound: judges
Irregular nouns	Memorize plural forms most used; consult dictionary on others, as needed	Child = children, mouse = mice (though "mouses" often used to refer to computers)
Compound nouns	1. Written as *one word*, add -s or -es	Keyboards, strongboxes
	2. Written as *two or more words*, with or without hyphens, make the **base word** plural	Attorneys-at-law, passers-by, courts martial
	Exception:	
	3. Some compound nouns are irregular; memorize words most used; consult dictionary on others	Ten-year-olds, tie-ups

Note: Adapted from *English Composition and Grammar: Complete Course*, by J. E. Warriner, 1988, Orlando, FL: Harcourt Brace Jovanovich. Copyright 1988 by Harcourt Brace Jovanovich.

the field of psychology, this confusion increases, because an additional definition and a different pronunciation of *affect* are added to the ones used in everyday speaking and writing.

- *Effect* as a *verb* means to bring something about: "The medication *effected* a great change in the child's behavior."
- *Effect* as a *noun* means the result of action taken: "Unfortunately, the medication also had one side *effect*."
- *Affect* as a *verb* means to influence or produce a change: "The therapeutic story *affected* him deeply."
- *Affect* as a *noun* (especially in psychology) is pronounced differently from the verb, with emphasis on the first syllable. It means an expressed or observed emotional response: "The assessor took special note of the client's flat *affect*."

TABLE 9.6   Plural Noun Endings, Part II: Special Situations

Nouns	Rules and Exceptions	Examples
Ending in –y	1. Keep the -y after a *vowel* and add an -s	Stay + -s = stays
	2. Change the -y to -i after a *consonant* and add -es	Theory + -s = theor*i*es
Ending in -o	1. Keep the -o after a *vowel* and add an -s	Ratio + -s = ratio*s*
	2. Keep the -o after a *consonant* and add either -s or -es. Memorize words most used; consult dictionary on others	Piano + -s = piano*s*; Hero + -es = hero*es*
Ending in -f or -fe	1. Retain the -f and add -s **Or**	Roof + -s = roof*s*
	2. Change the -f to -v and add -s or -es. Memorize words most used; consult dictionary on others.	Shel*f* = shel*ves*
Same singular or plural	Some plural nouns remain the same as singular; memorize words most used; consult dictionary on others	Deer, salmon, sheep, series, species
Foreign words	Some foreign words used in English take the same plural as in the original language; memorize words most used; consult dictionary on others	Addend*um* = addend*a* (pl.) Symposi*um* = symposi*a* Alumn*us* = alumn*i* Cris*is* = cris*es*
Numbers, letters, and symbols	1. Plurals of *numbers*, add -s or -es with **no apostrophe**; use with figures or words	1990s; W-2s; twos and threes; sixes
	2. Plurals of *letters* or *symbols*: add -s or -es with **no apostrophe**	IQs; URLs; WISCs (NISes)
	Exception:	
	3. Sources differ on *plurals of single letters* of alphabet or when referring to the *plural of a word as a word*. One solution: **use apostrophe** if dropping it could confuse reader by forming an unintended word.	A's (dropping apostrophe would leave you with "As") I's (dropping apostrophe would leave "Is")

Note: Adapted from *English Composition and Grammar: Complete Course*, by J. E. Warriner, 1988, Orlando, FL: Harcourt Brace Jovanovich. Copyright 1988 by Harcourt Brace Jovanovich.
Adapted from Publication Manual of the *American Psychological Association (6th ed.)*, 2010, Washington, DC: American Psychological Association. Copyright 2010 by APA.

TABLE 9.7 Numbers: As Figures or Words?

	Rule	Examples
Base rule	1. *Spell out* numbers below 10.	One, two, three
	2. *Use figures* for numbers 10 and above.	10, 11, 12
Use figures	3. *Use figures* before a unit of measurement, percentages, and ratios.	A 12-inch ruler; in the 8th percentile; a ratio of 2:1
	4. *Use figures* to represent time, date, age, and *exact* sums of money (see Rule 8 for exception).	5:30 p.m.; June 18; 35 years old; $5.25
	5. *Use figures* to indicate a specific place in a series, book, table, or in a list of four or more numbers.	Chapter 9; Table 9.7; pages 1, 2, 3, 4, and 5
Use words	6. *Use words* when a number begins a sentence or title.	Two clients cancelled appointments last week.
	7. *Use words* for common fractions.	One-half of the tests
	8. *Use words* for *indefinite* numbers (days, months, years).	About four days ago
Combine figures and words	9. *Combine figures and words* when two numbers appear one after the other.	2 ten-minute tests

Note: Adapted from *Publication Manual of the American Psychological Association* (6th ed.), 2010, Washington, DC: American Psychological Association. Copyright 2010 by APA.

If you plan to use the word *affect* in its psychological meaning in an assessment report, ask yourself whether your intended reader is familiar with this usage. If you are not certain, consider rephrasing your sentence. If the reader has to stop to use the dictionary, you have broken the flow of communication and your reader still may not find the correct definition. Better to use a word or description in everyday English (e.g., "The client's facial expression, gestures, and voice showed little or no emotion"). Although rephrasing takes a few more words, the clarity will help your reader understand you.

Other Words Easily Confused

Many other words in everyday usage can be mistaken for each other. Table 9.8 lists only a few, defines them, and gives examples of correct usage.

As with *there*, *their*, *they're* in Table 9.8, confusion in spelling can arise between the possessive form (e.g., *your*, *its*) and a contraction (e.g., *you're*, *it's*). Chapter 10 discusses possessives, contractions, and use of apostrophes; see especially Table 10.8. See Chapter 2 for more general information on contractions.

Abbreviations and Acronyms

An *abbreviation* refers to any shortened form of a word or phrase, such as *Dr.* for *doctor* or *NY* for *New York*. In most cases, use title abbreviations with names but spell out the word in a sentence, for example, "*Dr.* Jones sent a report to the client's *doctor*." An *acronym* can be thought of as a special type of abbreviation. In its primary definition, an acronym is an actual word that is formed using the initial letter(s) of a series of words and can itself be pronounced as a word: Radar (*r*adio *d*etection *a*nd *r*anging), AIDS (*a*cquired *i*mmune *d*eficiency *s*yndrome), NATO (North Atlantic Treaty Organization), and amphetamine (alpha-methyl-phenethylamine) are examples. Expanded versions of acronyms, however, include those pronounced only as letters (APA for the *A*merican *P*sychological *A*ssociation; USA for *U*nited *S*tates of *A*merica) and those that can be pronounced as either words or letters (IRA for *i*ndividual *r*etirement *a*ccount). The APA *Publication Manual* (2010) explicitly permits using abbreviations that are not labeled as "abbreviation" in Merriam Webster's Collegiate Dictionary, 2005. These words, including *IQ* and *AIDS*, need no further explanation in the text.

In the world of psychological assessment, various test names have become acronyms that are pronounced as words (WISC, WIAT), and others are referred to by their letters (CVLT, PAI). When using any of these professional acronyms in a written report, spell out the full name and edition the first time you use it, immediately followed by the acronym and edition in parentheses: e.g., Wechsler Individual Achievement Test, third edition (WIAT-III). Subsequently, you can simply use the acronym.

TABLE 9.8   Common Words: They Sound Alike but Mean Different Things

Word	Meaning	Example of Correct Usage
Altogether	Completely	The assessor was not *altogether* sure that the boy understood her directions.
All together	In the same place; taking collective action	She gathered the completed tests and questionnaires *all together* in a large folder.
Complement	To complete or bring something to perfection	The assessor's thoroughness *complemented* her sensitivity with clients.
Compliment	To make a positive statement (*verb*) A statement that says something positive (*noun*)	The attorney *complimented* the assessor on her thoroughness. She thanked him for the *compliment*.
Principal	The head of an entity The main person or idea among several A debt minus interest	The attorney was a *principal* in the firm. The *principal* reason he sought an assessment was to understand his anger. How much *principal* remains on the mortgage?
Principle	A basic truth or motivating force A standard of good behavior	She understands the *principles* of a thorough assessment. The judge declared that the client had no *principles*.
Stationary	Not movable	Her large desk was heavy and *stationary*.
Stationery	Writing materials	She kept *stationery* in the top desk drawer.
There	In that place	Place the completed forms *there*.
Their	Belonging to—shows possession by more than one	*Their* appointment is scheduled for 2 p.m. tomorrow.
They're	"They are"—contraction of the two words	*They're* scheduled for 2 p.m. tomorrow.

Note: All definitions from *Webster's New World College Dictionary* (4th ed.), 2001, Cleveland, OH: Wiley; and *American Heritage Dictionary of the English Language* (4th ed.), 2000, Boston, MA: Houghton Mifflin Harcourt.

If you mention the term only once or twice, though, using the full name each time with no acronym is probably clearest for the reader.

A few Latin abbreviations in common usage may be used in writing your report in Standard English:

- e.g., = for example
- etc. = and so forth
- i.e., = that is
- vs. = versus

The Latin abbreviations are used parenthetically:

"The child appeared to find it hard to concentrate (*e.g.,* fidgeting, jumping up to go to the window, asking for a different pencil, *etc.*)"

If you use the English equivalent, do so within the sentence:

"The child appeared to find it hard to concentrate; *for example,* he fidgeted, jumped up and went to the window, asked for a different pencil, *and so forth.*"

Capital Letters

Just as a new paragraph signals a shift in topic from the prior one, a capital letter at the beginning of a sentence performs a similar function. It tells the reader that this sentence will present a new thought, either wholly or as expansion from the previous sentence. Capital letters are used at other times, too, though style manuals can differ widely on use of capitals. Table 9.9 and the following bullet list it give standard capitalization rules. Some that are specific to APA are listed separately in Table 9.10. These combined lists and tables will likely be ample for use in assessment reports. But if you deal with publications that use other style manuals, you might run into conflicting rules in some of these areas (Bates, 2000).

Also capitalize the following:

Particular places, things, trade names, organizations, and countries and languages
- Place: San Francisco, California

TABLE 9.9 Capitals: First Words, Pronoun *I*, Proper Names, and Titles

What to Capitalize	Example
First word of sentence	*The* assessor sighed and sat back in his chair.
First word of complete sentence after a colon	The assessor sighed and sat back in his chair: *Scoring* was complete and he could now begin to integrate data.
First word of a direct quotation	*"Have* I taken all the tests?" asked Samuel.
Pronoun *I*, wherever it appears in sentence	*I* think you have finished them all, unless *I* find another on the list.
Proper names	*Samuel Smith* has finished direct testing.
Family relationship as part of a name (but not when simply indicating a relationship)	Samuel's *Uncle Earl* is his primary guardian. (Samuel relied on his *uncle, Earl.*)
Title as part of a name (but not as a descriptor)	Samuel's physician is *Dr.* Deborah Jones. (Deborah Jones is Samuel's *doctor.*)

Note: Adapted from *English Composition and Grammar: Complete Course,* by J. E. Warriner, 1988, Orlando, FL: Harcourt Brace Jovanovich. Copyright 1988 by Harcourt Brace Jovanovich.
Adapted from Purdue University, 2005–2011, *"A little help with capitals."* Retrieved from http://owl.english.purdue.edu/owl/resource/592/1/.

- Thing: Golden Gate Bridge
- Trade name: McKesson
- Organization: Society for Personality Assessment
- Country and language: Japan, Japanese

Historical periods and events, special events, ethnic groups, and specific religious terms

- Historical period and event: Middle Ages; Vietnam War
- Special event: Olympic Arts Festival
- Ethnic groups: African-American; Serbo-Croatian
- Religious terms: Methodist, Bible, Buddha, God (Exception: Use lowercase when speaking generically: "She said she wasn't sure which *god* to pray to." "When it came to writing, the dictionary was her *bible.*")

Days, months, directions, and seasons

- Day: Thursday
- Month: April
- Directions: Only when referring to a specific part of the country: "He moved to the Northwest." (Exception: No

TABLE 9.10   Capitals in APA Usage

What to Capitalize	Examples
• Titles of books:	
First word and other major words (noun, verb, pronoun, adjective, adverb plus any words of four letters or more)	*In Our Clients' Shoes: Theories* and *Techniques* of *Therapeutic Assessment*
First word after hyphen or colon	*Individualizing Psychological Assessment: A Collaborative* and *Therapeutic Approach*
• Trade names of drugs, but not generics	*Lamictal* (generic lamotrigine) *Xanax* (generic alprazolam)
• Complete titles of tests, published and unpublished	Rorschach Inkblot Test
Exceptions:	
Do not capitalize words that refer to subscales (e.g., test, scale)	Rorschach Oral Dependency *scale*
Do not capitalize generic use of test names	the inkblot test
• University departments and academic courses when referring to specific ones	Educational Psychology Department, University of Texas at Austin
Exceptions:	
Do not capitalize in generic use	a psychology course/department
• Title preceding a number or letter that indicates a specific item in a series.	Table 1.1; Figure 1.1

Note: Adapted from *Publication Manual of the American Psychological Association* (6th ed.), 2010, Washington, DC: American Psychological Association. Copyright 2010 by APA.

capitals when the word is a compass direction: "She lives just north of the city limits.")

■ Seasons: Only when part of a title: "She registered for the Spring Conference." (Exception: No capital when referring to a season in general: "The client delayed the assessment till spring.")

The rules listed in Table 9.10 are a few that are specific to the APA *Publication Manual.*

One rule of thumb for capitalizing is that if an item is one-of-a-kind and a proper noun, it will likely be capitalized. At present, the Internet and the World Wide Web fall into that category, although you may run into some cases where a writer will not capitalize it. Nevertheless, capitalizing makes sense until the day arrives when (a) we have more than one Internet or Web or (b) they otherwise become demoted to a common noun.

When Not to Capitalize

While capitals help us recognize the beginning of new thoughts and the distinction between proper nouns and common ones, we need lowercase letters in the bulk of our writing. A sentence written in all capital letters is very difficult for the eye to make sense of. A single word highlighted by all CAPS (or bolding, italics, or underlining) can be useful for emphasis; but a whole capitalized sentence throws too much emphasis onto the statement.

As our world has embraced e-mails and texting, using all caps has become a variable in effective communication. When a large company first handed out text-only devices to its staff, they were in the middle of an urgent project. Two people not well acquainted found themselves in a close working relationship. Male and female, of different ages, they communicated mainly through texting, but after several texts back and forth, the anxious, flustered woman called the man and asked why he was yelling at her. Confused, he asked why she thought he was yelling. "Because your texts are all in caps," she said. He laughed, apologized, and told her he did not yet know how to shift his texting to lowercase.

Spelling Variations and Modern Usage

Contemporary English spelling is based for the most part on that of the 15th century; however, pronunciations have shifted over time, and some of those changes have affected spelling (English Language: Orthography, para. 2). In addition, advertising usage has shortened some words for space (*thru* instead of *through* or *nite* instead of *night*). Both of these examples of shortened versions are considered informal and simplified spellings of the originals and not Standard English (Webster's, 2001; American Heritage, 2000). At present, adhere to standard spelling of these and other words in your reports unless those newer spellings become standard.

The English language is always in transition, but it may take centuries for shifts to be accepted. *All right* and *alright* provide an example. *All right* is standard in all uses. *Alright* is nonstandard and not even recognized as a real word, despite its use by well-known writers of the 20th century. That combination has only been around for about 100 years, whereas other words that began as two combined back in the Middle Ages (e.g., *all ready* became *already*) (American Heritage, 2000). So, at this point in the evolution of the English language, using "alright" in reports would likely be viewed as a mistake. Better to stick with the standard *all right*.

10

Guiding the Reader
Punctuate and Connect for Clarity

> I was working on the proof of one of my poems all the morning, and took out a comma. In the afternoon I put it back again.
>
> **Oscar Wilde, Irish dramatist and poet (1854–1900)**

One experienced assessor-writer had exceptional command of the English language. She could write to a report's recipient in articulate and specific language that enabled the reader to both understand and connect with her observations. But psychological writing involves difficult concepts and at least a few long sentences. Those long sentences, of course, require punctuation for clarity. Each of us has one or more challenges in our writing, and this assessor-writer struggled a bit with punctuation. She scattered commas like birdseed, hoping the right bird would find the right seed.

Accurate punctuation and connecting words between clauses enable the reader of your assessment report to follow the information you provide. You will likely be aware of punctuation as you write, though connecting words may not be as conscious for you at that stage of the report. When you edit and proof, however, take a closer look at the connecting words in your sentences and the punctuation you have chosen to use with them: They are related. Based on whether your sentences are constructed of independent or dependent clauses, you will use different connectors and punctuation. We will look first at the difference between those types of clauses and then at the differences in the three types of connectors. The bulk of the chapter, then, goes through various forms of punctuation and explains when and how to use each to attain clarity in your reports.

Independent and Dependent Clauses

As first mentioned in Chapter 6, a clause is a group of words that is part of a sentence. Each clause contains both a subject and a verb, but not every clause is independent (Warriner, 1988). (See Table 6.2, Sentence Structure.)

- An *independent clause* stands alone; it contains all the words necessary to make complete sense: "He finished administering the remaining subtests last week."
- A *dependent clause* does not make sense on its own and so must always be combined with an independent clause: "After he finished administering the remaining subtests last week,…"

With the addition of *after*, the original independent clause becomes incomplete and dependent. What happened "after" must be spelled out in a clause following the comma, such as, "After he finished administering the remaining subtests last week, *he scored them.*"

Connecting for Clarity

The word "conjunction" means "the act of joining something together" or "the state of being joined together" (American Heritage, 2000). In English grammar, a conjunction joins words, phrases, clauses, or sentences. (See the end of this chapter for a discussion about beginning sentences with conjunctions.) Different conjunctions may require different punctuation. For that reason, we will briefly identify three types of conjunctions before discussing punctuation.

- *Coordinating conjunctions* tie together thoughts that are of *equal* importance and are given equal emphasis in the sentence. They are *for, and, nor, but, or, yet,* and *so.*
- *Subordinating conjunctions* connect thoughts that are *unequal* in the sentence. One clause in the sentence cannot stand alone and relies on another clause to complete its meaning.

TABLE 10.1   Conjunctions: Coordinating, Subordinating, and Correlating

Type	What it Does	Example	Sample Sentence
Coordinating	Connects equally important ideas	*For, and, nor, but, or, yet,* and *so*	Testing was complete, *but* scoring took longer than anticipated.
Subordinating	Connects unequal ideas; focus is on the clause that stands alone	*After, although, as, because, before, if, since, though, unless, while*	*Although* testing was complete, the assessor faced many hours of scoring.
Correlating	Pairs that link and balance ideas	*Either...or, neither...nor, whether...or, both...and, not only...but also*	*Not only* testing, *but also* scoring must be complete before writing the report.

Note: Adapted from *English Composition and Grammar: Complete Course,* by J. E. Warriner, 1988, Orlando, FL: Harcourt Brace Jovanovich. Copyright 1988 by Harcourt Brace Jovanovich.

> These conjunctions include *after, although, before, though, unless,* and *while,* among others.
>
> ■ *Correlating conjunctions* are paired words that link and balance words, phrases, and clauses. These conjunctive pairs include *either...or, neither...nor, whether...or, both...and,* and *not only...but also.*

Table 10.1 gives examples of using each of the three types of conjunctions.

Punctuation Marks: How and Why We Use Them

Punctuate means "to break in here and there, interrupt, emphasize, accentuate" (Webster's, 2001; American Heritage, 2000). A perfectly clear and comprehensible sentence can be written with no punctuation other than a final period. Nevertheless, as ideas and words begin to come together and build on each other, punctuation within a sentence is not only required by rules of grammar, it can also aid the reader. A range of tiny pauses and subtle inflections guides the listener when hearing speech; so, too, with punctuation marks on the written page. The reader's eye and internal "ear" are guided by accents and pauses placed in the flow of words.

Periods and Semicolons

A period shows that you have completed a full thought. You have written a complete sentence that (a) has a subject and a verb and (b) stands alone. While another sentence will likely follow and may expand on it, you can rest assured that that single sentence is self-sustaining.

A semicolon, on the other hand, forms a direct link between the statements on either side of the semicolon, with the second statement expanding on the first. Most sources, including the APA *Publication Manual* (2010), agree that a semicolon should be used in two cases:

1. Between closely related independent clauses *not* joined by a coordinating conjunction (*for*, *and*, *nor*, *but or*, *yet*, or *so*)
2. To separate items in a list that already contains commas

Two more standard uses of the semicolon (Warriner, 1988; Writing Center, 2009) are not mentioned by APA. In these two cases, rely on your judgment and do what is clearest for the reader:

3. Between independent clauses linked by a coordinating conjunction, when either sentence already contains commas and the sentence would be confusing without the semicolon
4. Between independent clauses that are closely related and linked by a transitional expression such as *however*, *therefore*, *consequently*, *otherwise*, *nevertheless*, and *hence*.

See Table 10.2 for examples of all four uses.

When the reader goes through your report, ending punctuation will provide a clue to varying lengths of brief pauses in reading. These pauses can subtly inform the reader about the closeness of the link between sentences and clauses. The British term for a period at the end of a sentence is "full stop." With the full stop/ period as a starting place, remember the following:

■ At the end of a complete sentence, indicate the longest pause, a *full stop/period*.
■ At the end of a clause that will link to the next one, indicate a moderate pause by a *semicolon*.

TABLE 10.2 Using Semicolons

When to Use a Semicolon	Example
1. Between independent clauses *not* joined by coordinating conjunction (*for, and, nor, but, or, yet,* or *so*)	Testing was complete; scoring took longer than anticipated.
2. For clarity, to separate items in a list that already contains commas	Edward completed many measures, including the Delis-Kaplan Executive Functioning Tests (EFT): Trail-Making Tests, Design Fluency Test, Verbal Fluency Test, Color-Word Interference Test, and Tower Test; Grip Strength; and Finger Tapping Test.
3. For clarity, between independent clauses linked by a coordinating conjunction, when either sentence already contains commas	For Edward, problematic areas include organization of materials, monitoring, shifting, and initiating; **and** these executive dysfunctions will likely hinder his academic performance, accomplishing tasks, and follow-through.
4. Between independent clauses— closely related and linked by transition (e.g., *however, therefore, nevertheless*)	Edward's test results show problems with organization, initiating, and monitoring; **therefore**, he will likely have difficulties with follow-through.

- The shortest pause of the three is shown by a *comma*, which is used within sentences.

Commas

A comma is the most frequently used punctuation mark. It gives a visual separation of the written elements and can also indicate a brief pause for the reader to consolidate ideas that went before it. Both qualities are especially useful in complex sentences. As with other areas of grammar, style manuals can differ on comma use. Complicating things further, the assessor-writer may write for a psychological publication governed by the APA *Publication Manual* (2010) and may also score the Written Expression subtest of the Wechsler Individual Achievement Test, 3rd edition (WIAT-III) (Wechsler, 2009) in his or her practice. These activities insert additional variables into the question of correctly using commas.

Aiming for clarity, we will start by examining so-called optional commas. The WIAT-III scoring guidelines say, "Use a grammar reference source for information about optional commas" (Wechsler, 2009, p. 127), and further state that the assessor should not penalize for either use or omission of optional or stylistic commas. Defining *optional* becomes slippery, however, when you add APA conventions and grammar rules of standard American English to the mix.

1. The serial comma that follows the last word in a series, and precedes *and* or *or*, can be optional in standard usage and in the WIAT-III but is required by APA.
2. A comma after a short introductory phrase is required by WIAT-III but APA does not address it.
3. The comma between two short, independent clauses can be optional in standard usage, but both APA and WIAT-III require it.

Standard usage also has other optional or stylistic commas not addressed by either APA or WIAT-III. The best way to get your mind around the rules for commas in the varying approaches is to see them side by side, in Table 10.3, and then look for examples in Table 10.4.

Comma rules not addressed by APA are likely ones not often encountered in scientific writing, and the items missing from the WIAT-III template are those least quantifiable for scoring. Perhaps the most stylistic of the rules listed are the final two entries in Table 10.3: Each of them requires that the writer be especially clear about what s/he writes and how commas can affect both meaning and clarity. In the case of the final rule, that of preventing misreading, sometimes a comma will not save the sentence and you must simply revise it. Table 10.4 again lists the comma rules, this time with examples of using each.

Recognizing Fragments and Run-on Sentences

Written Expression scoring on the WIAT-III places special emphasis on recognizing and penalizing fragmented or run-on sentences. Understanding and avoiding those will also improve the effectiveness of report writing.

A *sentence fragment* capitalizes and punctuates a partial sentence as if it were a whole sentence. The fragment may lack words (subject, verb, or both), or it may begin with a word that creates an dependent clause with no following independent clause to make the sentence stand alone.

TABLE 10.3 Using Commas: A Comparison of Approaches

Rule	APA	WIAT-III	Standard American
To separate items in a series of three or more	Required	Last comma optional	Last comma may be optional
To separate two or more coordinate adjectives in front of a noun	Not addressed	Required	Required
Between two independent clauses connected by coordinating conjunctions *for, and, nor, but, or, yet,* or *so*	Required	Required	May be optional if clauses short
Before and after nonessential phrases	Required	Required	Required
Following an introductory element that comes before an independent clause	Not addressed	Required	May be optional if word/clause is short
Separating dates and addresses	Required	Not addressed	Required
After greeting in a personal letter and after the title following a name	Not addressed	Not addressed	Required
Before a quotation preceded by a verb of communication (*said, asked,* etc.)	Not addressed	Not addressed	Required
To set off modifiers that can be placed anywhere in the sentence without confusion	Not addressed	Not addressed	Required
To indicate contrasting elements or a shift	Not addressed	Not addressed	Optional
When necessary to prevent confusion or misreading	Not addressed	Not addressed	Optional

Note: Adapted from *Publication Manual of the American Psychological Association* (6th ed.), 2010, Washington, DC: American Psychological Association. Copyright 2010 by APA.
Adapted from *Wechsler Individual Achievement Test* (3rd ed.), *Examiner's Manual,* by D. Wechsler, 2009, San Antonio, TX: Pearson. Copyright 2009 by Pearson Publishing.

TABLE 10.4   Using Commas: Examples

Rule	Example
To separate items in a series of three or more	He completed the *CVLT-II, the WCST, and the Gordon Diagnostic System.*
To separate two or more coordinate adjectives in front of a noun[a]	His parents are an *older, professional* couple.
Between two independent clauses connected by *for, and, nor, but, or, yet,* or *so* (acronym to aid memory: *FANBOYS*)	Testing was complete, *but* scoring took longer than anticipated.
Before and after nonessential phrases (if dropped, meaning of sentence remains clear):	
• Interrupters	On Tuesday, *a rainy day,* we finished testing.
• Name as direct address	Do you know, *Edward,* what time it is?
• Word/phrase that explains adjacent word	The client, *Edward,* finished testing on Tuesday.
Following an introductory element that comes *before* an independent clause:	
• Dependent clause introduced by subordinating conjunction (but no comma if dependent clause comes after)	*Because of the time change,* Edward was late. **But:** Edward was late *because of the time change.*
• Introductory word/phrase	*On the other hand,* he finished quickly.
• Word/name	*Edward,* do you know what time it is?
Separating dates and addresses	*December 16, 1990,* is the client's birth date. He lives with his parents at 1234 Lily Lane, Green Ridge, CA.
After greeting in a personal letter	*Dear Edward,*
After the title following a name	James L. Smith, *M.D.,* is Edward's father.
Before a quotation preceded by a verb of communication (*said, asked,* etc.)	His father *said,* "Edward feels relieved to find out why he struggled with school."
To set off modifiers that can be placed anywhere in the sentence without causing confusion	*Sighing loudly,* Edward finished the test. Edward, *sighing loudly,* finished the test.

(continued)

TABLE 10.4   Using Commas: Examples (continued)

Rule	Example
To indicate contrasting elements or a shift	Edward was inattentive, *not hyperactive.* He seemed relieved by the news, *even happy.*
When necessary to prevent confusion or misreading	Let's finish Edward before we leave. **Or** (depending on context) Let's finish, Edward, before we leave.

Note: Adapted from *Publication Manual of the American Psychological Association* (6th ed.), 2010, Washington, DC: American Psychological Association. Copyright 2010 by APA.

Adapted from *Writing with Precision: How to Write so That You Cannot Possibly Be Misunderstood,* by J. D. Bates, 2000, New York, NY: Penguin. Copyright 2000 by Penguin.

Adapted from *English Composition and Grammar: Complete Course,* by J. E. Warriner, 1988, Orlando, FL: Harcourt Brace Jovanovich. Copyright 1988 by Harcourt Brace Jovanovich.

Adapted from *Wechsler Individual Achievement Test* (3rd ed.), *Examiner's Manual,* by D. Wechsler, 2009, San Antonio, TX: Pearson. Copyright 2009 by Pearson Publishing.

[a] See "Placing Adjectives" in Chapter 8 for discussion of coordinate vs. cumulative adjectives.

A *run-on sentence* is not merely a sentence with questionable punctuation that runs on at length. The term *run-on* means that the sentence allows two or more separate ideas to run together. It may take one of two forms:

1. *Comma splice,* joining two independent clauses with a comma rather than a semicolon
2. *Fused sentence,* with no punctuation or connecting word between the ideas

Table 10.5 summarizes and gives examples of these errors and how to correct them.

Colons

A colon announces that something important follows: It alerts the reader to look for that important point or expansion in the next clause. Using colons can be straightforward if you take the most conservative approach. The APA *Publication Manual* (2010) calls

TABLE 10.5   Correcting Fragments and Run-on Sentences

The Problem	Incorrect	Correct
Sentence fragment:		
Capitalizes/punctuates as if it were a complete sentence:		
• Lacks subject, verb, or both	Left the office after finishing the test. (No subject)	*The client* left the office after finishing the test.
• Starts with word that creates dependent clause not followed by independent clause	After he finished the test. (*After* creates dependent clause)	After he finished the test, *the client left the office.*
Run-on sentence:		
Allows two or more ideas to run together		
• *Comma splice* joins two independent clauses with a comma not a semicolon	The client finished the test, he left the office.	The client finished the test**;** he left the office.
• *Fused sentence* uses no punctuation or connecting word between ideas	The client finished the test he left the office.	The client finished the test**, so** he left the office.

Note: Adapted from *English Composition and Grammar: Complete Course,* by J. E. Warriner, 1988, Orlando, FL: Harcourt Brace Jovanovich. Copyright 1988 by Harcourt Brace Jovanovich.
Adapted from *Wechsler Individual Achievement Test* (3rd ed.), *Examiner's Manual,* by D. Wechsler, 2009, San Antonio, TX: Pearson. Copyright 2009 by Pearson Publishing.

for only one grammatical use of the colon, with some additional caveats, as listed in Table 10.6.

The same rules apply to sentences that lead into a vertical list of items, such as a list of tests administered:

- If the sentence leading into the list is a complete thought and stands alone, *use a colon* after that lead-in sentence.
- If the clause leading into the list does not stand alone, *use no colon or other punctuation mark* at the end of that phrase.

(APA, 2010; Warriner, 1988)

TABLE 10.6   Using Colons

When to Use a Colon	Example
Only after an *independent clause* (a sentence that stands alone with subject and verb)	He completed three tests during the session: [follow by expansion, as shown below]
Caveat 1: If the clause that follows after the colon is also a complete sentence, *capitalize* the first letter after the colon.	He completed three tests during the session: *They* were the CVLT-II, the WCST, and the Gordon Diagnostic System.
Caveat 2: If the clause is not a complete sentence, *do not capitalize* the first letter.	He completed three tests during the session: *the* CVLT-II, the WCST, and the Gordon Diagnostic System.

Hyphens and Dashes

A hyphen is "a mark (-) used between the parts of a compound word or the syllables of a divided word, as at the end of a line" (Webster's, 2001). It can help your reader clearly understand your meaning. Contemporary writing avoids unnecessary hyphens, though at times they are called for. Knowing when to use a hyphen can be confusing, since words evolve. They may start out as two words, at some point become joined by a hyphen, and then eventually become all one word. And as with other areas of grammar, expert sources may conflict on when to use hyphens.

Before considering use of hyphens, we first take into account whether the words are verbs, nouns, or adjectives in a sentence. Their role in the sentence affects the decision to combine or separate words:

- When used as a *verb*, write two words separately: "Did her car *break down*?"
- When they are a *noun* or *adjective*, combine into one word: *Noun*: "The couple had a *breakdown* in communication." *Adjective*: "The area was designated a Superfund *cleanup* site."

(Strauss, 2011).

A dictionary is the definitive expert on how to write a word, whether all one word, hyphenated, or two words separated but without a hyphen. If a term appears in a recent dictionary (with or without hyphens), that is its current accepted usage. Unfortunately, dictionaries can differ in this usage as can style manuals. APA's

TABLE 10.7 Using Hyphens

When to Use a Hyphen	Example
• With compound modifiers: a single description of a thought or thing;	
• Placed *before* a noun but not *after*	*13-year-old* girl versus "The girl was *13 years old*"
• Adjective + noun	*High-income* family versus "The family had *high income*"
• Adverb + adjective	*Well-known* attorney versus "The attorney is *well known*"
Exceptions:	
Do not hyphenate an adverb ending in *-ly* even when it precedes a noun.	*Stylishly dressed* client
Do not hyphenate with superlatives.	*Better composed* essay; *higher rated* student
• With fractions spelled out: *before* a noun but not *after*	*One-third* payment, but "The fee was *one third* paid"
• With compound numbers spelled out	From *twenty-one* through *ninety-nine*
• With a number + word:	
• *Before* a noun but not *after*	*Third-grade* student, but "The student is in *third grade*"
• With words/compounds starting with *self*	*Self-*esteem, *self-*report, *self-*respect, *self-*medicating
Exceptions for *self* words:	*Self*ish, *self*less, *self* psychology
• With prefixes *ex-* and *all-*	*Ex-*husband; *all-*purpose
• With all prefixes before a capitalized noun or adjective	*Pro-*American; *post-*World War II; *non-*Jungian
• With prefixes ending in same vowel as the base word's first letter	*Extra-*ambitious; *semi-*independent
Exception: Words resulting in double *e* are usually not hyphenated	Preeminent
• With coequal nouns	*Assessor-writer; writer-editor*
• With words that might be misread	*Resign, reform, resent* (e.g., *resent*—to send again or to feel hurt? For clarity, "send again" would be hyphenated as *re-sent*)

(continued)

TABLE 10.7   Using Hyphens (continued)

Note: Adapted from *Publication Manual of the American Psychological Association* (6th ed.), 2010, Washington, DC: American Psychological Association. Copyright 2010 by APA.
Adapted from *Writing with Precision: How to Write so That You Cannot Possibly Be Misunderstood*, by J. D. Bates, 2000, New York, NY: Penguin. Copyright 2000 by Penguin.
Adapted from *English Composition and Grammar: Complete Course*, by J. E. Warriner, 1988, Orlando, FL: Harcourt Brace Jovanovich. Copyright 1988 by Harcourt Brace Jovanovich.
Adapted from *The Blue Book of Grammar and Punctuation*, by J. Strauss, 2011. Retrieved August 21, 2011, from http://www.grammarbook.com/punctuation/hyphens.asp. Copyright 2011 by GrammarBook.com.

Publication Manual (2010) recommends *Merriam-Webster's Collegiate Dictionary*, 2005, as the standard. Although using only one dictionary will provide consistency, referring to other dictionaries can confirm and give broader context to the usage. If a combined term is not in a dictionary, treat the words as separate and use the guidelines shown in Table 10.7.

One final thought on deciding when to use a hyphen: If each word in a phrase could stand alone with the noun, and the sentence would still mean the same, you may not need a hyphen. But if all are required for the sentence to make sense, then keep the hyphen (Bates, 2000). In the example, "She uses up-to-date testing software," no single word in the hyphenated phrase would make sense ("up software," "to software," or "date software") and so none would mean the same thing as all the words together. In this case, the hyphens are necessary.

A *dash* is either of two marks (— or –) that are used in printing and writing. They indicate (a) a break in the sentence, (b) a parenthetical element, or (c) they connect numbers that show a range, such as date or time (Webster's, 2001). In APA usage, the dash shows a sudden interruption in sentence continuity (e.g., "He completed three tests—the CVLT-II, the WCST, and the Gordon Diagnostic System—during the session").

Apostrophes

Apostrophes show possession or indicate missing letters in a word. They are not used to form plurals, with a couple of small exceptions that are noted in the following discussion. Use has shifted over time and style manuals can differ. British versus American usage also can vary when forming the possessive of proper names ending in *s*. This handbook refers to American usage and suggests that usage err on the side of clarity and simplicity.

To start, we will refer again to the APA *Publication Manual* (2010):

- To form possessive of a *singular* name: Add apostrophe and *s* (Exception: Add the apostrophe alone when the name ends in an *s* that is not pronounced).
- To form possessive of a *plural* name: Add only the apostrophe.

The APA *Publication Manual* (2010) refers to apostrophe use only in the above-listed situations. Other uses that follow are ones in standard usage and aim for clarity for the reader. Also use apostrophes to show

- Possession with indefinite pronouns *one, everybody, everyone*: (e.g., *one's*)
- Missing letters, as in contractions (*cannot = can't*; *I had = I'd*)
- Plurals of lowercase letters but not uppercase except to avoid confusion
- Plurals of combined uppercase and lowercase abbreviations or ones with interior periods

Use *no apostrophe* to show possession with personal pronouns *his, hers, its, ours, yours, theirs* or with the relative pronoun, *whose*. Table 10.8 summarizes uses of the apostrophe and gives examples.

Quotation Marks

Style manuals differ in use of quotation marks, and American usage can vary from British usage. Table 10.9 shows when to use quotation marks and Table 10.10 shows how to use them. Rules in both tables adhere to APA and standard American English usage (APA, 2010; Warriner, 1988).

For block indentations of 40 or more words

- Do not use quotation marks around the quote.
- Start on new line of the document.
- Place *double* quotation marks around any material quoted within the block quotation.

TABLE 10.8   Using Apostrophes

When to Use an Apostrophe	What You Do	Example
To form possessive of a singular name	Add apostrophe and *s* at the end	*Edward's* testing is complete.
Exception: When the singular name ends in an *s* that is not pronounced	Add apostrophe only	*Jacques'* testing begins on Monday.
To form possessive of a plural name	Add apostrophe only	The *Smiths'* questionnaires were completed last week.
To form possessive with indefinite pronouns *one, everybody, everyone*	Add apostrophe and *s* at the end	*Everyone's* questionnaire was completed last week.
To indicate missing letters, as in contractions	Add apostrophe only in place of letter	He *cannot* keep the appointment. He *can't* keep the appointment.
To form plurals of single lowercase letters but not uppercase	Add apostrophe and *s* to the letter	The report's subsections were indicated by *a's, b's* and *c's.*
Exception: When no apostrophe with uppercase causes confusion	Add apostrophe and *s* to the letter (if citing letter that needs apostrophe along with those that do not, as in example, use apostrophe with all, for consistency)	*Edward's* grades slipped from *A's* to *C's* (with no apostrophe, "A's" would become the word "As")
To form plurals of combined upper- and lowercase abbreviations **or** those with interior periods	Add apostrophe and *s* to the abbreviations	PhD's, Ph.D.'s, M.B.A.'s **But** MBAs because uppercase letters only, with no periods
Use no apostrophe to show possession with personal pronouns *his, hers, its, ours, yours, theirs* or with the relative pronoun, *whose*	Add nothing	*Whose* scores on the CVLT-C were higher, *his* or *hers*?

Note: Adapted from *Chicago Manual of Style Online*, 2010c, Chicago, IL: University of Chicago. Retrieved August 8, 2011, from http://www.chicago-manualofstyle.org/16/ch07/ch07_sec014.html.
Adapted from *English Composition and Grammar: Complete Course*, by J. E. Warriner, 1988, Orlando, FL: Harcourt Brace Jovanovich. Copyright 1988 by Harcourt Brace Jovanovich.

TABLE 10.9   When to Use Quotation Marks

When to Use	Example
• With a direct quotation, but not a paraphrase	Direct: Edward said, "I can't do this math problem." Paraphrase: Edward said that he couldn't do the math problem.
Exception: Use no quotation marks with long quotations (40 or more words); block indent instead	See example of block indent in text following Table 10.10.
• To indicate a word or phrase that is colloquial, invented, or expresses irony	Paraphrase: Jane said that sometimes she feels "spacey."
But: Use quotes only first time word is mentioned	The assessor asked what spacey felt like to her.
• To set off the title of a shorter work, such as an article or chapter	The assessor suggested they read *The Gift of ADHD* by Lara-Honos Webb, especially Chapter 1, "Difference Is Not a Disorder or a Deficit."

TABLE 10.10   How to Use Quotation Marks

How to Use	Example
Double quotation marks:	
• Place before and after direct quotation	In an interview, Jane said, "I wish I made better grades."
• Place periods and commas *inside* closing quotation marks	The attorney said, "Send your report as soon as it's finished."
• Place colons, semicolons, question marks, and exclamation points *outside* closing quotation marks	In an interview, Jane said, "I wish I made better grades"; she spoke in a low, sad tone.
• Place inside only if part of the quoted material)	The attorney asked, "When will the report be finished?"
Single quotation marks:	
• Place before and after material that is a quotation within a quotation	In her report the assessor wrote, "Jane said in an interview, 'I wish I made better grades.'"
• Use same rules for ending punctuation as listed here for double quotation marks	See previous examples for double quotation marks.
• Block indent long quotations	See example given in text.

The following is an example of a block indentation quote with quoted material within the block:

> Jane said in an interview, "I wish I made better grades." Seating her in the front of the classroom or in a location that limits surrounding distractions will likely benefit Jane's learning. While giving instructions, break down multiple-part instructions into smaller components.

Ellipsis

Ellipsis refers to "the mark or series of marks used in writing to show an omission" (American Heritage, 2000). We use an ellipsis when quoting material but leaving out unessential information. Various sources address how to use them in this way. We will call this the grammatical use of ellipses and look at that use first, followed by another use having more to do with style.

Grammar: When you omit material from a quoted, original source because it is unessential to your meaning, you will use three spaced ellipsis points (...) to show where the material is omitted. If the omission falls between two sentences, use four ellipsis points (....) (APA, 2010).

Style: Ellipsis points can also be used to indicate an incomplete thought or trailing off into silence.... In creative writing, the ellipsis often indicates that a character is pausing in his or her speech and can be used to indicate a melancholy feeling (Wikipedia, 2011a). With that stylistic definition, we can see why ellipses should be used judiciously in an assessment report. If you are directly quoting a person you interviewed and they paused in this manner, by all means use the ellipsis. But any other stylistic use indicates the assessor-writer's own mood and response and may be considered out of place in a report.

Connecting Words Revisited: Special Challenges

Early in this chapter, we discussed connecting words and how they affect the flow of a sentence. To close this chapter, we will look at confusions in using some of these connectors and discuss how to clarify usage.

Although, Though, While

Although and *though* can generally be used interchangeably (e.g., *Although* he had finished the test, he did not leave; *Though* he had finished the test, he did not leave). *Although* most often occurs at the beginning of a phrase; *though* may also be used to begin a phrase and is more usual than *although* in other sentence locations and as a link between words and phrases (e.g., Late *though* he was, the client took care completing the questionnaire).

Depending on which source you refer to, *while* may also have a similar meaning to *although/though*, but it's not the first or even second definition listed. *While*'s first definition is "during or throughout the time that" (American Heritage, 2000), which links it to time passing (e.g., *While* he took the test, he drummed his feet against the desk). The APA *Publication Manual* (2010) points out that confusion can result from using *while* to mean *although*; it suggests using *while* to refer to "events happening simultaneously," as in the example given here, and using *although* to mean "in spite of the fact that" (p. 84.).

Since

The first usage listed for *since* is "from then until now" (American Heritage, 2000), which also links this word to time passing (e.g., *Since* he finished the test, he has waited for his parents to pick him up). Its third definition is "because," but as in the last paragraph's discussion of *while*, APA suggests using *since* in its time-related sense only (2010, p. 84). If you choose to use the less precise version of either word, review your sentence to make sure the reader will not confuse how you are using it.

Like Versus Such as

When we include examples in our writing or draw a comparison between items, we use either the word *like* or the phrase *such as*. Reference sources can differ on differentiating between the two; sometimes the opinion for one or the other is based on the sound of the chosen word/phrase in everyday speech. *Such as* may strike some as more formal than *like*, and they choose to keep the sound of their writing more informal. But if we look at the meanings of the two in certain sentences, a difference is apparent.

- *Such as* gives examples that are included in a larger subject: "During the assessment, Edward completed many tests *such as* the CVLT-II, the WCST, and the Gordon Diagnostic System." (*Such as* tells the reader that these are specific tests Edward took among many others.)
- *Like* indicates that an item (or list of items) resembles or is similar to others not named: "Edward's therapist, Dr. Jones, said she found clients like Edward gratifying to work with." (*Like* tells the reader that Dr. Jones has other clients who are also good to work with.)

In some sentences, either term might work depending on what you intend to say. Be precise in what you mean and choose the one that fits (Fogarty, 2010).

That Versus *Which*

When to use *that* or *which* in a sentence can challenge any writer. The difference lies in whether the word introduces a clause that is essential or nonessential to the sentence's meaning. *That* always introduces an essential clause; *which* may introduce either. Sources including Strunk and White (2000) and the APA *Publication Manual* (2010), however, suggest a simplified approach: Since *that* is reserved for essential clauses, they suggest using *which* only with nonessential ones.

- *That:* "The tests *that Edward completed on Wednesday* varied widely." (The phrase beginning with *that* is essential to the meaning of the sentence; it refers specifically to the "the tests completed on Wednesday," not any others).
- *Which:* "The tests, *which Edward completed on Wednesday*, varied widely." (The phrase beginning with *which* is not essential, since the emphasis is on the array of tests, not on when he finished them. The essential part of the sentence is "The tests varied widely.")

Notice that a comma always precedes a nonessential clause starting with *which,* but no comma is used before an essential clause beginning with *that.*

Beginning a Sentence With a Conjunction

An assessor friend reviewed a portion of this book and commented on a sentence that began with the conjunction "but." He said he would use a comma to connect it with the previous independent clause. That choice is a reliable one, and many of us were taught in school to never begin a sentence with a conjunction. Yet, as with split verbs and split infinitives discussed in Chapter 8, gray areas exist. "Fowler called the notion that sentences shouldn't start with conjunctions a 'prejudice that lingers from a bygone time…the supposed rule is without foundation in grammar, logic, or art'" (Garner, 2009, p. 187). Garner also points out that starting a sentence with a conjunction (*and, but, so, yet,* etc.) gives "clear signals to the reader" (p. 187); that is, these straightforward words tell the reader clearly what is coming next. As with the choice to split verbs or infinitives, however, be aware that your reader—including a teacher or editor—may require sentences that do not begin with conjunctions.

I selectively choose to use conjunctions to start sentences, rather than always connecting independent clauses with a comma. It allows me to keep sentences shorter. And it provides a shift in the rhythm of reading. (The last two sentences would also be correct if connected by *and*, preceded by a comma: "It allows me to keep sentences shorter, and it provides a shift in the rhythm of reading.") Staying aware helps you to choose the best alternative, as it does with other decisions in effective writing.

PART **III**

BEYOND THE REPORT

Extending Clear and
Effective Communication

The formal written report is not the only avenue the assessor can travel to effectively communicate results. The type of psychological assessment known as Collaborative/Therapeutic Assessment often uses a direct letter to the person assessed, a metaphorical story, or both. The first chapter in Part III discusses those forms of written feedback. The other chapter in this section discusses basic tenets of effective spoken communication, including cues transmitted nonverbally. Throughout the assessment process, information in these two chapters can assist in creating a connection between assessor and client. These steps create synergy with the topics discussed in Parts I and II, as shown in Figure P3.1.

Collaborative/Therapeutic Assessment (C/TA) combines aspects of two subsets of traditional psychological assessment:

■ *Collaborative Assessment* (CA) is the model developed by Constance T. Fischer of Duquesne University. The CA process involves the client as a full partner at each step of the evaluation. The client is encouraged to tap into self-knowledge, to trust it, and to communicate it to the assessor as a

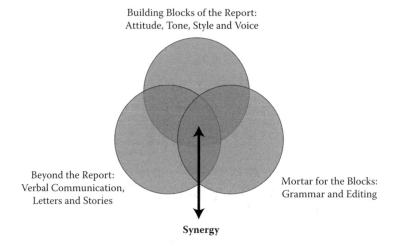

Building Blocks of the Report:
Attitude, Tone, Style and Voice

Beyond the Report:
Verbal Communication,
Letters and Stories

Mortar for the Blocks:
Grammar and Editing

Synergy

FIGURE P3.1   Synergy of topics in Parts I, II, and III.

part of the process. This approach intends to humanize the assessment procedure and make it more understandable for the client (Fischer, 1994).

- *Therapeutic Assessment* (TA) is the semistructured approach developed by Stephen E. Finn and his colleagues at the University of Texas at Austin. TA has been referred to as mainly an attitude about psychological assessment (Finn, 2007). This attitude moves the goal of the assessment beyond collecting data for use in understanding the client and toward creating the positive change s/he seeks in life.

In combination, Collaborative/Therapeutic Assessment encourages the client to work as a team with the assessor throughout the evaluation process. They may jointly

1. Formulate questions to answer
2. Co-interpret meaning and impact of results
3. Collaborate on the written documents summarizing the assessment
4. Agree on the best next steps to take after the assessment

Some practitioners use the term without a slash—CTA. This choice implies an approach in which collaborative assessment necessarily *is* therapeutic.

C/TA's approach underscores the importance of clear and effective written and spoken communication in the practice of assessment. Research indicates that giving combined written and verbal feedback to the person assessed promotes better understanding of the results (Lance & Krishnamurthy, 2003). A more recent meta-analysis (Poston & Hanson, 2010) validates the meaningful therapeutic effect of personalized and collaborative feedback of assessment results.

The chapter on personal letters and metaphorical stories does not attempt a comprehensive discussion of the tenets of C/TA. Rather, it focuses on how to create letters and stories as the written product of an assessment. All skills discussed are useful for assessors who decide to write a summary letter directly to the person they have evaluated. The assessment process includes verbal interaction throughout, and so the chapter on effective verbal and nonverbal communication closes the book with information useful to all assessors.

CHAPTER **11**

Continuing the
Therapeutic Goals
Writing Letters and Stories

Detail makes the difference between boring and terrific writing.… As a writer, words are your paint. Use all the colors.

Rhys Alexander, American professor of English

The preface to Part III gives a brief overview of Collaborative/
Therapeutic Assessment (C/TA), a subset of psychological assessment. It also mentions studies validating the use of combined written with oral feedback (Lance & Krishnamurthy, 2003; Poston & Hanson, 2010). Two documents have evolved within C/TA: one a variation of the traditional assessment report and the other an extension of it. Chapter 11 expands and refines the process of report writing into those two documents: (a) a direct letter to the person assessed when he or she is the primary audience for the report, and (b) a metaphorical story that embeds essential mental or cognitive health information into a narrative. Chapter 3 defines *story* as the telling of a happening or connected series of happenings, either true or fictitious. A standard assessment report, a letter, or a story fit this definition. Chapter 11 discusses when an assessor might choose to write the more informal letter and how the letter's tone differs from that in a standard report. The components and steps in creating a story as therapeutic intervention for child, adolescent, or adult finish the chapter.

Letter to the Individual Assessed: An Overview

Collaboration presupposes an attitude that each member of the team—assessor, client, family member, therapist, physician, or teacher—contributes uniquely and is respected by the other members. As discussed in previous chapters of this book, that need for respect carries over into written documents, be they standard report, letter, or story. The introduction mentioned the idea of indexing testing results to the client's life and interests when writing a report (Fischer, 1994). A letter or story to the person assessed provides a direct method of accomplishing this integration. In C/TA, the letter goes beyond restatement of facts. It emphasizes the collaborative interaction of assessor and client and discusses both meaning and personal impact of the data and process. The skill of narrative can be especially valuable in a letter of this type. It enables the assessor-writer to speak to issues and changes in the client's life as reflected in the assessment experience and results.

These summary letters appear to be a natural outgrowth of the decision to make psychological reports accessible to clients (S. E. Finn, personal communication, May 2011). Over 30 years ago, psychologist and assessor Constance Fischer began responding to client requests for a written summary by crafting letters for them; she also encouraged graduate students, in certain situations, to do the same. Summary letters are written with an eye toward continuing the therapeutic goals of the assessment (C. T. Fischer, personal communication, May 2011). The assessor encourages the client's response to the written form and, collaboratively, they work to modify areas that the client finds inaccurate or otherwise problematic. This process and use of a letter in place of a report has been called a "growing trend toward integrating assessment with therapy" (Groth-Marnat, 2009a, p. 583). One branch of C/TA, the semistructured form of Therapeutic Assessment developed by psychologist and assessor Stephen Finn and colleagues, specifically builds the summary letter around the questions that a client poses of the assessment (Finn, 2007). This approach, too, encourages the client to comment on drafts of the letter, thereby involving them "in co-editing the new story that emerged from the assessment" (p. 11).

Tone in Letters Written as Feedback

Chapter 2 discussed formality in tone in various written applications. Of the three levels of formality discussed in that chapter (popular/casual, conversational, and formal), tone in letters that take the place of a report will usually range from conversational to formal. The assessor-writer will choose the tone based on the document's primary reader, also taking into account any potential secondary readers. A letter addressed to an individual will carry a more personal feel than a standard report, though it may retain many of the formal qualities. (Refer to Chapter 2 and Table 2.2 for degrees of formality in writing.)

Even very data-rich assessments, such as those that evaluate neuropsychological issues, may use a letter as written report if the intended audience is the person assessed. In these cases, providing a certain amount of technical detail in the letter is essential to casting light on assessment findings for the client. More extensive technical information may become addenda to the letter (Fischer, 1994). On occasion, the assessor-writer might also choose to address a third-party referral source—attorney, school, or referring therapist—in letter format. As with a letter directly to the client, the assessor-writer will select the tone most appropriate: conversational, conversationally formal, or fully formal.

If you are conducting a clear-cut Collaborative/Therapeutic Assessment, however, you will likely choose to write a report in the form of a letter using a less formal tone. You will still plan your document's format, whether it is grounded in answering questions or in some other approach to providing salient information. You will also rely on effective style and grammar, as discussed throughout this book. By careful word choice, use of contractions, and juxtaposing material (see Chapter 2), your tone will likely be as conversational as you can make it without becoming artificial. And your letter will intend more than simply reporting data. In deciding whether to write a letter instead of a report, consider the questions in Table 11.1.

Can a Letter of Written Feedback Be "Therapeutic"?

Perhaps because this type of letter evolved out of C/TA, it has sometimes been informally referred to as a "therapeutic letter" (Allyn, 2010, 2011), though that term does not appear in the work of Finn or Fischer. Can a letter be therapeutic, intentionally or unintentionally? *Therapeutic* means "having healing powers" and

TABLE 11.1 Letter Versus Standard Report

Questions to Ask	Report	Hybrid Letter	Letter
Who is the audience?	Third party	Third party/client	Client
What is the goal of the written form?	Transmit data	<<<Hybrid>>> Aspects of both	Collaboration; extend assessment effects
How should the document be structured?	Standard report sections	<<<Hybrid>>> Aspects of both	Answer questions; other individualized approach
What tone should it take?	Formal	<<<Hybrid>>> Aspects of both	Conversational

"serving to cure or heal" (American Heritage, 2000; Webster's, 2001). An assessor-writer may intend therapeutic impact only to the extent that the letter continues therapeutic goals of the assessment, as Fischer says in the personal communication cited earlier in this chapter. That written letter, however, gives the client ongoing reference to the assessment results and process long after the event has passed. According to a study by Lance and Krishnamurthy (2003), "[H]aving continual access to this information in written form…is most central to enhanced self-awareness" (Results and Discussion section, para. 2). Perhaps by this yardstick the name "therapeutic letter" could be considered accurate.

But what about more technically focused letters or those written to third parties? Do these have any impact beyond the transmitting of information? Can any have components of "therapeutic"? Those who research and validate methods and outcome in a field such as psychology may be considered the official arbiters of a term such as *therapeutic* and how it is applied. Nevertheless, those clinicians who practice in the field also have their opinions and attitudes based on the results of methods they use, including the written report. Their feedback on reports, though, may arrive months or years later and may come from individuals who read the report but were never meant to. This gives the clinician a glimpse of the impact a document can have well down the line. (See also the Weiner and Engelman quotes in the "Ordering Sections and Content" section of Chapter 5.)

That being the case, we might reasonably assume that even third-party letters can be avenues for therapeutic messages to the person assessed—directly, if and when they are shown the report,

TABLE 11.2   Contrasting Phrases

Standard Report Language	versus Collaborative/Therapeutic Phrasing
Client functions within the superior psychometric range of intelligence.	You are very smart — more than most of your classmates. But sometimes you don't seem to think logically, especially when you are anxious.
Demonstrates the comorbidity of depressive-like symptoms.	Unhappy moods can affect your ability to pay attention or focus. They may interfere with doing your schoolwork in a way that reflects how smart you are.
Tests imply frontal system involvement as may be observed in those with ADHD.	Moods are not the only reason for your problems with paying attention. Some lower test scores indicate that additional attention problems are a result of ADHD.

and indirectly, through the actions taken by the person receiving the report or letter. The tone of your letters to referring professionals can encourage their view of assessments as avenues of help for the person assessed. Clear, accurate, and sensitive framing of information can help you to help them, even at one remove.

Table 11.2 revisits some phrases first used in Chapter 5 to show the differences in phrasing between the C/TA approach and standard report language.

A Clinician's Approach: Assessing Personal Warmth in Letters to the Person Assessed

"Neurodiversity" is a recently identified concept referring to the fact that every one of us is neurologically unique. This term implies that as with cultural, ethnic, or other types of diversity, each person needs to be recognized, respected, and celebrated as an invaluable and distinct individual (Engelman, 2011b). These distinct ways of being in the world can influence the ways in which people hear or relate to other people and information. A collaborative/therapeutic assessor and client may agree on the questions that the assessment will seek to answer. Clients may even welcome the idea of a letter written directly to them. But other qualities can influence the way that report is received and so will affect the assessor's choice of form and tone. Warmth and openness may be perceived and valued differently by different people—differences that stem from background and experience.

TABLE 11.3 Client Letters: Response to Information and Acceptance of Warmth

	Response to Information	Acceptance of Warmth	Degree of Warmth
Level 1	Easily heard and accepted	Very receptive/ seeks connection	High
Level 2	Mostly accepted, after consideration	Somewhat hesitant, though receptive	Moderate to moderately high
Level 3	Not easily accepted	Not receptive/ self-contained	Very low to low

Varying degrees of warmth—defined as "friendliness, kindness, or affection" (American Heritage, 2000)—and a personal quality in the report may not be welcome or acceptable to some people. You, the assessor-writer, will best know when warmth is acceptable and to what degree.

In deciding how warm a tone to take in letters, Engelman has informally applied Finn's (2007) three levels of the client's ability to hear and accept information, discussed in Chapter 2 of this book. She has found that background, culture, and personality can influence where the person assessed falls in the acceptance-of-warmth levels shown in Table 11.3. In addition, she takes into account the person's likely response-to-information levels and assesses the degree to which those levels parallel the ones accepting warmth. Depending on the fit, the degree of warmth in her writing then moderates accordingly. Warmth of tone may also vary between that in the overall letter and that in sections covering specific topics.

Engelman has extended this assessment of tone to third-party letters, adjusting for the forum and use of the letter and her knowledge of the professional receiving the letter. Keeping her reader clearly in mind and writing in a way she believes they can hear, lends a quality of "therapeutic" to the letter even if not overtly so (D. H. Engelman, personal communication, May 2011).

Metaphor: A Bridge Between Fact and Truth

Without getting into a complicated philosophical discussion of "fact" versus "truth," we might simply make one assumption: History and data from your assessment provide the *facts*, while

TABLE 11.4   Simile Versus Metaphor

	Comparison	How Does it Do This?	Examples
Simile	Explicit	Uses words such as *like* or *as*	The road *was like* a ribbon of moonlight. The surface of the pond is *as* smooth as glass.
Metaphor	Implied	Does **not** use *like* or *as*	The road *was* a ribbon of moonlight. The surface of the pond *is* glass.

the sense you make of analyzing and integrating those facts with the person's life form the *truth* of their situation. And to quote American writer, Orson Scott Card (n.d.), "Metaphors have a way of holding the most truth in the least space." When used thoughtfully, metaphor can lend power and meaning to both letters and stories. We can begin to understand metaphor as a figure of speech by starting with a different one, simile.

- *Simile* is an *explicit* comparison of two things that are usually unlike (Garner, 2009). It uses words such as *like* or *as* to set up the comparison: "She defends her daughter *like* a mother lion."
- *Metaphor*, on the other hand, gives an *implied* comparison without using *like* or *as* (Garner, 2009). Between two unlike things, it implies an important similarity. To do this, a word or phrase that is usually applied to one thing describes the other: "She *is* a mother lion defending her daughter."

Table 11.4 summarizes these differences.

Since simile can be viewed as a subset of metaphor (McArthur, 1992), the following discussion will speak of metaphor as a broad class. Metaphors derive power from overlapping connotations between two words. For example, a geographical road map shows routes for traveling from one place to another. Referring to your assessment report as a "map" indicates that you believe it can help the person get from one place to another in life. The overlapping connotation is that each keeps the person from getting lost. Metaphorical references allow you to suggest meaning without landing directly on it. Metaphor in literary use goes back centuries. It appears in the earliest known literature from

Mesopotamia, likely written nearly 3,000 years ago (Wikipedia, 2011b). Aristotle used it in his *Poetics* around 335 BCE (trans. 1907). Metaphor's use in literature comes and goes—sometimes in fashion and other times not. Metaphor is not simply a literary figure of speech, however; it also has life context.

Conceptual Metaphor: Everyday Life

Residual arguments say that metaphor has no meaning beyond the superficial comparison of two dissimilar things (Davidson, 1978/1984). Nonetheless, nonliterary metaphor has long been used, and growing research supports its expanded meaning in everyday life. Cognitive linguists George Lakoff and Mark Johnson began work in this area over 30 years ago with their book *Metaphors We Live By* (1980). They wrote of metaphor as primarily related to human thought and action and only secondarily as an artifact of language. They wrote that "metaphors as linguistic expressions are possible precisely because there are metaphors in a person's conceptual system" (p. 6).

Conceptual or cognitive metaphor shows up in our everyday language and refers to the way we understand one idea in terms of another. This common usage moves metaphor closer to concrete terms on the continuum of abstract-to-concrete discussed in Chapter 3. One of the clearest examples of an everyday use of metaphor is the way we speak of argument as a war or a struggle: "He *shot down* that argument" or "She *attacked* all the points he made." Another everyday conceptual metaphor is that of time-as-money. We speak of *wasting* time, *spending* time, *investing* time, *running out of* time, and *budgeting* time, as if it were money.

The conceptual metaphors of argument-as-war or time-as-money are called *structural metaphors*, because the concepts of argument and time are structured metaphorically in relation to war and money. *Orientational metaphors*, on the other hand, do not deal with only one concept; instead they organize related systems of concepts with respect to one another. Many of them have to do with spatial orientation: up-down, front-back, on-off, etc. In the following examples, *up* and *good* are the positives and *down* and *bad* are the negatives:

More is up and Less is down
- *More* = His income *rose* last year.
- *Less* = Turn the heat *down*.

TABLE 11.5 Conceptual Metaphors: Structural or Orientational

Type of Metaphor	How it Works	Format	Example
Structural	Sets up comparison between two different things	Parallel equation: Argument-as-war	He *attacked* her argument.
		Time-as-money	She *invested* time in studying.
Orientational	Organizes concepts into related systems	Spatial system: More is up	His job responsibilities *increased.*
		Less is down	Her case load *dropped.*
		Good is up	Client satisfaction rate is *up.*
		Bad is down	His mood has been *declining.*

Note: Adapted from *Metaphors we live by*, by G. Lakoff & M. Johnson, 1980, Chicago, IL: University of Chicago Press. Copyright 1980 by University of Chicago Press.

Good is up and Bad is down
- *Good* = Things are looking *up*.
- *Bad* = Things are at an all-time *low*.

The *physical basis* for these usages is that if you add *more* of something to a pile, the level goes *up* (Lakoff & Johnson, 1980). Table 11.5 presents qualities and examples of both orientational and structural metaphors.

Other conventional, structural metaphors that give shape to our everyday concepts include ideas, love, and life:

- Ideas are food, as in "I just can't *swallow* that idea." Ideas are also people, plants, or products.
- Love is magic, as in "She *cast her spell* over me"; it is also a physical force, a patient, madness, and war.
- Life is a container, as in "He had a *full* life."

Life is also a story. Lakoff and Johnson write that this conventional metaphor is "deeply-rooted in our culture" (1980, p. 172). If we say to someone, "Tell me the story of your life," he or she will likely create a more-or-less linear narrative, often beginning in childhood. S/he will craft it around people, settings, episodes of peaks and valleys, and how s/he conceives that those episodes are related. When the person tells the story, s/he selects the facts she believes are pertinent, deselects others, and likely believes that she expresses the full truth of the story.

But what if that person's life has always been out of balance, so that the logic of the cultural metaphor of a coherent life story doesn't fit? Or what if his or her life changes unexpectedly and dismantles the logic of the narrative? That person may view the metaphor of his or her life as "a tale told by an idiot...signifying nothing" (Lakoff & Johnson, 1980, p. 174). We might assume that this person's nonconventional metaphor (life is a tale signifying nothing) means that the conventional, conceptual metaphor of life-is-a-story does not really exist in our culture. But it does the opposite: The nonconventional metaphor actually evokes the original one by unspoken reference. The conventional metaphor assumes that we make sense of our life episodes; the nonconventional exception points out the impossibility of making sense of them in that one case. The *absence* of the conventional metaphor in a person's life points out its *presence* in our wider culture.

When you write a letter to a client, the conceptual metaphors discussed here, and many others, can easily find their way in. These metaphors might be either those you think will benefit the client or those you note in the client's own speech, and many will simply arise unbidden from our language. For instance, if you refer to the assessment findings and your letter to the client as a "road map," you evoke the cultural metaphor of life-is-a-*journey*. If you write of the client's "changing her story," you call up life-is-a-*story*. And if you observe that he "fell into a depression" but now "his spirits have begun to rise," you employ the orientational metaphor of sad-is-*down* and happy-is-*up*. In this way, metaphor transfers meaning from one thing to another, whether it is in Shakespeare's description of Hamlet's unhappy life as "a rank and unweeded garden that grows to seed" (1603/1936 version, Act I, ii, 135–136) or Robert Frost's extended metaphor of life-as-a-journey in his poem "The Road Not Taken" (Frost, 1915/1969).

Metaphor and the Brain

Evolving research has begun to pinpoint parts of the brain that are involved when a person understands and responds to metaphor (Sapolsky, 2010; UC San Diego, 2005). These brain regions seem to combine literal with figurative experiences. For example, a portion of the frontal cortex called the anterior cingulate is involved in the subjective experience of pain. The anterior cingulate will activate when you are in pain. It will also activate if you see a loved one in pain. These neural circuits apparently do not separate *real* experiences from *symbolic* ones. If damaged, those parts of the brain will no longer recognize the figurative truth in metaphor; instead, they will focus exclusively on the literal meaning of a statement like "the grass is always greener."

Since you may not have a brain scan of your client to work from, your assessment of their response to metaphor will rely on observations. What words and expressions do they use? Are they literal, figurative, or some combination? Which of your own phrases and ways of speaking seem to connect most with them? Proceeding through the assessment, you will gather more impressions on the person's response to metaphor. If you decide to work with metaphor, keep in mind two things:

1. *Avoid mixing metaphors.* They can be confusing and unintentionally humorous. For example, Garner (2009) gives the illustration of "He's really got his hands cut out for him," which combines "He's got his hands full" with "He's got his work cut out for him" (p. 534). If you choose to mix them for effect, be conscious of that choice and its impact.
2. *Beware "dead" metaphors.* Mixed metaphors often arise when we unconsciously string together dead metaphors. Metaphors can have a shelf life. Once they have been overused to the point that they lose their metaphorical resonance, they pass their expiration date.

Table 11.6 lists a few dead metaphors and some words or phrases to use in place of them (Fiske, 1994).

These expired metaphors have an afterlife as clichés that we continue to use in speech because they are a quick way to communicate. But we should be selective in the way we use them in

TABLE 11.6 "Dead" Metaphors and What They Mean

Metaphor	Meaning
Chip on his shoulder	Bitterness, hostility, indignation
Chilled to the bone	Frigid, glacial, ice-cold
Follow the crowd	Adapt, comply, submit
Food for thought	Something to think about; ideas to consider
Grist for the mill	All can be useful; things can be used to advantage
Raise a red flag	Alert, caution, forewarn
Sharp as a tack	Brilliant, insightful, perceptive
Under a cloud	Disgraced, distrusted, suspect

writing. While an apt metaphor will enliven the written document, a dead metaphor will drain the life from it. In choosing metaphors for letters, you will likely draw on conceptual metaphors as discussed previously. Metaphors used in stories can bear a more literary stamp.

Therapeutic Stories

Prose refers to ordinary speech and writing, the documents we write every day, the speech with which we interact. But Aristotle also described prose as the "art which imitates [character, emotion, and action] by use of language alone..." (transl. 1907, 1, I, par. #5). This description may apply to a letter or a standard assessment report but certainly does apply to stories. The therapeutic story can be an extension of the therapeutic letter as well as an individual intervention. For a child, adolescent, or adult, the story incorporates key assessment findings into a fictional construct, though one recognizable as paralleling some aspects of the client's life. It employs metaphor as both a figure of speech and context for the client's life experience. The same rules of effective writing that we have explored throughout this book apply to writing stories. In addition, we add imagination to integrate the facts of the assessment findings with metaphors that will speak to the reader.

For centuries, mythology has enabled humankind to make sense of our world and experiences. That mythology manifests in images painted on ancient cave walls and in stories told around fires and, eventually, written in books. Mythologist, writer, and teacher Joseph Campbell wrote that myth's ability "to touch and

TABLE 11.7   Fable and Allegory in Therapeutic Stories

	Fable	Allegory
Definition	Fictional story intended to teach. Characters may be animals, mythical creatures, plants, or forces of nature that speak and act like humans.	Fictional story meant to teach, with hidden or symbolic meanings. May also represent abstract ideas, such as a blindfolded figure holding scales aloft to indicate impartial justice.
Used with	Usually children	Usually adolescents or adults
Sample Context	Child dealing with ADHD and anger-management issues	Client seeking diagnosis, but has self-diagnosed and is fearful of confirmation
	Talking mythic creatures: Nature spirits: fairies, elves, gnomes	*Abstract metaphors/mythology:* Hero's journey through dark forest; dog as supportive, valued companion on journey—represents client's real pet
	Wise teacher: Elf Queen— reflects assessor	*Mentor/message-giver:* Lady of the Lake from Arthurian myth—represents assessor as well as client's therapist

inspire deep creative centers dwells in the smallest nursery fairy tale" (1949, p. 4). Psychology has long used stories as intervention in counseling children (Tharinger et al., 2008). Its more recent use as feedback in Collaborative/Therapeutic Assessment seems a logical outgrowth.

Stories for children are usually *fables*, and those written for adolescents or adults are more often *allegories* structured around complex or extended metaphors. See Table 11.7 for definitions and examples (American Heritage, 2000; Webster's, 2001).

Children's Stories: Fables

The first stories written as an extension of Collaborative/ Therapeutic Assessment were for children. The process intended to provide children some form of direct assessment feedback without overwhelming them. As in the rest of C/TA, Fischer (1994, 2011) and Finn (2007) led the way through their own work and teaching. Other early C/TA practitioners either

TABLE 11.8   Writing a Fable for a Child

Step	Its Components	What it Does
Create storyboard[a]	Child as main character (as animal or mythic creature)	Establishes the metaphorical context for the story and the events within it
	Name similar to child's or otherwise meaningful	
	Wise character represents assessor	
	Parents as characters	
	Setting/culture/events	
Introduce the challenge	Similar to child's actual problem: based on questions, findings, and change child/family is ready for	Models steps to successful change
Maximize effectiveness	Awareness and collaboration: invites parent participation (consultation, writing, revision)	Can serve as intervention for parents as well as child
Recognize constraints	Acknowledges real context: may reflect child's solo issues (e.g., school/learning problems) not family system	Reflect realistic possibilities for child's change
Present the fable	Child chooses the reader. Ask child for changes. Remind child that story is hers/his to keep.	Gives child something concrete to refer to as life/change progresses

Note: Adapted from "Providing psychological assessment feedback to children through individualized fables" by D. J. Tharinger et al., 2008, *Professional Psychology: Research and Practice, 39,* 610–618. Copyright 2010 by APA.
[a] Term comes from filmmaking: A large board shows sketches of scenes in sequence that outlines the action of a film.

independently developed variations of this approach or soon adopted it. Over the past two decades, an increasing number of assessors have begun to work with this form of feedback (Tharinger et al., 2008).

As with letters written directly to clients, fables may use questions posed of the assessment as the starting point. With children, the questions will most likely come from the parents, who may also collaborate with the assessor on writing or revising the fable. Table 11.8 summarizes the steps to creating a child's story, as discussed in detail by Tharinger et al. (2008). This approach is taught by psychologist and assessor Deborah Tharinger at the University of Texas at Austin.

After completing a thorough and exhaustive assessment, writing a fable may seem an overwhelming extra step for the assessor. But Tharinger et al. (2008) point out the rewards of the process, not the least of which is to understand the results of the assessment at a deeper level. The summary and integration demanded by the fable take the assessor into the heart of a situation and allow her or him to communicate it clearly to the child through metaphor.

Adult and Adolescent Stories: Allegories

More recently, stories have also been used as feedback with adolescents and adults (Allyn, 2011; Engelman & Allyn, 2007, in press). Intuitively, metaphorical stories for adults, or even teenagers, may not seem appropriate or effective. Children, for the most part, drop easily into the world of a story. But by the time we move through adolescence and reach adulthood, our willing suspension of disbelief has often taken an extended vacation. For that reason, not every adolescent or adult is a good candidate to receive an allegory of his or her life and situation. We all started as children, however, and if given a chance, that child inside often loves a story still, though one geared to adolescent or adult understanding.

You, as the assessor, will get to know the person assessed on a deep level. You will understand the client's level of acceptance for metaphor. And you will know your own abilities and willingness to work in this creative format, either on your own or in collaboration with a writer. Neuropsychologist and assessor Diane Engelman has spoken of her decision to collaborate with me, a creative and technical writer: "[B]y the time I'm done with an assessment, I'm done…I've no energy left to convert the results into a story" (Engelman & Allyn, 2007, p. 2, para. 2). You may decide to write stories yourself. But if you choose to create stories with a writer, the process adds an additional level of collaboration to the assessment. I have written of the unusual dynamic of collaborating on the story with one degree of separation (Engelman & Allyn, due to publish February/March 2012). I never meet the client, so all interaction is with Engelman. Not a simple process, surely, but one that is both gratifying and worthwhile.

After you have decided that an adolescent or adult would respond to and benefit from a story as part of the feedback process,

TABLE 11.9 Writing an Allegory for an Adult or Adolescent

Step	Its Components	What it Does
Select messages	1–3 main findings to embed in the story	Clarifies takeaway from assessment
Define the metaphors	Percepts from testing Personal interests from questionnaire or interview Client as main character: name of character different from client's but often with same meaning or shared culture Level of abstraction/complexity of metaphors	Establishes creative context for story
Select the mentor	May be person from history, mythology, or family Represents therapist, assessor, or other person client respects	Both refines and expands metaphorical construct based on this essential character
Develop the work plan	Three sections: Story flow of action/dialogue Images from testing Messages: mental health or cognitive—always include hope	Creates structure for allegory
Draft and refine story	Make it crisp, clear, and succinct: 3–4 double-spaced pages. "Longer" does not necessarily mean "better."	Holds reader's attention
	Label as "Draft 1, 2, 3" etc., never "Final."	Invites client to change story
Present the story	Client chooses reader (self, assessor, therapist, or silent reading). Assessor leads following discussion. Assessor asks client for changes. Assessor reminds client that the story is theirs to keep.	Provides second intervention following earlier session to discuss findings

the steps in Table 11.9 will guide you through. These steps apply whether writing yourself or working with a collaborator.

Narrative and Dialogue

Finally, here are a few words on the structure of your story. Your story will likely rely on both narrative flow and dialogue between characters. Narrative will paint a picture of the setting and describe actions of characters that move along your plot. It will also describe the physical appearance of characters and insight into your main character's response to what occurs in the story. It is a summary technique that allows you to convey a lot of detail in a shorter space and yet can cover a long period of time. You will format narrative into logical paragraphs in the same way as your everyday writing.

Dialogue, on the other hand, places the characters and the reader in "real time." The back-and-forth quality of dialogue slows down the pace and asks the reader to step into the experience of each character during conversation. For that reason, dialogue requires a bit more attention to formatting and flow. When each character speaks, in turn, his or her dialogue starts on a new line on your page. The actual words of the character are set off by quotation marks that separate the character's words from informational notes about his or her movements and quality of speech—for example, *"Thank you," she said quietly, as she sat on the grass.* (See Chapter 10 for where to place quotation marks with other punctuation following a line of dialogue.)

Integrating the facts and truth of your assessment into a story may seem to use a different skill set than writing your report. But as I said in Chapter 5, good writing is good writing. You will rely on the same grammatical guidelines and aspects of style in writing both.

CHAPTER **12**

Richness, Texture, Safety, and Risk
Communicating Verbally

In the effort toward clear expression, thought also becomes clearer.

Constance T. Fischer, American
psychologist and professor

C hapter 12 explores basic tenets of clear yet sensitive spoken communication. It also examines nonverbal cues because they affect verbal communication. The chapter reviews and reinforces certain basics of effective personal interaction and places it in the assessment context. Sensitivity in interaction forms a critical foundation for Collaborative/Therapeutic Assessment (C/TA) and, indeed, can apply to any conversation within the field of psychological assessment. Political scientist and communications theorist Harold Lasswell provides the chapter's context with his oft-quoted frame for communications: "Who says what to whom in what channel with what effect" (Wikipedia, 2011c). As with written communication, spoken interaction requires clarity, precision, accuracy, and compassion. Unintentional use of loaded words can be as powerfully negative when spoken as when written—maybe more so, because of the addition of intonation and nonverbal cues. The chapter incorporates linguistic and sociological perspectives on verbal and nonverbal communications; it also draws on information from the areas of risk perception and risk communication.

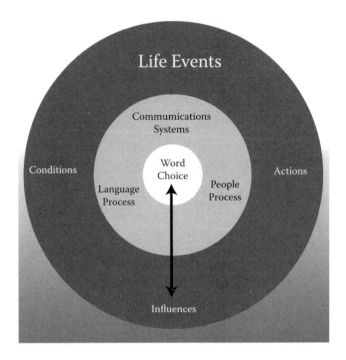

FIGURE 12.1 Creating communication.

Figure 12.1 sets a context for communications systems. As the diagram shows, communicating involves a people process as well as a language process. Before you reach the point of choosing words and phrases to speak, multiple aspects of life events affect you and the person you are communicating with. You experience

- *Conditions*: the external environment, surroundings, and circumstances in which you each function
- *Actions*: the individual behavior and conduct of each of you and of other people important to your interaction, either directly or indirectly

These combine to create

- *Influences*: the power of you or the other to affect one another and the interaction

As a system, none of these aspects stands isolated from the others. Each contributes to your eventual way of speaking to the other—your formality, phrasing, word choice, and voice.

Written Versus Spoken Communication

Spoken communication can be very different from the written form. As far back as the late 1800s, a well-known writer and speaker noticed this difference. Author and lecturer Mark Twain edited his extensive works for verbal presentation. On one occasion, he began to tell a story he had not presented in some time. He did not have his edited lecture text available and so started to read from the original story text instead. He quickly put the book away saying, "It wouldn't read," and simply told the story from memory (Hurwitt, 2011). Spoken communication often relies on more casual sentence structure and informal words. The words Twain had written for publication did not translate well to the more interactive mode of verbal presentation.

Speaking requires a listener, just as writing requires a reader. An audience—for whom you either write or speak—can feel "dangerous" or "safe" to you (Elbow, 1998). A person's attention is easier to get and hold in one-on-one discussion, such as an assessment feedback session. If you believe your listener is paying attention and thinks you have something valuable to say, you will likely feel safer. Nevertheless, your own sense of safety in the communication process may also be influenced by the other person's level of fear and hostility. And in the case of an assessment, hostility could stem from his or her reluctance to hear the results. At the extreme end of that spectrum, the communication process could feel dangerous to you, the assessor, if you sense the "shoot the messenger" dynamic in play. In turn, the other person in the communication interaction—the person assessed—can also feel degrees of safety and danger with you as the listener. (More on the impact of fear on communication is presented later in this chapter.)

That tension between safety and danger in communication brings up a strong similarity between writing and speech: Both require the care and consciousness in word choice and phrasing discussed throughout this book, most especially in Chapters 1, 2, and 3. Sensitivity in word choice is essential in C/TA, where collaboration and the therapeutic impact of the process are a focal point. The other components of written tone (formality, arranging material, and juxtaposition) also require attention in the verbal as well as in the written form. If anything, tone becomes stronger in speaking because of the richer communication cues provided by both verbal and nonverbal signals.

Richness and Texture in Communication

Spoken language contains more degrees of richness than does written. "Information richness" is a framework to assess "the ability of information to change understanding within a time interval" (Daft & Lengel, 1986, p. 560). The richer the medium of communicating, the more cues it gives the listener about the meaning and importance of what is being said. The more cues for the listener, the more quickly a message is received and understood. Figure 12.2 provides a diagram of that increasing richness, with "least rich" being the medium of written communication and "most rich" in face-to-face communication.

In war zones, unique passwords sometimes replace the face-to-face communication cue. Often these passwords are chosen because they are difficult for the enemy to pronounce. When a person approaching in the dark pronounces the correct password without difficulty, "We then virtually 'see' his face" (D.E. Balding, personal communication, May 2011).

Face-to-face communication is most rich because of the warmth that can be conveyed interpersonally and the immediate

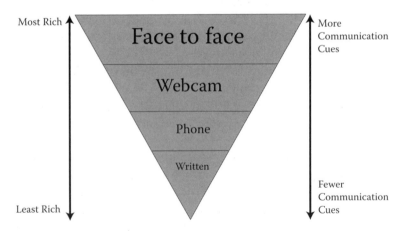

FIGURE 12.2 Richness and cues in communicating.

response possible between the speaker and listener. The listener can ask for instant clarification of anything confusing. Face-to-face, both speaker and listener have other cues to help them understand each other, such as tone of voice and body language. Body language enables you, the assessor, to continually check whether your client's nonverbal response indicates confusion or distress. Tone of voice allows you and the client to monitor attitude coming from the other. Visual cues and tone of voice may be available to a lesser extent with webcam and videoconferencing. Phone, too, can allow you to pick up shifts in tone of voice, although you must use active, careful listening to counteract the loss of visual cues.

Less-rich formats are not inferior forms of communication. They are simply better suited to more clearly defined uses. For instance, when a message is straightforward, as in setting an appointment time, then phone or written communications are reliable. But the more complex and difficult the message or material, the more it demands richness of medium, face-to-face when possible. When a written assessment report follows the rich face-to-face feedback session, it backs up what has already been communicated verbally. The assessor first communicates complex material in rich form and then provides the less-rich written form for future reference. With only written feedback, however, great care is needed to compensate for the loss of richness in communication cues.

"Voice" in Speech

Chapter 4 discussed voice in writing and the qualities that contribute to it. Speech more readily displays a person's unique voice due to the multiple cues it carries. A person is much likelier to have voice in speech than in writing—it is the sound and texture of "them" (Elbow, 1998).

Sociolinguist Deborah Tannen has called intonation "the music of talk" (Tannen, 1986, p. 38). Intonation is composed of various signals. The listener must perceive them correctly in order to keep the conversation flowing. Pacing, pauses, loudness, and changes in pitch all modify our words. Even minute differences in these signals can affect the ways that we understand each other. We speak automatically based on years of conversation. We do not always listen carefully. Because of those reflexes, we can miss cues in this music of talk that would tell us that the other person is singing from different sheet music than we.

Pacing and Pauses

Some people speak faster than others or take longer pauses between each person's turn in speaking. Pacing is the rhythm of taking turns in speech. Think of the brief transmission delay in some cell phone conversations. Even when speaking with someone whose pacing you are familiar with, that cell phone lag throws normal conversation off balance. Then factor in conversational pauses, those natural, brief delays between speakers in a conversation. If you and your client are from different parts of the country—or the world—one of you may speak faster than the other. In addition, a "normal" pause to one of you may seem too long or too short to the other person (Samovar & Porter, 1995). When two people do not pick up each others' vocal cues, their expectations can conflict over how long a pause is normal. One person does all the talking and wonders why the other says next to nothing; the other person wonders why the talker will not pause long enough to give him an opening (Tannen, 1986). In the same way, when someone who speaks very rapidly converses with someone who paces her words more slowly, an imbalance in expectations can easily occur.

Loudness and Pitch

Levels of loudness go up and down as we speak. Anger, other emotions, and vocal emphasis can all influence how loudly we speak. But each person has a vocal baseline from which s/he increases or decreases volume. Some people's baselines are louder than others due to a number of variables, including family dynamics, where they live, difficulty with hearing, or simply the vocal apparatus they were born with. As with pauses, different expectations of what is "normal" accompany loudness (Samovar & Porter, 1995). A person whose family context says that loudness expresses excitement will unsettle the person who believes that loudness always indicates anger (Tannen, 1986).

Pitch, too, has a baseline in each person. It can be influenced by our upbringing, including where we lived. A person from a background that uses wide variety in pitch may find monotonous the speech of someone who was raised speaking with less variety (Tannen, 1986). We shift pitch according to the emphasis we put on words spoken. For example, pitch at the end of a question goes up (*italics indicates the rising pitch*):

"How are *you?*"

If we have not seen the person in awhile, however, the raised pitch might shift to a different word:

"How *are* you?"

Pitch can also send subtle signals and perhaps betray impressions we do not intend. Assume that a client asks you how much longer her teenager's assessment will take. The son drives himself to the appointments; he has been late more than once; and you have mentioned it to the parent as well as the son. You might respond to the parent with relatively little pitch in the phrase, "We are somewhat behind, since John was late again." But if unexpected pitch intrudes and you say, "We are somewhat *behind*, since John was late *again*," your pitch reveals your frustration and even disapproval. Only you can judge which version of pitch will communicate best to a given client.

Interruptions and Overlap

Our rate of speaking and what we each consider to be normal pauses between speakers affect how we interrupt or overlap others in conversation (Samovar & Porter, 1995). As with other qualities of intonation, our perception of interruptions may rely on where we were raised. For example, people living in one part of the country may view interrupting as impolite, while those in another may view it as showing enthusiasm or support for what is being said. A person viewed as appropriately talkative and supportive in one location may be seen as impolite and aggressive in another (Tannen, 1986).

Differences in the way we use and perceive all aspects of intonation, gesturing, and facial expressions can contribute to our stereotyping others, either by culture or gender (Tannen, 1986). One gender split in American conversation can come in the area of interrupting. Many men view speaking as a process of taking turns, in which each speaker says all he has to say and then allows the other a turn. For many women, conversation is often more about the personal interaction, and they view comments not as interruptions but as support for the speaker.

These different styles illustrate *report-talk* versus *rapport-talk* (Tannen, 1990).

Report-Talk Versus Rapport-Talk

Report-talk is a way to get and hold attention by showing knowledge about a topic and to "maintain status in a...social order" (Tannen, 1990, p. 77). *Rapport-talk*, on the other hand, is about establishing and negotiating relationships. The first is used to "manage contest" in a public setting, the second to "create community" in a private one (p. 210). Aspects of each, however, can show up in the opposite forum. Report-talk occurs in a private setting when minimal give and take occurs between two people. Rapport-talk takes place in a public setting when a speaker works to establish interaction with a group. Neither method is right or wrong, but knowing the difference enables us to recognize when a person relies more heavily on one style than the other.

In verbal feedback following an assessment—indeed, during the verbal interactions of the whole assessment process—recognizing conversational differences can aid your interactions. Understanding differences in the way you and your clients use "the music of talk" and knowing whether report-talk or rapport-talk is more dominant for each of you can help you communicate in ways they will more readily hear. Table 12.1 summarizes qualities in conversation, including intonation and approach.

Nonverbal Cues

In many cases, we find it easier to establish human connection in the spoken word than in the written form. Verbal communication's powerful, silent companions are rich, sometimes unconscious, nonverbal cues and context. Nonverbal communication and culture are linked—both are invisible and learned (Samovar & Porter, 1995). When used well, nonverbal cues enable us to transmit a message and the listener to receive its meaning. If we make a statement and are met by a blank stare, we have no idea if our listener does not understand, disagrees, or is simply distracted. But if s/he shakes her head and gestures that we lost her or, alternatively, gives a nod and smile of recognition, we take it

TABLE 12.1 Qualities in Conversation

Quality	What It Is	What Affects It
Intonation:		
Pacing	Rate of speech; rhythm of taking turns	Country, region, culture, and/or gender may affect all forms of intonation
Pauses	Delay between speakers or within speech	
Loudness	Volume of delivery, from loud to soft	
Pitch	Rise or fall on words, high to low	
Interruption/ overlap	Beginning to talk before other has finished; comments of outrage or sympathy	
Approach:		
Report-talk	Usually public: to show knowledge, give information, manage contest	Forum (public or private) or gender may affect which approach is used
Rapport-talk	Usually private: to establish and negotiate relationships; create community	

Note: Adapted from *That's not what I meant! How conversational style makes or breaks relationships,* by D. Tannen, 1986, New York, NY: Ballantine. Copyright 1986 by Ballantine.
Adapted from *You just don't understand! Women and men in conversation,* by D. Tannen, 1990, New York, NY: William Morrow. Copyright 1990 by William Morrow.

as a signal of what is needed next in the interaction. While *verbal* feedback plays a major part in communication, *nonverbal* cues can also give the necessary feedback that transmission was received and understood, as shown in Figure 12.3.

Unfortunately, human communication is not as clear-cut as the diagram shows. Still, allowing for the unavoidable "filters" through which we each comprehend (e.g., personal perceptions, stress, cultural bias, etc.), the transmit-receive-feedback loop provides a useful frame. It reminds us that we do not truly know a person has understood until we receive some sort of confirmation, verbal or nonverbal. In the communications model shown in Figure 12.3, the term *feedback* is not meant to describe a one-way

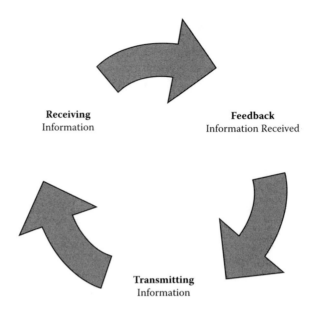

Receiving
Information

Feedback
Information Received

Transmitting
Information

FIGURE 12.3 Communications process: Transmitter–receiver–feedback loop.

process, but rather a two-way exchange. It presupposes that both parties are active partners in the dialogue. It assumes that they each give feedback to the other indicating that they do or do not understand what is being communicated. This process includes seeking clarification and expressing disagreement or confusion. The communications feedback loop creates a dialogue, not a monologue.

With their training, psychologists become uniquely qualified in effective nonverbal communication: (a) nonverbal cues, such as gestures, posture, expressions, eye contact, and distance, and (b) active listening, including sensitivity to what is *not* said. See Table 12.2 for a summary of these cues.

Active Listening

As with active and passive voice in sentence construction (see Chapters 3 and 4), active and passive listening have different qualities and impacts.

TABLE 12.2 Nonverbal Communication

Cue	What It Is	What It Does
Nonverbal		
Distance	"Personal space" between people—can vary by culture	Allows connection; too close can trigger discomfort in other person
Eye contact	Holding or avoiding someone's gaze	Opens flow of communication; can cause discomfort if intense
Facial expression	Smiles, frowns, and other signs	Transmits attitude and mood; silent commentary; however, receiver may not always pick up meaning
Gestures	Natural use of hands, limbs, etc., to illustrate thought or speech	Humanizes speech—softens or sharpens
Posture	Leaning toward or away from someone; turning your back	Establishes or breaks connection
Active listening	Presence; feedback to show understanding; includes attention to what is *not* said	Facilitates communication; encourages problem-solving and understanding

- *Passive listening* can occur with one eye on the clock while making a mental list of grocery items; the listener may nod absent-mindedly from time to time but is otherwise not fully present.
- *Active listening*, on the other hand, requires that the listener let the speaker know s/he understands what is being said by verbal or nonverbal feedback.

Active listening has a goal: to solve a problem, for example, or to understand the other person. It requires that the listener play an active role even when silent. One maxim when performing in the theater says that the hardest part of acting is *re*acting. When you have nothing to say during another person's long speech, your character must stay present—must hear all those words and make sense of them as if for the first time, every time. If your mind wanders to your grocery list, you could easily miss your cue to speak, leaving the other person dangling like a limp marionette. Active listening in human communication shares that requirement to stay present.

Communicating When Fear Equals Risk

Anyone who has dealt with a personal crisis—and that likely includes all of us—knows how fear can tangle and confuse communication. Earlier in this chapter, we touched on how a speaker might perceive his or her listener as safe or dangerous. Another sort of fear may be at play for an assessment client, and that fear could affect his or her communication with the assessor. Work done in the field of risk communication over the past 30+ years has underscored the importance of recognizing and mitigating fear in order to clearly communicate. The mechanism for that communication combines compassion, clarity, concrete words and images, and collaboration.

The U.S. Environmental Protection Agency, other agencies, and industry widely use a model developed by communications professor Peter Sandman in communicating environmental risk. Sandman has more recently applied his model to communicating about risk of infectious diseases (Sandman & Lanard, 2003). During crises such as the Three Mile Island nuclear incident, scientists and communicators realized that the public's perception of risk was out of balance with the statistical probability of actual risk. Sandman's model gives weight to a person's fear, dread, or misery about a threat as well as the threat itself. The original model aligns 12 factors that most people view as "safe" versus those they consider "risky." In communicating with people about an issue, those factors influence both the content of information and the process used for interaction (Sandman, 1987).

In psychological assessment, the person assessed may carry fear or dread of the assessment process or its outcome. At least four of Sandman's risk factors can be applied to the assessor's interaction with an assessment client. Always allowing for differences in people and situations, the answer to the questions in Table 12.3 may influence the extent to which the client finds the assessment process risky.

- Perception of safety in the assessment aligns with the process being *voluntary, fair, familiar,* and *controlled by the person assessed.*
- Perception of risk in the assessment aligns with the process being *required, unfair, unfamiliar,* and *controlled by others.*

TABLE 12.3   Perception of Risk

Factor	Question
1. Volition	Is the assessment *voluntary* or *required* (by family, school, court, etc.)?
2. Familiarity	Has the person had a previous evaluation and so finds the process *familiar*, or is it completely *unfamiliar*?
3. Fairness	Does the person assessed believe it's *fair* or *unfair* that s/he is undergoing the assessment?
4. Control	Is the process of the assessment *controlled by the person* or *controlled by others*?

Even in the best case, where the assessment is *voluntary* and viewed as *fair* and *familiar*, the process still will not fully *be controlled by* the person assessed. Just that one issue could raise the person's fear about the assessment, increasing his or her perception of risk. Worst case, the assessment would be *involuntary, unfamiliar*, viewed as *unfair*, and *controlled by others*. The person's fear and risk perception would likely increase proportionally. The dynamics in these four areas can explain actions as basic as someone balking at dates the assessor proposes for testing. Balking gives the client more seeming control over the situation and, perhaps, helps him or her better deal with the imbalance in the other three.

Previous chapters emphasize the need for care and precision in writing the assessment report. The current chapter discusses the factors in effective spoken and nonverbal communication, such as in a feedback and discussion session. Whether written, spoken, or nonverbal, communication concerns the link with another human being. Writing and speaking effectively enable us to clearly communicate important ideas in a way that another person can hear. Both, when done well, reinforce the qualities discussed in earlier chapters: sensitivity, compassion, respect for the subject and/or reader, clarity, accuracy, specificity, and careful word choice. That approach, ultimately, is what this book is about.

Glossary of Terms: Grammar, Style, and Communication

Abbreviation: Any shortened form of a word or phrase.

Absolute: Word describing a quality that a thing or person either does or does not have, with no gradations (e.g., *unique, perfect, infinite*).

Abstract: Word or phrase referring to intangible concept with no physical shape (e.g., *hope, kindness, love*)—we know it through thought process, not through our senses. Contrast **concrete**.

Abstraction ladder: Progression of related words or phrases ranging upward from most concrete to most abstract. See also **abstract; concrete**.

Acronym: Special type of abbreviation; formed by using the initial letter(s) of a series of words, which together can be pronounced as a word (e.g., radar [*r*adio *d*etection *a*nd *r*anging]).

Active listening: Process in which a listener provides ongoing indication of receiving and understanding the information transmitted by another person.

Active verb: Shows movement; the subject takes some action—writes, sits, walks, etc. Also called *dynamic* verb. See also **linking verb**.

Active voice: Sentence structure that shows subject of sentence performing some action (e.g., "He *drove* the car"). Contrast **passive voice**. See also **narrative voice; stylistic voice; voice**.

Adjective: Qualifies or alters meaning of a noun or pronoun. See also **compound adjective; coordinate adjective; cumulative adjective**.

Adverb: Qualifies or alters meaning of a verb, an adjective, or another adverb.

Agreement: Match between a sentence's subject and verb, as reflected by number (singular or plural) and person (*I, you, he/she*, etc.).

Allegory: Fictional story meant to teach, with hidden or symbolic meanings; may also represent abstract ideas. See also **extended metaphor**.

Antecedent: The word to which a pronoun refers (e.g., "Tom drove the car. He arrived late": *Tom* is the antecedent of *he*).

Article: Three words used as adjectives that indicate (a) one of a general group (*a, an*) or (b) a specific person or thing (*the*).

Attitude: The writer's internalized, often unconscious view of a subject or person, reflecting feelings as well as thoughts.

Base verb: The basic form of a verb listed in a dictionary (e.g., *write, test, finish*). See also **infinitive**.

Clause: Grouping of words that contains a subject and verb and is part of a sentence. See also **dependent clause; independent clause**.

Collective noun: Group of persons or things viewed as a unit (e.g., *army, jury, family*).

Comma splice: Form of run-on sentence that incorrectly joins two independent clauses with a comma rather than a semicolon. See also **run-on sentence.**

Communication: Content and context of spoken or written interaction between people.

Complex metaphor: Combines multiple simple metaphors together or builds one on the other for greater effect. See also **metaphor**.

Complex sentence: Made up of one independent clause and one or more dependent clauses. See also **clause; dependent clause; independent clause; sentence**.

Compound adjective: Two or more adjectives that describe a noun; one adjective limits the other in some way (e.g., *small-business* consultant.)

Compound-complex sentence: Composed of two or more independent clauses and one or more dependent clauses. See also **clause; dependent clause; independent clause; sentence**.

Compound noun: Made up of more than one word (e.g., *keyboard, attorney-at-law*).

Compound sentence: Made up of two or more independent clauses and no dependent clause. See also **clause; dependent clause; independent clause; sentence**.

Compound subject: Two subjects, joined by such words as *and* or *or*, that take the same verb.

Conceptual metaphor: Structures and equates one concept in terms of another (e.g., *wasting time* equates time with money.) See also **metaphor**.

Concrete: Word or phrase that describes something we perceive through our ability to taste, smell, touch, hear, or see (e.g., *sandwich, pencil, scoring manual*). Contrast **abstract**.

Conjunction: Joins words or groups of words. See also **coordinating conjunction; correlating conjunction; subordinating conjunction**.

Connotation: Idea or meaning attributed to a word, as opposed to its direct dictionary definition. Contrast **denotation**.

Coordinate adjective: Carries equal weight with other adjectives in describing the noun in a sentence; separated from other adjectives by commas (e.g., an *older, professional* couple). Contrast **cumulative adjective**.

Coordinating conjunction: Joins words or groups of words that represent equally important ideas (e.g., *for, and, nor, but, or, yet,* and *so* = the acronym FANBOYS).

Correlating conjunction: Pair of words that link or balance ideas (e.g., *either...or; both...and*).

Cumulative adjective: Builds on other adjectives in describing the noun; no commas separate them (e.g., *several bangle bracelets*). Contrast **coordinate adjective**.

Cumulative sentence: See **loose sentence**.

Denotation: Direct meaning of a word, as from the dictionary. Contrast **connotation**.

Dependent clause: Does not express a complete thought or stand alone if removed from a whole sentence. Contrast **independent clause**. See also **clause**.

Descriptive writing: Describes a person, place, or thing.

Dynamic verb: See **active verb**.

Ellipsis: A series of dots used within or between sentences; shows omission when quoting factual material or indicates melancholy or trailing off into thought in creative writing.

Essential clause: A group of words necessary to the meaning of a sentence; the sentence would not make sense without the clause. Contrast **nonessential clause**.

Extended metaphor: Continues an implied comparison of two unlike things through a series of sentences, a story, or a poem. See also **allegory; metaphor.**

Fable: Fictional story intended to teach; characters (animals, mythical creatures, plants, etc.) speak and act like humans.

Fused sentence: Form of run-on sentence containing two or more ideas without punctuation or connecting word(s) between the ideas. See also **run-on sentence.**

Indefinite pronoun: Does not refer to a specific antecedent and often expresses the idea of quantity (e.g., *all, few*, or *many*).

Independent clause: Expresses a complete thought and makes sense if removed from a sentence. Contrast **dependent clause.** See also **clause.**

Infinitive: Basic form of a verb, such as that listed in a dictionary, preceded by the word *to* (e.g., *to write, to test, to finish*). See also **base verb.**

Information richness: Extent of communication cues given to a listener or reader to help them understand information.

Informative writing: Gives information or explains.

Intensifier: An adverb that emphasizes adjectives or other adverbs by showing degree (e.g., *very* flat, *extremely* hot, *really* tired).

Jargon: Specialized vocabulary used by those in the same profession.

Juxtaposition: Aligns written material side by side for comparison or contrast, influencing tone.

Knowledge telling: Creates text by combining knowledge of content and writing process in a simple, linear manner.

Knowledge transforming: Creates text by combining knowledge of content with continual analysis and adjustment of writing process and goals.

Linking verb: Shows a state or condition; describes the subject of the sentence rather than showing the action the subject takes (e.g., *is, seems, appears*).

Loose sentence: States facts upfront, then follows with elaborations. Also called a *cumulative* sentence, since elaborations build on the basic sentence. See also **periodic sentence.**

Metaphor: Figure of speech that implies similarity between two dissimilar things without using *like* or *as*. Contrast **simile.** See also **complex metaphor; conceptual metaphor; extended metaphor.**

Modifier: Word, phrase, or clause that limits another word, a phrase, or a clause; adjectives and adverbs are modifiers.

Mood: Verb form or inflection in grammar that shows the speaker's or writer's attitude through sentence structure. Different moods make a statement or ask a question, issue a command, or express a wish or doubt.

Narrative stance: Perspective the writer takes in communicating with reader; reflected in choice of writing in first, second, or third person and in level of emotional distance from the subject matter. See also **narrative voice**.

Narrative voice: Reflects point of view as shown by the pronouns used in writing a document: first person (*I, we*), second person (*you*), or third person (*he, she, they, it*). See also **active voice; passive voice; stylistic voice; voice; narrative stance**.

Narrative writing: Relates a series of events.

Nonessential clause: A group of words not necessary to the meaning of a sentence and often set off by commas; the sentence would still make sense without the clause. Contrast **essential clause**.

Noun: Names a person, place, thing, action, quality, etc. (e.g., *client, test, office, kindness*).

Object: Word that receives the action taken by the subject of a sentence (e.g., "She drove the *car*"). Contrast **subject**. See also **active voice**.

Parallel structure: Using the same pattern of words, parts of speech, verb forms, or word endings in a sentence to compare, contrast, or correlate ideas.

Passive voice: Sentence structure that moves the object of the sentence to the subject position (e.g., "She drove the *car*" becomes "The *car* was driven by her). Contrast **active voice**. See also **narrative voice; stylistic voice; voice**.

Periodic sentence: Sets context of the sentence before giving the facts; creates a mini-narrative. See also **loose sentence**.

Persuasive writing: Attempts to convince the reader.

Point of view: See **narrative voice**.

Predicate: Words in a sentence that tell what the subject is doing or being. Contrast **subject**. See also **verb**.

Prefix: Single letter or a group of letters or syllables added to the beginning of a word to change its meaning.

Preposition: Connects nouns and pronouns to other words in a sentence (e.g., *for, in, of, on, to,* and *with*).

Pronoun: Replaces a noun; takes different forms depending on whether it is the subject or object of a sentence (e.g., *he/ him, she/her, they/them, who/whom*). See also **antecedent; indefinite pronoun; noun**.

Proposition: The underlying premise of a sentence or paragraph; reflects the writer's unspoken ideas about the subject and intent of the written document.

Rapport-talk: Interaction between people focused on establishing and building relationships; individuals comment freely back and forth.

Report-talk: Interaction between people focused on showing knowledge about a topic; individuals take turns speaking.

Risk perception: Subjective experience of a situation that influences a person's view of its potential risk to his or her well-being.

Run-on sentence: Allows two or more separate ideas to run together by incorrect punctuation (*comma splice*) or missing punctuation (*fused sentence*). See also **comma splice; fused sentence; sentence fragment**.

Sentence: A group of words with a subject and verb that expresses a complete thought. See also **complex sentence; compound-complex sentence; compound sentence; simple sentence; topic sentence**.

Sentence fragment: Partial sentence that is capitalized and punctuated as if it were complete; may lack subject, verb, or both. See also **run-on sentence**.

Simile: Figure of speech that explicitly compares two dissimilar things by using *like* or *as*. Contrast **metaphor**.

Simple sentence: Composed of one independent clause and no dependent clause. See also **clause; sentence**.

Smothered verb: Combining an active verb with a form of *to be*, which converts the verb to a noun and smothers its power (e.g., "The client *authorized* the discussion" becomes "*Authorization* for the discussion *was given by* the client.")

Style: (a) A writer's personal way of putting thoughts into words or (b) the conventions of writing according to a certain set of guidelines (e.g., the APA *Publication Manual*).

Stylistic voice: Combines attitude, tone, and style into writer's unique way of communicating. See also **active voice; narrative voice; passive voice; voice.**

Subject: In a sentence, the person, place, idea, or thing that takes action or exists; usually a noun or pronoun. Contrast **subject, compound subject; noun; predicate; pronoun.**

Subordinating conjunction: Connects unequal ideas in a sentence (e.g., *after, although, because*).

Suffix: Single letter or a group of letters or syllables added to the end of a word to change its meaning.

Tense: Verb form that shows the time of an action or state of being in a sentence (e.g., present, past, future).

Tone: Qualities in writing or speaking that express the writer's or speaker's attitude toward a subject or person.

Topic sentence: States a paragraph's main idea, usually at the beginning.

Verb: Shows action or state of being in a sentence. See also **active verb; linking verb; smothered verb.**

Voice: Individual way of communicating in written or spoken word. See also **active voice; narrative voice; passive voice; stylistic voice.**

References

Allyn, J. B. (2010, March). All words are not created equal: Communicating effectively in therapeutic assessment. In D. H. Engelman (Chair), *Choosing the right words: Verbal and written feedback in therapeutic assessment.* Paper session conducted at the annual meeting of Society for Personality Assessment, San Jose, CA.

Allyn, J. B. (2011, March). Metaphor in life, letters, and stories. In D. H. Engelman (Chair), *Making a difference: The power of metaphor in collaborative/therapeutic assessment.* Paper session conducted at the annual meeting of Society for Personality Assessment, Boston, MA.

American Heritage Dictionary of the English Language (4th ed.). (2000). Boston, MA: Houghton Mifflin Harcourt.

APA. (2010). *Publication manual of the American Psychological Association* (6th ed.). Washington, DC: American Psychological Association.

APA. (2011). Supplemental material: Writing clearly and concisely: General guidelines for reducing bias. Retrieved August 8, 2011, from http://supp.apa.org/style/pubman-ch03.00.pdf

Aristotle. (1907). Poetics. In Daniel C. Stevenson (Ed.), S. H. Butcher (Trans.), *Internet Classics Archive*, Web Atomics, 1994–2000. (Original work published 350 BCE). Retrieved August 8, 2011, from http://classics.mit.edu/Aristotle/poetics.mb.txt

Bates, J. D. (2000). *Writing with precision: How to write so that you cannot possibly be misunderstood.* New York, NY: Penguin.

Bereiter, C., & Scardamalia, M. (1987). *The psychology of written composition.* Hillsdale, NJ: Erlbaum.

Braaten, E. (2007). *The child clinician's report-writing handbook.* New York, NY: Guilford Press.

Campbell, J. (1949). *The hero with a thousand faces.* New York, NY: Barnes & Noble Books.

Cameron, C., & Moshenko, B. (1996, October). Elicitation of knowledge transformational reports while children write narratives. *Canadian Journal of Behavioural Science.* Retrieved August 8, 2011, from http://findarticles.com/p/articles/mi_qa3717/is_199610/ai_n8737059/

Card, O. S. (n.d.). Brainyquote.com. Retrieved August 8, 2011, from http://www.brainyquote.com/quotes/quotes/o/orsonscott108637.html

Changes in the language since Shakespeare's time. (n.d.). In *Cambridge history of English and American literature in 18 volumes* (1907–1921): *Vol. 14. The Victorian Age, Part 2.* Retrieved August 8, 2011, from http://www.bartleby.com/224/1503.html

Chicago manual of style online. (2010a). Chicago, IL: University of Chicago. Retrieved August 8, 2011, from http://www.chicagomanualofstyle. org/CMS_FAQ/Abbreviations/Abbreviations08.html

Chicago manual of style online. (2010b). Chicago, IL: University of Chicago. Retrieved August 8, 2011, from http://www.chicagomanualofstyle.org/CMS_FAQ/Pronouns/Pronouns14.html

Chicago manual of style online. (2010c). Chicago, IL: University of Chicago. Retrieved August 8, 2011, from http://www.chicagomanualofstyle. org/16/ch07/ch07_sec014.html

Daft, R. L., & Lengel, R. H. (1986). Organizational information requirements, media richness, and structural design. *Management Science, 32*, 554–571.

Davidson, D. (1984). What metaphors mean. In *Inquiries into truth and interpretation.* Oxford, U.K.: Oxford University Press. (Reprinted from D. Davidson, 1978, *Critical Inquiry, 5*, 31–47)

Donders, J. (1999). Pediatric neuropsychological reports: Do they really have to be so long? *Child Neuropsychology, 5*(1), 70–78.

Elbow, P. (1998). *Writing with power: Techniques for mastering the writing process.* New York, NY: Oxford University Press.

Elbow, P. (2007, November). Voice in writing again: Embracing contraries. In *College English,* 70.2, 168–188. Retrieved August 8, 2011, from http://works.bepress.com/cgi/viewcontent.cgi?article= 1022&context=peter_elbow&sei-redir=1#search="peter+elbow+ voice"

Emmons, R. H. (1975). An effective writing formula for unsure writers. *Air University Review,* September-October. Retrieved August 8, 2011, from http://www.airpower.au.af.mil/airchronicles/aureview/1975/sep-oct/emmons.html

Engelman, D. H. (2011a). How collaborative/therapeutic assessment works [Web page *Collaborative/Therapeutic Assessment*]. Retrieved August 8, 2011, from http://www.dianeengelman.com/collaborative-therapeutic-assessment.html

Engelman, D. H. (2011b, March). Collaborative/therapeutic assessment, brain-based issues, and the DSM-IV-TR. In D. H. Engelman (Chair), *In your client's brain: Cognitive testing in collaborative/therapeutic assessment.* Workshop conducted at the annual meeting of Society for Personality Assessment, Boston, MA.

Engelman, D. H., & Allyn, J. B. (2007, March). Collaborative creativity: Ways in which an assessor works with a writer to craft therapeutic stories. In D. H. Engelman (Chair), *Creative approaches within therapeutic assessment.* Symposium conducted at the annual meeting of the Society for Personality Assessment, Arlington, VA.

Engelman, D. H., & Allyn, J. B. (February/March 2012). Collaboration in neuropsychological assessment: Metaphor as intervention with a suicidal adult. In S. E. Finn, C. T. Fischer, & L. Handler (Eds.), *Collaborative/therapeutic assessment: A casebook and guide.* Hoboken, NJ: John Wiley and Sons.

English language. (2010). In *Encyclopædia Britannica.* Retrieved September 1, 2011, from http://www.britannica.com/EBchecked/topic/188048/English-language

Finn, S. E. (2007). *In our clients' shoes: Theory and techniques of therapeutic assessment.* Mahwah, NJ: Erlbaum.

Fischer, C. T. (1994). *Individualizing psychological assessment.* Hillsdale, NJ: Erlbaum.

Fischer, C. T. (2011, March). Language matters: How to evoke life worlds. In C. T. Fischer (Chair), *Conceptual developments in psychological assessment.* Symposium conducted at the annual meeting of the Society for Personality Assessment, Boston, MA.

Fiske, R. H. (1994). *Thesaurus of alternatives to worn-out words and phrases.* Cincinnati, OH: Writer's Digest Books.

Flower, L., & Hayes, J. R. (1981). A cognitive process theory of writing. *College Composition and Communication, 32*(4), 365–387. Retrieved September 1, 2011, from http://kdevries.net/teaching/teaching/wp-content/uploads/2009/01/flower-hayes-81.pdf

Fogarty, M. (2010). "Like" versus "such as." In *Grammar girl: Quick and dirty tips for better writing.* Retrieved September 1, 2011, from http://grammar.quickanddirtytips.com/like-versus-such-as.aspx

Fowler, H. W. (1906). *The king's English.* Oxford, U.K.: Clarendon Press.

Frost, R. (1969). The road not taken. In E. C. Lathem (Ed.), *The poetry of Robert Frost.* New York, NY: Henry Holt. (Original work published 1915)

Franzblau, R. N. (1966). *New York Post.* Retrieved August 30, 2011, from http://www.quotelady.com/subjects/honesty.html

Garner, B. A. (2009). *Garner's modern American usage* (3rd ed.). New York, NY: Oxford University Press.

Gerard, P. (2000). *Writing a book that makes a difference.* Cincinnati, OH: Story Press.

Goldfinger, K., & Pomerantz, A. M. (2010). *Psychological assessment and report writing.* Los Angeles, CA: Sage.

Graham, S., & Harris, K. R. (2000). The role of self-regulation and transcription skills in writing and writing development. *Educational Psychologist, 35*(1), 3–12.

Groth-Marnat, G. (2009a). *Handbook of psychological assessment* (5th ed.). Hoboken, NJ: Wiley.

Groth-Marnat, G. (2009b). The five assessment issues you meet when you go to heaven. *Journal of Personality Assessment, 91*(4), 303–310.

Hayakawa, S. I., & Hayakawa, A. R. (1990). *Language in thought and action.* New York, NY: Harvest/Harcourt.

Hurwitt, R. (2011, March 24). Still a fire in voice of Twain. *San Francisco Chronicle*, pp. F1, F5.

Kiehl, K. A., Liddle, P. F., Smith, A. M., Mendrek, A., Forster, B. B., & Hare, R. D. (1999). Neural pathway involved in the processing of concrete and abstract words. *Human Brain Mapping, 7,* 225–233. Retrieved September 1, 2011, from http://www.themindinstitute.org/pubs/kiehlhbm99.pdf

Koller, D. (2004, January). Origin of the name "Google." Retrieved September 1, 2011, from http://graphics.stanford.edu/~dk/google_name_origin.html

Lakoff, G., & Johnson, M. (1980). *Metaphors we live by.* Chicago, IL: University of Chicago Press.

Lamott, A. (1994). *Bird by bird: Some instructions on writing and life.* New York, NY: Pantheon.

Lance, B. R., & Krishnamurthy, R. (2003, March). *A comparison of three modes of MMPI-2 test feedback.* Paper presented at the annual meeting of the Society for Personality Assessment, San Francisco, CA.

Landon, B. (2008). *Building great sentences: Exploring the writer's craft.* Chantilly, VA: The Teaching Company.

Lichtenberger, E. O., Mather, N., Kaufman, N. L., & Kaufman, A. L. (2004). *Essentials of assessment report writing.* Hoboken, NJ: Wiley.

McArthur, T. (1992). *Oxford companion to the English language.* New York, NY: Oxford University Press.

Merriam-Webster's online dictionary. (2011). Definition of "hopefully." Retrieved September 1, 2011, from http://www.merriam-webster.com/dictionary/hopefully

Narrative therapy. (n.d.). About narrative therapy. Retrieved September 1, 2011, from http://www.narrativetherapycentre.com/index_files/Page378.htm

Oxford Dictionaries online. (2011). How many words are there in the English language? Retrieved September 1, 2011, from http://www.oxforddictionaries.com/page/93

Poston, J. M., & Hanson, W. E. (2010). Meta-analysis of psychological assessment as a therapeutic intervention. *Psychological Assessment, 22*(2), 203–212.

Purdue University Online Writing Lab. (2005–2011). A little help with capitals. Retrieved September 1, 2011, from http://owl.english.purdue.edu/owl/resource/592/1/

ReadabilityFormulas.com (2011a). Flesch-Kincaid grade level readability formula. Retrieved September 1, 2011, from http://www.readabilityformulas.com/flesch-grade-level-readability-formula.php

ReadabilityFormulas.com (2011b). Flesch reading ease readability formula. Retrieved September 1, 2011, from http://www.readability-formulas.com/flesch-reading-ease-readability-formula.php

ReadabilityFormulas.com (2011c). The Gunning fog index readability formula. Retrieved September 1, 2011, from http://www.readabilityformulas.com/gunning-fog-readability-formula.php

Richardson, L. (1990). *Writing strategies: Reaching diverse audiences.* Newbury Park, CA: Sage.

Samovar, L. A., & Porter, R. E. (1995). *Communication between cultures* (2nd ed.). Belmont, CA: Wadsworth.

Sandman, P. M., (1987). Risk communication: Facing public outrage. *Environmental Protection Agency Journal,* November, 21–22. Retrieved September 1, 2011, from http://www.psandman.com/articles/facing.htm

Sandman, P. M. (2004). Tell it like it is: 7 lessons from TMI. *International Atomic Energy Agency Bulletin, 47*(2). Retrieved September 1, 2011, from http://www.iaea.org/Publications/Magazines/Bulletin/Bull 472/htmls/tmi2.html

Sandman, P. M., & Lanard, J. (2003, October 20–21). *Risk communication recommendations for infectious disease outbreaks.* Report prepared for the World Health Organization SARS Scientific Research Advisory Committee, Geneva, Switzerland. Retrieved September 1, 2011, from http://www.psandman.com/articles/who-srac.htm

Sapolsky, R. (2010, November 14). This is your brain on metaphors. *New York Times.* Retrieved September 1, 2011, from http://opinionator. blogs.nytimes.com/2010/11/14/this-is-your-brain-on-metaphors/

Sartre, J.-P. (1988). What is writing? In *What is literature? and other essays* (J. Mehlman, Trans.). Cambridge, MA: Harvard University Press. (Original work published 1947)

Shakespeare, W. (1936). The tragedy of Hamlet, prince of Denmark. In W. A. Wright (Ed.), *The complete works of William Shakespeare.* Garden City, NY: Garden City Books. (Original work published 1603)

Seligman, M. E. P. (1991). Appendix on good scientific writing. In J. Baron & R. Rescorla, *How to write a research report in psychology.* Retrieved September 1, 2011, from http://www.psych.upenn.edu/~baron/labrep.html

Strauss, J. (2011). The blue book of grammar and punctuation. Retrieved August 21, 2011, from http://www.grammarbook.com/punctuation/hyphens.asp

Strunk, W., & White, E. B. (2000). *The elements of style* (2nd ed.). New York, NY: Longman.

Taavitsainen, I., & Pahta, P. (2004). *Medical and scientific writing in late medieval English.* Cambridge, U.K.: Cambridge University Press.

Tannen, D. (1986). *That's not what I meant! How conversational style makes or breaks relationships.* New York, NY: Ballantine.

Tannen, D. (1990). *You just don't understand! Women and men in conversation.* New York, NY: William Morrow.

Tharinger, D. J., Finn, S. E., Wilkinson, A., DeHay, T., Parton, V. T., Bailey, K. E., et al. (2008). Providing psychological assessment feedback to children through individualized fables. *Professional Psychology: Research and Practice, 39*, 610–618.

Twain, M. (1918). Fenimore Cooper's literary offenses. In M. Twain *Literary essays* (pp. 60–77). New York, NY: P. F. Collier and Son.

University of California–San Diego. (2005, May 27). Grasping metaphors: UC San Diego research ties brain area to figures of speech. *Science Daily.* Retrieved September 1, 2011, from http://www.sciencedaily.com/releases/2005/05/050526092321.htm

Warriner, J. E. (1988). *English composition and grammar: Complete course.* Orlando, FL: Harcourt Brace Jovanovich.

Webster's new world college dictionary (4th ed.). (2001). Cleveland, OH: Wiley.

Wechsler, D. (2009). *Wechsler individual achievement test* (3rd ed.), *Examiner's manual.* San Antonio, TX: Pearson.

West, W. C., & Holcombe, P. J. (2000). Imaginal, semantic, and surface-level processing of concrete and abstract words: An electrophysiological investigation. *Journal of Cognitive Neuroscience, 12*, 1024–1037. Retrieved September 1, 2011, from http://neurocog.psy.tufts.edu/manuscripts/18.West%26Holcomb.pdf

Wikipedia. (2011a). Ellipsis. Retrieved September 1, 2011, from http://en.wikipedia.org/wiki/Ellipsis

Wikipedia. (2011b). Epic of Gilgamesh. Retrieved September 1, 2011, from http://en.wikipedia.org/wiki/Epic_of_Gilgamesh

Wikipedia. (2011c). Harold Lasswell. Retrieved September 1, 2011, from http://en.wikipedia.org/wiki/Harold_Lasswell

Wikipedia. (2011d). I before E except after C. Retrieved September 1, 2011, from http://en.wikipedia.org/wiki/I_before_E_except_after_C #cite_note-3

Wikipedia (2011e). Gunning fog index. Retrieved from http://en.wikipedia.org/wiki/Gunning_fog_index

Wilford, J. N. (1999, April 6). Who began writing? Many theories, few answers. *New York Times.* Retrieved September 1, 2011, from http://www.nytimes.com/library/national/science/040699sci-early-writing.html

Williams, J. (2004). Neologism history and evaluation: Gender neutral pronoun FAQ. Retrieved September 1, 2011, from http://www.aetherlumina.com/gnp/history.html#net

Writing Center at the University of Wisconsin–Madison (2009). The writer's handbook: Using semicolons. Retrieved September 1, 2011, from http://writing.wisc.edu/Handbook/Semicolons.html

Zinsser, W. K. (1980). *On writing well: An informal guide to writing nonfiction* (2nd ed.). New York, NY: Harper & Row.

Zinsser, W. K. (2009). Writing English as a second language. *The American Scholar*. Retrieved September 1, 2011, from http://www.theamericanscholar.org/writing-english-as-a-second-language/

Zuckerman, E. L. (2005). *Clinician's thesaurus: The guide to conducting interviews and writing psychological reports* (6th ed.). New York, NY: Guilford Press.

Zumbrunn, S. (2010). *Nurturing young students' writing knowledge, self-regulation, attitudes, and self-efficacy: The effects of self-regulated strategy development (SRSD)*. Doctoral dissertation, University of Nebraska–Lincoln. Retrieved September 1, 2011, from http://digitalcommons.unl.edu/cehsdiss/71/

Index

A

Abbreviations, 142
Abstract terms, 35, 36. *See also* Abstraction
    Ladder
Abstraction Ladder, 38–40, 41*t*
Accessibility in writing, 41
Accuracy, 34–35
Acronyms, 142, 144
Active sentence structure, 48, 50, 53
Active voice, 51, 52, 53, 97
Adjectives
    absolutes, 129–130
    articles, 120
    comparison, degrees of, 126–127
    compound, 122
    overused, 129
    overview, 120
    placing in a sentence, 122–123
    quantity, of, 120, 122
Adverbs
    awkward, 129
    comparison, degrees of, 126–127
    overused, 129
    overview, 124
    splitting verbs with, 124–125
Affect *versus* effect, 138–139, 141
Alexander, Rhys, 173
Allegories, 187–188
Although, 166
Ambiguity, 128
APA *Publication Manual*, 59, 64, 65, 68, 74,
        134, 137, 142, 152, 154, 156, 159,
        161, 162, 166, 167
Apostrophes, 161–162
Articles, 120
Assessment reports
    conversational, 73
    formatting; *See* Formatting reports
    linking verbs, use of, 46, 47
    personal letter form, 59, 73, 175–177
    standard phrases, 89
    subtleties, 28–29
Attitude, 5
    defining, 6, 17
    manifestations of, 12
    overview, 6–7
    own writing, toward, 7–9
    reader, relationship to, 12–15
    subject and audience, toward, 7, 9–10, 11
    subliminal influences on, 10–11
Audience, 5
    influence of on writing, 9, 10
    knowledgeable readers, 24
    lay readers, 24
    multiple, 69–70
    secondary, 10
    types of, 72
    writer's knowledge of, 9–10
Awkwardness, 128

B

Block indentation, 162, 165
Body language, 195
Brevity, 97
Buddha, 12
Bureaucratic writing, 49

C

Campbell, Joseph, 184–185
Capitalization, 144–147
Card, Orson Scott, 179
Clarity, 23, 25–26, 33, 34–35, 97
Clutter in writing, 43–44
Collaborative Assessment (CA), 169–170
Collaborative/Therapeutic Assessment
    (C/TA), 13, 73
    communication approach, 171
    fables written for children, 185–187
    overview, 169–170
Collective nouns, 107–108
Communications
    clear, 2–3
    conditions of, 192
    context of, 192
    effective, 3, 5–6
    face-to-face, 194–195
    influences of, 192
    richness in, 194–195
    specificity, 35–37
    spoken, 193–194
    written, 193–194, 195
Compassion in writing, 40
Concrete terms, 37–38
Conjunctions, 150–151, 168
Connotation, 26–27
Contractions
    use of, influence on tone, 22

Creativity, 77, 78
Critical thinking, 77

D

Data gathering, 11
Deductive assessment, 71
Denotation, 26
Dependent clauses, 85, 150, 154
Descriptive writing, 2
Dialogue, 189
Drafts, initial, 78

E

E-mail, 147
E.g., 144
Editing, 78, 79
    unnecessary phrases, 92–93
Effect *versus* affect, 138–139, 141
Elbow, Peter, 9–10, 44, 49, 57, 63
Ellipses, 165
Energetic writing, 44–45
Engelman, Diane, 69, 187
Etc., 144
Evaluating writing, 78

F

Fables, 185–187
Feedback, 187
Fiction narrative, 55
Fillers, 92, 93
Finn's model, 29–30
Finn, Stephen, 29
First person, 53, 55, 59
Fischer, Constance, 48, 169, 191
Flesch Reading Ease, 95, 97
Flesch-Kincaid Grade Level, 94–95, 96
Formal report, standard. *See* Assessment
        reports
Formatting reports, 55
    font, 68–69
    order of sections, 69–71
    outline, use of; *See* Outlining
    overview, 68
    section types, 72–74
Fragments, sentence, 154
Franzblau, Rose N., 12

G

Gender neutrality, 111–113
Grammar. *See also* Punctuation
    complexity of, 34–35

jargon, 65
    mood of, 101
    origins, 63–64
Groth-Marnat, Gary, 2, 35, 41
Gunning's fog index, 95–96

H

Harvey, V. S., 35
Hayakawa, S. I., 38
Hemingway, Ernest, 31
Hopefully, use of, 130
However, use of, 130–131

I

I.e., 144
Independent clauses, 84–85, 150, 152, 154
Inductive assessment, 71
Information richness, 194
Informative writing, 2
Intonation, 195–196

J

Jargon, 41, 42–43, 44*t*, 65
Juxtaposition, 28, 194

K

King, Stephen, 5
Knowledge telling, 7, 9*t*
Knowledge transforming, 7, 8, 9*t*

L

Lamott, Anne, 67
Lasswell, Harold, 191
Like *versus* such as, 166, 167
Listening, active, 200–201
Lists, bulleted, 35
Lists, numbered, 35
Literary writing, 1–2

M

Meaning, explicit, 27
Meaning, implicit, 27
Metaphors, 38, 178–180. *See also* Similes
    brain, relationship between, 183–184
    conceptual, 180, 182
    context provided by, 184
    conventional, 181–182
    figure of speech, as, 184
Microsoft Word, 93, 94

Milne, A. A., 133
Modifiers, misplaces, 129
Mythology, 184–185

N

Narrative stance, 58
Narrative voice, 53
Narrative writing, 2, 189
Neurodiversity, 177
Neutrality, 59–60
Nonverbal cues, 198–200
Nuance, 27. *See also* Connotation
Numbers and numerals, use of, 137

O

Object (of a sentence), 84
Objectivity, 59
Outlining, 74, 76–77
Ownby, R. L., 2

P

Pacing in speech. *See* Speech
Paragraphs
    forming, 88, 89
    main idea, 88
    overview, 87, 88
    topic sentences, 88
Parallel structure, 90–92
Passive sentence structure, 48, 49–50, 50, 53
Passive voice, 45, 47–48, 49–50, 51, 52, 53,
        93, 97
Persuasive writing, 2
Phonics, 134
Plural nouns, 136–137
Point of view, 53. *See also specific points of view*
Precision in writing, 45
Predicates, 83
Prefixes, 135, 136
Prepositions, 116–117
Pronouns, 53
    antecedents, 110
    gender neutrality, 111–113
    indefinite, 111
    object, as, 114–115
    overview, 109
    selecting, 110
    subject, as, 114–115
Proofreading, 79–80
Prose, 184
Punctuation
    apostrophes, 161–162
    colons, 157–158

commas, 153–154
dashes, 161
definition, 151–152
ellipses, 165
hyphens, 159, 161
overview, 149–150
periods, 152
quotations marks, 162–163
semicolons, 152
Pyramid of effective writing, 3

Q

Quotations, 43–44
Quotations marks, 162–163

R

Readability
    Flesch Reading Ease, 95, 97
    Flesch-Kincaid Grade Level, 94–95, 96
    Gunning's fog index, 95–96
    overview, 93–94
Redundancies, 92
Risk, perception of, 202–203
Run-on sentences, 157
Ruskin, John, 17

S

Sartre, Jean-Paul, 27
Second person, 53, 55, 59
Seligman, Martin, 81
Sensitivity in writing, 40, 73
Sentences
    compound, 85–86
    fragments, 154
    logic in, 129
    loose, 86
    order, 84–86
    periodic, 86
    run-on, 157
    structure of, 48, 49–50, 53, 81–82, 83
    topic, 88
    varying, 86–87, 94
Similes, 179
Simplicity, 97
Since, 166
Socrates, 12
Specificity, 35–37
Speech
    interruptions, 197–198
    intonation, 195–196, 197
    loudness, 196–197
    overlap, 197–198

pacing, 196
pauses, 196
pitch, 196–197
rapport-talk, 198
report-talk, 198
Spell check, 79–80, 94, 134, 138
Spelling, 133–134
    effect *versus* affect, 138–139, 141
    modern usage, 148
    variations, 147
Split infinitives, 131
Style
    defining, 31–32
    psychological assessments, role in, 32–33
Subheadings, use of, 35
Subject (of a sentence), 83, 84
    -verb agreement, 99, 100, 105–106,
        108–109
    compound, 107
Subtext, 27
Such as *versus* like, 166, 167
Suffixes, 136
Sumerians, 1

T

Tannen, Deborah, 195
Technical reports, 41
Texting, 147
That *versus* which, 167
Therapeutic stories, 184–185
There, their, they're, 142
Third person, 53, 54, 59
    objective, 54–55
    subjective, 55
Though, 166
To be, use of, 45, 47–48, 126
To, too, two, 138
Tone, 5
    accuracy and, 23
    attitude revealed by, 59
    clarity and, 23
    conversational, 20
    defining, 17–18, 19
    formal, 20–21, 22
    linguistics, in, 18
    music, in, 18
    painting, in, 18
    perception of, 177, 178
    popular/casual, 20
    speaking, 194, 195

    subtleties in, 28–29
    word choice, 22
    written, 194
Transitions, 88, 89
Twain, Mark, 193

V

Variety in writing, 25–26
Verbs, 44
    -subject agreement, 99, 100, 105–106,
        108–109
    action, 125
    active, 45
    can *versus* may, 103
    few *versus* less, 103–104
    lay *versus* lie, 104
    linking, 45–46, 47, 125
    pairs, 101–102
    passive, 45, 47–48, 50–51
    raise *versus* rise, 104
    set *versus* sit, 104
    tenses, 100
    used to *versus* use to, 102–103
Voice
    active; *See* Active voice
    consciousness of, 60
    narrative; *See* Narrative voice
    neutral, 59–60
    passive; *See* Passive voice
    stylistic, 55–58
Voltaire, 12
Vs., 144

W

Wechsler Individual Achievement Test,
    third edition (WIAT-III), 39, 85,
    153–154
Which *versus* that, 167
While, 166
Whole-word recognition, 134
Wilde, Oscar, 149
Word choice
    sensitivity in, 27
    tone, impact on, 22
Word count tool, 93–94

Z

Zinsser, William, 34, 97

The Spiritual Condition of Infants

A Biblical-Historical Survey and Systematic Proposal

ADAM HARWOOD

WIPF & STOCK · Eugene, Oregon

THE SPIRITUAL CONDITION OF INFANTS
A Biblical-Historical Survey and Systematic Proposal

Wipf & Stock
An Imprint of Wipf and Stock Publishers
199 W. 8th Ave., Suite 3
Eugene, OR 97401

www.wipfandstock.com

ISBN 13: 978-1-60899-844-9

Manufactured in the U.S.A.

Contents

Foreword • vii

Acknowledgements • xi

Abbreviations • xiii

INTRODUCTORY SECTION

1 Does It Matter if Infants Are Guilty of Sin? • 3

2 What Are the Boundaries? • 7

3 Grudem's Tentative Solution • 13

BIBLICAL SECTION

4 What Do Infants Receive from Adam? • 31
   (Romans 5:12–21)

5 Does God Judge Our Sinful Nature or Our Sinful Actions? • 41
   (Psalm 51:5 and Ephesians 2:3)

6 Are Infant Deaths Due to the Guilt of Other People? • 50
   (Genesis 6:5–6 and 2 Samuel 12:23)

7 What Is the Knowledge of Good and Evil? • 56
   (Genesis 2–3 and Deuteronomy 1:39)

8 John the Baptist: Salvation or Anointing? • 65
   (Luke 1:15)

9 The Children with Jesus: Baptism or Blessing? • 69
   (Mark 10:13–16)

10 Holy Children: Covenant or Blessing? • 74
    (1 Corinthians 7:14)

HISTORICAL SECTION

11 The Eastern Church Fathers • 83
    (Irenaeus, Gregory of Nazianzus, and Gregory of Nyssa)

12 The Western Church Fathers • 96
    (Tertullian and Cyprian)

13 Augustine • 105

14 The Magisterial Reformers • 113
    (Luther, Zwingli, and Calvin)

15 The Anabaptist Reformers • 126
    (Hubmaier and Marpeck)

16 Nineteenth-Century Baptists • 135
    (Boyce, Strong, and Mullins)

17 Twentieth-Century Baptists • 145
    (Hendricks and Erickson)

    Conclusion • 153

    Bibliography • 165
    Name and Subject Index • 177
    Scripture Index • 180

Foreword

THE CASKET WAS so tiny that one funeral director carried it from the hearse to the grave site. The baby had lived only five days and now the parents, Asian educators who had recently immigrated to America, sat alone in two chairs as the funeral director and I completed the retinue. Though the funeral director was abundantly experienced, the loneliness of the scene, the brokenness of the mother, and the obvious absence of hope took a toll on him. Obviously he wished to say as little as possible. I read from the Psalms, spoke briefly of the goodness and the love of God. The mother never looked up but wept softly, her eyes affixed on her shoes. The father gave me a glance, which suggested his preference for brevity. I offered prayer to God, seeking His comfort for both.

Before I could apprehend the words, I heard myself ask the mother, "Are you content to leave this child here or do you wish to see him again?" The director turned and walked quickly away. The father, obviously startled, gave me a stare so cold that it made the winter day seem warm by comparison. The mother's head jerked upward as though a shock had been administered, and through her cascading avalanche of tears, she spoke for the first time: "Can I see my baby again?"

At seven that evening, the door to their home opened, and the father, without mirth or warmth, motioned me into the family room where his wife was already sitting. I was aware that the professor/father was an agnostic and almost certainly considered what I was doing to be cruel. When I departed shortly after 10:00 p.m., both parents still fought with the sorrow of the last three days, and both were weeping. But despair had vanished from their visage, and the hope and comfort of Jesus had filled the vacuum of bitterness in their souls.

Often have I relived and contemplated that scene. Amid all the sorrows of life, the loss of a baby is surely among the most poignant experiences any woman can face. Was the minister in this case heartless to raise the question of a renewal of relationship for mother and child in a remote future? For various reasons, some would doubtless conclude that chutzpah is the only appropriate term to describe the minister's actions.

Whatever one may think about what transpired that day, all thoughtful people who are individuals of faith must ask the question: What happens to the infant at the moment of death? Is he annihilated? Does he journey to limbo? If a non-elect infant, does he spend eternity separated from God in hell? Can this be altered by a hurried post-mortem baptism? Or is there evidence to believe that although in some sense we are all "born in sin" (Ps. 51:5), the infant awakens from death's clutch in heaven in the presence of God? If all are "born in sin," is the infant guilty before God from birth and if so, how is that guilt assessed? The Bible speaks lucidly on some subjects. Unfortunately the teachings of Scripture on these issues are less apparent to our fallen minds. But "less apparent" does not mean "less important."

In this sensitive and perceptive monograph, *The Spiritual Condition of Infants*, Adam Harwood, assistant professor of Christian studies at Truett-McConnell College in Georgia, is the pathfinder who leads us on a delightful journey through the maze of historical persuasions considering insights from the patristic era from such lights as Irenaeus, Cyprian, Augustine, and others. The perspectives of the famous Reformers Luther, Zwingli, and Calvin are assessed together with unique insights gleaned from radical Reformers Hubmaier and Marpeck, little-known but thoughtful contributors to this issue.

Theologians of the nineteenth and twentieth centuries, James P. Boyce, A.H. Strong, E.Y. Mullins, William Hendricks, and Millard Erickson are critical to the discussion and receive careful attention. Harwood discovers greater affinity with some of these theologians than with others, but the analysis offered is painstakingly fair and thoughtful.

Harwood is an evangelical thinker in the finest sense of the term *evangelical*. What is at stake here is not merely the spiritual state of the infant but an understanding of the evangel itself. Further, while instructed by the wisdom of the theologians of the past, terminal conclusions must be informed by the testimony of the sacred Scripture. While other texts are cited, ten texts from the Old and New Testaments are selected as the most critical assessments of themes related to the fields of biblical anthropology, hamartiology, ecclesiology, and soteriology as they impinge on the question of infants standing before God—particularly prior to what has often been delineated as an age of accountability.

Harwood's conclusion that an infant is born with a sin nature, which makes the commission of rebellious acts inevitable, though the infant as yet carries no guilt, is not unusual or novel. How he arrives at this conclusion is unique and will be convincing to many. The study is crucial not only because it seeks to determine the state of the infant prior to awareness of sin and salvation but also because its conclusion impacts questions such as infant salvation, appropriate time of baptism, comfort of grieving parents in time of loss, and the instruction of the church.

This volume fills a void in the contemporary church. Few have addressed this question at any length, and almost none have addressed it so perceptively. Theologians will profit from the book. Pastors, too, will read with great pleasure and receive guidance. Because of Harwood's lucid style, parents will enjoy his insights, and more than a few will be profoundly comforted in an hour of bereavement. Adam Harwood has blessed the church and honored the Lord in the preparation of this critical study.

Paige Patterson
Southwestern Baptist Theological Seminary

Acknowledgements

COMPLETING A RESEARCH DOCTORATE is a herculean task. My wife, Laura, is gracious and supportive. On many weeknights and Saturdays from September 2001 to December 2007, I was secluded either in the seminary library or in my office. Many nights during those six years, whether because of ministry responsibilities or academic deadlines, Laura usually put our four children (Anna, Nathan, Jonathan, and Rachel) to bed without me. This book is a revision of my Ph.D dissertation, which was written during the last two years of that period.

I am thankful for the church family at Tate Springs Baptist Church in Arlington, Texas, which encouraged, subsidized, and prayerfully supported my academic pursuits as I ministered the Word of God and shared my life with them. Bart McDonald, the pastor, and Terry Jeffries, the administrator, along with other staff members, leaders, deacons, and church members were all good friends and faithful co-laborers. It was a blessing to serve at a church which encouraged and provided ministry opportunities for seminary students. This proved beneficial to both the student and the church. God taught me at Tate Springs to love the congregation you serve.

Several professors at Southwestern Baptist Theological Seminary (SWBTS) in Fort Worth, TX, provided input at various stages of the development of the dissertation. Dr. James Leo Garrett Jr. provided assistance as I developed my prospectus. My doctoral supervisor, Dr. Paige Patterson, guided me through the process of developing, submitting, and refining the prospectus. Following the prospectus stage, he read carefully and provided detailed feedback on each chapter. Patterson has been a blessing and encouragement in my life and ministry. I am thankful and humbled that he penned a foreword for this book. Drs. Malcolm Yarnell and Thomas White both provided feedback and direction early in my research, critical and pointed feedback as committee members during the defense of my thesis, and counsel and friendship in subsequent years. Dr. Kevin Kennedy corrected my misunderstanding of a secondary source.

Dr. George Klein taught me that although I had spent eleven years with Kate Turabian's style manual, I didn't know her as well as I thought I did.

Few people read dissertations. They are filled with technical jargon, difficult sentences, and copious footnotes. In order for the content of the dissertation to be accessible to a wider audience, I needed to convert it into a readable book. As the book made this transition, I wanted to pass it by several sets of eyes. I wanted to test its readability as well as its pastoral integrity. I am thankful for the following friends who were willing to read and provide feedback on this manuscript: Jason Brown, graduate student at Southeastern Baptist Theological Seminary, Wake Forest, NC; Vernon Burger, executive director of His Voice Global, Dallas, TX; Marilyn Byrum, English teacher, Mansfield, TX; Dr. Scott Callaham, chaplain at US Naval Academy, Annapolis, MD; Dr. Dongsun Cho, professor at SWBTS, Ft. Worth, TX; Pat Findley, pastor, Hamlin Memorial Baptist Church, Springfield, MO; Laura Harwood, speech-language pathologist, Gainesville, GA; Phil Hudgins, retired newspaper editor, Gainesville, GA; Michael Staton, pastor, First Baptist Church, Mustang, OK; and Dr. Earl Waggoner, professor at Golden Gate Baptist Theological Seminary, Mill Valley, CA.

Other people read portions of the book and provided feedback as those smaller portions appeared as paper presentations at meetings of the Evangelical Theological Society or in classroom discussions where I taught theology courses at The College at Southwestern in Fort Worth, TX, or at Truett-McConnell College in Cleveland, GA. Although there have been several opportunities for people to provide feedback, suggestions, and corrections, the responsibility for the end result is—of course—mine. All of the comments above are meant to dispel the notion that this book is mine alone. I wish to share all of the credit but none of the blame. Any errors, omissions, or inaccuracies are mine alone.

I am thankful for the constant support of my parents, Jim and Kay Harwood, and mother-in-law, Betty Holland. I am grateful for the hard work invested by my copyeditor, Amy Bauman, of Bauman Wordsmiths, Oakland, CA. Thank you to Dr. K. C. Hanson and his team at Wipf & Stock, Eugene, OR.

I dedicate this book to all parents who have suffered the loss of an infant. You have walked one of the darkest of life's journeys. May the God of hope fill you with all hope, joy, and peace as you continue to trust him (Rom 15:13).

Abbreviations

ACW	Ancient Christian Writers
ANF	Ancient-Nicene Fathers
BAG	Walter Bauer, W. F. Arndt, and F. W. Gingrich, *A Greek-English Lexicon of the New Testament*, 2d. rev. ed.
BDB	F. Brown, S. R. Driver, and C. A. Briggs, *A Hebrew and English Lexicon of the Old Testament*
CHALOT	William L. Holladay, *A Concise Hebrew and Aramaic Lexicon of the Old Testament*
CR	Corpus Reformatorum
ESV	English Standard Version
ETS	Evangelical Theological Society
FC	Fathers of the Church
HCSB	Holman Christian Standard Bible
LCC	The Library of Christian Classics
LCL	Loeb Classical Library
LW	Luther's Works
LXX	Septuagint
NASB	New American Standard
NET	New English Translation
NIV	New International Version
NKJV	New King James Version
NPNF	Nicene and Post-Nicene Fathers of the Christian Church
NPNF2	Nicene and Post-Nicene Fathers of the Christian Church, Second Series
PG	Patrologiae Cursus Completus: Series Graecae
PL	Patrologia Cursus Completus: Series Latina
SWJC	Selected Works of John Calvin
TWOT	*Theological Wordbook of the Old Testament*

INTRODUCTORY SECTION

Does It Matter if Infants Are Guilty of Sin?

I REMEMBER THE HEAT of the Texas summer as I stood in a black suit at the graveside. As a church staff member, I had attended many funerals. But this was different. The casket was only two feet long. When the father knelt down to gently lay a spade of dirt on the small metal box containing the body of his two-week old son, the grief was almost unbearable. This shouldn't be, I thought. Parents shouldn't have to bury their child. And it certainly shouldn't happen twice. But three years earlier, this young couple had laid their eleven-month-old son to rest. In all, the couple has welcomed four boys into their family, but complications due to a genetic disorder claimed the second- and third-born sons. Each died before his first birthday. Fortunately God can bring healing and hope to even the darkest situations. And this family, thankfully, continues to experience God's healing, his grace, and his strength in the midst of their trial.

My wife and I have never experienced this type of tragedy in our home, but from what I have read and witnessed in the lives of our friends, few experiences are more painful or perplexing than the death of an infant. In the moments immediately following such a tragedy, the pastor can offer the family the ministry of his presence and words of love. And those parents, family, and friends can be assured that the child is with God in heaven.

But a time may come when they will be ready to talk about the deeper issues surrounding infant salvation. If they ask, "Where is my baby?" and you, as pastor, answer, "Heaven," then you need to be able to provide biblical justification. After all, as harsh as it might seem, infants are just like the rest of us in one respect: They are part of sinful humanity. And sinful humanity is separated from a holy and just God. The aim of this book is to draw attention to this issue and to survey both what we can know from the Bible and what Christian pastors and teachers throughout history have taught about the spiritual condition of infants.

The Bible presents a dilemma concerning infants. On the one hand, Gen 3 and Rom 5 detail humanity's fall into sin and the horrible legacy for subsequent generations. We all have a relationship with the first Adam, and that relationship results in our being sinners. Even before we can understand the difference between right and wrong, we are sinful people. The Bible also informs us that every person will spend the rest of eternity somewhere—either with God in heaven or apart from God in hell. Although we are all hopeless and helpless in our sin, the good news is that God did not abandon his broken creation. Instead, his son, Jesus, who was and is fully God and fully man, lived and died and was raised to provide the forgiveness of sin and to offer peace between God and man (1 Cor 15:1–4; 1 Tim 2:5–6).

But the sad part of the good news is that not everyone will be forgiven of his or her sin. Jesus spoke of a broad gate and road, which lead to destruction, and the *many* who would find them (Matt 7:13). He warned about the danger of being thrown into hell (Luke 12:5). In John 3:36, God warns that people who reject the son will not see eternal life. Evangelicals, even with the broadest definition of that term, believe that people who go to heaven will have heard, at some point in their lives, the saving message of the Gospel: that Christ died for our sins. And those people who have heard that message will have responded by turning from their sin and to Christ for salvation. Faith is a gift of God, but it must be received or recognized or somehow expressed in a person's life.

The dilemma arises when considering the death of an infant. In this book, an infant is defined as a person who is one year old or younger (including the preborn). Infants are part of sinful humanity. So, even if they don't yet *know* they are sinners, they have inherited a sinful nature, which they will inevitably and certainly act upon later in life and knowingly commit sin against God. But people who do not mature into early childhood never have a chance to hear, understand, and respond to the Gospel. It's not just that they *do not* hear and respond to the Gospel (as is the tragic case with some older children and adults); infants *cannot* hear and respond to the Gospel.

It seems wrong to think that those who die in infancy would spend eternity in hell, apart from the loving God of the Bible. But it seems equally wrong to think that the holy God of the Bible would welcome sinful people—no matter how young—into heaven. Thus, the dilemma before us: How does God welcome some, or any, sinful infants into heaven? The Bible does not explicitly answer this question. When Anabaptist leader Balthasar Hubmaier (1480–1528) was asked about the eternal destiny of unbaptized infants, he wrote, "I confess here publicly my ignorance. I am not ashamed not to know what God did not want to reveal to us with a clear and plain word."[1] Because the Bible does not directly address the issue, we can only build a case for how we think God deals with people who die in infancy.

Numerous books already have been written to address the question of infant salvation.[2] But this book is different because it deals with the spiritual condition of *living* infants. Are infants sinners, or have they only inherited a sinful *nature*? Are infants guilty of sin only because they have inherited a sinful *nature,* or must they knowingly *commit* a sinful thought or action in order to be judged a sinner by God? Are infants currently separated from God and in need of his forgiveness, or will they *become* guilty of sin the first time they become aware of the difference between right and wrong, yet choose to do wrong? Is it consistent for evangelicals to insist that some people who die in their infancy will be welcomed into heaven apart from a confession of Jesus as Lord while claiming that an adult who fails to make such a confession will be eternally lost? This is the dilemma that arises when considering the spiritual condition of infants.

What are the issues that are so difficult to reconcile? They are the sin of infants and the judgment of God. Are infants guilty of sin or not? If you believe that people need to hear and respond to the Gospel to be saved, *and* you say that infants are guilty of sin, then the consistent viewpoint is that all infants who die without hearing and responding to the Gospel will be separated from God. But almost *no* theologian says that all people who die in their infancy go to hell. Nearly all theologians hold out hope that some, or all, people who die in their infancy go to heaven. But the majority of those theologians also say that infants are guilty of sin. That means we're left with this inscrutable situation in which a person seeks to align his doctrinal system so that it can maintain both unconfessed guilt and entrance into heaven. That's not easy.

1. Hubmaier, *On the Christian Baptism*, 140.

2. See, as examples: Hayford, *I'll Hold You in Heaven*; Lightner, *Safe in the Arms of Jesus*; McDavid, *Infant Salvation*; MacArthur, *Safe*; Nash, *When A Baby Dies*; Warfield, *The Development of the Doctrine of Infant Salvation*; Webb, *The Theology of Infant Salvation*.

Let me illustrate for you the difficulties that resulted when one theologian tried to make sense of the issue. Ronald Nash was a well-respected theologian and philosopher who taught at Christian colleges and seminaries for forty years and authored more than thirty books. He attempts to deal with this difficult subject in his 1999 popular work entitled *When a Baby Dies*. Nash insists that infants are guilty because of their sinful *nature*.[3] So, infants are guilty. However, Nash writes that "divine judgment is administered on the basis of sins committed in the body." He cited as an example 1 Cor 6:9–10, which includes sexual sins and notes that this *excludes* infants.[4] Because God judges sinful actions, which exclude infants, they are *not* guilty. However, he writes, infants are guilty due to their sinful *nature*. So, infants *are* guilty. Nash cites David Russell, who notes that infants don't know the difference between good and evil and are incapable of personal sin.[5] Nash also cites John Cumming, who argues that the indictments of Romans 1 are "clearly dealing with responsible adults."[6] So, infants are *not* guilty. What we see is that this otherwise consistent and clear theologian and philosopher insists that infants are at the same time guilty before God and *do* need to be saved but will *not* be judged.[7] How can a person be judged when, at the very same time, he will *not* be judged? As Nash's analysis demonstrates, this is not a simple topic.

Before turning to the relevant passages in the Bible and summarizing the views of various pastors and teachers throughout church history, it is important to draw figurative lines in the sand that identify what I do mean and what I don't mean. In the next chapter, I'll attempt to articulate those doctrinal boundaries.

3. Nash, *When a Baby Dies*, 20–21.

4. Ibid., 60–61.

5. Russell, *Infant Salvation*, 47, cited in Nash, 62.

6. Cumming, *Infant Salvation*, 36, cited in Nash, 63.

7. Nash, 87–100.

2

What Are the Boundaries?

IN MY JUNIOR HIGH school years, I remember playing football and other tackling games with kids in my Beaufort, South Carolina, neighborhood. Besides being one of the slower and less-coordinated kids in the neighborhood, I was also frustrated at times by boundary disputes. I would think I had made a touchdown only to have it called back because a player on the opposing team claimed I had stepped out of bounds. As we players would talk it over, it would become clear that the two teams had begun to play before clearly marking the boundaries of play. In order for any game to be competitive and fun, I now see, all of the players should agree on the boundaries: you're out if you step here or here or here, you score a goal by crossing this line, etc.

In a similar way, I want to mark out our boundaries of play for this study of the spiritual condition of infants. To do this, I'll state some assumptions to clarify what I mean and what I don't mean. My assumptions are these:

1. A person is a person no matter how small.[1]

2. Infants have a sinful nature because of their descent from the first Adam.

3. God can welcome infants with a sinful nature into heaven.

4. If number 3 occurs, then it is through the person and the work of Christ.

Let's look at these four assumptions more closely:

A person is a person no matter how small. If the Bible does not clearly address the spiritual condition of an infant, then why does it matter?

---

1. I am indebted to Theodore Geisel for this clever phrase, which was a repeated line in the 2008 movie *Horton Hears a Who* (20th Century Fox).

Two reasons. First, every child, including those who have not yet been born, is made in the image of God. Second, every child, again including the preborn, has a soul. If for those two reasons alone, the spiritual condition of infants is a matter of eternal significance. And it matters for a large swath of humanity.

The number of people throughout history who never made it to age one is not certain, but the possible number is staggering.[2] If you affirm that human life begins at the moment of conception, then you must view every fertilized ova as a person. Sadly lives can be lost in many ways within the first several months of conception:

- A fertilized ovum may never have been implanted in the walls of the uterus.

- A fertilized ovum may have been implanted, but the pregnancy still results in a miscarriage.

- An abortion is medically induced.

After birth, infants face many dangers outside of the womb, including sudden infant death syndrome (SIDS) and a high infant-mortality rate in countries with limited medical access. The tragic upshot is that many people do not make it out of infancy. Bioethicist Gilbert Meilander estimates that the majority of people who are conceived do not live beyond their infant years.[3] Whatever the actual numbers, because every person is created in the image of God and has a soul, then the spiritual condition of infants is worthy of consideration.

Infants have a sinful nature because of their descent from the first Adam. In this section, I will rule out Pelagianism, which is the false idea that infants are sinless. From the moment of conception, infants have an inherited sinful nature. I'm not talking about *guilt*, only sin. Infants do not inherit guilt.

Pelagianism was named after the British monk Pelagius. He was accused of teaching that people are born without sin. To keep man from

---

2. Conservative estimates in 2010 of the number of infant deaths in our country due to abortion since Roe v. Wade (1973) begin at forty million people. Those are conservative estimates and only count abortions in the United States. Abortions occur worldwide and occurred before 1973. That figure of forty million people does not count the millions of miscarriages and stillbirths worldwide that have occurred throughout the thousands of years of recorded human history.

3. Meilander, *Bioethics*, 30.

wrongly blaming God for his sin, Pelagius argued that people do not receive from Adam an organic transmission of sin, but an example of disobedience.[4] Consequently, he reasoned, people could avoid committing sin, and Augustine (354–430) was right in arguing that Pelagius was wrong.[5] Councils of bishops were inconsistent in dealing with Pelagius. One group of bishops condemned his teachings in Carthage in 410; another group acquitted him in 415 in Lydda; still another in 418 issued a decree against his teachings.

This study affirms the condemnation of Pelagianism. The Bible is clear that Jesus is the only person among all of humanity who is without sin. All other people are sinful. I do not attempt to argue that infants are sinless. I will attempt, however, to show that infants inherit a sinful nature and later acquire their own guilt after they know the difference between right and wrong but knowingly choose to do wrong. This view operates under the umbrella of Christian orthodoxy, and we will see this view in the writings of some Greek fathers and, more recently, among groups such as Methodists and Baptists. Pelagianism was condemned not because of a denial of inherited guilt but because of a denial of inherited sin. Pelagian said that infants are sinless, and this view has rightly been rejected by Christians for 1,600 years.

God can welcome infants with a sinful nature into heaven. The conviction that God saves people who die in their infancy is nearly the universal response given by Christian leaders to Christian parents in a pastoral setting. And rightly so. The difficulty lies in developing the theology behind this conviction while maintaining fidelity to Scripture's clear declarations of God's wrath and judgment against sinful humanity. How does God receive sinful people to himself (even infants) who have not yet heard the message of the Gospel? The question of the eternal destiny of people who die in their infancy strongly correlates to similar questions about people who are mentally incompetent—and unevangelized adults. Although interesting, I will not attempt to develop these related issues. Instead, I'll simply state my conviction that infants and the mentally incompetent are probably in the same spiritual condition, which is sinful, not guilty. Unevangelized adults, however, are both sinful and guilty. The difference is not whether these groups have access to the message of the

4. Hall, *Learning Theology with the Church Fathers*, 134.
5. Nash, *When A Baby Dies*, 43–44.

gospel, but whether or not they have knowingly acted out of their sinful nature.[6]

Universalism is the wrong idea that all will finally be saved by God in Christ. Origen was condemned for his view of Apokatastasis,[7] which he expressed in *On First Principles*. More recently, Karl Barth taught that God fully accomplished the universal reconciliation of himself to man through Christ.[8] Evangelicals do not affirm the ultimate salvation of all humanity.[9] At this point, a distinction should be made. It is possible to argue a universal salvation among all people who die in their infancy. That is not the idea that is being rejected. What is being rejected is the idea that all who die as infants will be saved because every person, regardless of age or religious conviction or election by God, will finally be granted eternal salvation by God. If God saves all who die in their infancy, then it could be for any number of reasons, but not simply because infants are numbered among the human race. Universalism should be rejected as a solution to the questions of infant salvation and the spiritual condition of infants.

Another proposal that must be rejected when considering the eternal destiny of infants is the concept of a postmortem opportunity for salvation. In his effort to insist on the need for an infant to exercise personal faith, Baptist theologian A. H. Strong (1836–1921) identified the time of an infant's opportunity for salvation as after its death. He wrote, "(S)ince there is no evidence that children dying in infancy are regenerated prior to death, either with or without the use of external means, it seems most probable that the work of regeneration may be performed by the Spirit in connection with the infant soul's first view of Christ in the other world."[10] Nearly a century later, another Baptist (or former Baptist) theologian, Clark Pinnock, would speculate that people who die in their infancy are "given time to grow up and mature, so then a decision can be made."[11]

6. For more on the accessibilism and the relationship among infants, mentally incompetent people, and unevangelized adults, see Tiessen, *Who Can Be Saved?*

7. For more on Origen's view of *Apokatastasis*, see Harmon, *Every Knee Should Bow*.

8. Barth, *The Humanity of God*, 60–62.

9. For seven theories, or varieties, of Universalism, see Erickson, *Christian Theology*, 1025–27.

10. Strong, *Systematic Theology*, 663.

11. Pinnock, *A Wideness in God's Mercy*, 168.

Yet another Baptist, Millard Erickson (b. 1932) disagrees. He appeals to the "chasm" mentioned in the parable of the rich man and Lazarus (Luke 16:19–31) in order to reject a postmortem opportunity for salvation.[12] In the parable, Abraham explains to the rich man that people are unable to cross over the chasm from one side to the other. Ronald Nash cited that passage, as well as Heb 9:27 and Rev 20:11–13, when he wrote, "Postmortem judgment is based on premortem conditions." In other words, judgment after death is based on the life lived before death. Nash also writes, "Physical death marks the boundary of human opportunity for salvation."[13] Canadian professor of theology and ethics Terrance Tiessen argues that his view is different from that of Strong or Pinnock. He believes infants meet Christ at death rather than after death.[14] But this nuanced difference does not keep his view from being placed in the same general category. All varieties of postmortem opportunity for salvation should be rejected.

If God does welcome infants into heaven, then it is through the person and the work of Christ. Every person needs to hear and respond to the message of the gospel. Even if you disagree with my attempt to distinguish between an infant's sinful nature and his guilt, then I trust that you will still be able to affirm that my positions on sin and salvation conform to the historic, orthodox Christian statements of faith.

In the Bible, God declares that we are all sinners who are separated from God and dead in our sin. But the good news—the gospel—is that while we were still sinners and without hope, Christ died for us (Rom 5:8). His death is the only death that would satisfy God's righteous wrath against us. Jesus gave himself as our substitute and became sin for us so that we might be made right with God (2 Cor 5:21; 1 Peter 2:24). That good news is better than good news. It is *great* news. God calls people to himself and calls them to repent of their sin and turn to him. He gives them the ability to believe and to call on him and to respond to his offer of salvation. And all who call on the name of the Lord will be saved (Rom 10:13). Believers have been saved by God's grace alone through faith alone in Christ alone (Eph 2:8–10; Titus 3:4–5). In addition to loving God with all of their heart (Matt 22:37), believers are called to tell the

---

12. Erickson, *Christian Theology*, 1027.

13. Nash, *When A Baby Dies*, 43–44.

14. See Tiessen, *Who Can Be Saved?*, 216–29.

nations—and all people—of God's grace and forgiveness, which are available through the sacrificial death, burial, and resurrection of Jesus Christ. All people need to hear the message of the cross—the Gospel—because it is the power of God for salvation (Rom 1:16; 1 Cor 1:18). But what about infants? Are all of these affirmations about sin and salvation true in every way about infants—who seem to be a special case? In the next chapter, I'll present and examine Wayne Grudem's proposals for understanding what we can know from the Bible about the special case of infants.

3

Grudem's Tentative Solution

IT WAS JANUARY 2006, and I picked up my ringing kitchen phone. On the other end, was a theology professor who was serving as the chairman of the upcoming regional meeting of the Evangelical Theological Society (ETS). He was calling because I had submitted a paper proposal for that meeting entitled, "Grudem on Infant Guilt: A Critique of Wayne Grudem's Proposed Solution to the Dilemma of Inherited Guilt for People Who Die in Infancy." Because my paper disagreed with Grudem at certain points, the chairman called to clarify my position.

"Do you know that Grudem will be a main speaker at this meeting?"

I replied that I did.

"And do you know that he might sit in and listen to your paper presentation?"

I told him that I hoped so because I would love the chance to interact with him and hear his feedback on my critique. I assured the chairman that I had a great deal of respect for Dr. Grudem and would maintain a peaceable attitude when discussing those points on which we might disagree.

Although I had not met Wayne Grudem before 2006, he had already mentored me for a decade through his book, *Systematic Theology*. This was the first systematic theology on which I cut my teeth as a young believer. I appreciate Grudem's high view of God, his dependence on the Scripture for his theological formulations, and the usefulness of his work for the church. As a Bible study teacher, an associate pastor, and now as a college professor, I have often used his book as a reference to guide me through difficult theological issues. So I approached this meeting as an opportunity to interact with a man whom I held—and continue to hold—

in high regard. But Dr. Grudem and I disagree on the matter of inherited guilt. In this chapter, we'll look at this issue more closely.

IS INHERITED SIN ALSO INHERITED GUILT?

Wayne Grudem begins to deal in his *Systematic Theology* with the spiritual condition of infants in his chapter on sin. He does this when he defines sin as *"any failure to conform to the moral law of God in act, attitude, or nature."*[1] People fail to obey God's laws by both their sinful *actions* and their sinful *nature*. Next, Grudem considers the doctrine of inherited sin, but he begins his examination with a subsection entitled, "Inherited Guilt: We Are Counted Guilty Because of Adam's Sin." It is precisely this leap from inherited *sin* to inherited *guilt* that I question.

There are some difficulties that accompany the view that humans inherit not only the *sin* but also the *guilt* of Adam. But before dealing with these difficulties, one question must first be asked: What is the basis for the view that humans inherit Adam's guilt?

The view that God considers all humans to be guilty of sin because of our relationship to Adam is an Augustinian-Calvinist viewpoint. Whether the view is Augustinian or Calvinist depends on whether you view humanity's relationship with Adam as either seminal or federal. The seminal view of union with Adam (also known as the Augustinian or the realistic view) teaches that all humans existed in Adam seminally because he was the first person and the head of the human race. Stated another way, seminalism depends on the understanding that the human race existed in the loins of Adam; therefore, the human race is guilty of sin because we were present in him when he committed that first sin in the garden of Eden.

Another view of union with Adam is federalism (also known as the Calvinist or representative view). The federal view teaches that Adam acted as our representative, and so human beings are counted guilty not because we were seminally present in Adam but because Adam acted as the representative of the human race.[2]

According to seminalism, all people are naturally generated of Adam and therefore possess both a corrupt nature and the guilt of Adam's original sin. In federalism, Adam was the representative of humanity and was

1. Grudem, *Systematic Theology*, 490. Italics his.
2. Murray, *The Imputation of Adam's Sin*, 24–40.

guilty of sin, and for that reason every person is guilty. Grudem blends seminalism and federalism into an Augustinian-Calvinist mix when he explains: "When Adam sinned, God thought of all who would descend from Adam as sinners." He says also, "As our representative, Adam sinned, and God counted us guilty as well as Adam."[3]

In the Augustinian-Calvinist view, all people are guilty of Adam's sin either because Adam is their ancestor (seminal view) or because Adam is their representative (federal view). Either way, the words of Rom 5:12b, "death spread to all men, because all sinned"[4] are to be understood in the following way: all people are guilty before God and under the judgment of death because of the sin of Adam. Certain difficulties present themselves for the Augustinian-Calvinist view when one considers the nature of sin and God's judgment. Does the Bible convey the idea that guilt before God is a thing that is passed on at conception (seminalism), a status that we hold due to the actions of another person (federalism), or as our willful disobedience against God in thought, attitude, or action? The Bible seems to present the view that guilt before God is a result of willful disobedience against him rather than simply inheriting guilt or being represented by a guilty person. In the Bible, does God usually judge a person for the sins of another person or for his own sinful thoughts, attitudes, and actions? For this study, the question is this: Will God hold me responsible and guilty for the sins of the first Adam or for my own sins?

ROMANS 5:12

Grudem quotes Rom 5:12 as follows: "Therefore . . . sin came into the world through one man and death through sin, and so death spread to all men because all sinned." He then explains that "through the sin of Adam 'all men sinned.'" In a footnote, he appeals to the aorist verb form of the word translated "sinned" (*hēmarton*) as evidence that the sin of all humanity was a "completed past action." He explains, "Paul must be meaning that when Adam sinned, God considered it true that all men sinned in Adam."[5]

---

3. Grudem, *Systematic Theology*, 494–95.

4. Unless otherwise noted, all biblical quotations in this book have been taken from the New American Standard Bible (NASB).

5. Grudem, *Systematic Theology*, 494 n. 9.

Grudem's grammatical argument concerning the verb tense of *hēmarton* in Rom 5:12 is very much like that of John Murray. Although Murray retired from Westminster Theological Seminary shortly before Grudem began his work there as a student, Murray had taught theology there for nearly forty years. In *The Imputation of Adam's Sin*, Murray argues that the aorist form of *hēmarton* is evidence that Paul viewed in the sin of Adam the sin of all humanity. Murray objects to the "Romish interpretation" that sinfulness is passed on to children by parents at conception because passing on sinfulness involves present action, but *hēmarton* must be understood to be an historical aorist, referring to a "once-for-all historical inception."[6]

The grammatical presupposition that forms the basis of both Murray and Grudem's theological conclusions is based on a narrow understanding of the aorist verb tense. This kind of interpretation was exposed as inadequate in a 1972 article written by Frank Stagg. In the article, Stagg challenges the view that was often espoused by pastors and theologians that the aorist tense always refers to either a single action or a once-for-all action. He provides examples from the New Testament that support his claim that the verb "can properly be used to cover any kind of action: single or multiple, momentary or extended, broken or unbroken, completed or open-ended." Stagg explains that the aorist "simply points to an action without describing it."[7] Stagg is not alone in his view of the aorist verb tense. Dallas Theological Seminary Department Chair and Professor of New Testament Studies Buist M. Fanning writes that the aorist tense "presents an occurrence in summary, viewed as a whole from the outside, without regard for the internal make-up of the occurrence."[8] The observations of those two New Testament professors are cited to suggest that the case for an Augustinian-Calvinist reading of Rom 5:12 cannot be based on the verb tense alone.

Murray and Grudem's theological conclusions are based in part but not in full on this particular view of the aorist. Grudem also argues that Paul wrote that death came because all men sinned (completed past action). But because not every person had been born (much less sinned) at the point of Paul's writing, Paul must have meant that all men sinned

6. Murray, *The Imputation of Adam's Sin*, 15–16.

7. Stagg, "The Abused Aorist," 222–32. I am grateful to Paige Patterson for bringing this article to my attention.

8. Fanning, *Verbal Aspects in New Testament Greek*, 97.

in Adam's sin.[9] If, however, the aorist tense does not necessarily refer to a completed past action, then the Augustinian-Calvinism is not the only possible view.

Elaine Pagels the Harrington Spear Paine Professor of Religion at Princeton University, explains the historical situation of Augustine's misreading of the phrase *eph' hō* as "in whom" rather than "in that" or "because" in Rom 5:12. She writes, "Augustine read the passage in Latin, and so either ignored or was unaware of the connotations of the Greek original; and thus he misread the last phrase as referring to Adam. Augustine insisted that it meant that 'death came upon all men, *in whom* all sinned.'" She contrasts that view with John Chrysostom and argues that it was Augustine's view of sin and death that was in the minority at the time.[10]

So, it is possible to understand from Rom 5:12 that sin entered the world through one man, Adam, but that men die not because of the sin of Adam but because of *their own* acts of sin. Consider the verse again with such an interpretation in mind: "Therefore...sin came into the world through one man and death through sin, and so death spread to all men because all sinned."

Even if the arguments above cast some doubt on Grudem's reading of Rom 5:12, it is important to note that a doctrine of inherited guilt due to all of humanity sinning in Adam *can* be construed apart from appealing to the aorist form of *hēmarton*.

GRUDEM RAISES AND ANSWERS THE FAIRNESS OBJECTION

Grudem ends his section on inherited guilt by raising and then answering the objection that it is not fair for God to hold people responsible for the sin of Adam. Grudem offers three statements in reply. First, those who object to inheriting Adam's guilt have committed actual sins, for which God could hold that person responsible. Second, it is not a conclusive argument to state that if another person would have been in Adam's place, he too would have rebelled against God. Third, it is equally unfair for Adam's sin to be imputed to us as it is for Christ's righteousness to be imputed to us.[11]

---

9. Grudem, *Systematic Theology*, 494, n. 9. Italics mine.

10. Pagels, *Adam, Eve, and the Serpent*, 109. See also Pelikan, *The Christian Tradition*, 299, and Fitzmyer, *Romans*, 413–16.

11. Grudem, *Systematic Theology*, 495.

I agree with Grudem's first responses to the objections he offers. It is true that people do have *actual* sins for which they are guilty—even if they don't like being linked in their *nature* with Adam. I also agree with Grudem that arguing how we would or would not act if we were in Adam's place is difficult to prove either way. I also agree that Christians would be wise to seek God's justice rather than fairness. God's justice, for example, allows him to accept the death of Jesus Christ as propitiation for sin (Rom 3:24–25). A simple appeal to fairness would mean that the innocent are saved and the guilty are punished. In that system, guilty people cannot be forgiven of their sin.

In addition to these arguments that Grudem has raised against inherited guilt, it is important to consider Ezek 18:20. This verse is clear: The soul who sins dies. So a person is not held responsible for the sins of *another* person, but only for *his own* transgressions. That means that a person would not be held guilty for the sin of Adam in the same way that he is not held guilty for the sin of his parents or grandparents. Are there consequences of the sins of others that can affect us? Yes. But that is not the same thing as being counted guilty of sin solely because of the actions of another person.

Although I agree with Grudem that those who reject inherited guilt also commit actual sins, that logic runs into difficulty because it necessarily excludes infants. Exactly what kind of actual sin can an infant commit?

I agree with Grudem that it is equally unfair for us to be represented by Christ as it is to be represented by Adam. It is at this point that the insights of Baptist theologian Millard Erickson are helpful. Erickson discerns a need to understand Rom 5 in a way that incorporates human ratification of the actions of both representatives in order to avoid universalism. In other words, if Grudem's view is correct that all inherit Adam's guilt, then all should inherit Christ's righteousness. If, however, it is necessary for humans to *ratify* the work of Christ by *appropriating* the salvation offered by Christ, then it is likewise necessary to ratify the sin of Adam in order to fall under condemnation and guilt. Consider the following explanation offered by Erickson: "Until the first conscious or responsible moral action or decision by a person, there is no imputation of the Adamic sin, just as there is no imputation of Christ's righteousness until there is a conscious acceptance of that work."[12] Erickson demonstrates that passive acceptance of the imputation of Adam's sin raises difficulties for maintaining an exclusivist view of salvation. When asked for further comment to the critique of his view of infants, Grudem stated the following to me in an e-mail: "I think it's possible that God imputes guilt to every person, even all infants, but that he only imputes Christ's forgiveness to those who are elect. This then does not lead to universalism."[13]

Grudem ends his section on inherited guilt with the admission that not all evangelicals hold to his Augustinian view of inherited guilt. Arminians, for example, reject inherited guilt. He concedes, though, that all evangelicals "agree that we receive a sinful disposition or a tendency to sin as an inheritance from Adam."[14]

INHERITED CORRUPTION

Grudem's next section is entitled, "Inherited Corruption: We Have a Sinful Nature Because of Adam's Sin." He explains that humans inherit a sinful nature because of Adam's sin. He quotes Ps 51:5, "Behold, I was brought forth in iniquity, and in sin did my mother conceive me" as David's way of explaining that "even before he was born, he had a sinful disposition." Grudem writes, "Here is a strong statement of the inherent tendency to sin that attaches to our lives from the very beginning." As further evidence for this point, Eph 2:3 affirms that "we were by nature children of wrath."[15] In both our nature and our actions, we lack any spiritual good and are unable to perform any spiritual good before God.[16]

Although infants display a "tendency to sin," that does not necessarily mean that infants are guilty of sin. Consider, for example, the assessment of Stanley Grenz: "Consequently, although all persons inherit a sinful disposition, only those who have given expression to the fallen nature through wrong choices stand under condemnation. The sentence falls only on those whose deeds mark them as guilty. On this basis, we

---

12. Erickson, *How Shall They Be Saved?*, 250.

13. E-mail dated 19 July 2006.

14. Grudem, *Systematic Theology*, 496.

15. Ibid.

16. Ibid., 497.

conclude that persons who do not develop the moral potential do not fall under the eternal condemnation of the righteous God."[17]

In his 1987 Dallas Theological Seminary dissertation, Thomas Cragoe argues that infants are guilty of sin because of their *nature,* although the Bible teaches that God judges people according to their *actions.* Nash and Grudem make the same argument.[18] Grudem suggests that because infants have not yet committed sinful actions for which to be judged, their sinful nature alone must be the basis of God's judgment against them. But if the Bible addresses God judging only the sinful *actions* of people—not their nature—and if infants are not yet responsible, moral agents, then is it appropriate to assign guilt to infants who possess only an inherited sinful nature?

GUILTY INFANTS

In the preceding subsections, I have attempted to establish Grudem's doctrine of sin, which forms the basis of his position on the spiritual condition of infants. In his next section, "Actual Sins in Our Lives," Grudem asks and answers the following question: "Are Infants Guilty Before They Commit Actual Sins?" He begins by noting Erickson's argument for the age of responsibility, or age of accountability, but quickly dismisses it. Grudem writes that "even before birth, children have a guilty standing before God and a sinful nature that not only gives them a tendency to sin but also causes God to view them as 'sinners.'"[19]

Grudem acknowledges that the biblical texts that refer to the judgment of sin refer to a person's *actions* rather than his *nature.* Further, people who die in or prior to infancy have not acted in ways that would bring God's judgment. So, Grudem reasons, the basis for God's judgment against an infant are those Scriptures that refer to a sinful *nature* (such as Ps 51:5 and Eph 2:3) rather than those that refer to sinful *actions.*[20]

Grudem's logic, then, is as follows: The Scriptures that speak of God's final judgment of the human race refer to his judgment of actions. People who die in infancy cannot be judged sinful according to their actions, so

17. Grenz, *Theology for the Community of God,* 209.

18. See Cragoe, "An Examination of the Issues of Infant Salvation," 77; Nash, *When a Baby Dies,* 60–61; and Grudem, *Systematic Theology,* 499–500.

19. Grudem, *Systematic Theology,* 499.

20. Ibid., 499–500.

God will judge them to be sinful according to their nature. Wouldn't a better conclusion, though, be that the basis of God's judgment on people who die in infancy is the same as those who die later in life, their sinful thoughts, attitudes, and actions?

Grudem's commitment to Augustinian-Calvinism leads him to include the sinful nature in his understanding of God's judgment of sin, rather than only sinful thoughts, attitudes, and actions, which he acknowledges as the explicit teaching of Scripture. Grudem follows Murray in his grammatical understanding of *hēmarton* in Rom 5:12, that people die because of Adam's sin rather than because of their own sin. This is one possible way, but not the only way to understand this important verse. Another challenge to Grudem's view comes from Erickson's suggestion that one must ratify the work of Adam in order to become guilty in the same way that one must ratify the work of Christ in order to be redeemed. A final difficulty with Grudem's position is that if God judges people for their sinful actions, then why would he alter his standard in order to judge infants, who have no condemnable actions, according to their nature?

GRUDEM ON INFANT SALVATION

The Prebirth Salvation of Guilty Infants

After establishing their sinful nature as the basis for God's judgment, Grudem asks if those who die in infancy can be saved. He begins by stating that if infants are saved, such an event would be due to the work of Christ and regeneration by the Holy Spirit, not infants' innocence or their own righteousness. Grudem makes an interesting move at this point. He writes that "it certainly is possible for God to bring regeneration (that is, new spiritual life) to an infant even *before* he or she is born."[21] He then cites two unique people as examples, John the Baptist, who would be filled with the Holy Spirit in his mother's womb (Luke 1:15) and David, who is quoted in Ps 22:10 as stating, "Since my mother bore me you have been my God." Then Grudem states the following: "It is clear, therefore, that God is able to save infants in an unusual way, apart from their hearing and understanding the gospel, by bringing regeneration to them very early, sometimes even before birth." Although he is careful to provide the disclaimer that "this is not the usual way for God to save people," Grudem

---

21. Grudem, *Systematic Theology*, 500. Emphasis mine.

does state that since God brought salvation to John the Baptist before he heard the gospel and trusted Christ, such a transaction could occur more often. He writes, "And this leads us to conclude that it certainly is possible that God would also do this where he knows the infant will die before hearing the gospel."[22]

It is surprising that Grudem would cite as examples for normative Christian experience David—the one God had chosen to rule over all of Israel and Judah—and John the Baptist, the forerunner of the Christ who was miraculously born to a barren senior adult. The lives of David and John the Baptist were unique. Sadly the death of infants is not unique. Every day infants die without a chance to hear and respond to the gospel. In what way do the unusual circumstances surrounding the lives of King David and John the Baptist lead us to believe that God would in the same way fill many infants with his Spirit? Does it matter that to support the idea that God saves people who die in their infancy, Grudem uses the biblical examples of King David and John the Baptist, neither of which died in their infancy but in their adult years?

The Pre-Confession Salvation of Guilty Infants

Surprisingly, Grudem allows for some people to come into relationship with God apart from confessing an explicit faith in Christ. Rather than simply appealing to election, which is a common move among many evangelicals, Grudem writes that infants "show an instinctive trust in their mothers and awareness of themselves as persons distinct from their mothers. Thus we should not insist that it is impossible that they would also have an intuitive awareness of God, and if God gives it, *an intuitive ability to trust in God* as well."[23] It would have been less problematic for him to argue that people who die in infancy are part of the elect. In that way, there would be no reason to suggest that infants can somehow place their faith in God. By arguing for an intuitive ability to trust God, Grudem apparently is attempting to preserve the idea that a person needs to trust God rather than simply affirming that those who die in infancy are part of a chosen group. The resulting problem is that now these infants are said to be trusting God without confessing Christ. This conclusion would support the position of the inclusivist, who similarly argues that

22. Ibid.

23. Grudem, *Systematic Theology*, 500 n. 19. Emphasis mine.

God saves adults who died before they had a chance to hear the gospel.[24] Grudem is clear at other times, though, that people are saved only when they hear (or read) and respond to the gospel of Christ.[25]

If infants and adults share a sinful condition because they have inherited Adam's guilt, then they are sinners by nature (even if infants have not yet committed actual sins) and both infants and adults who die apart from explicit faith in Christ should die in their sin. If an exception is to be made for infants who die without hearing and responding to the gospel, then why would such an exception not be made for the man who dies without hearing and responding to the gospel? Do the infant and the one who has no exposure to the gospel not possess the same "intuitive ability to trust in God?"

Some Infants Will Likely Not Be Saved

Grudem is careful to base his justifications for both an infant's guilt and hope for salvation on biblical grounds. Also he is in a minority of scholars who either imply or state that some people who die in infancy will or might end up in hell. Consider his following comment: "Regarding the children of unbelievers who die at a very early age Scripture is silent. We simply leave that matter in the hands of God and trust him to be both just and merciful."[26] So, Grudem affirms both inherited guilt and a Christian parent's hope for his infant's salvation but indicates that non-Christian parents of those who die in infancy lack such an assurance.

24. An inclusivist believes that some are included by God in salvation through Jesus Christ even apart from explicit knowledge of or acknowledgment of him during their lifetime. For a defense of inclusivism, see Pinnock, "An Inclusivist View," 93–123.

25. Consider, for example, the following statements of Grudem in *Systematic Theology*: "The necessity of Scripture means that the Bible is necessary for knowing the gospel." (116); "The conclusion is that saving faith comes by hearing (that is, by hearing the gospel message), and this hearing of the gospel message comes about through the preaching of Christ. The implication seems to be that without hearing the preaching of the gospel of Christ, no one can be saved." (117); also, Grudem argues that "it is fair of God to condemn people who have never heard of Christ" (117 n. 3). Grudem makes exclusivist statements about the gospel but allows infants to be saved in an inclusivist manner, in which they are saved without hearing and responding to the gospel.

26. Ibid., 501.

The Household Sanctification of Guilty Infants

Without using the phrase, Grudem advocates a view of household sanctification. After making a qualification that the Bible is silent on the issue,
he cites twelve verses of Scripture in support of the following statement:
"(I)t is God's frequent pattern throughout Scripture to save the children
of those who believe in him." Although some children of believers grow
up to reject the Lord, God normally brings these children to himself. For
that reason, it seems reasonable to Grudem that God would deal in the
same way with the children of believers who die in their infancy.[27]

Although Grudem disagrees with his view being characterized as
one of household sanctification,[28] his view bears striking resemblance to
the belief. First, Grudem's view holds that many children of Christian parents experience salvation as a result of their birth into a particular family.
Two of the twelve passages cited are Gen 7:1 and Heb 11:7, which recount
God's command for Noah and his "household" to enter the ark and the
subsequent experience of "the salvation of his household." Another passage that Grudem cites in support of his view is 1 Cor 7:14, a classic text
used to defend the practice of infant baptism. The verse is as follows: "For
the unbelieving husband is sanctified through his wife, and the unbelieving wife is sanctified through her believing husband; for otherwise your
children are unclean, but now they are holy." The argument on that issue
can go something like this: An infant is not able to make a confession of
faith in Christ. So, an infant with Christian parents is sanctified by the
faith of his parents.

Space constraints do not allow for the examination of the other nine
verses,[29] but Grudem's assertion is that, as a whole, they support the view
that God normally brings believers' children to saving faith later in life, so
the same can be inferred for believers' children who die in their infancy.

Grudem combines David's confession that he will one day go to his
infant son (2 Sam 12:23) with David's expectation that he himself eventually will be with the Lord in heaven (Ps 23:6) as evidence that believers will see their deceased infant children in heaven. Although Grudem
states that the condition of unbelievers' infant children is not explicitly

---

27. Ibid., 500.

28. Grudem, Response.

29. The nine verses are as follows: Josh 2:18; Ps 103:17; John 4:53; Acts 2:39; 11:14(?);
16:31; 18:8; 1 Cor 1:16; Titus 1:6. Grudem questions the contribution of Acts 11:14 for
this issue and even includes the question mark in his list of supporting verses.

addressed in Scripture, Grudem trusts God to be "just and merciful." He goes further when he writes of those from unsaved households who die in their infancy, "If they are saved, it will be on the basis of Christ's redeeming work," and, like the prebirth regeneration of John the Baptist, it "will be by God's mercy and grace."[30] Although Grudem clearly stated that all infants inherit guilt and therefore God's condemnation, he seems unwilling to declare that God's judgment will actually occur among infants—even in the case of an infant who dies in a household of unbelievers.

IMPLICATIONS OF GRUDEM'S VIEW

Grudem's views of infant guilt and salvation have important implications for the doctrine of salvation. It must be asked, "If God will save the infant who dies without having a chance to hear and respond to the Gospel, then will he likewise save the man who also dies without having a chance to hear and respond to the gospel?" It seems that Grudem allows for infants to have an unconscious faith. In his view, infants possess a saving faith apart from their own awareness of such faith. He provides the following three arguments to bolster this view: the prebirth salvation of guilty infants, the preconfession salvation of guilty infants, and the household sanctification of guilty infants.[31] In all three instances, the hope of heaven is held out for an infant who is allegedly guilty of a sinful nature (he admits that infants do not commit actual sins) and therefore under God's condemnation.

Next, Grudem's view of household sanctification seems to allow for salvation by physical birth rather than by receiving, or believing, in, Christ. In this way, his view seems to allow an exception to the teaching of Scripture, such as John 1:12–13, which states, "But as many as received Him, to them He gave the right to become children of God, even to those who believe in His name, who were born, not of blood nor of the will of the flesh nor of the will of man, but of God." According to that verse, a person who has been born of God has received Jesus and believed in him. I doubt that anyone would argue that an infant can knowingly receive and believe in Jesus. If you argue that an infant can unknowingly receive and believe in Jesus, then you are arguing for an inclusivist soteriology.

30. Grudem, *Systematic Theology*, 501.

31. Unconscious faith and the phrases to describe his three arguments are my terms, not the terms of Grudem.

Other passages that deal with the justification of a person and mention confession, repentance, or belief include John 3:16, Acts 2:38, and Rom 10:9–10.

The present topic has significant implications for people who attempt to comfort parents who have lost children due to miscarriage, abortion, or other untimely deaths in infancy. Grudem's position can provide comfort for Christian parents but not for those who are lost at the time of the infant's death. Some of the possible pastoral difficulties are listed below.

If only one spouse was a believer, then would the entire household be sanctified? What if unbelieving parents lost a child in infancy and, as a result of that grief, they later came to a saving faith in Christ? Will they see that infant in heaven? Also, at what point should a child place his faith in Christ? Certainly there is some point when household sanctification ends. If not, then that child could live until the age of 55 and still have the hope of heaven. A sanctification that ends, resulting in a child being found at a later date under the condemnation of God seems to equate to some kind of age of accountability, which is an idea that Grudem rejects. A final problem with this view of household sanctification is the following situation: An infant from an unbeliever's home who dies as a result of an abortion ends up in hell, but an infant from a Christian home who dies in a similar way ends up in heaven. Is it just that infants are either condemned or redeemed depending on the corresponding unbelief or belief of their parents?

Wayne Grudem's tentative solution to the question of the spiritual state of those who die in infancy is that infants are guilty sinners due to Adam's sin, but if they die before hearing and responding to the gospel, they can likely be saved by God's grace. This is especially likely if they have Christian parents.[32] After stating that "all men sinned in Adam" and all are counted "guilty because of Adam's sin,"[33] Grudem notes "the inherent tendency to sin."[34] The result of this tendency is that "even before birth children have a guilty standing before God."[35] People who die in infancy will be judged by God for their sinful *nature* rather than for their sinful *actions*. Because of God's mercy and due to the work of both Christ and

32. Grudem, *Systematic Theology*, 500–01.

33. Ibid., 494.

34. Ibid., 496.

35. Ibid., 499.

the Holy Spirit, even guilty people who die in infancy may be saved. In support of this view, Grudem cites his arguments for the prebirth salvation of guilty infants, the preconfession salvation of guilty infants, and the household sanctification of guilty infants.

Wayne Grudem is a well-respected, contemporary theologian. He has edited a major Bible translation and written with skill on difficult issues such as evangelical feminism, theories of Bible translation, and the use of the gift of prophecy in the church. He attempted in *Systematic Theology* to address an issue that the Bible does not address directly, the spiritual condition of infants. When I raised concerns about his view at the 2006 ETS meeting, Grudem was gracious and humble. After my thirty-minute presentation, which was largely an effort to question his proposal on infants, he publicly conceded that the spiritual condition of infants is one of the "secret things" of God (Deut 29:29).[36] He then autographed my copy of his *Systematic Theology* and engaged me in private conversation about my own view of infants. It was when he asked me, "What do you think?" that I realized that I had constructed only a negative statement. Even if I had succeeded in stating what I believe the Bible does *not* teach about infants, I was unprepared to write a positive statement about what the Bible *does* teach about infants. This book, which is based on my 2007 PhD dissertation, is an attempt to answer Dr. Grudem's question.

36. Grudem, Response.

BIBLICAL SECTION

4

What Do Infants Receive from Adam?
(Romans 5:12–21)

"Therefore, just as through one man sin entered into the world, and death through sin, and so death spread to all men, because all sinned—for until the Law sin was in the world, but sin is not imputed when there is no law. Nevertheless death reigned from Adam until Moses, even over those who had not sinned in the likeness of the offense of Adam, who is a type of Him who was to come. But the free gift is not like the transgression. For if by the transgression of the one the many died, much more did the grace of God and the gift by the grace of the one Man, Jesus Christ, abound to the many. The gift is not like that which came through the one who sinned; for on the one hand the judgment arose from one transgression resulting in condemnation, but on the other hand the free gift arose from many transgressions resulting in justification. For if by the transgression of the one, death reigned through the one, much more those who receive the abundance of grace and of the gift of righteousness will reign in life through the One, Jesus Christ. So then as through one transgression there resulted condemnation to all men, even so through one act of righteousness there resulted justification of life to all men. For as through the one man's disobedience the many were made sinners, even so through the obedience of the One the many will be made righteous. The Law came in so that the transgression would increase; but where sin increased, grace abounded all the more, so that, as sin reigned in death, even so grace would reign through righteousness to eternal life through Jesus Christ our Lord."—Rom 5:12–21

Tuesday nights are special nights in the Harwood home. My older children are now ten and twelve. Every Tuesday night, I take one of them out for an hour or so just to spend some time together. Usually we'll get ice cream cones, but the idea is for each of them to have one-on-one time with dad a couple of times during the month. (Soon, I'll need to figure out how to work my preschoolers into a similar schedule.)

Yesterday, I took my oldest child on her special day. In a break from our routine, we visited various stores looking for a desk for her room. During the car ride home, she commented about the trouble she was having with some of her teeth. Her mom has great teeth, but I don't. She got her bad teeth from me. She also got her extra-thick, dark hair from me. But she got the freckles on her nose from her mom. In this chapter, we'll consider something that was passed on to us. But it wasn't passed on to us from our parents. It came all the way from the first Adam. Sin. But did we also receive his guilt?

Romans 5:12–21 is probably the most important biblical text to consider in this study because it directly links Adam's sin with human sinfulness. But it's important to draw meaning out of the text rather than read meaning into it. New Testament scholar Joseph Fitzmyer issues this warning when he cautions readers of Rom 5 to be careful to determine what Paul was saying rather than what the church later *said* that Paul was saying. The Catholic scholar explains that the doctrine of original sin (the view that all people inherit both the sin and the guilt of Adam) is a Christian idea rather than an explicit Pauline teaching. This doctrine was developed from later Augustinian writings and solidified through the Sixteenth Council of Carthage, the Second Council of Orange, and the Tridentine Council. Also original sin developed as a doctrine in the western tradition but not in the eastern tradition.[1]

In Rom 5:12–21, Paul parallels the work of one man, Adam, with the work of the God-man, Jesus. Sin and death entered the world and came to all people through one man, Adam (v. 12). Between the time of Adam and Moses, who was given the law, sin and death reigned in the world (vv. 13–14). In this way, there were lawbreakers even before the giving of the law. Adam, though, was a pattern of the one (Jesus Christ) who was to come (v. 14). The parallel between the actions of Adam and Christ is presented in verses 15–19. Adam's trespass, one act of sin, brought judgment, condemnation, and death for all people. We are all sinners because of Adam's disobedience. Conversely God's grace is demonstrated in Christ's one act of righteousness, which brought grace, justification, and

---

1. Fitzmyer, *Romans*, 408–09.

righteousness for many people. We are made righteous because of Christ's obedience. Verses 20 and 21 mention that when the law was given, sin increased and reigned in death. But God met that with an increase of grace so that "grace might reign through righteousness to bring eternal life through Jesus Christ our Lord" (NIV).

There is widespread agreement in Christian circles that every person is sinful because of people's relationship to Adam. But there are two views of how Adam's sinful actions are imputed (passed on) to us. These are known as the immediate and the mediate views of imputation. Both views teach that all people are sinful and guilty before God due to our relationship to Adam. And both views read Rom 5 as a parallel of Adam and Christ, in which Christ reverses through his obedience the condemnation that resulted from Adam's disobedience. The difference comes when considering precisely whether a person *becomes* or *is always guilty* of sin and thus under the condemnation of sin and death.

This first view is known as immediate imputation. In this book, I'll refer to it as either the view of inherited guilt or the Augustinian-Calvinist tradition. According to this view, the final phrase in Rom 5:12, "because all sinned," means that all people are guilty because all people sinned *in Adam*. The view of inherited guilt teaches that all people were either present in or represented by Adam when he sinned in the garden. Therefore, Adam is to blame for the sin and guilt of humanity.

The second view is known as mediate imputation. I'll refer to it as either the inherited sinful nature view or moral responsibility. This view affirms that everyone is *sinful* because of Adam, but it denies that we are *guilty* due to the sin of Adam. Instead, we are guilty and fall under condemnation only when God judges our own sinful thoughts, attitudes, and actions. That is the position for which I am advocating. Below, I will summarize and critique the arguments for the first view, immediate imputation, and then present a case for the inherited sinful nature view.

THE INHERITED GUILT VIEW

In 1959, John Murray published *The Imputation of Adam's Sin*, which is a biblical-historical examination of Rom 5:12–21. Murray begins his study of the passage by identifying the clause *eph' hō pantes hēmarton* ("in that all sinned" or "because all sinned") in verse 12. Murray sees in this phrase an explanation for why death came to all people. The reason is because all sinned *in Adam*.

Murray writes that a person who thinks that people die only because of their own sin have adopted a Pelagian view.[2] In Pelagiansim, Adam is a prototype, one who sinned and died and was followed by others who will do the same. But the inherited sinful nature view should not be called a Pelagian view because it affirms the full sinfulness of humanity from the time of conception, which Pelagianism denies.

Interestingly, Murray begins his study by acknowledging that "the construction of verse 12 does not disprove this interpretation." Murray's comment that the construction of Rom 5:12 "does not disprove" the Pelagian view is a devastating admission. The main argument of Murray's work is that all people are counted guilty because of their association in the mind of God with the sin of Adam. If Rom 5:12 doesn't disprove the mediate view, then Murray's entire argument is suspect.

Murray reads Augustinian-Calvinism into Rom 5:12. This is because he teaches that the phrase *eph' hō pantes hēmarton* ("because all sinned") means that all of humanity sinned in Adam. Augustine understood the phrase *eph' hō pantes hēmarton* to mean "in whom all sinned" rather than "because all sinned" or "with the result that all sinned." It is not clear whether this resulted from his use of the Old Latin and Vulgate versions of Rom 5:12 or from the influence of western theologians. University of Durham Emeritus Professor of Divinity James D. G. Dunn writes that the "dominant consensus" is that this phrase is "best taken as 'for this reason, because.'"[3] This translation choice is affirmed by the following English versions of the Bible, which translate the phrase, "because all sinned": ESV, HCSB, NASB, NIV, NKJV, and the NET[4] What that means is that people who hold to the Augustinian-Calvinist view must add these italicized words to the text so that Rom 5:12 ends as follows: "because all sinned" *in Adam*.

2. In *The Imputation of Adam's Sin*, Murray presents the following views: Pelagian, Roman Catholic, Calvin's Interpretation, and the Classical Protestant Interpretation. In this study, I am not attempting to summarize and critique every nuance of Murray's argument but to interact with his main argument for the immediate view and against the mediate view of imputation.

3. Dunn, *The Theology of Paul the Apostle*, 95 n. 76. In support of his view, Dunn cites Cranfield, *The Epistle to the Romans*, 274–81.

4. In fairness to Murray, it should be noted that none of those English translations were in existence when Murray first published his study.

Murray argues against what he calls the Pelagian view. As previously demonstrated, Murray misuses the term *Pelagian* because he actually argues against the mediate view of imputation. First, he writes, some infants die without "actually and voluntarily" sinning. Second, verses 13 and 14 state that death reigned over those who did not sin in the likeness of Adam's transgression; in other words, death reigns universally. Third, verses 15–19 repeatedly state that many died because of the trespass of the one person—rather than stating that many died because of their own individual and personal trespasses. Fourth, the Pelagian view violates Paul's analogy between two men, Adam and Christ. Since the justification of men is brought about by the act of one man, Christ, then the condemnation of men being brought about by each man's individual sin would destroy the comparison of one man to one man.[5]

The Death of Some Infants Before They Commit Sinful Acts

Murray's first objection is that some infants die without "actually and voluntarily" sinning. This is true. However, it does not follow that an infant's death is a result of his or her personal sin. In the *International Critical Commentary* on Romans, C. E. B. Cranfield allows for a distinction between Adam's sin being passed to infants and the guilt they later incur after they commit sinful actions when he writes the following: "It has also sometimes been argued that *pantes [hēmarton]* must include those who have died in infancy, and that the contention that infants participate by seminal identity in the primal sin of Adam is more intelligible than the contention that they commit actual sins. But those who die in infancy are a special and exceptional case, and Paul must surely be assumed to be thinking in terms of adults."[6] In Cranfield's estimation, Paul was dealing with adults in Rom 5:12 not infants.

One of the arguments later in the book of Romans (chapter 8) is that all of creation is presently in a state of corruption but there is a future hope of glory when it will be set free and renewed (vv. 18–25). The death of infants is one of those instances in which all of God's creation is being subjected to bondage and futility prior to the future revelation of glory.

I will suggest in my examination of Gen 6 that infants both inside and outside of the womb suffered death as a consequence of God's judg-

5. Murray, *The Imputation of Adam's Sin*, 9–12.
6. Cranfield, *The Epistle to the Romans*, 279.

ment against the human race carried out in the flood during the time of Noah. Genesis 6:5 states that this judgment came as a result of the wicked actions and thoughts of humans. Murray's view would require us to think that all of the infants who were swept up by the flood of God's judgment were killed because of the sinful nature that infants possess from the time of their conception. The inherited sinful nature view, however, understands that the deaths of those infants were a result of God's general judgment against the sinful thoughts, attitudes, and actions of men rather than his particular judgment against their sinful nature.

The Death of People Who Did Not Participate in Adam's Sin

Murray's second objection is that the "because all sinned" phrase of Rom 5:12 cannot refer to individual transgression. The reason is that verses 13–14 state that death reigns apart from the existence of the law even among those who did not commit Adam's sinful act. In other words, people who did not participate in Adam's sin still die. Therefore, people do not experience death because of their individual sin against God but because they share in the sinful act and judgment declared against Adam, which was death.

Murray is correct in affirming that people experience death as a result of the sinful disobedience of Adam. But it doesn't follow that because people experience death they are guilty of and responsible for the sin of Adam. Advocates of both views of imputation agree that sin is passed from Adam to all humanity. The difference is that the inherited guilt view ties all death to guilt of and participation in Adam's actions. The inherited sinful nature view, which is the argument of this book, is that death is a result of Adam's sin. And the effects of sin, including death, impact all people. But this does not make us guilty of Adam's sin. We are guilty and under condemnation only for our own sins, which we commit after we know the difference between right and wrong and choose to do wrong.

Murray's third and fourth arguments suggest that we sinned in Adam because of the link between death and Adam's sin mentioned in verses 15–19 and the Adam-Christ parallel in the passage. So, Adam's one sin results in the death of all people because all people are guilty of Adam's one sin before they are guilty of their own sin. The inherited sinful nature view, however, teaches that death is an effect of Adam's sin and is experienced by all of creation. We experience the consequences of Adam's sin, but that does not make us guilty of Adam's sin.

The remainder of Murray's work is a historical presentation of the two major views of union with Adam (realistic and representative) and the two major views of imputation (mediate and immediate). After providing detailed arguments from the writings of various theologians, Murray casts his lot with the representative view of our union with Adam. He then defines that view in such as way as to affirm both Augustine's seminalism and Calvin's federalism.[7]

THE INHERITED SINFUL NATURE VIEW

Murray's presentation of the two major views of imputation provides an important distinction. The major difference between the two views is that the inherited sinful nature view excludes the imputation of guilt while the other view includes it.[8] Murray cites as advocates of this sinful nature view some Calvinist theologians who were associated with New Divinity, also known as New England Theology. Samuel Hopkins (1721–1803), for example, was a Congregational minister and a brother-in-law of Jonathan Edwards. Hopkins taught this view of imputation because he thought that infants possess evil inclinations and will eventually sin, but that they become guilty of Adam's sin only when they actually join his rebellion.[9]

Timothy Dwight (1752–1817) was another advocate of the inherited sinful nature view. He was a Congregationalist minister and one of the early presidents of Yale College. Dwight wrote, "When I assert, that in consequence of the Apostacy [sic] of Adam all men have sinned; I do not intend, that the posterity of Adam is guilty of his transgression. Moral actions are not, so far as I can see, transferable from one being to another. The personal act of any agent is, in its very nature, the act of that agent solely; and incapable of being participated by any other agent. Of course, the guilt of such a personal act is equally incapable of being transferred, or participated."[10]

7. Ibid., 22–41.

8. Ibid., 42–70.

9. Hopkins, *The Works of Samuel Hopkins*, 216–18, cited in Murray, *The Imputation of Adam's Sin*, 48–50.

10. Dwight, *Theology Explained and Defended*, 478, cited in Murray, *Imputation*, 51. Original punctuation in place; first sentence is italicized in the original.

Hopkins and Dwight were in agreement that infants are sinful but not guilty. Murray, however, disagrees. He explains that the analogy between Adam and Christ in Rom 5 favors the view of inherited guilt, in which there is an "immediate conjunction of the sin of Adam" with the death of all (vv. 12, 15, 17), the condemnation of all (vv. 16, 18), and the sin of all (vv. 12, 19).[11]

Murray concludes his study by stating the following conclusions: First, all humans were conceived of in God's mind and associated with Adam when he sinned. Second, people do not become but always are sinners. Third, Adam's sin is imputed to people from the moment that they come into existence. Fourth, all people are considered to have sinned in Adam. Fifth, Adam sinned by transgressing God's law. Sixth, imputation includes depravity.[12] These conclusions, though, are statements of the Augustinian-Calvinist viewpoint, which are read into rather than exegetical conclusions that are drawn out of the text of Romans.

Murray's book is a helpful study of the historical perspectives on this issue and provides an argument that we inherit both sin and guilt from Adam (inherited guilt). But his arguments don't rule out the possibility that we inherit from Adam sin but acquire our own guilt and condemnation the first time we knowingly sin (inherited sinful nature).

DUAL CAUSALITY

Before leaving this discussion of Rom 5, I should raise the point that many scholars who have written commentaries on this book advocate for a both/and rather than an either/or position on the question of how a person becomes guilty.

In the Anchor Bible commentary, Fitzmyer observes in Rom 5 an "antithetical parallelism" between Adam and the resulting death and Christ and the resulting life. Fitzmyer identifies the "dual causality" of both one's relationship to Adam and one's own sinful actions for understanding the phrase "all have sinned" (v. 12). Fitzmyer also explains that including infants among the all who sinned of Rom 5:12 was not an idea that Paul had in mind.[13]

---

11. Murray, *The Imputation of Adam's Sin*, 65–70.

12. Ibid., 91–93.

13. Fitzmyer, *Romans*, 406–13.

Dunn affirms an idea similar to Fitzmyer's dual causality when he writes that "Paul was operating with a double conception of death," in which death is "an *outcome* of Adam's first transgression" and also "a *consequence* or even penalty for one's own individual transgressions."[14] To the voices of Fitzmyer and Dunn should be added the voice of New Testament scholar Leon Morris. In an article on sin and guilt in Pauline literature, Morris writes, "All commit their own sins, to be sure, but in some way all are also caught up in the sin of Adam, for 'by the one man's trespass the many died' (Rom. 5:15)."[15]

Wheaton College Blanchard Professor of New Testament Douglas Moo provides another example of this view of dual causality. He writes in his commentary on Romans, "Paul can therefore say both 'all die because all sin' and 'all die because Adam sinned' with no hint of conflict because the sin of Adam is the sin of all. All people, therefore, stand condemned 'in Adam,' guilty by reason of the sin all committed 'in him.'"[16]

In his commentary on Romans, Baylor University Distinguished Professor of Religion Charles Talbert explains, "Adam's sin caused all to sin (v. 19), all to be condemned (v. 18), and all to die (vv. 15, 17). At the same time, [Paul] said 'all sinned' (v. 12). Paul, then, did not answer the question about 'how' that later interpreters have attempted."[17] If Talbert is correct, then it is impossible to know from this passage alone exactly how our sin, condemnation, and death are all linked to Adam's sinful actions.

GOD JUDGES ACTIONS

It is also helpful to notice the context of Rom 5. In Rom 3:10, we see a classic statement of man's unrighteousness (sinfulness). What follows in Rom 3:11–18 is not a summary of man's sinful *nature* but his sinful *actions*. Humankind is indicted for its failure to understand or seek God (v. 11); for turning aside and failing to do good (v. 12); for speaking sinful words (vv. 13–14); and for killing, destroying, failing to live peaceably, and failing to fear God (vv. 15–18). These are all indictments by God against sinful *actions* rather than a sinful *nature*. The significance? The

---

14. Dunn, *The Theology of Paul the Apostle*, 96. Emphasis his.

15. Morris, "Sin, Guilt," 878.

16. Moo, *Romans 1–8*, 338.

17. Talbert, *Romans*, 155.

Augustinian-Calvinist tradition argues for human guilt based upon a sinful *nature,* but Paul argues for human guilt based upon sinful *actions.*[18]

The dilemma that the view of inherited guilt creates is that a person is considered guilty before God before committing any sinful actions. God's judgment in Scripture, though, is clearly manifested against sinful actions not against a sinful nature.[19] Fitzmyer, Dunn, Morris, Moo, and Talbert do not assign only one cause of judgment and death. Instead, they consider the causes for the sin, guilt, and death upon humanity to be found in both our link to Adam as well as our individual sinful actions.

CONCLUSION

The inherited guilt view teaches that people are sinful and guilty because of the sin of Adam. The inherited sinful nature view teaches that people receive from Adam a sinful nature but later become guilty due to their own sinful thoughts, attitudes, and actions. This third view, dual causality, affirms aspects of both views to be true. We are sinful and guilty because of Adam's sin as well as our own. But could it be that infants are a special case? For, infants do not knowingly commit sinful, thoughts, attitudes, or actions for which to be judged. If that is the case, then they are excluded from God's judgment and thus are sinful in their nature but not guilty of committing any sin.

18. See also Grudem, *Systematic Theology,* 499–500.

19. For an extended argument from the beginning of Romans that at the final judgment God judges according to works, see Bell, *No One Seeks for God,* 132–83.

Does God Judge Our Sinful Nature or Our Sinful Actions?
(Psalm 51:5 and Ephesians 2:3)

TECHNOLOGY CAN PROVIDE A window into a mother's womb. My mom tells me that when she carried me in her body in 1974, ultrasound equipment provided a fuzzy, snowy, black-and-white image in which you could hardly see the infant. Ultrasound technology was in its infancy; they didn't make pictures of those sessions. In 2005, while my wife, Laura, was pregnant with our third child, a friend in our church gave us a gift certificate for a free session at her workplace. Our friend worked at a facility that uses ultrasound technology to capture 3-D pictures and videos. So Laura invested a couple of hours for a video session with our infant who was six months old in the womb.

The video clips picture Baby Jonathan with an orange tone and a black background. One clip pictures Baby Jonathan from mid-chest to the top of his head. Eyes closed, his mouth opens and his tongue shoots out for a moment. You can see his features clearly. Nose. Cheeks. Forehead. His right hand is in view, making a fist with thumb out, ready to insert into his mouth. They took images from behind, images from beside, and images from below. You can see all ten of Jonathan's fingers and all ten of his toes.

This technology was not available to us when Laura carried our first two children. We considered it a novelty at the time of Jonathan's video session. But last month, as we celebrated Jonathan's fifth birthday, we realized that what was unnecessary as an expense was appreciated as a gift. The images from that session are treasured among our keepsakes. And while I enjoy these pictures and videos as a dad, I also value them as a teacher. In a sermon on contentment (1 Tim 6), I showed a clip of our video to illustrate that we, as humans, bring nothing into the world (v. 7). In a classroom lecture on the incarnation, I showed another clip to prompt the students to think about the full humanity of Jesus, who once lived in his mother's womb.

Those images of Baby Jonathan in his mother's womb could also introduce this chapter on the spiritual condition of infants. The common claim is that people are guilty of sin from the time of their conception. Psalm 51:5 and Eph 2:3 are frequently cited to support this claim. But in this chapter, we'll see that these verses affirm infant *sinfulness* but not infant *guilt*.

PSALM 51:5

"Behold, I was brought forth in iniquity,
And in sin my mother conceived me." —Ps 51:5

Old Testament scholar Franz Delitzsch wrote that in Ps 51:5, "hereditary sin is here more distinctly expressed than in any other place."[1] It would be difficult to overstate the importance of this verse when considering the spiritual condition of infants.

What was the original context and meaning of Ps 51:5? The superscription names David as the author of Psalm 51 after his sin with Bathsheba and his confrontation by Nathan. David was making a statement about the presence of sin in his life from the earliest possible time. He wrote that he was brought forth in *ʿāwōn* ("iniquity") and conceived in *ḥēṭ* ("sin"). What are iniquity and sin?

A Concise Hebrew and Aramaic Lexicon of the Old Testament (*CHALOT*) defines *ʿāwōn* as "activity that is crooked or wrong." Similarly it desines *ḥēṭ* as "fault (against men)" and "sin (against God)." The Brown-Driver-Briggs (BDB) Hebrew lexicon defines the word *ʿāwōn* as used in this verse as "guilt of iniquity." But the lexicon notes that it is difficult to distinguish between this definition and its primary definition, which is simply "iniquity." English translation committees for the following Bible editions omitted the notion of guilt when they rendered *ʿāwōn* in Ps 51:5 as "iniquity": KJV, NKJV, ASV, RSV, ESV, and NASB. Similarly, the NIV rendered *ʿāwōn* as "sinful." But the NRSV and HCSB versions rendered *ʿāwōn* as "guilty."

1. Delitzsch, *Biblical Commentary on the Psalms*, 137.

Under the BDB lexicon's definition of ʿāwōn as "guilt of iniquity," there is the subcategory "as a condition." In other words, when this word is used, it can imply guilt as a condition of iniquity. However, none of the instances in which ʿāwōn is understood in this way referred to infants. Instead, all of the Scriptures refer to actions that were accomplished by people who had matured beyond their infancy. Joshua 22:20 refers to the ʿāwōn of Achan, an adult. Jeremiah 31:30 refers to accountability for one's own sinful actions, not simply being born with a sinful nature. Ezekiel 3:18–19 and 33:8–9 refer to specific immoral behaviors, such as extortion and robbery. Infants do not and cannot perform any of those actions. So the use of the word ʿāwōn in the Old Testament indicates that it can refer to either iniquity or the guilt of iniquity. But in the cases in which there is a condition of guilt, there are no other Scriptures that clearly refer to infants.

The *Theological Wordbook of the Old Testament* (*TWOT*) states that one understanding of ʿāwōn can include guilt as a consequence for "past misdeeds."[2] But who argues that infants have committed misdeeds for which they can accumulate guilt? If not, then Ps 51:5 should be read as David's statement that he was brought forth in a condition of sin but not of guilt.

Many scholars who comment on the meaning of Ps 51:5 refer to the *sinfulness* of humans from their origins but not their *guilt*. Delitzsch, for example, writes that "the meaning is merely, that his parents were sinful human beings, and this sinful state (*habitus*) has operated upon his birth and even his conception, and from this point has passed over to him."[3] In his study of Psalm 51, Edward Dalglish observes that "the psalmist is relating his sinfulness to the very inception of life; he traces his development beyond birth (*chuwl*) to the genesis of his being in his mother's womb–even to the very hour of conception (*yacham*)."[4] Old Testament scholar Bruce Waltke writes that it "supports the notion that at the time of conception man is in a state of sin (. . .)."[5] In his commentary, Mitchell Dahood writes, "All men have a congenial tendency toward evil."[6] In his

2. Harris, Archer, and Waltke, *TWOT*, 2:651.

3. Delitzsch, *Biblical Commentary on the Psalms*, 137.

4. Dalglish, *Psalm Fifty-One*, 121.

5. Waltke, "Reflections from the Old Testament," 12.

6. Dahood, *Psalms II*, 4.

detailed study of David's prayers, Michael Goulder notes that "critics are almost unanimous in taking v. 5 to refer to the universality of human sin, transmitted from generation to generation."[7] In his commentary, Hans-Joachim Kraus writes, "'*Āwōn* and *ḥēṭ* have from the hour of birth been the determining forces under who signature life began. The petitioner wants to say that the primordial cause, the root cause of my existence, is interwoven with corruption."[8] None of these Old Testament scholars glean from the text that humans are guilty of sin from birth. Instead, they affirm that sinfulness is present at the first moment of life.

EPHESIANS 2:3

"Among them we too all formerly lived in the lusts of our flesh, indulging the desires of the flesh and of the mind, and were by nature children of wrath, even as the rest." —Eph 2:3

Ephesians 2:3 states that we "were by nature children of wrath." Many theologians point to that phrase in order to teach that God judges the sinful *nature* of people rather than their sinful *actions*. If that is true, then the spiritual condition of infants is guilt before God due to their sinful nature. If something different is meant by that phrase, then the implications for the spiritual condition of infants could be very different.

First, I will examine the work of two theologians, Wayne Grudem and Thomas Cragoe, who appeal to Eph 2:3 in order to teach that infants are guilty due to their sinful nature. Second, I will consider whether the idea of infant guilt was the original meaning of the text or a theological assumption read into the text. Third, I will consider briefly the nature of wrath and judgment in Paul's writings to determine whether God judges people according to their sinful actions or their sinful nature.

Wayne Grudem states that humans inherit a sinful nature and cites as biblical evidence for that position Eph 2:3. Grudem writes that the verse teaches that both in our nature and in our actions, we lack any spiritual good and are unable to perform any spiritual good before God.[9] To this point, Grudem's assessment is consistent with the thesis of this book. Grudem's conclusion, though, about the spiritual condition of in-

---

7. Goulder, *The Prayers of David*, 53.

8. Kraus, *Psalms 1–59*, 503.

9. Grudem, *Systematic Theology*, 496.

fants progresses beyond such statements in the Scripture and reads into them an Augustinian-Calvinist view of inherited guilt. Grudem reasons that because those who die in or prior to infancy have not yet committed sinful *actions* for which God would judge them, God must judge them on the basis of their sinful *nature*.[10] So, the result of Grudem's assessment is that God judges some people (those who die in or prior to infancy) on the basis of their sinful nature but judges others (all other people) on the basis of their sinful actions. Certainly, God is able to make judgments about sin in any way that he chooses. It is not clear, though, that Grudem has correctly identified the way that God has chosen to judge sin.

Thomas Cragoe cites Eph 2:3 as a biblical text to argue that infants have a spiritual need to be saved. Cragoe cites F. F. Bruce[11] in support of the view that in this verse, Paul is teaching that "all humans are inherently subject to condemnation." Also, Cragoe cites various uses of *physis* ("nature") in the BAG Greek-English lexicon (2d. rev. ed.), in which "the term carries the connotation of a natural endowment or condition inherited from one's ancestors." Cragoe also cites four secondary sources to support the following conclusion of Eph 2:3: "By natural constitution and physical descent, all human beings are deserving of the wrath of God." Further, Cragoe adds, "Infants are born in a condition of separation from God, a state which carries with it both guilt and condemnation."[12]

In a surprising move, Cragoe seems to disagree with his own conclusion. After arguing that infants are guilty due to their imputed sinful nature, he disagrees with that conclusion when he writes, "Since infants are incapable of both faith and acts of sin (wherein the child knowingly chooses sin, becoming personally guilty), they cannot be judged guilty at the great White Throne judgement, where judgement is based upon rejection of Christ and works of evil."[13] So, Cragoe concludes that God does not judge infants guilty because they do not knowingly choose to sin, which is the argument of this book. But Cragoe's interpretation of Eph 2:3 isn't consistent with his conclusion. Cragoe argues that infants are by their nature separated from God in a condition of both guilt and condemnation. If that is the case, then infants must be considered guilty before

---

10. Ibid., 499–500.

11. Bruce, *The Epistles*, 284–85.

12. Cragoe, "An Examination of the Issues of Infant Salvation," 35–37.

13. Ibid., 77.

God. However, Cragoe excuses those who die in their infancy from such a judgment by distinguishing between original and personal sin.

Cragoe explains that original sin refers to that corrupt nature that is received from Adam, resulting in both physical and spiritual death. Just as infants passively receive the sin of Adam, all people who die in their infancy passively receive the righteousness of Christ in order "to cover the guilt associated with original sin." Cragoe offers two ideas to support this conclusion. First, Cragoe speculates that because infants are passive, they do not obstruct the mercy and grace by any sin or reject this work of regeneration in them. Second, the atonement of Christ remits both "halves" of the curse for infants (the physical and spiritual halves). Cragoe attempts to ground this argument in the New Testament term for regeneration, *palingenesia*, which he understands as a reference in Matt 19:28 to the restoration of all things that passively participate in Adam's curse.[14]

Personal sin, however, is different from original sin. Personal sin is acquired at "the age of moral accountability" when a child knowingly sins. At that point, the child incurs personal guilt. Cragoe explains, "Having knowingly sinned, the person must now savingly believe in the substitutionary death and resurrection of Christ for the forgiveness of sins (plural—denoting the sins of personal transgression)."[15] A failure to personally appropriate the atonement for the forgiveness of these sins will result in eternal death, which is different from the judgment of spiritual death against original sin.

In his work, Cragoe attempts to both affirm and deny the Augustinian-Calvinist view of inherited guilt. On the one hand, Cragoe points to Eph 2:3 and other verses to establish the guilt of all people, including infants. On the other hand, he argues that God judges only those people who knowingly commit sinful actions. In order to maintain this view, he must divide God's judgment against sinfulness and guilt into two groups. God judges original sin, and God judges personal sin. The most serious difficulty with this division of sin into original and personal is that it suggests an uninvited application of the atonement. What I mean is this: In Cragoe's view, all people who die in their infancy passively receive the effects of the atonement of Christ to cover their inherited sin and guilt.

14. Ibid., 78–85.
15. Ibid., 82. Emphasis his.

This means that every person who dies in or prior to infancy will be justified and enjoy everlasting life with God in heaven apart from hearing and responding to the Gospel of Christ. If God saves all guilty infants who die without their hearing and responding to the gospel, then does God save all guilty adults in a similar way?

Is infant guilt the original meaning of Eph 2:3 or a theological assumption read into the text? In the first chapter of Ephesians, Paul reveals God's plan for redeeming and sealing his elect for salvation. In the first three verses of chapter 2, Paul states (v. 1) and describes (vv. 2–3) the spiritual condition of the believers *before* their salvation. In his excellent commentary on Ephesians, Harold Hoehner writes that they "walked according to the temporal values of the world (2:2a)," "walked according to the ruler of the power of the air (2:2b)," and "lived in the desires of the flesh and the mind" (2:3). This outline focuses on the sinful actions of people rather than on their sinful nature. Hoehner thinks that *physis* ("nature") in the phrase "and were by nature children of wrath" refers to a person who is under wrath due to his relationship to an ancestor. He also thinks that *orgē* ("wrath") "clearly" refers to the wrath of God. Hoehner cites Rom 1:18–3:20 and John 3:36 as similar passages for understanding God's wrath. Finally, he writes, "Paul makes it very clear in Romans that it is their willful acts of transgression and disobedience that bring this wrath."[16]

Although Hoehner acknowledges the ancestral aspect of *physis*, Hoehner does not think Paul means that every person has been born guilty and is under God's wrath. Rather, all people have been born sinful and because of their sinful actions, which come naturally, they are under God's judgment and wrath. Robert Webb makes a similar conclusion when he argues that infants are not sinless and morally neutral. Rather, they are "blemished at birth with an internal *vitium* which insures [*sic*] a development into a manhood more or less deflected from the moral ideal." After quoting Eph 2:3, Webb writes, "There is then a defect, a *vitium*, in the native heart of all men which leads to an unholy 'conversation,' and brings into a state of 'wrath.'"[17]

When exploring the meaning of Eph 2:3, the flow of Paul's argument must also be considered. Paul was writing to remind the believers what

---

16. Hoehner, *Ephesians*, 309–324.

17. Webb, The Theology of Infant Salvation, 75–77. Italics his.

kind of people they were *before* they were believers. He was not commenting on the spiritual condition of infants but of adults who had previously been unbelievers. Markus Barth affirms as much in his commentary when he writes, "Eph. 2:3 certainly does not assert that because of their procreation and a physical transmission of poison of sin, even babies are condemned. Paul speaks here about adults and to adults (. . .). 'Children of wrath' is a Semitic idiom for condemned and cursed men, not a reference to babies."[18]

Hoehner, Webb, and Barth all read Eph 2:3 as teaching that people are by nature sinners, which eventually results in their being subject to God's wrath. They are careful to distinguish between the sinful nature and the eventual wrath. The reason they make this distinction is that God's wrath does not come due to one's sinful nature but due to the actions that arise out of one's sinful nature.

Consider the following passages in Paul's letter to illustrate this concept. In Rom 1, God's wrath is revealed not against the sinful nature of mankind. Rather, God's wrath is revealed against the following: "ungodliness and unrighteousness of men, who suppress the truth in unrighteousness" (v. 18), failing to honor or thank God (v. 21), claiming wisdom (v. 22) but choosing idolatry (vv. 23–25), and homosexuality (vv. 26–27). Consider 1:28–32 with this question in mind, "Does God judge our sinful nature or our sinful actions?"

> And just as they did not see fit to acknowledge God any longer, God gave them over to a depraved mind, to do those things which are not proper, being filled with all unrighteousness, wickedness, greed, evil; full of envy, murder, strife, deceit, malice; *they are* gossips, slanderers, haters of God, insolent, arrogant, boastful, inventors of evil, disobedient to parents, without understanding, untrustworthy, unloving, unmerciful; and, although they know the ordinance of God, that those who practice such things are worthy of death, they not only do the same, but also give hearty approval to those who practice them.

Ronald Nash argues for infant guilt due to Adam's sin but also maintains that God judges people for their sinful thoughts and actions. He writes that "divine judgment is administered on the basis of sins committed in the body" and cites as an example 1 Cor 6:9–10, a passage that in-

---

18. Barth, *Ephesians 1–3*, 231.

cludes sexual sins. Nash argues that this obviously excludes infants from this judgment.[19]

CONCLUSION

Paul's understanding of the circumstances of God's wrath combined with the context of Eph 2:3 favors the view that judgment comes as a result of sinful actions rather than a sinful nature. Because infants are unable to commit sinful actions, they are therefore not subject to God's judgment and wrath. This understanding of Eph 2:3 combined with a view of Ps 51:5 as referring to sinfulness rather than guilt should lead a person to ask the following question: On what biblical grounds should an infant be considered guilty of sin?

19. Nash, *When a Baby Dies*, 60–61.

6

Are Infant Deaths Due to the Guilt of Other People?
(Genesis 6:5–6 and 2 Samuel 12:23)

Is the death of some infants evidence of their guilt of sin? As discussed in chapter 4, John Murray thinks so. Following the Augustinian-Calvinist tradition, Murray teaches that infants are guilty of Adam's sin. And one of his supporting arguments is that some infants die without "actually and voluntarily" sinning. But in this chapter, we will consider two instances in which infants died without any mention of their guilt. If in these two cases the infants die as a result of God's judgment against the sin and guilt of another person, then the logic of the Augustinian-Calvinist tradition proves to be flawed. Stated another way, some infants die but it cannot be established that those infants die because of their guilt in Adam. Another possibility is that infants die because of the sweeping consequences of God's judgment against sin.

GENESIS 6:5–6

> "Then the Lord saw that the wickedness of man was great on the earth, and that every intent of the thoughts of his heart was only evil continually. The Lord was sorry that He had made man on the earth, and He was grieved in His heart." —Gen 6:5–6

What is the context and meaning of Gen 6:5–6? Following the account of the creation (chapters 1–2), the fall of Adam and Eve (chapter 3), and the rise of evil from the first murder by Cain to the bragging about multiple murders by Lamech (chapter 4), Moses then presents a genealogy from Adam to the sons of Noah (chapter 5) and in Genesis 6 begins the flood narrative. Genesis 6:14 has generated controversy mainly because scholars disagree on the identity of the "sons of God" who took women as their wives and fathered the "fallen ones." They disagree about whether or not women procreated with fallen angels, but there is consensus on the broad idea that whatever happened on earth to that point displeased God. Genesis 6:5–6 reveals the reason God flooded the earth: "Then the Lord saw that the wickedness of man was great on the earth, and that every intent of the thoughts of his heart was only evil continually. And the Lord was sorry that He had made man on the earth, and He was grieved in His heart."

So God brought destruction and judgment on his creation because of man's great wickedness and continually evil thoughts. The statement that God regretted making man should be understood as anthropomorphic language, or ascribing human emotion to God, in order to express God's remorse over man's sinful condition (see also Num 23:19 and 1 Sam 15:29). The text does not state that God was angry but that he was grieved. As Claus Westermann writes in his commentary, "It is painful for God to be the judge of His people."[1]

The relevance of these verses is that they reveal one of the most graphic statements on the human condition in the Bible. Humans are not referred to as innocent, good, or sometimes evil. God declared that their wickedness was great and that their thoughts were *only* evil *all* the time. It must be asked, though, if God was making this judgment about infants. They were not explicitly mentioned in God's declaration of humanity's evil. Perhaps that is because they were not guilty of the wickedness and evil thoughts that God had witnessed. Or, they may not have been named because God saw no wickedness or evil thoughts among them.

Although the biblical narrative of the flood does not explicitly mention infants drowning in the waters of God's judgment, every person who was not in the ark with Noah and his family was killed. It is reasonable to speculate that among the victims of the flood were infants, who were neither able to exhibit wicked behavior nor think sinful thoughts. Although they were not performing the actions that God condemned, they were swept up in the flood of His judgment against human wickedness. This opens the possibility that God's judgment against wicked humanity sometimes includes infants, although they are not old enough to commit sinful actions or think sinful thoughts. The judgment experienced by the infants in Noah's day was not a result of their sinful nature but of the

---

1. Westermann, *Genesis 1–11*, 410.

sinful thoughts and actions of other people who were older and knew the difference between good and evil, or the difference between right and wrong.

2 SAMUEL 12:23

"But now he has died; why should I fast? Can I bring him back again? I shall go to him, but he will not return to me."
—2 Sam 12:23

In 2 Sam 12:23, David makes a powerful statement. What is the context and meaning of that statement? Chapter 11 recounts the events of David lusting after and committing adultery with Uriah's wife, Bathsheba, while the Israelite army was off to war. Bathsheba became pregnant and David brought Uriah back from the front lines of war, hoping he would lay with his wife and their adulterous affair would not be discovered. When Uriah failed to have sexual relations with his wife, David ordered Uriah to be sent to the most dangerous area of battle and abandoned in order to kill him. Uriah *was* killed and David took Bathsheba into his house. The Scripture reports, "But the thing that David had done was evil in the sight of the Lord" (11:27b).

In chapter 12, the prophet Nathan confronted David with a story that enraged the king, but actually it was a retelling of the king's sinful actions. Nathan declared that because David struck down Uriah and took his wife and despised the Lord, the sword would never leave his house (v. 10), others would lie with his wives (v. 11), and all of this would be done for others to see (v. 12). After David admitted his sin, Nathan pronounced forgiveness and assured David that he would not die (v. 13). Then, the prophet makes the following statement, "However, because by this deed you have given occasion to the enemies of the Lord to blaspheme, the child also that is born to you shall surely die" (v. 14).

The child born to David and Bathsheba became sick. David fasted, but the child died. When David learned of the child's death, he rose, washed, and worshipped the Lord (vv. 15–21). When asked by his servants why he fasted before the child's death but was now eating, David explained his reasoning that "the Lord may be gracious to me, that the child may live" (v. 22). David continued, "But now he has died; why should I fast? Can I bring him back again? I will go to him, but he will not return to me" (v. 23).

The words of 2 Sam 12:23 are relevant to the present study because the passage seems to provide implicit teaching about the spiritual condition of infants. David made a statement about his child who had died. What was the relationship between David's sin and his son's death? Is it possible to discern from verse 23 what David understood about his child's spiritual condition? What are the implications of the answers to these questions?

Antony Campbell states the dilemma as follows: "What troubles many readers is rather that while the sinful king lives, the innocent child dies."[2] The present study suggests that although infants are born with sin that originated in Adam, infants are not accountable to God for the guilt of Adam. The concept of personal guilt for individual actions and thoughts of sin is critically important for this study. If David's child who died had been judged guilty of David's sin, then that would count against the present thesis. If, however, the child died as a result of David's sin, not as a result of the child's sinful nature, then the present thesis stands. The death of David's son could be understood in the same way as the death of infants in the days of the flood; they were all victims of God's righteous judgment against the sinful thoughts and actions of other people.

If David sinned, then why did his child die? Campbell puts it this way: "The suggestion that the dead child is a substitute for David may be morally objectionable; it is unsupported in the text—verse 14 portrays punishment not substitution." Campbell cites Deut 24:16 as evidence that children are not to be put to death for the crimes of their parents. He suggests that other verses that describe the Lord visiting the iniquity of the parents on the children (such as Exod 20:5; 34:7; Num 14:18; and Deut 5:9) refer to "the long-term consequences of sin."[3]

In his discussion of the ancient Near Eastern concept of divine retribution, Ben F. Philbeck Jr. notes that "the ancients saw behind every force of nature the presence of an inscrutable god." Philbeck cites certain judgments in the books of 1 and 2 Samuel as originating from the Lord, but implies that secondary causation may better explain other instances of judgment. Significantly, he fails to cite the death of David and Bathsheba's son as an example of divine retribution. Commenting on the text that records the son's death, Philbeck writes, "The idea that God punishes a

2. Campbell, 2 *Samuel*, 118.
3. Ibid., 118–19.

child for the sin of its parents is modified in other Old Testament passages." He then cites Exod 20:5–6, which notes that consequences of sin
are passed on to succeeding generations, and Ezek 18:1–4, 20, which indicates that each person is punished for his own sin. Philbeck continues,
"David recognized that he had been responsible for the misfortune which
fell upon others" and that David "was unable to halt the consequences of
his deeds." So the Bible teaches, Philbeck says, that while individuals are
held accountable to God for their own sin, they are still affected by the
consequences of the sins of others.[4]

Stephen B. Chapman applies Klaus Koch's "act-consequence model"[5]
to this story and arrives at a similar conclusion. Chapman writes, "Despite
being announced by a prophet, the death of David's son is treated by the
narrative as the unavoidable consequence of a violation of the created
order, not as the direct intervention of God."[6]

Antony Campbell views the death of David's child as a time in which
the Lord "struck" a person (see Exod 32:35; 1 Sam 4:3; 25:38; and 2 Chr
13:20 and 21:18). But McCarter, Nutkowicsz, Philbeck, and Chapman
all understand David's sin to be the immediate cause of his infant son's
death.

Mark Biddle suggests that sin is an organic system of wrongdoing
that involves more than a blemish against the individual sinner; it has
an "afterlife" of real impact on the world.[7] Biddle notes that even after
forgiveness is granted to the sinner, "the chain of causation is sometimes,
sadly, unable to interrupt the sequence (. . .)." He cites this account of
David's sin and the loss of his son as an example of sin's afterlife. He notes
that Nathan assured David that his wrongdoing had been taken away
but does not mention the consequences. Rather, David has by his sinful actions "loosed something in the world that God will not or cannot
call back. Sin has taken on its own life, and forgiveness cannot reverse its
course in the world."[8] Although Biddle errs in viewing the effects of sin as
more powerful than God Himself, I think that Biddle is correct in viewing

---

4. Philbeck, "1–2 Samuel," 8–9.

5. Koch, "Is There a Doctrine of Retribution," 57–87.

6. Chapman, "Reading the Bible as Witness," 184.

7. Biddle, *Missing the Mark*, vxiii.

8. Ibid., 130–31.

the negative consequences of one's own sin as sometimes spilling over into the lives of other people.

What does verse 23 indicate about David's understanding of his infant son's spiritual condition? Philbeck writes that David's comment suggests only that David understands that he, like his son, will one day die and they will be together in Sheol.[9] Wayne Grudem cites this verse in support of his argument that believing parents can have confidence that they will be reunited in heaven with their children who die in infancy. Grudem argues against the view that David was only referring to death by citing the "language of personal reunion," in which "David does not say, 'I shall go to *where he is,* but rather, 'I shall go *to him.*'" Grudem combines this statement with statements such as Ps 23:6, which imply that David anticipates being in the presence of the Lord after death, in order to conclude that David expects to one day be with his son in heaven.[10] Whether or not David spoke of his son being in the grave or in heaven is uncertain, but it is certain that David expected one day to be with him. Even if David understood his son to be in heaven, it is impossible from this text to know whether the infant child would be in heaven because he was never guilty of Adam's sin or whether he was guilty of Adam's sin but was subsequently cleansed of that guilt.

CONCLUSION

David and Bathsheba's child, who was not old enough to commit any sinful actions, did not die as a punishment for his own sin but as a consequence of David's sin. The circumstances surrounding this infant's death, as well as the infants lost during the flood, affirm the argument of this book. Infants are not guilty of the sin passed on to them by their parents, but infants are sometimes subject to the sweeping consequences of God's judgment against the sinful behavior of their parents.

9. Philbeck, "1–2 Samuel," 114.

10. Grudem, *Systematic Theology,* 501.

7

What Is the Knowledge of Good and Evil?
(Genesis 2–3 and Deuteronomy 1:39)

A T YALE UNIVERSITY, THE study of infants is serious business. Paul Bloom, professor of psychology, conducts research at the Infant Cognition Center on the renowned campus and publishes his findings in academic journals such as *Nature* and *Science*. In 2010 he wrote an article for *The New York Times Magazine* entitled "The Moral Life of Babies." He and his team conducted clinical studies that assessed an infant's response to puppets that were either helpful or hurtful to each other. The study revealed that infants reached for the helpful puppets and showed an aversion to the hurtful puppets. Against the traditional view among psychologists and sociologists, this suggests that infants are not born with a "blank slate." Instead, infants are born with an innate, although undeveloped, sense of morality.[1]

Although Bloom and his team assume a Darwinian worldview in which people evolved from lower life forms, their observations of infants are consistent with a Christian worldview in which infants have an inborn but undeveloped sense of right and wrong. In this chapter, we will consider two Bible passages that refer to the knowledge of good and evil, Gen 2–3 and Deut 1:39. The phrase "knowledge of good and evil" is used in slightly different ways in those passages, but when taken together, the passages should give us more information about the spiritual condition of infants.

GENESIS 2–3

Because the issue is raised frequently in the academic study of Gen 1–11, I will begin by disclosing my presupposition of the truthfulness and his-

---

1. Bloom, "The Moral Life of Babies."

torical reliability of the account in Gen 2–3. The narrative indicates that two things happened because Adam and Eve ate the fruit from the tree of the knowledge of good and evil: shame over their nakedness and death. What is the significance of this tree? What is the relationship between the sin of Adam and Eve and the consequent shame over their nakedness and their eventual death?

The tree of the knowledge of good and evil was present in the garden of Eden (2:9), and God declared that death would come to man after he ate from it (2:17). Adam and Eve were naked and unashamed (2:25) until they ate of the tree and their eyes were opened to their nakedness (3:7). When Adam and Eve admitted to God that they had eaten from the tree from which he had forbidden them to eat, God declared negative consequences for the serpent (3:14–15), the woman (v. 16), and the man (vv. 17–19). That judgment included "enmity" between her seed and the seed of the serpent (v. 15). The Lord God makes the statement in 3:22 that "the man has become like one of Us, knowing good and evil." As a result of eating from the tree of the knowledge of good and evil, God expelled the man from the garden (v. 22) and set cherubim to guard the gate so that he could not enter and eat of the tree of life, thus living forever.

What was the significance of the tree? There was a particular knowledge gained by eating from that tree. What kind of knowledge? The knowledge of good and evil. There are three major possibilities for the type of knowledge gained by eating from that tree. They are sexual desire,[2] advancement in all knowledge,[3] and the idea of moral autonomy. The first and second views do not seem best to explain the events of the narrative because sexual desire was created by God, and it does not follow that Adam and Eve advanced in their general knowledge as a result of their sin. This third view, the idea of moral autonomy, seems best to explain the significance of the tree.

In his commentary on Genesis, Victor Hamilton surveys various Old Testament passages to build a case that "good and evil" is an idiom that refers to the ability to make legal decisions. For example, the generation in the wilderness who had no knowledge of good and evil (Deut 1:39) were "not legally responsible for their actions." Also, Solomon prayed in 1

2. Gordis, "The Knowledge of Good and Evil," 123–38.

3. Wenham, *Genesis* 1–15, 63–64, understands good and evil as opposites, implying that the knowledge encompasses everything. See also Wallace, *The Eden Narrative*, 115–32.

Kings 3:9 that he might be able to discern between good and evil, which indicates a request for wisdom in his decision making. By eating from the tree of the knowledge of good and evil, Adam and Eve reflected their desire to decide for themselves what was best. Hamilton writes, "This is a decision God has not delegated to earthlings." He also writes, "When man attempts to act autonomously he is indeed attempting to be godlike."[4] Kenneth Mathews, professor of Old Testament at Beeson Divinity School, agrees. He writes that the knowledge of good and evil was a "divine wisdom" and the action of Adam and Eve taking from it reflects their desire for moral autonomy.[5] By eating from the tree of the knowledge of good and evil, Adam and Eve made a decision to reject God's rule over their lives.

What does it mean that if man ate from the tree he would die? The Augustinian-Calvinistic tradition interprets Paul's references to Adam in Rom 5 and 1 Cor 15 to mean that Adam's sin and death would be passed on to all future generations. Because the narrative itself does not claim that future generations would experience death as a result of inherited sin, there is some disagreement on this issue. In his commentary on Genesis, Walter Bruggemann argues against the Augustinian-Calvinist view, which he terms a "mechanistic connection of sin and death." In support of his interpretation, Bruggemann notes that no one died in Gen 2–3, Paul's reflections in Rom 5 are based on 4 Ezra rather than Genesis, and that Paul's purpose in referring to the first man was not in order to describe the world but to proclaim the Gospel. Bruggemann explains that in the garden, death was a "boundary," which became a "threat."[6]

Although it is true that no one died in Gen 2–3, the eventual result of Adam and Eve's sinful disobedience is their death. Leander Keck notes that "Gen. 3:19 and 22–24 imply that death was part of their punishment." Adam and Eve's exclusion from access to the tree of life after gaining the knowledge of good and evil demonstrates that death was God's judgment against their sinful disobedience.[7] Terje Stordalen also appeals to the im-

---

4. Hamilton, *The Book of Genesis*, 163–66.

5. Mathews, *Genesis 1–11:26*, 205.

6. Bruggemann, *Genesis*, 42–48.

7. Keck, *Romans*, 149. Cf. Barr, *The Garden of Eden*, 57–73, who understands their exclusion from the tree of life to symbolize God's design for humans from the beginning rather than his judgment against their sinful disobedience.

agery of the tree of life to argue that exclusion from the garden equates to exclusion from life. In this way, the result of their sin was death.[8]

The sinful nature view does not question the relationship between the sin of Adam and inevitable, universal death. Rather, the sinful nature view questions the charge that universal death implicates every person in the *guilt* of the sin of Adam. C. John Collins strikes a blow to the doctrine of inherited guilt when he notes that the only explicit mention in the Genesis narrative of something being passed on to future generations is the comment in 3:15 that there would be enmity between the seed of the woman and the seed of the serpent. Collins argues from the singular form of the Septuagint (LXX) word for offspring in 3:15, *sperma*, that this is actually a promise of a personal redeemer. If that is the case, then the only thing passed explicitly in the Gen 2–3 narrative to future generations is the promise of a battle between Satan and Christ.[9]

Although sin results in death, it is not necessary to believe that the sin of Adam resulted in the *guilt* of all of humanity. Rather, the early chapters of Genesis indicate only that the sin of Adam and Eve resulted in their *eventual death*. Paul's comments in Rom 5 point toward the origin of sin with Adam, but the first chapter of that letter indicates that God's wrath comes as a result of our *behavior* rather than our *nature* (suppressed the truth [v. 18], worshipped the creature [v. 25], sinful actions [vv. 26–31] although they knew God's laws [v. 32]). The effects, or judgments, of Adam and Eve's sin are not immediately and fully felt by people. Infants, for example, do not experience the toil of working the ground or the pains of childbirth. These are effects of sin which, if infants live long enough, they will eventually experience.

Like Barr[10] and Stern,[11] Old Testament scholar Bruce Waltke connects Adam and Eve's taking from the tree with their later discovery of and shame over their nakedness. He refers to this as ethical awareness and defines it as "the capacity to create a system of ethics and make moral judgments."[12] Perhaps this is why infants display no shame when they are physically naked. They have not yet attained moral autonomy. In other

8. Stordalen, *Echoes of Eden*, 291–92.

9. Collins, "A Syntactical Note," 139–48.

10. Barr, *The Garden of Eden*, 62–65.

11. Stern, "The Knowledge of Good and Evil," 407–17.

12. Waltke, *Genesis: A Commentary*, 86.

words, infants are not ashamed of their nakedness because they have not yet reached for the forbidden fruit. They do not possess the moral knowledge required in order to either make or recognize moral choices before God.[13] But the human predicament is this: Given the time and capacity to mature, they will gain that moral knowledge. And when a person is able to distinguish between moral good and evil, his eyes are opened to his spiritual nakedness before God, and he experiences shame over his guilt. If this interpretation of the text is correct, then it is still necessary to explain why infants who have an undeveloped moral knowledge and who lack the accompanying shame and guilt sometimes die.

It is sometimes claimed that the death of some infants is evidence of their guilt, because death is a wage of sin. John Murray, for example, argues for the imputation of Adam's sin and guilt upon all of humanity by noting that infants die without "actually and voluntarily" sinning.[14] It is true that some people will die in their infancy, but it is an inappropriate leap to state that the reason that some infants die is because of their guilt. An infant has no ability to distinguish between good and evil, but this does not remove either the presence of an inherited sinful nature or the fallen condition of the world. In other words, infants' ignorance of the presence of sin in their nature and in the world does not exempt them from the broad wave of horrible consequences of sin. In this way, all infants are affected by sin and some are affected by the consequences of sin to such a degree that some infants will lose their life before they make it into childhood. Such a death, though, is not because of any guilt.

It is sin rather than guilt that is passed from Adam to all of humanity, and people are in a fallen condition from the moment of conception. The presence of sin in a person who is unable to make moral judgments (for example, an infant) makes that person subject to the effects of the presence of sin (in this case, death) but not guilty of sin. In this way, people begin life as infants who are sinners but not guilty of sin because they lack a developed moral knowledge, which results in a lack of shame or guilt over sin.

13. I am grateful to David Holland for pointing me to this possible correlation between a lack of knowledge of good and evil and a lack of shame about physical nakedness among young children.

14. Murray, *The Imputation of Adam's Sin*, 10.

DEUTERONOMY 1:39

> "Moreover, your little ones who you said would become a prey, and your sons, who this day have no knowledge of good or evil, shall enter there, and I will give it to them, and they shall possess it." —Deut 1:39

Deuteronomy 1:39 raises the following questions: Who were these "little ones" and "sons?" What is the meaning of the phrase "have no knowledge of good or evil?" What was the significance of this group entering the land when the rest of the generation had been prohibited? What, if anything, does this verse imply about whether infants receive only sin from Adam or both sin and guilt?

The first three chapters of Deuteronomy contain the address of Moses to the Israelites in which he describes their journey from Horeb (Sinai) to the plains of Moab. A survey of the contents of the first chapter follows, which should adequately set the context for verse 39.

After an introduction (1:1–5), Moses reports God's instructions for them to depart (vv. 6–8) and for him to appoint judges from among the tribes (vv. 9–18). They leave Horeb and upon arriving at Kadesh-Barnea, the spies who had been sent out from Israel become fearful and sin by failing to trust Yahweh, who had promised to go before them and fight for them (v. 19–33). Their response angers God, who swore on oath that none of that "evil generation" would see the land sworn to their forefathers (vv. 34–35). God then notes the following exceptions to his prohibition of entering the land: Caleb and his sons (v. 36), Joshua (v. 38), and "your little ones . . . your sons" (v. 39). Through Moses, God commands them to go into the desert (v. 40). They attempt to confess their sin and obey God's earlier instructions (v. 41), but it is too late. God states that they should not attempt to fight their enemies because he will not be present with them and they would lose (vv. 42–43). They ignore the warning, engage the Amorites in battle, and are soundly defeated (v. 44). They cry out to God, but he does not listen (v. 45). Finally they obey God's earlier command to travel into the desert (2:1).

Who were the "little ones" (*ṭap*) and "sons" (*bēn*) mentioned in Deut 1:39? In this verse, these words refer to the younger offspring of the disobedient generation. Numbers 14 is the parallel passage, so those verses will be considered, too. In Num 14:3, the people complained that their "little ones" (*ṭap*) would become "plunder." In 14:31 God speaks to Moses and Aaron in response to the complaint of the people. God states that he would bring their "children" (*tap*) into the land. If Num 14:3 and 31 are to be read together, then the people complained that their "little ones" would become "plunder" and God restated their complaint as a judgment that their "children" would become "prey." This phrase in Num 14:31 parallels exactly the statement in Deut 1:39, "your little ones who you said would become a prey."[15]

In Deut 1:39, the statement is made that their sons "have no knowledge of good or evil." By reading Num 14:29 and 33 with Deut 1:39, you can see God's judgment against the rebellion of his people. The older generation would die in the desert rather than enter the Promised Land. The sons who would be allowed to enter the land were identified in one text as having no knowledge of good or evil (Deut 1:39) and were identified in the other text as under the age of twenty years (Num 14:29).

By reading Deut 1 and Num 14 as parallel accounts, it seems clear that God judged the men who were twenty and older for their sinful action of grumbling against God. The "sons" who would be allowed to enter the land were those males under the age of twenty. Weinfeld translates the phrase in Deut 1:39 as "who do not yet know good from bad" and thinks it refers to males "not yet of responsible age." In support of this view, he compares the phrase to Isa 7:15, cites the parallel passage in Num 14:31, and notes the age of twenty years as a time of accountability (Exod 30:14 and Num 1:3). Weinfeld adds, "According to rabbinic tradition, man is not accountable before the age of twenty (*y. Bik.* 2:1; *y. Sanh.* 11:7; 30b; *b. Sabb.* 32b)."[16]

Although not guilty of the sin of the older generations, they would nevertheless suffer consequences for that generation's unfaithfulness, specifically a forty-year delay in entering the land. McConville offers a similar interpretation of Deut 1:39 when he writes,

---

15. McConville, *Deuteronomy*, 72, and Weinfeld, *Deuteronomy* 1–11, 151, see this parallel, note the absence of the phrase in the LXX, and conclude that the phrase was omitted. Lohfink, "Canonical Signals," 30–37, sees the same parallel but suggests that the MT in final form is the result of an earlier Hebrew manuscript tradition, to which the Samaritan Pentateuch added the phrase "which you said would become a prey" (although he reads it "of which you said, 'it shall become booty!'") and to which the LXX added the phrase "who this day have no knowledge of good or evil." Regardless of the direction in which the textual tradition developed, there is agreement that Deut 1:39 and the verses from Num 14 refer to the same episode.

16. Weinfeld, *Deuteronomy*, 151.

The next generation is now characterized as not knowing the difference between right and wrong. That is, at this moment of decision ('today'), they are not yet morally responsible (cf. Is. 7:15). This is different from an assertion of innocence as such. They are, indeed, guiltless with respect to their failure to enter the land at the first command. They, therefore, become recipients of the promised gift of land, and will 'inherit' it.[17]

Pastor and author John MacArthur holds a similar interpretation of Deut 1:39 and links that with the spiritual condition of infants today. He writes, "The Israelite children of sinful parents were allowed to enter fully into the blessing God had for His people. They were in no way held accountable, responsible, or punishable for the sins of their parents. Why? Because they had no knowledge of good and evil, right or wrong." After quoting Ezek 18:20, MacArthur continues, "The same is true today. A child may be conceived out of wedlock. A fetus may be aborted by an ungodly mother. A child may be beaten to death by an ungodly father. But before God, that child does not bear culpability for the sins of the parents. The children were considered 'innocent' of sin. They had not rebelled; they had no 'say' regarding the Israelite's rebellion and unbelief. In a profound way, God blessed their innocence."[18]

The understanding of Deut 1:39 explored in this chapter suggests a number of things concerning the nature of sin, guilt, and judgment. First, the "little ones" and "sons" were those Israelites who were at a childhood age—explicitly under twenty years old—when the older generation of Israelites disobeyed God. Although not held guilty for the sins of their fathers, the younger generation nevertheless experienced some of the negative consequences or wages of sin. They wandered in the desert, unable to inherit the Promised Land until the last person of the older generation died. In a similar way, infants today are not held responsible for the actions of previous generations, up to and including Adam. Like the younger generation in the Deuteronomy/Numbers account, infants experience the consequences of sin for which they are not counted guilty. Infants, for example, can experience illness, abuse, and even an early death, none of which are the result of their own sinful actions, but a result of the sinful actions of those who went before them, up to and including Adam.

17. McConville, *Deuteronomy 1–11*, 72.
18. MacArthur, *Safe in the Arms of God*, 45.

CONCLUSION

The concept of the knowledge of good and evil is presently being explored at Yale's Infant Cognition Center but it was first observed in the garden of Eden. After Adam and Eve ate from that tree, the results of their disobedience included shame and death. But it is not necessary to affirm the Augustinian-Calvinist view of inherited guilt. Rather, an inherited sinful nature view teaches that if a person lives long enough to be able to distinguish between good and evil, his eyes will be opened to his spiritual nakedness before God. The result is shame and guilt. Death, however, is a consequence that is experienced by some people even before they develop the ability to exercise moral autonomy.

Deuteronomy 1:39 cites a particular event in history when God set aside judgment for a group of people based upon their age and their lack of moral discernment. Although this younger generation (including infants) experienced some of the consequences of the sins of the older generations, they were not considered guilty by God because they had not yet developed this knowledge of good and evil.

8

John the Baptist: Salvation or Anointing?
(Luke 1:15)

I N HIS CHAPTER ON sin in *Systematic Theology*, Wayne Grudem states that "even before birth children have a guilty standing before God."[1] Grudem then asks if infants can be saved before they have a chance to hear and understand the gospel. Grudem answers his question by explaining that if infants are saved, it is only by the redemptive work of Christ and the regenerative work of the Holy Spirit. Further Grudem provides two examples from the Scriptures of people that he suggests were regenerated *before* their physical birth, John the Baptist and David. In other words, Grudem thinks that these two men were born spiritually before they were born physically.

LUKE 1:15

"For he will be great in the sight of the Lord; and he will drink no wine or liquor, and he will be filled with the Holy Spirit while yet in his mother's womb." —Luke 1:15

The statement is made proclaiming that John would be filled with the Holy Spirit "even from his mother's womb" (Luke 1:15b). In Ps 22:10, David declares, "Since my mother bore me you have been my God." Although Grudem admits that "this is not the usual way for God to save people," we "cannot know" how many infants God saves before their physical birth.[2]

---

1. Grudem, *Systematic Theology*, 499.

2. The translations of Luke 1:15b and Ps 22:10 are that of Grudem, *Systematic Theology*, 500.

In this chapter, I will attempt to determine the nature of John's filling of the Holy Spirit in Luke 1:15 and apply the findings to the present study.[3]

In the first chapter of Luke's gospel, an angel of the Lord appeared to Zacharias (Zechariah in the NIV and other translations) as he performed his priestly duties in the temple (1:8–11). Zacharias is told that his wife, Elizabeth, will bear a son, who will be great and "will be filled with the Holy Spirit while yet in his mother's womb" (v. 15b). What does it mean that John the Baptist would be filled with the Holy Spirit? Does this refer to an instance of prebirth salvation? If so, does this establish a paradigm for understanding the spiritual condition of infants?

Let us consider the last question first. Whatever is discovered about the relationship between the Holy Spirit and John the Baptist, it is important to remember that John was unique in God's plan. The things discovered about John's relationship as an infant with the Spirit will not necessarily have a bearing on the relationship between other infants and the Spirit. There are at least eight factors, which can be found in the immediate context of Luke 1:15, that demonstrate John's uniqueness. First, like the Old Testament heroes Isaac, Joseph, Samson, and Samuel, John was born to a barren woman (v. 7).[4] Second, his birth was announced by an angel of the Lord (v. 13). Third, John was named by God rather than his father (v. 13). Fourth, it is announced that Zacharias would have "joy" and "gladness," terms that are often associated with responses to God's work (v. 14). Fifth, the corporate rejoicing in verse 14 can be understood as an "eschatological joy."[5] Sixth, it is stated that John the Baptist will be "great in the sight of the Lord" (v. 15). Seventh, John will turn many Israelites back to God (v. 16). Eighth, John will prepare the way for the Messiah (v. 17). Whatever one's conclusion is about John's relationship to the Holy Spirit, he must certainly be understood as an infant who represents the "exception"[6] rather than the rule. Stated another way, the example of the

---

3. I will not consider Ps 22:10 for two reasons. First, I dealt in a previous section with another psalm of David, Ps 51:5, in which he refers to being sinful from the time of his birth. Second, the principle objections that will arise in this chapter can be applied to Grudem's view of Ps 22:10 as fetal salvation.

4. Marshall, *The Gospel of Luke*, 49. See also Brown, *The Birth of the Messiah*, 273, who notes that the births of Samson (Judg 13:4–5) and Samuel (1 Sam 1:9–15) also involved a statement of abstinence from wine.

5. Bock, *Luke 1:1—9:50*, 83.

6. This is the term used by Zuck, *Precious in His Sight*, 19.

relationship between John the Baptist in his infancy and the Holy Spirit is not the best example for establishing a paradigm for the relationship between the Holy Spirit and all other infants, or even the infant children of believers.

What was meant by the statement that "he will be filled with the Holy Spirit while yet in his mother's womb" (1:15b)? New Testament scholar Darrell Bock follows another respected scholar, I. Howard Marshall, in his comments in 1:15a about John's abstinence from wine. They think this statement does not refer to the Nazirite vow because of the lack of commands regarding the hair.[7] Instead, John is one who has been "set apart to God" and has a "prophetic role." The Spirit's presence in the womb represents "God's sovereign choice of one to serve him,"[8] or "prenatal sanctification."[9] Catholic scholar Raymond Brown also considers the statement in 1:15b as a reference to John as a prophet of God. Brown views John as having been filled with the "prophetic Holy Spirit."[10] There is justification for considering John to have been a prophet. First, he is commonly regarded as the last of the Old Testament prophets. Second, the circumstances of his birth resembled that of the prophet Samuel. Third, Jesus called John "more than a prophet" (7:26).

It is clear from the comments on this passage, that this sampling of New Testament scholars share a common view of the mention of the Holy Spirit in Luke 1:15 as a designation of John as God's prophet. If that is true, then Grudem's suggestion—that the presence of the Holy Spirit on the infant John represents salvation—presents an anachronistic ("against history") reading of the Holy Spirit in salvation history. Before the coming of the Holy Spirit upon Jewish believers at Pentecost (Acts 2), the Spirit came upon individuals in order to accomplish tasks such as speaking the word of the Lord or acting in his strength. The presence of the Holy Spirit as a promised seal was not revealed until after the death of John the Baptist.

What is the relevance of the above observations for the present study? First, the statement that John would be filled with the Holy Spirit while in the womb was not a promise that God had brought John to sav-

---

7. Bock, *Luke 1:1—9:50*, 85. Cf. Marshall, *The Gospel of Luke*, 58.
8. Bock, *Luke 1:1—9:50*, 85–86.
9. Marshall, *The Gospel of Luke*, 58.
10. Brown, *The Birth of the Messiah*, 274–75.

ing faith as an infant. Instead, this was a comment about John's role as a prophet of God. Second, Luke 1:15b does not imply that God can save infants because God did not send his Spirit to indwell believers until after the death of John the Baptist. I affirm that John was chosen by God and filled with his Holy Spirit even before birth. In that sense, John was in a relationship with God. I disagree, though, with the notion that John's prebirth experience somehow provides a template for understanding the spiritual condition of all infants. Luke 1:15b does not teach that God can save infants today before they are physically born. If there must be an application made of this text to the spiritual condition of infants, then it could be argued that the passage teaches that God sometimes fills infants before the time of their physical birth with his Spirit in order for them to function later as his prophets.

CONCLUSION

Some scholars cite Luke 1:15b as a rare occasion in which God saves a person before his or her physical birth. It was demonstrated, though, that this passage actually tells the story of God filling John the Baptist with his Spirit as an infant in order for John to later function as one of his prophets. Rather than an instance of infant salvation prior to physical birth, this passage is an example of the prebirth anointing of one of God's chosen prophets in the tradition of Jeremiah (Jer 1:5).

9

The Children with Jesus: Baptism or Blessing?
(Mark 10:13–16)

"And they were bringing children to Him so that He might touch them; but the disciples rebuked them. But when Jesus saw this, He was indignant and said to them, 'Permit the children to come to Me; do not hinder them; for the kingdom of God belongs to such as these. Truly I say to you, whoever does not receive the kingdom of God like a child will not enter it at all.' And He took them in His arms and began blessing them, laying His hands on them."
—Mark 10:13–16

ANYONE WHO HAS GROWN up attending church has seen them. Whether it was a pencil sketch or an acrylic painting, whether it was realistic or cartoonlike, you have seen them. In Sunday School rooms and illustrated children's Bibles of all types, you have seen images of Jesus welcoming the children. What, if anything, does this episode tell us about the spiritual condition of infants?

In Mark 10, Jesus' disciples rebuked people who were bringing children to be touched by Jesus (v. 13). The response from Jesus was indignation at his disciples and an invitation to allow the children to come to him. Not only does Jesus allow them to come to him, but he speaks against anyone who prohibits them and declares that it is to "such as these" that the kingdom of God belongs (v. 14). Then Jesus pronounces a "truly, truly" statement that people must receive the kingdom like a child or not enter (v. 15). Then he took the children in his arms, blessed them, and laid hands on them (v. 16). What can be discerned from this passage about the spiritual condition of infants?

Mark 10:13–16 (and parallels in Matt 19:13–15 and Luke 18:15–17) is important for the present study because it is one of the few first-century

writings about children.[1] The present section will consider the age of the
children and why they went to Jesus. Next, I will explain why this passage
should not be used as a proof-text in support of infant baptism. Finally, I
will offer an explanation of the meaning of the text and its application to
the present research.

The text does not reveal the exact age of the children who encountered Jesus but certain deductions can be made about the range of their
age based upon the events in the text. Mark and Matthew refer to *paidion*
("children") being brought to Jesus. This word alone doesn't clear things
up because in the New Testament, *paidion* is used to refer to both a newborn baby (John 16:21) and a twelve-year old girl (Mark 5:39–42). One of
the parallel passages, Luke 18:15–17, provides an interesting insight because two different words are used to refer to the same group of children.
Luke writes that the *brephos* ("infants")[2] were brought to him, but Jesus
commanded them to permit the *paidion* ("children") to come to him.

In his book *The Baptism of Disciples Alone*, Fred Malone argues that
the pronoun *auta* ("them") in Luke 18:16 should be understood as re-
flexive so that the children who were being restrained from coming to
Jesus were the *brephos*.[3] His conclusion is that the *brephos* mentioned in
verse 15 are old enough to respond to Jesus' call. Although the pronoun
in verse 16 can be understood to refer to the *brephos* in verse 15, it does
not follow that the *brephos* were the ones who were being kept from coming to Jesus. The reason for my disagreeing with Malone at this point is
that Jesus makes the following statement in verse 16: "Permit the children
(*paidion*) to come to Me." Jesus was clearly asking for the children to be
admitted and not prohibited from being in his presence. In Luke's account, Jesus called for the *brephos*, who were being brought to him, and
he ordered that the *paidion* be allowed to come to him. According to the
uses of the two words that have been surveyed in this section, *brephos*
refers only to infants, but *paidion* can refer either to infants or children

1. Donahue and Harrington, *The Gospel of Mark*, 301. For more on the first-century
sociocultural attitudes about children, see Bakke, *When Children Became People*.

2. Luke uses this word six times (Luke 1:41, 44; 2:12, 16; 18:15; Acts 7:19). The first
two occurrences refer to John the Baptist in the womb, the next two refer to Jesus in the
manger, the fifth occurrence is a parallel of the text in question, and the sixth refers to
the death of newborns at the time of Moses' birth (see Exod 1:15–2:5). The other gospel
writers, even in Matthew's record of the birth of Jesus, never used the word *brephos*.

3. Malone, *The Baptism of Disciples Alone*, 153.

up to twelve years old.[4] By reading Mark 10:13–16 in light of the nuanced uses of the two words in the texts above, it seems reasonable to suggest that the children who had an audience with Jesus varied in age. Some of them may have been as young as newborns, but others may have been up to twelve years old.

The children were brought to Jesus so that he could touch them (Mark 10:13). The result was that Jesus "took them in His arms and *began* blessing them, laying hands upon them" (v. 16b). Earlier in the gospel of Mark, the writer tells the stories of the expectation for healing by the father of a sick girl (5:23), and the woman who had bled for twelve years (5:28). There was a first-century belief in the power for healing by the touch of a spiritual man. The text, however, does not mention any sick children. It is more likely that the request was that Jesus bless the children.[5] Whether the blessing was especially significant or a standard blessing, precedent is found in Gen 48:14–18 for such an action in order to conferring God's blessing. These children were brought to Jesus to be touched by Jesus. He not only touched them but also blessed them and laid his hands upon them.

Mark 10:13–16 and its parallel passages have been used to support the practice of infant baptism. Joachim Jeremias, for example, argues that infants of believers and infants in the community were baptized by AD 70.[6] Jeremias argues that Jesus referred in John 3:5 to water baptism and that—read along with Mark 10:13–16 and two statements from Justin— early Christians made the connection to infant baptism. As further evidence, Jeremias writes that *kōluein* ("to hinder") is a technical term connected to water baptism (Acts 11:17).[7]

---

4. The definitions provided for these two words in the standard Greek-English lexicon BAG confirm these observations.

5. Donahue and Harrington, *The Gospel of Mark*, 299, notes the following "two dimensions" in New Tesatment times to receiving a blessing: physical contact with a holy person so that there can be a transfer of power and having a holy person call upon God to confer a blessing on a person. Consider also that according to Jeremias, *Infant Baptism in the First Four Centuries*, 49, the Babylonian Talmud records in *Sopherim* 18.5 that Jewish parents brought their children to scribes for prayer and blessing on Yom Kippur.

6. Jeremias, Die *Kindertaufe*, 68. Aland, *Did the Early Church Baptize Infants?*, 95 n. 3, notes that the English edition of this work does not include this important and startling claim.

7. Jeremias, *Infant Baptism in the First Four Centuries*, 50–53.

Kurt Aland directly refutes the two major arguments of Jeremias, which are that Mark 10:13–16 depends on John 3:5 and that *kōluein* is a technical term related to water baptism. On the first argument, Aland admits that there is an "external parallel" of the "truly, truly" statements, but the phrase occurs so often in the gospels that there is no special significance to the use of the phrase in both texts.[8] Also, the idea of being born again (John 3:5) is not the same as the concept in the Synoptic Gospels (Matthew, Mark, and Luke) of receiving the kingdom of God like a child (Mark 10:15). Further evidence against dependence of Mark 10:13–16 on John 3:5 is that Nicodemus was an old man, but Jesus spoke in Mark 10 about children.

Against the notion that *kōluein* is a technical term related to water baptism, Aland notes that this verb is used twenty-three times in the New Testament and "rarely" refers to baptism. He adds that the word should only be understood as a technical term related to baptism when the context is clearly a situation of water baptism, which is not the case in Mark 10:13–16.[9] Aland seems to have rendered the arguments of Jeremias for infant baptism to be untenable.[10] Consider also the following common-sense observation about the parallel passage Matt 19:13–15 by Fred Malone: "In fact, if any passage in Scripture teaches the fallacy of paedobaptism this one does. Neither Jesus nor His disciples baptized these children even though they had a perfect opportunity to do so. Instead, Jesus and the disciples only blessed them."[11]

In Mark 10:13–16, children of unknown ages (perhaps as young as infants and as old as twelve years) were brought to Jesus so that he could offer them a physical touch. His disciples rebuked those who brought the children, and Jesus used that event as a chance to teach his disciples about both the significance of children and the reception of the kingdom of God as a gift.[12] It is not possible to determine whether or not Jesus viewed the

8. The phrase translated "truly, truly" occurs thirty-one times in Matthew, fourteen times in Mark, seven times in Luke, and twenty-five times in John. Aland, *Did the Early Church Baptize Infants?*, 98.

9. Ibid., 96–99.

10. Although arguments for infant baptism can be made from a covenantal view of theology, a pursuit of that trajectory would fall outside of the scope of the present study and so will not be engaged. For more on this debate, see Wellum, "Baptism," 97–161.

11. Malone, *The Baptism of Disciples Alone*, 153.

12. Donahue and Harrington, *The Gospel of Mark*, 301. Cf. Rowe, *God's Kingdom*

infants in the group as guilty of sin, but he did welcome them. Although the actions of Jesus were not a declaration of their innocence, or even a sinful-yet-guiltless condition, he did not call them to repentance or attempt to baptize them with water. He simply welcomed the children, blessed them, and pointed to them as an example for how one should receive the kingdom of God.

CONCLUSION

In Mark 10:13–16, Jesus blessed young children. Although it is not certain whether or not Jesus considered them guilty of sin, he neither called them to repentance nor attempted to baptize them with water. Rather, he blessed them and pointed to them as an example of how a person should receive the kingdom of God.

---

and God's Son, 156, who writes, "To receive 'like a child' means to receive a gift with a trusting and dependent attitude, rather than trying to earn a reward by one's status or achievements."

10

Holy Children: Covenant or Blessing?
(1 Corinthians 7:14)

> "For the unbelieving husband is sanctified through his wife, and
> the unbelieving wife is sanctified through her believing husband;
> for otherwise your children are unclean, but now they are holy."
> —1 Cor 7:14

The final New Testament passage to consider when exploring the biblical
teaching on the spiritual condition of infants is 1 Cor 7:14. In this section of Paul's letter, he gives instructions concerning various situations in
which believers find themselves. Some of them are single and desire marriage (vv. 1–9). Others are believers and married but desire to separate
from their spouse (vv. 10–11). In the immediate context of the verse in
question, Paul addresses a situation in which one person in the marriage
is a believer and the other person is an unbeliever. Paul writes, "For the
unbelieving husband is sanctified through his wife, and the unbelieving
wife is sanctified through her believing husband; for otherwise your children are unclean, but now they are holy." How should these comments be
understood? What does Paul mean when he writes that an unbelieving
spouse "is sanctified" through the believing spouse? Is this a reference to
salvation or to something else? What does Paul mean when he writes that
the children are holy? Does this mean that infants in such a home should
be considered believers?

Some Protestants hold a doctrine that is known by various titles,
such as the doctrine of covenant succession, children in the covenant, or
practical covenant theology. Benjamin Wikner defines covenant succession as "the Scriptural teaching that the children of believers (covenant
children) are expected to succeed in the faith of their parents, and this is

accomplished through the divinely ordained means of covenant."[1] This view teaches that there are corresponding blessings and curses upon the children of believing parents according to the example and nurture that the parents provide their children.[2] In this way, believing parents should train their children in godliness even from infancy and treat their children as believers because they are participants in the covenant. After providing quotations from Reformers such as Henry Bullinger, Caspar Olevianus, John Calvin, and Ulrich Zwingli to establish its legitimacy, Thomas Trouwborst makes the following summary statement:

> The Reformers understood our children as fully Christian. That is, the children of the covenant did not merely have certain advantages of being in the covenant or the church, but they had salvation entire—whether described by forgiveness of sins, regeneration, being covered by the blood of Christ, justified, sanctified, or members of the kingdom of heaven. Since this is what they possessed, they did not need to obtain these blessings for the first time at some future point. They were members in good standing in Christ's church and were expected to continue as such through faithful parental training in complete reliance on the work of the Holy Spirit.[3]

Although that view of covenant succession has been challenged by Anabaptists, Baptists, and the larger circle of evangelical groups throughout the centuries that associates salvation with a "model of conversion experience," the doctrine of covenant succession is common in present-day Reformed churches.[4]

According to the doctrine of covenant succession, Paul clearly taught in 1 Cor 7:14 that children are holy due to their participation in the covenant. This view is supported by a theological statement produced by the Synod of Dort (1618–19), which supplied the (in)famous TULIP acronym.[5] Canon 1.17 states that "the children of believers are holy, not

---

1. Wikner, "Introduction," in *To You and Your Children*, xix.

2. See Rayburn, "Parental Conditions," in *To You and Your Children*, 3–27.

3. Trouwborst, "From Covenant to Chaos," in *To You and Your Children*, 76.

4. Ibid., 101. For examples of those who hold to the doctrine of covenant succession in present-day Reformed churches, see Venema, "The Doctrine of the Sacraments and Baptism," 21–86; *To You and Your Children*, ed. Wikner; and Lusk, *Paedofaith*.

5. TULIP stands for: Total Depravity, Unconditional Election, Limited Atonement, Irresistible Grace, and Perseverance of the Saints.

by nature, but in virtue of the covenant of grace" and further states that
"godly parents ought not to doubt the election and salvation of their children whom it pleases God to call out of this life in their infancy." In other
words, children of believers are believers due to the covenant, and any
who die will be in heaven due to the covenant. At the end of that statement, the following verses are cited for biblical support: Gen 17:7, Acts
2:39, and 1 Cor 7:14. Charles A. McIlhenney clarifies the significance of
those verses when he writes that children with believing parents would
be holy because they would be in Christ due to the Abrahamic covenant,
which was recorded in Gen 17 and restated in Acts 2.[6]

The doctrine of covenant succession should be commended for
both its desire to affirm God's promises in both the Old and the New
Testaments and also for its call for believing parents to nurture in their
children a heart of repentance and faith. But the doctrine of covenant
succession is inadequate because it imports an extra-biblical viewpoint
into its reading of the Bible. The viewpoint which colors their reading of
the covenantal texts in Scripture is the wrong-headed assumption that the
children of believers are themselves believers due to a covenantal status.[7]

So, all readers must decide whether or not 1 Cor 7:14 teaches that infants with at least one believing parent are included in the covenant. Also,
readers must make a judgment about whether or not the sanctification
results in the salvation of the child. This section will proceed with those
two categories in view, covenant and salvation. McIlhenney's interpretation of the verse, for example, fits the categories of covenantal/salvific. He
sees the covenant in the background and considers all children of believing parents to be believers.

One major difficulty with the covenantal/salvific view is that if one
understands every occurrence of the words *sanctified* and *holy* as references to salvation, then consistency demands that both the unbelieving

6. McIlhenney, "Will My Child Go to Heaven?", 184–85.

7. For an excellent response to the in-creeping of covenant succession into evangelical theology and its implications for the doctrine of baptism, see *Believer's Baptism*. After
explaining that their volume was not written in response to those who view paedobaptism as salvific, Schreiner and Wright write in the "Introduction," 7, "Our desire, rather,
is to respond to evangelical paedobaptists, primarily in the Reformed tradition, who
baptize infants not because they believe that baptism regenerates the child but because
they believe that baptism brings the child into the covenant community where he or she
will have the blessing of hearing the gospel preached as they grow up as members of the
church."

spouse and the children mentioned in 1 Cor 7:14 should be included in the covenant and considered to be believers. McIlhenney, though, is clear on this issue when he writes, "The believing parent sanctifies the unbelieving parent, but that does not mean that the unbelieving spouse is saved."[8] Why would the sanctifying work of God within the covenant save the child but not the spouse? Fred Malone[9] criticizes G. I. Williamson's conclusions about 1 Cor 7:14 for the same reason. Malone writes, "Williamson is inconsistent in his hermeneutic because he will not call the unbelieving spouse a Christian as he does the children."[10] In arguing against 1 Cor 7:14 as implicit support for infant baptism, New Testament professor Thomas Schreiner concurs that Paul did not mean that these "holy" children were either believers or part of the covenant.[11]

In his commentary on 1 Corinthians, Gordon Fee points to the words "sanctified" and "holy." He notes that forms of the verb *hagiazō* ("to make holy") have already appeared in 1:30 and 6:11 "as a metaphor of salvation." Fee continues, "But whatever it means here, it cannot carry that force, not only because the idea that marriage can effect salvation for the pagan partner would be nonsense to Paul but also because v. 16 completely disallows such a sense." Fee then cites Paul's use in Rom 11:16 of "holy." In that verse, if part of an offering to God of dough is holy, then the whole batch is holy. Israel had not yet been fully converted, but because of their original belief, they were still considered "holy." Similarly, the setting apart for God of the marriage by the belief of one spouse sanctifies both partners.[12] Through this intertextual reading, Fee exposes as wrong-headed this equating of "sanctified" and "holy" with salvation, which supports the misguided, covenant succession view of 1 Cor 7:14.

Commenting on the verse in question, Paige Patterson notes that the meaning of *hagiazō* depends upon the context of the word. He cites as an

---

8. McIlhenney, "Will My Child Go to Heaven?", 185.

9. According to the categories above, Malone argues in *The Baptism of Disciples Alone*, 141–49, for a noncovenantal/nonsalvific view.

10. Malone, *The Baptism of Disciples Alone*, 143.

11. Schreiner, "Baptism in the Epistles," 95. Wilson, "Baptism and Children," 286–302, argues that Baptists claim that every conversion be dramatic and that the exact moment of conversion can be discerned. Against Wilson's view, Schreiner, "Baptism in the Epistles," 95 n. 67, defends believer's baptism by explaining that "the Baptist does argue that baptism should only take place when there is evidence that God has indeed worked savingly in the hearts of children."

12. Fee, *The First Epistle to the Corinthians*, 299–301. Quotations on 299.

example 1 Pet 3:15, in which believers are commanded to "sanctify" the Lord God in their hearts. He then quips, "God has no need for sanctification" and explains that although the word often refers to salvation that is clearly not always the case. Patterson reads 1 Cor 7:14 in context with the rhetorical questions in verse 16 and concludes that the unbelieving spouse and children in question would not receive salvation, but would be recipients of God's blessings due to their familial relationship with the believer.[13] What kind of blessing was available to the unbelieving spouse? Collins answers that "a Christian married to a non-Christian should remain committed to his or her spouse on the grounds of a well-founded hope of their conversion."[14]

In addition to the blessings that an unbelieving spouse and a child in that household would receive under the care of a believing parent, it is also true that Paul was making a statement about the legitimacy of a marriage between a believer and an unbeliever. Fred Malone discerns in 1 Cor 7:14 Paul's response to the commands in Ezra 10:2–3 to put away the wives and children of mixed marriages. Paul responds by telling the believing spouse to remain in the marriage. This difference between the command in the Old Testament and the command in the New Testament is due to the sanctifying work of Christ in a marriage. Rather than the unbeliever defiling the believer with sin, as was the case in the Old Testament, the believer's holiness now contaminates (sanctifies) the unbeliever.[15]

Garland supports this idea through the blending of the following four concepts: marriage as becoming one flesh (Gen 2:24 cited in 1 Cor 6:16), the holiness of believers as God's temple (1 Cor 3:16–17 and 6:19), the transferability of holiness (Exod 29:37; 30:29 and Lev 6:18) and the "concept of family solidarity." Uniting with a prostitute, which is not God's will, would result in corruption. Instead, the sexual union of marriage, which is in accordance with God's will, facilitates a transfer of holiness

13. Patterson, *The Troubled, Triumphant Church*, 119–20. Although Patterson holds a non-covenantal/non-salvific view, a similar conclusion on the meaning of "sanctified" as set apart rather than saved is made by Collins, *First Corinthians*, 265–72, who holds a covenantal/non-salvific view.

14. Collins, *First Corinthians*, 272. Cf. Garland, *1 Corinthians*, 295; Fee, *First Epistle to the Corinthians*, 306; and Patterson, *The Troubled, Triumphant Church*, 121.

15. Malone, *The Baptism of Disciples Alone*, 144. In Ezra, the Israelite men knowingly married foreign women. In the Corinthian church, the original circumstances may not have been the same. Thanks to Scott Callaham for pointing out to me those different contexts.

from the believing spouse to the unbeliever. Because Paul argues for believers to remain in a mixed marriage, he mentions the condition of their children in order to assert something like this: The children produced by your marriage to an unbeliever are holy; the unbeliever's relationship to you makes him/her holy; marriages between holy people should be maintained (vv. 10–11); therefore, mixed marriages should be maintained.[16]

CONCLUSION

So, what does 1 Cor 7:14 imply about the spiritual condition of infants? This passage is cited by some people who teach a covenant view of salvation and infant baptism. Their argument is that the sanctification mentioned by Paul refers to the children of believers being protected by God due to the faith of their parents. In this chapter, I attempted to demonstrate some of the difficulties in affirming a covenantal view of salvation and infant baptism.

The examination above indicates that infants in a household with one or more believing parents enjoy a life which has been affected by a "setting apart" by God due to their relationship with the believing parent. This "setting apart" is neither participation in the covenant nor individual salvation but the ability to enjoy blessings that are bestowed upon the children of believers. These blessings are not explicitly mentioned but might include the opportunity to hear and respond to the gospel early in life, protection from rampant sin, and other ancillary benefits of growing up in a household in which God is feared and his Word is held in high regard.

16. Garland, *1 Corinthians*, 288–90.

HISTORICAL SECTION

In this part of the book, I will survey the views of pastors and teachers who have addressed the spiritual condition of infants throughout church history. I will consider church fathers from both the Eastern (Irenaeus, Gregory of Nazianzus, and Gregory of Nyssa) and the Western (Tertullian and Cyprian) traditions. Next I will consider the view of Augustine, who has undoubtedly been the most influential figure on this subject. Due to space constraints and their restatement of previous positions, I will not consider any viewpoints from the medieval period, which dates from the fifth to the fifteenth centuries. The study will resume with representatives from the reforming movement, which can loosely be characterized as magisterial reformers (Luther, Zwingli, and Calvin) and Anabaptist reformers (Hubmaier and Marpeck). The historical survey will conclude with the following Baptist representatives from the nineteenth century (James P. Boyce, A. H. Strong, and E. Y. Mullins) and twentieth century (William Hendricks and Millard Erickson).

11

The Eastern Church Fathers
(Irenaeus, Gregory of Nazianzus,
and Gregory of Nyssa)

THE THEOLOGICAL WORLD OF the patristic period can be roughly divided into the Eastern and Western traditions. Some of the differences between these traditions are widely known. As examples, the Eastern fathers tended to read and write in Greek, but the Western fathers worked in Latin; the Eastern fathers thought of salvation in terms of theosis, deification, or divinization, but the Western fathers thought in terms of justification. Another major distinction is that Eastern theologians denied the idea of inherited guilt, but Western theologians affirmed it. Consider this summary by the International Theological Commission of the Roman Catholic Church, "For the Greek Fathers, as the consequence of Adam's sin, human beings inherited corruption, possibility and mortality, from which they could be restored by a process of deification made possible through the redemptive work of Christ. The idea of inheritance of sin or guilt—common in the western tradition—was foreign to this perspective since in their view sin could only be a free, personal act."[1]

In this chapter, I will examine some of the writings of Irenaeus, Gregory of Nazianzus and Gregory of Nyssa in order to determine the views of these pre-Augustinian, Eastern theologians on the spiritual condition of infants. I will attempt to demonstrate by their writings that these Eastern theologians considered infants to be free from the guilt and condemnation of Adam's sin. These three theologians are only representatives of the Eastern view. Other writings could be surveyed for their statements on the spiritual condition of infants. Consider, for example,

---

1. International Theological Commission, "The Hope of Salvation," 729.

83

the following remark from John Chrysostom (374–407): "We do baptize infants, although they are not guilty of any sins."[2]

IRENAEUS

Robert M. Grant calls Irenaeus of Lyon (ca. 140–200) "the most important Christian controversialist and theologian" between the time of the apostles and the time of Origen.[3] He was familiar with most of the New Testament and the writings of the apostolic fathers. Irenaeus knew Justin, Tatian, and Theophilus. Irenaeus had met Polycarp, a disciple of John, and had served as the second bishop of Lyon, a city in present-day southern France.

The theological viewpoint of Irenaeus was shaped in reaction to the heresy of Gnosticism, which taught that the material world was the result of an error by a pair of aeons.[4] According to this system, the world should not exist and needs to be redeemed. Against this wrongheaded view of the world and the origin of sin, Irenaeus affirms that the Creator God sent his Son to redeem fallen humanity. In *Proof of the Apostolic Preaching*, Irenaeus sketched the biblical storyline of God as a good and transcendent creator and man as the one who rebelled against God's commands.[5]

How did Irenaeus understand the original state of humanity prior to the fall and the subsequent need for redemption? Should his view of the pre-fall condition of humanity be translated into his understanding of the spiritual condition of infants? Although not explicitly about infants, the following passage by Irenaeus seems to correlate Adam and Eve's status prior to the fall with that of the innocence and purity of childhood:

> Adam and Eve were naked and they were not ashamed, for they were innocent and had only thoughts that were pure, like those of children. Nothing entered their minds that could cause evil desires or shameful impulses to take birth in their souls. They still retained the integrity of their nature because that which had been breathed into them at the moment of creation was the breath of life. Now, as long as this breath retained its intensity and force, it sheltered their

2. John Chrysostom *On Infants*, in *Later Christian Fathers*, 169.

3. Grant, *Irenaeus of Lyons*, 1.

4. For more on his concern over the Valentinians, see Grant, *Irenaeus of Lyons*, 21–28.

5. Rondet, *Original Sin*, 38–39.

thought and their mind from evil. That is why they embraced each other with caresses, just like children.[6]

Based on the passage above, O. M. Bakke thinks that Irenaeus saw a relationship between Adam and Eve's lack of sexual desire and the innocence of children.[7] It could be argued that the statements comparing Adam and Eve with children were meant only euphemistically rather than as a precise theological statement on the spiritual condition of children. But even if the phases are understood as euphemisms, they still carry the meaning that childhood is a time of innocence and purity. Further, the passage speaks of Adam and Eve as being "sheltered" from evil.

In addition to his view of the human condition prior to the fall, it is helpful to consider his view of the atonement. Irenaeus is probably best known for his view of salvation, which is known as recapitulation. For Irenaeus, Adam was the prototype of humanity and the cross of Christ came in the fullness of time in order to reverse the previous curse and restore our likeness to God.[8] The comparisons between the first garden and the cross of Christ abounded in his writings. As examples: neither Adam nor Jesus had earthly fathers, both Eve and Mary were virgins but the latter was obedient while the former was not, and just as Adam sinned on the sixth day so Christ died on the sixth day.[9] As Rondet writes, "Jesus is the new Adam; Mary, his mother, is the new Eve."[10] The cross brought about a recapitulation, or resumption, of what was lost in the garden.

In arguing against those who taught that Jesus only ministered publicly for one year, Irenaeus espoused the view that Jesus experienced in the incarnation every age of life in order to sanctify every stage of life. The quotation is as follows:

> For He came to save all through means of Himself—all, I say, who through Him are born again to God—infants, and children, and boys, and youths, and old men. He therefore passed through every age, becoming an infant for infants, thus sanctifying infants; a child for children, thus sanctifying those who are of this age, being at the same time made to them an example of piety, righteous-

---

6. Irenaeus *Proof of the Apostolic Preaching* 14, in ACW 16:53–54.

7. Bakke, *When Children Became People,* 69.

8. Irenaeus *Against Heresies* 3.21.10, in ANF 1:454.

9. Ibid., 3.22.3–4; 5.23.2, in ANF 1:455; 1:551–52.

10. Rondet, *Original Sin,* 42.

ness, and submission; a youth for youths, becoming an example
to youths, and thus sanctifying them from the Lord. So likewise
He was an old man for old men, that He might be a perfect master
for all, not merely as respects the setting forth of the truth, but
also as regards age, sanctifying at the same time the aged also, and
becoming an example to them likewise.[11]

The significance of the above quotation is that Irenaeus mentions
the salvation of infants, but that is not the focus of the text, and he does
not elaborate on how infants are saved. Terrance Tiessen understands
this comment to mean that "Irenaeus did consider infants in need of
saving grace."[12] He notes the references to this passage in support of infant baptism by Alexander Roberts and Adelin Rousseau but adds that
"many Christians who do not believe in baptismal regeneration (e.g.
Presbyterians and Baptists) believe in an 'age of accountability' prior to
which children who die are saved through the efficacy of Christ's atonement, apart from a personal act of faith."[13]

The dating of the origin of the practice of infant baptism in the
early church has been the subject of much discussion. Tertullian wrote
On Baptism between 200 and 206, offering alternatives to the practice of
baptizing infants. Between thirty and fifty years later, Origen (185–254)
defended the practice in two different works. Origen wrote that infants
benefited by the practice because they shared in the "stain" of Adam's sin
and because it was the "custom of the Church," which originated with
the apostles.[14] If infant baptism was already practiced in the early church
by 200,[15] then it is possible that the statement by Irenaeus that one must

---

11. Irenaeus *Against Heresies*, in ANF 1:391.

12. Tiessen, *Irenaeus on the Salvation of the Unevangelized*, 216.

13. Roberts, undesignated footnote in ANF 1:391, and Rousseau, et. al, *Contre les
Hérésies*, 287, in Tiessen, *Irenaeus on the Salvation of the Unevangelized*, 216 n. 5.

14. Origen *Commentary on Romans* 5.9, in FC 103; and *Homilies on Leviticus* 7, in
FC 83.

15. Bakke, *When Children Became People*, 240. Against this view, see McKinion,
"Baptism in the Patristic Writings," 168, who presents evidence from this period to support his conclusion that "the baptism of believers only was the normative practice in the
second century, with the possible exception of emergency baptisms of mortally ill infants
later in the century." McKinion, 180, thinks Origen was apologizing for the practice.
Wright, "Recovering Baptism for a New Age of Mission," 57, argues that it was not a
"common practice, until after Augustine, perhaps in the sixth century."

be "born again to God" is a technical reference to baptism.[16] Joachim Jeremias argues that the phrase was a technical reference to baptism but Kurt Aland argues against that view.[17]

The occurrences of infant baptism as early as the middle of the second century forced the church to reflect critically about its justification for the practice. Consider the following observation by David F. Wright about the order of reflection and practice on this issue of infant baptism:

> There is no doubt that the custom of infant baptism was the single most powerful catalyst of the formulation of doctrines of original sin, and that the direction of argument moved from the accepted practice of infant baptism to the truth of the doctrine, and not vice-versa. We have here an unmistakable illustration of the axiom *lex orandi lex credenda* ["the law of worship is the law of belief"]. The church baptizes babies who, it is agreed, have not sinned *in proporia persona* ["in person"]; therefore, we must believe that they are baptized for the cleansing or remission of original sin. Original sin must be part of the faith of the church; why else does the church baptize babies?[18]

The focus of Irenaeus' argument throughout *Against Heresies* 2.22 was neither on infant baptism nor on the salvation of infants; it was to persuade his readers that Jesus ministered publicly for over twenty years and was over fifty years old when he died.[19] So, the incarnation was significant for Irenaeus due to Jesus attaining various ages, including infancy, but the patristic father does not elaborate on the idea of infant salvation. When Irenaeus mentioned the sanctification of other groups (children, youth, and old men), he wrote of Jesus being an example to them. But he did *not* mention Jesus being an example to infants. Perhaps that was

---

16. Irenaeus *Against Heresies* 2.22.4, in ANF 1:391.

17. Jeremias, *Infant Baptism in the First Four Centuries*, 72–75; Idem, *The Origins*, 62–63; Aland, *Early Church*, 58–59.

18. Wright, "How Controversial," 51. See also Bakke, *When Children Became People*, 241; International Theological Commission, "The Hope of Salvation," 729; McKinion, *Life and Practice*, 10; Newman, *A History of Anti-Pedobaptism*, 8–9; and Wiley, *Origins*, 60–61.

19. Irenaeus *Against Heresies* 2.22.5–6, reasoned that although Jesus was thirty at the time of his baptism, he was acknowledged at the time of his entrance into Jerusalem as a master teacher, which meant that he was nearly fifty. Irenaeus argued that by the time of his death, Jesus was over fifty years old. This explains why the Jews asked how he, being not yet fifty years old, had seen Abraham.

because he viewed infants as being unable to consider human examples. Without further explanation by the original author or a wider context for understanding the comment, interpretations will abound on this mention of infant sanctification. A Universalist would understand his statement to mean that Jesus had redeemed all of humanity through the incarnation but a covenant theologian would understand the sanctification to refer only to the children of believing parents. Although the means and nature of infant sanctification in this passage are unclear, this Eastern theologian affirmed that the incarnation of the Son of God positively impacted all of humanity, from the youngest to the oldest.

GREGORY OF NAZIANZUS

Gregory of Nazianzus (ca. 330–390) is known today as one of the Great Cappadocians, the others being the brothers Gregory of Nyssa (ca. 330–394) and Basil of Caesarea (d. 379). Gregory of Nazianzus was born to Gregory, bishop of Nazianzus, and Nona. His father held heretical views such as rejecting the Trinity, but he was corrected by Nona and he converted prior to being installed as a bishop.[20] Gregory was dedicated by his mother, who had made that promise before his birth.[21] Although he was dedicated to God as an infant and raised by Christian parents, he was not baptized until he entered the monastic life at the age of thirty.[22] He served as a presbyter in Nazianzus and then as a bishop. His struggle against Arianism culminated in his influence on the Council of Constantinople, which in 381 affirmed the divinity of both the Son and the Holy Spirit.[23] He spent the remainder of his life out of the scrutiny of ecclesial or civic office.

Although he wrote many poems, which were later sung as hymns, and letters, Gregory's theology was preserved in his orations.[24] His contribution, which is relevant to the present study, is found in a sermon known

20. Browne and Swallow, "Prolegomena," 187.

21. Gregory of Nazianzus, *Oration* 18, in NPNF2 7:258.

22. Adult baptism was common among the church fathers. Jeremias, *Infant Baptism in the First Four Centuries*, 88, presents the following approximate ages for the time of baptism of the following theologians: Basil of Caesarea, twenty-eight; Ambrose, forty; John Chrysostom, fourteen to twenty-four; Jerome, sixteen to twenty-six; Rufinus, twenty-five; and Augustine, thirty-three.

23. González, *The Story of Christianity*, 187–88.

24. Rondet, *Original Sin*, 98.

as *Oration* 40, or "The Oration on Holy Baptism," which he preached in Constantinople on January 6, 381. In this sermon, Gregory noted that baptism "cuts off all the veil that is derived from birth."[25] He did not expound on the nature of the veil, but the editors identify it in a footnote as "Original Sin." I will attempt to demonstrate from an examination of *Oration* 40 that Gregory affirms the doctrine of original sin but rejects the doctrine of inherited guilt.

Gregory urged the hearer to "fortify yourself [before death] with the Seal."[26] He called for young and old to be baptized. He urged the congregation, "Have you an infant child? Do not let sin get any opportunity, but let him be sanctified from his childhood; from his very tenderest age let him be consecrated by the Spirit." He then cited the example of Anna [*sic*], who "consecrated" Samuel after his birth and raised him as a priest, who would trust in God.[27] Rather than the cleansing of Adamic guilt, this sanctification of infants to which Gregory referred is the same consecration to the Lord that he and the prophet Samuel experienced as newborns. In *Oration* 40, Gregory does not call for infants to be baptized. Rather, he mentions that infants are sanctified by their consecration to the Lord.

Baptism, he explains, is a benefit to a person in any stage of life, married or single, rich or poor. Gregory refuted the idea that the parable of the workers in the vineyard who begin their day at different times but receive equal pay refers to people who were baptized earlier or later in life. The argument Gregory refuted was that delaying baptism was a way to avoid laboring in the church, because believing and receiving baptism later in life leads to the same reward. Gregory also dismissed the idea that God, in his mercy, would "take the desire of Baptism instead of Baptism." God, he told his congregants, does not regard the unbaptized as baptized.[28]

25. Gregory of Nazianzus, *Oration* 40.2, in NPNF2 7:360.

26. Gregory of Nazianzus, *Oration* 40.15, in NPNF2 7:364. The "Seal" was one of his many terms for baptism. Other references to baptism in *Oration* 40.4 include: the clothing of immortality, the enlightenment, the gift, the grace, illumination, the laver of regeneration, and unction.

27. Gregory of Nazianzus, *Oration* 40.17, in NPNF2 7:365.

28. Gregory of Nazianzus, *Oration* 40.18–22, in NPNF2 7:365–67. The Roman Catholic Church recently articulated its "hope," based largely upon the influence of Karl Rahner, that God accepts such a desire for infants who die without having been baptized. The idea is that God substitutes for those infants the baptism of water with either a baptism of blood (likening an infant's death to that of a martyr) or a baptism of desire (citing either an infant's "unconscious desire" to have been baptized or the desire of the church

Three groups of people do not receive baptism and the result for each of them is different. The first group will not receive the "gift" of baptism because they despise it; they will suffer punishment for their sins, which include their "contempt of baptism." The second group will not receive baptism due to their foolishness or neglect; they will suffer but to a lesser degree because of their lack of malice. The third group is "not in a position to receive it, perhaps on account of infancy." They "will be neither glorified nor punished by the righteous Judge, as unsealed and yet not wicked, but persons who have suffered rather than done wrong."[29] It seems by this remark that Gregory regards unbaptized infants as worthy of neither justification nor judgment before God.

Gregory exhorted his hearers to be baptized now rather than waiting until another holy day such as Easter or Pentecost or when a family could witness their baptism.[30] Next he anticipated the following objection: "(W)hat have you to say about those who are still children, and conscious neither of the loss nor of the grace? Are we to baptize them, too?" He answered with the following affirmative, clarifying remark, "Certainly, if any danger presses. For it is better that they should be unconsciously sanctified than that they should depart unsealed and uninitiated."[31] In support of his remark, he cited eighth-day circumcision on "children before they had use of reason" and anointing doorposts, "though applied to things which had no consciousness." He continued by telling other parents to wait until their children are at least three years old, when they can listen to instruction and be able to answer questions about baptism. In this passage, infant baptism seems to be a concession for parents whose child approaches death prior to being able to hear and understand the gospel. I agree with Steven McKinion, who writes of this text, "Reading Gregory's allowance for infant baptism as a pastoral accommodation is supported by his immediate appeal to avoid the practice in other than emergency situations."[32]

---

for them to have been baptized). See International Theological Commission, "The Hope of Salvation," 732–33.

29. Gregory of Nazianzus, *Oration* 40.23, in NPNF2 7:367.

30. Gregory of Nazianzus, *Oration* 40.24–25, in NPNF2 7:368–69.

31. Gregory of Nazianzus, *Oration* 40.28, in NPNF2 7:370. McKinion, "Baptism in the Patristic Writings," 183, suggests that while *uninitiated* could mean "unsaved," it could also mean "not initiated into the life of the church."

32. McKinion, "Baptism in the Patristic Writings," 183.

This section of the sermon ends with perhaps the most significant statement for the present study. Gregory preached, "For this is how the matter stands; at that time they begin to be responsible for their lives, when reason is matured, and they learn the mystery of life (*for of sins of ignorance owing to their tender years they have no account to give*), and it is far more profitable on all accounts to be fortified by the Font, because of the sudden assaults of danger that befall us, stronger than our helpers."[33]

Gregory held forth in the passage above the following two ideas: First, people are not born with the responsibility of Adam's sin. Rather, they become morally responsible at the point in life at which their reason matures and "they learn the mystery of life." Second, they are not responsible for sins committed prior to this time of responsibility. Infancy is obviously included in the earliest period of life; Gregory called this period the "tender years," which is a time *prior* to people becoming "responsible for their lives." All sins committed during these "tender years" are regarded by God as "sins of ignorance," for which the person will not have to give an account.

Because Gregory affirmed "the veil that is derived from birth" and a "birth to a corruption"[34] due to humanity's connection to Adam, he would affirm that infants inherit sin. Gregory understood sin to have a negative impact even upon infants, who are neither to be praised nor condemned; they are neither innocent nor guilty because they have yet to knowingly act out any kind of behavior. When their faculties of reason mature and they attain moral knowledge, their sins are no longer passed over by God due to their ignorance but judged due to their responsibility. I agree with David L. Smith's nuanced definition of original sin applied to Gregory's theology, "While (Gregory of Nazianzus) had a doctrine of original sin, in that what occurred in Eden affected human nature, he did not demonstrate any linkage of that sin to guilt; that was determined by human free will."[35]

GREGORY OF NYSSA

Gregory of Nyssa (ca. 335–394) was the younger brother of Basil and friend of the other Cappadocian, Gregory of Nazianzus. Gregory married

---

33. Gregory of Nazianzus, *Oration* 40.28, in NPNF2 7:370. Italics mine.
34. Gregory of Nazianzus, *Oration* 40.2, 29, in NPNF2 7:360, 370.
35. Smith, *With Willful Intent*, 27.

but committed himself to a celibate, monastic lifestyle after the death of his wife. His brother, Basil, placed the bishopric of Nyssa on him. But Gregory was content with a life of solitude and contemplation. However he eventually stepped into the public forum against the Arians. Gregory was a leading participant at the Council of Constantinople in 381, served Emperor Theodosius as an advisor, and eventually returned to a life of obscurity in the monastic life.[36] He is known as a "Father of the church" and was given the title "Father of Fathers" at the second Council of Nicea in 787.

When Augustine was accused of teaching that Adam's sin was passed to his descendants, he appealed to numerous theologians, including Gregory of Nyssa.[37] Was Augustine justified in appealing to Gregory to support his view of original sin? Gregory's writings are relevant to the present study because of his writings about the origin and nature of sin as well as a work entitled *On Infants' Early Deaths*. In this section, I will survey these writings in order to reconstruct his view of the spiritual condition of infants.

Gregory addressed the origin and nature of sin in *The Great Catechism*. First, human sin and evil did not originate with God. Second, Gregory interpreted the creation account literally rather than allegorically.[38] Third, he taught that humans were created to be immortal but became mortal as a result of their sin.[39] Fourth, God allowed evil to increase before dealing with it.[40] Fifth, Gregory's teaching on the origin of human sin emphasized the redemption at resurrection.[41] Gregory's remarks on the origin and nature of sin are relevant if infants experience their own

36. González, *The Early Church to the Dawn of the Reformation*, 185–86.

37. Augustine, *Answer to Julian* 2.10.33, in WSA I/24.

38. See McClear, "The Fall of Man and Original Sin," 181, who writes that "he always treats Adam and Eve as historical characters." Also Azkoul, *St. Gregory of Nyssa*, 118, who writes of Gregory's understanding of a literal six days of creation and the fall of Adam "on a historical day, in a historical place."

39. Gregory of Nyssa, *The Great Catechism* 8, in NPNF2 5:482–85.

40. Gregory of Nyssa, *The Great Catechism* 19, in NPNF2 5:491.

41. Gregory of Nyssa, *The Great Catechism* 15, in NPNF2 5:487–88. Consider the following remark of Rondet, *Original Sin*, 95, "Gregory says repeatedly that man's primitive state cannot be properly understood outside the context of the resurrection. The resurrection of the body will bring man back to what his primitive state must have been: at the resurrection, there will be no more marriages, there will no more be man or woman, human beings will be as the angels of heaven."

fall as they mature in their knowledge of good and evil, which somehow reflects the pre-fall state of Adam and Eve.

Gregory implicitly addressed the issue of the spiritual condition of infants in his work entitled *On Infants' Early Deaths*, which was written in response to an inquiry on the subject by Hierius.[42] Gregory wondered "what we are to think of those who are taken prematurely, the moment of whose birth almost coincides with that of their death." He began his inquiry by stating that the question is a "mystery, as ostensibly too great for human conjecture to be employed upon."[43] Still he attempted to address in this text both the destiny of those who die in infancy as well as a justification for God allowing such a thing to occur.

Humans were made in the image of God and are therefore destined to participate in the divine nature. All of creation belongs to one of two spheres, either immaterial (intelligible) or material (sensible). Still humans are unique because they are made of both material as well as immaterial aspects. Although their purpose is to glorify God along with angels, the human soul has been clouded by ignorance and, as a result, no longer partakes in the divine.[44] One can be purified of ignorance and once again participate in the divine by struggling and finally achieving virtue. Bakke writes, "Gregory emphasizes that one's eternal fate depends on the individual's effort to live a virtuous life," which presupposes an individual's free will, one interpretation of humans having been created in the image of God.[45]

In addition to this concept of free will, Gregory established the notion that God will judge people according to their deeds. Consider the following statement: "If the recompense of blessedness is assigned according to the principles of justice, in what class shall he be placed who has died in infancy without having laid in this life any foundation, good or bad, whereby any return according to his deserts may be given him?"[46] Because God judges people according to their deeds, people who die in their infancy are left out of that judgment because they have no deeds to judge. Gregory illustrated this by supposing that two men suffered from

42. Gregory of Nyssa, *On Infants' Early Deaths*, in NPNF2 5:372 n. 1.

43. Ibid., 373.

44. Ibid., 375–76.

45. Bakke, *When Children Became People*, 74.

46. Gregory of Nyssa, *On Infants' Early Deaths*, in NPNF2 5:376.

an eye infection. One used the prescribed treatments, but the other did not. The former regained his sight, but the latter did not. In the same way, Gregory explains, the men received "recompense" according to their actions. The one who used the medicine has "purged himself" of the ignorance of his soul but the one who neglected the cure fails to share in "the truly natural life." Infants, though, are in a different situation. Why? Gregory explains, "Whereas the innocent babe has no such plague before its soul's eyes obscuring its measure of light, and so it continues to exist in that natural life; it does not need the soundness which comes from purgation, because it never admitted the plague into its soul at all."[47]

In the analogy above, Gregory seems to argue that infants do not need to be cured of an infection that would keep them from sharing in the "natural life" because they never committed sinful actions. If the "natural life" is to be understood as sharing in the divine, theosis, or salvation,[48] then the implication of Gregory's view is that infants who die will be with God not because they have been forgiven of their inherited guilt but because their souls were never corrupted by their own sinful actions.

It would be an error, though, to conclude that Gregory viewed infants as virtuous. In response to the idea that people who died in their infancy had achieved virtue, Gregory argued previously that such a situation would be unjust. For virtue would have no value if an adult strived for a lifetime to achieve it but infants received it without making any effort.[49] How, then, does an infant achieve virtue? Gregory did not clearly address this question, which has led some to cite this work in order to support a view of postmortem salvation.[50] Such a case cannot be made, however, because Gregory taught no such view in this or any other work.

After Gregory dealt with the eternal destiny of these infants, he raised the issue of theodicy in this situation. Theodicy is a defense of God's justice in light of suffering and evil. Why does a loving God provi-

47. Ibid., 376–77.

48. Objecting to this Eastern father's view of salvation as theosis is not grounds for dismissing his apparent teaching that people who die in their infancy will be with God because they have not committed sinful acts.

49. Ibid., 374.

50. The following authors cite this work in order to argue for the possibility of postmortem offer of salvation for infants: Dyer, "The Unbaptized Infant in Eternity," 147; and Sanders, No Other Name, 298. They wrongly state that Gregory taught in On Infants' Early Deaths that people who die in their infancy mature before they appear before God. In this way, they are given an opportunity for salvation after their death.

dentially will the death of infants?[51] Gregory taught that Christian parents who have lost an infant can have this assurance: God, by His omniscience, knew that the child would have grown up to be evil. Rather than allowing that child's "evil dispositions" to mature and be realized, God expresses his care through the infants' death before they commit those evil acts.[52] This is an unwise but interesting move on the part of Gregory, because he employs an argument for middle knowledge over a millennium before the birth of the one who is credited with the origin of Molinism, Luis Molina.[53]

It is not clear that Gregory viewed infants to be in the same condition as Adam and Eve prior to the Fall. So, his writings on the origin of sin and the Fall provide little help in this study. However, in *On Infants' Early Deaths*, Gregory did address the spiritual condition of infants. They were neither good nor bad; infants who died would be with God because their souls had never been corrupted by their own sinful actions.

51. Consider the remark of Gregory of Nyssa, *On Infants' Early Deaths*, in NPNF2 5:373, "If nothing in this world happens without God, but all is linked to the Divine will, and if the Deity is skilfull [sic] and prudential, then it follows necessarily that there is some plan in these things bearing the mark of His wisdom, and at the same time of His providential care."

52. Ibid., 378–79.

53. Middle knowledge is the idea that God knows how people would have freely acted in any possible scenario. See Craig, "Middle Knowledge," 147. Gregory employs this type of thinking at this point by arguing that God acts based on his knowledge of how people would respond given a particular future, which was realized only in the mind of God.

12

The Western Church Fathers
(Tertullian and Cyprian)

I N THIS CHAPTER, I will examine some of the writings of Tertullian and Cyprian in order to determine the views of those pre-Augustinian, Western theologians on the spiritual condition of infants.

TERTULLIAN

Tertullian received legal training, as evidenced by the arguments in his works, especially in *Prescription Against the Heretics*. In *Against Praxeas*, which he wrote after he joined the Montanists[1] around A.D. 207, he used Trinitarian and Christological formulas, which were foundational for the later theological development of those doctrines.[2]

"Tertullian (ca. 145–ca. 220)," writes Charles Warren, "was the first Church Father on record to express an explicit concept of original sin."[3] Dale Moody, however, differs. Citing *On the Soul*, Moody writes, "Tertullian taught that the child is in the paradise of innocence until the age of puberty when it goes forth in to the world of guilt."[4] Which was the case? Did Tertullian teach that human beings are born with the sin and guilt of Adam or did he teach that people are born innocent? In this section, I will examine portions of *A Treatise on the Soul*, *Against Marcion*, and *On Baptism* in order to establish Tertullian's view on the spiritual condition of infants.

---

1. Rondet, *Original Sin*, 51, notes that the error of adopting Montanism did not negatively affect his doctrines of grace or original sin.

2. González, *The Story of Christianity*, 74–77.

3. Warren, *Original Sin Explained?*, 11.

4. Moody, *The Word of Truth*, 290.

Tertullian's view on the spiritual condition of infants can be seen in his view of the soul. He rejected Plato's idea of pre-existent souls[5] and argued that an infant in the womb has a soul.[6] Also, both the body and the soul were formed at conception.[7] Because there were many idolatrous and superstitious rituals performed at the birth of children to pagan parents, these children were not considered holy. Children of believers, even though they "were designed for holiness," still require the second birth mentioned in John 3:5.[8] Tertullian then makes this important statement, "Every soul, then, by reason of its birth, has its nature in Adam until it is born again in Christ; moreover, it is unclean all the while that it remains without this regeneration; and because unclean, it is actively sinful, and suffuses even the flesh with its own shame."[9]

The above statement can be better understood when a couple of issues are explored. First, Tertullian taught that every person has a soul with two human natures. The first is a good one from God that is more powerful than the second human nature, which came as a result of the corruption of Adam's sin.[10] Second, the flesh and soul are composed of different substances. Although every person must be reborn, the corruption of the flesh came as a result of the corruption of the soul. In other words, the corrupted nature of the soul eventually corrupted the flesh. Even though this passage has been cited as one of his "concise statements describing of original sin,"[11] there is no indication that there was a passing of guilt from Adam to his posterity, which is the hallmark of the Augustinian view of

---

5. Tertullian, *A Treatise on the Soul* 23, in ANF 3:203.

6. Tertullian, *A Treatise on the Soul* 25, in ANF 3:205–06.

7. Tertullian is wrongly, I think, labeled a traducianist. See, as examples: Rondet, *Original Sin*, 58–59, who writes, "The soul enters the body well before birth; indeed, adds Tertullian, it is given from the first moment of conception, for it comes from the parents, more precisely from the father." Rondet then cites as evidence Tertullian *Soul* 27. Also, Smith, *With Willful Intent*, 30, cites the same passage and claims that "he supported his theory of traducianism by talking about the physical effect of the male's seminal discharge showing a departure of some 'soul.'" Instead Tertullian taught in *Soul* 27 that the soul was created at the same time that the body was created (rather than the soul pre-existing in the father), and he referred to seminal fluid as "the soul-producing seed" (rather than the seminal fluid containing souls).

8. Tertullian, *A Treatise on the Soul* 39, in ANF 3:219–20.

9. Tertullian, *A Treatise on the Soul* 40, in ANF 3:220.

10. Tertullian, *A Treatise on the Soul* 39–41, in ANF 3:219–21. See also Osborn, *Tertullian*, 165.

11. This claim was made by Warren, *Original Sin Explained?*, 37 n. 3.

original sin. The text, however, is clear that humanity is located in Adam and unclean.

The second text that seems to support the Augustinian view of inherited guilt is found in *Against Marcion*. In the passage, Tertullian argued that God's judgments are just, writing,

> He required the sins of the fathers at the hands of the children, the hardness of the people made such remedial measures necessary for them, in order that, having their posterity in view, they might obey the divine law. For who is there that feels not a greater care for his children than for himself? Again, if the blessing of the fathers was destined likewise for their offspring, previous to any merit on the part of these, why might not the guilt of the fathers also redound to their children?[12]

Tertullian argued in the above passage that God would have been just in allowing the children to have suffered the punishment inflicted on the fathers in the same way that the children enjoyed the blessings given to the fathers. He continued his argument, though, by quoting Jer 31:29 and stating that "the father should not bear the iniquity of the son, nor the son the iniquity of the father, but that every man should be chargeable with his own sin." Still, he argued, God was just in placing on those sons the sins of their fathers.[13] Tertullian was not making an argument in that passage for the passing of guilt from Adam to the human race but from one set of fathers to a limited number of subsequent generations of sons. Further, the greater context of Tertullian's argument was that God is just; he cited that particular instance when God acted in such a way that He could have been charged as being unjust. Still, his argument went, God's justice as a good judge remains intact.

On Baptism provides the first of three texts in which Tertullian implied that infants are innocent before God. In this work, Tertullian urged that baptism should be delayed, especially for "little children." This keeps sponsors from the danger of failing to keep a promise before the Lord of raising the child in godliness and from the disappointment of seeing the child develop a wicked character. Still, he noted, Jesus taught that the children should not be forbidden from coming to Him. So, he wrote, "Let them 'come,' then, while they are growing up; let them become Christians

---

12. Tertullian, *Against Marcion* 2.15, in ANF 3:309.
13. Ibid.

when they have become able to know Christ. Why does the innocent period of life hasten to the 'remission of sins?'"[14]

In the above passage, Tertullian was not encouraging infants to be baptized.[15] Instead, he stated that infants should be allowed to "become Christians" at a later time in their life, specifically when they are "able to know Christ." This means that Tertullian placed an individual's knowledge of Christ *prior* to his baptism and since infants do not yet know Christ, that means they have not yet become Christians. In the passage, he also asks a question which implies that the infants do not have a need to be baptized because they are innocent. Bakke agrees when he writes the following comment about this passage, "Although Tertullian does not go into detail about the meaning of *innocens* ["innocent"], it is clear that he presupposes that infants have not sinned."[16]

In *On Baptism* 18, Tertullian's statement about the need to delay infant baptism suggests the following things about his view on the spiritual condition of infants: they are not candidates for baptism because they do not and are not able to know Christ. Although they are not yet Christians, they are innocent and do not need to be baptized.

The second text to be considered is found in his treatment on human souls. In *A Treatise on the Soul* 56, he argued against the view that any souls remain on the earth after a person's "premature" death. Specifically, he imagined scenarios in which an infant died "yet hanging on the breast" as did an "immature boy" and a "youth arrived at puberty." If all of them were to have reached the age of eighty, Tertullian reasoned, then it is not possible for them to age after they have died, because one can only age in a body. So, the soul of a person remains unchanged after that person's death. Further, there will be a judgment in which the good souls are consigned to the region of the good and the bad souls are consigned to the region of the bad. He ended that section with this question: "If you mean the bad, even now the souls of the wicked deserve to be consigned to those abodes; if you mean the good why should you judge to be unworthy of such a rest-

14. Tertullian, *On Baptism* 18 in ANF 3:678.

15. There is considerable debate about when the practice of infant baptism became common in the Early Church. On this issue, I follow Wright, "The Origins of Infant Baptism—Child Believers' Baptism?", 6–7, who examines the work of Aland and Jeremias on this passage and concludes that "Tertullian's objections were directed against a practice already prominent in the Carthaginian Church."

16. Bakke, *When Children Became People*, 69.

ing place the souls of infants and of virgins, and those which, by reason of their condition in life were pure and innocent?"[17] Although Tertullian referred to infants in this passage as pure and innocent, he referred to virgins in the same terms. It is still possible to claim that Tertullian considered infants to have never sinned because even though he cited virgins in the same sentence, he may have intended the term in a different sense. For example, virgins are innocent because they have never committed a sexual act and infants are pure because they have never committed a sinful act. Still, due to the linking of virgins and infants in the sentence, I do not think this passage leads to a conclusive judgment for this study.

The third passage to be considered is found within one of Tertullian's extended arguments in *Against Marcion*. In 4.23, Tertullian responded to Marcion's false distinction between the Old Testament Creator (who is characterized as unkind to children) and the New Testament Christ (who is kind to infants). Marcion charged that the Creator sent bears to attack the children who mocked Elisha, but Christ upheld infants as an example to his disciples. Tertullian responded, "This antithesis is imprudent enough, since it throws together things so different as infants and children—an age still innocent, and one already capable of discretion—able to mock, if not blaspheme."[18]

In the above passage, Tertullian argued for God's justice by making a distinction between infants (*parvulos*) and children (*pueros*).[19] Infants, he wrote, are "still innocent." Children, though, are "capable of discretion." Tertullian continued by noting that God demonstrated his love for infants by protecting the Hebrew infants from Pharaoh in Egypt (Exod 2:15–21). Tertullian's distinction between infants and children is significant for the present study. First, it is important to notice that he made a distinction, rather than just stating that God treats all pre-adults in the same way. Second, he claimed that infants are innocent but children are not. Rather than stating that all people are guilty of the sin of the first man, Tertullian noted in this passage that children can be held accountable to God for their actions but that infants are innocent before him, presumably because they have performed no actions for which they would need to give an account.

17. Tertullian, *A Treatise on the Soul* 56, in ANF 3:232.

18. Tertullian, *Against Marcion* 4.23, in ANF 3:386.

19. These Latin words were footnoted by the editor and translator of the work, Peter Holmes, in ANF 3:386 n. 7–8.

The previous three texts support the view that Tertullian understood infants to be innocent before God in the sense that they have not yet committed acts for which they are accountable to God. In *On Baptism* 18, Tertullian suggested that infants are not candidates for baptism because they do not and are unable to know Christ. Although infants are not yet Christians, they are innocent and do not have a need to be baptized. *A Treatise on the Soul* 56 led to no firm conclusion because Tertullian included virgins when he noted the purity and innocence of infants. In *Against Marcion* 4.23, Tertullian distinguished between infants and children, calling children "capable of discretion" but infants "still innocent."

So, what was Tertullian's view of the spiritual condition of infants? He was unwilling to hold infants accountable for any sinful actions. And in *A Treatise on the Soul* 56, he mentioned pure and innocent infants. But in chapter 40 of the same work, he explained that every soul is in Adam and unclean. I don't think that Tertullian's writings paved the way for Augustine's later formulation of inherited guilt.[20] Instead I find myself in agreement with Eric Osborne, who notes that Tertullian does not cite key Bible texts such as Ps 51:5 or Rom 5:12–19 and he does not see guilt as physically transmitted. Osborne concludes, "While Tertullian displays the origins of the idea, one cannot attribute the later doctrine of original sin to him."[21]

CYPRIAN

Cyprian (ca. 200–258) was a famous rhetorician in Carthage who served as a priest, studied Tertullian's writings daily and became the bishop of Carthage one year before the Decian persecution of 250.[22] He left town in order to maintain peace,[23] which resulted in an unsuccessful effort led by Felicissimus to have Cyprian removed from office. The persecution also caused the church to deal with the issue of whether and how to restore Christians who lapsed during a time of persecution.

---

20. See, for example, the following comment of Rondet, *Original Sin*, 61: Tertullian "advances a thesis that will have considerable repercussions; we are linked with Adam because all souls were first contained in his. This thesis, which is at the extremes of Christian Hellenism, will weigh heavily upon Augustinian theology."

21. Osborn, *Tertullian*, 167.

22. Quasten, *Patrology*, 2:340–41.

23. Cyprian, *Epistle* 4.1, in ANF 5:282.

During the Decian persecution, all subjects of the Roman Empire were compelled to sacrifice to false gods. The result was that some Christians participated in these pagan worship practices and even brought their infants and gave them elements of the pagan worship meal. Cyprian wrote of these parents that "their own destruction was not sufficient." Tragically, "infants also, in the arms of their parents, either carried or conducted, lost, while yet little ones, what in the very beginning of their nativity they had gained." On the day of judgment, Cyprian wrote, these infants who were forced to participate in these pagan worship meals will object that they did not take the meals of their free will. Rather, "the faithlessness of others has ruined us… while we were little, and unforseeing, and unconscious of such a crime, we were associated by others to the partnership of wickedness (…)."[24] In another passage, a nurse took an infant to a pagan ceremony, and the infant was forced to drink the wine but was not old enough to eat the meat. At a Christian observance of the Lord's Supper, the same infant tried to refuse the wine. It was forcibly given to her, and she vomited it from her mouth. Cyprian explained, "In a profane body and mouth the Eucharist could not remain."[25]

In the above passages, Cyprian does not question the practice of infants participating in the observance of the Lord's Supper. His objection was that an infant would be taken to a pagan worship service and made to participate in an act for which the infant would need to defend herself later. The above passages provide interesting material for the study of the nature and extent of children's participation in worship practices in the early church, for most of the literature of this period focuses on the practice of baptism rather than the Lord's Supper.[26] On the issue of the spiritual condition of infants, the passages imply only that infants will be judged by the knowledge that they have of their actions. Recall that Cyprian's view of these infants before God's judgment would be that they did not participate of their free will and were "unconscious of such a crime." To that extent, Cyprian's view is consistent with the present thesis that infants are not guilty before God due to the nature of God's judg-

24. Cyprian, *On the Lapsed* 9, in ANF 5:439.

25. Cyprian, *On the Lapsed* 25, in ANF 5:444.

26. Some of the secondary literature that addresses the subject of children and the Lord's Supper, or Eucharist includes: Jewett, *Infant Baptism and the Covenant of Grace*, 41–43; Holeton, *Infant Communion*, 4–7; Strange, *Children in the Early Church*, 103–07; and Bakke, *When Children Became People*, 246–51.

ment against sinful actions as well as these infants' inability to distinguish between good and evil.

Cyprian deals explicitly with the issue of the spiritual condition of infants in a letter on behalf of sixty-six bishops who met in a council to discuss a question raised in 253 by Fidus, an African bishop. Fidus supported the practice of baptizing infants at the age of eight days but objected to the practice of baptizing newborn infants who were only two or three days old. He apparently wrote that the bishops ought to "shudder" at the thought of kissing the infant's foot, which was part of the ceremony.[27]

In response to Fidus' inquiry, Cyprian wrote on behalf of the council that they were unanimous in their judgment "that the mercy and grace of God must be denied to no man born." Human beings have "divine and spiritual equality" regardless of their age. Rather than being unclean, the feet of a newborn baby should be considered clean because they are fresh from the creative hands of God. Further, although the eighth day was given significance because it was the day of Old Testament circumcision as well as the day of the Lord's resurrection, the significance of the eighth day ceased "with the giving to us of the spiritual circumcision." Further, just as Peter was prohibited from regarding any man as unclean (Acts 10:28), and adult men should not be hindered from receiving God's grace, even more so should infants not be kept from that grace. When mentioning an infant, Cyprian described it as one "who, recently born, has not sinned at all, except that, born carnally according to Adam, he has contracted the contagion of the first death from the first nativity."[28]

In the final comment above, Cyprian made a significant contribution to the study of the spiritual condition of infants. He acknowledged that infants had not committed any sinful actions. In that sense, they are innocent. However unlike his theological mentor, Tertullian, who stopped at that point to argue for delaying the baptism of infants, Cyprian continued thinking through the issue and arrived at the opposite conclusion. Cyprian posited that although infants were not guilty of committing any sinful actions, they were still in need of "baptism and grace" because they were born of Adam, thereby having "contracted the contagion of the first death." In his book *When Children Became People*, Bakke writes of Cyprian's view, "In other words, the newborn child is affected by the

---

27. Cyprian *Letter* 64.2–5, in FC 51:16–19.
28. Ibid.

fall of Adam. It is not unreasonable to assume that Tertullian would have approved Cyprian's thinking that infants are affected by Adam's fall. What distinguishes them sharply is that Cyprian links belief in original sin with the perception of the innocence of infants and (. . .) employs this position as an argument *against* postponing the baptism of children."[29]

Cyprian's view of the spiritual condition of infants, then, is that they are innocent of actual sins but guilty due to their relationship to Adam and that they receive God's grace through baptism, which cleanses them of their Adamic guilt. This judgment rendered by Cyprian and the council of sixty-six provided a firm theological foundation for Augustine's later doctrine of original sin as *inherited guilt*.[30]

CONCLUSION

Among the pre-Augustinian Western fathers, Tertullian is often cited in support of the view that infants inherit sin and guilt. However after examining the primary sources, it is not clear that he affirmed inherited guilt. Although Tertullian mentioned that their souls are unclean in Adam, he also questioned why there was a rush to baptize infants, referred to their innocent souls, and differentiated between infants and children based upon their capability to commit sin. Cyprian, though, clearly affirmed the guilt of infants. Although he noted that they are innocent of committing actual sins, they are guilty due to their relationship to Adam.

29. Bakke, *When Children Became People*, 72. Emphasis mine.

30. In support of this claim, see Kelly, *Early Christian Doctrines*, 176–77, who writes that Cyprian "linked the transmission of sinfulness with the process of generation is confirmed by his appeal to Ps. 51,5" in *Testimonies* 54.

13

Augustine

A UGUSTINE (354–430) HAS BEEN called "the framer of the doctrine of
original sin."[1] Both the Roman Catholic Church and the Protestant
tradition trace their basic understanding of the origin of human sinfulness to this church father.[2] The Roman Church points to Augustine as the
leading influence in the doctrinal formation at the Council of Carthage
in 418 and the Council of Trent, which in its fifth session developed its
"Decree on Original Sin."[3] The Protestant tradition also views Augustine
as a seminal figure who influenced subsequent theologians as they reflected on human sinfulness. Neither tradition, though, accepts all of his
viewpoints. For example, most churches in the Protestant tradition reject
his view of baptismal regeneration (salvation by grace mediated through
water baptism).[4] The Catholic Church rejects his teaching that unbaptized
infants who die will suffer God's judgment.[5]

1. Ellingsen, *The Richness of Augustine*, 72.

2. Pagels, *Adam, Eve, and the Serpent*, xxvi, writes that Augustine "offered an analysis in human nature that became, for better and worse, the heritage of all subsequent
generations of western Christians and the major influence on their psychological and
political thinking." See Pagels, *Adam, Eve, and the Serpent*, 98–126, for her argument that
Augustine overturned three hundred years of Christian interpretation on the account in
the garden. Rather than a story about the freedom of human choice, Augustine turned
the story into one about the enslavement of humans to sin.

3. International Theological Commission, "The Hope of Salvation," 731. Murray, *The
Imputation of Adam's Sin*, 12–17, cites Ambrosius Catharinus and Albertus Pighius as
examples of Roman Catholics at the time of the Council of Trent who held that the *transgression of Adam* is imputed to every person. The position of the church, though, was that
habitual sin is transmitted. Emphasis mine.

4. Smith, *With Willful Intent*, 35; Nash, *When a Baby Dies*, 46.

5. Although it has been moving toward this position since pre-Vatican II, it was
approved for publication by Pope Benedict XVI in 2007. See International Theological
Commission, "The Hope of Salvation," 731, for the "hope" that unbaptized infants will

What was Augustine's doctrine of original sin? Where is this doctrine found in his writings? How did this doctrine shape his view of the spiritual condition of infants? In this chapter, I will examine some of the writings of Augustine in order to determine what he taught about original sin and how these teachings either created or solidified[6] the notion that infants are guilty and under condemnation due to Adam's sin.

According to Gerald Bonner, Augustine's doctrine of original sin was a combination of two views that were predominant in his day and continue to be so in the present. The first viewpoint understands sin in medical terms; sin is a disease that has infected humanity. This was the predominant view in the Eastern church. The second viewpoint, which was more popular in the Western church, views sin in judicial terms; all of humanity is involved in both the sin and guilt of Adam. Bonner suggests that Augustine adopted a third view, which is a combination of the eastern and western views, when he writes, "Original Sin is both a disease and a crime. We all sinned in Adam, and share both the guilt and the penalty of his Fall."[7] Further, every person sinned in Adam because "all future generations were, in one sense, present in our progenitor's loins at the time of the Fall."[8] Where in the writings of Augustine can this doctrine of original sin be found?

Some scholars have suggested that original sin was a later development in Augustine's theology and formed in reaction to the Pelagian controversies.[9] A strong case can be made for this view from an examination of his writings. Although Augustine mentioned original sin in his earlier writings, he did not include in that concept inherited guilt until he reacted against the Pelagians. What are some examples of this earlier view

---

enjoy "eternal happiness" and the certain rejection for their condemnation. See also Dyer, "The Unbaptized Infant in Eternity" and Hall, *Learning Theology*, 156.

6. See Burnaby, "Introduction," 184–85, for evidence of the influence of Cyprian and Ambrose on Augustine's doctrine of original sin. Cf. Bonner, *God's Decree and Man's Destiny*, 35, who suggests that Augustine was not the originator of but the defender of this doctrine.

7. Bonner, *Augustine of Hippo*, 371. Cf. Stortz, "'Where or When Was Your Servant Innocent?'", 78–102, who exegetes Augustine's writings in order to develop a view of infants as "non-innocent," and as people who would become more accountable as they grew in their knowledge.

8. Bonner, *Augustine of Hippo*, 372.

9. This is the claim of Sage, "Le péché original," 75–112, and Burns, *The Development of Augustine's Doctrine*.

of original sin? In a letter written in 397 to Simplician, who succeeded Ambrose as the bishop of Milan, Augustine answered the new bishop's questions about Paul's teachings in Rom 7:7–25 and Rom 9:10–29. In commenting on the first passage, Augustine wrote that "inherited mortality . . . is the penalty of original sin."[10] In explaining the Rom 9 text on election, Augustine appealed to the extra-canonical creation account found in Ecclesiasticus in order to explain that all people have come "from inherited sin and the penalty of mortality."[11] In both of those explanations, Augustine traced the present problem of sin to the first sinner, Adam. But at this earlier time in Augustine's ministry, he identified that what is inherited from our first parent is not guilt but only mortality. In *On Genesis Against the Manicheans*, Augustine addressed the immortality to be gained that Adam lost in the garden. Again there is no statement of our guilt, but Augustine wrote in terms of our suffering the same loss that was experienced by Adam.[12] Even at the end of his life, Augustine took the opportunity in *Retractions* 2.1 to modify some of his views on the law and grace, but he did not clarify that guilt is inherited from Adam. It seems that when Augustine described the effects of Adam's sin on humanity, he did not always write about inherited guilt.

Scattered references to infants can be found throughout Augustine's voluminous body of work. Consider, for example, this statement from one of Augustine's sermons, "'Suffer little children to come unto me.' Let the little ones come, let the sick come to the Physician, the lost to their Redeemer; let them come, let no man hinder them. In the branch they have not yet committed any evil, but they are ruined in their root."[13] In that statement, Augustine distinguished between a child's sinless actions and their sinful nature. In his view, children can be "ruined" even before they commit any sinful action. Augustine also made a reference to children inheriting Adam's punishment in his monumental work, *City of God*. He wrote, "(W)hat existed as punishment in those who first sinned, became a natural consequence in their children."[14]

---

10. Augustine, *To Simplician* 1.1.10, in LCC 6.
11. Augustine, *To Simplician* 1.2.20, in LCC 6.
12. Augustine, *On Genesis Against the Manicheans* 6.24.35, in WSA I/13.
13. Augustine, *Sermon LXV*, in NPNF 6:454.
14. Augustine, *City of God* 13.3, in NPNF 2:246.

Because Augustine's most significant statements on the spiritual condition of infants are found in his writings against Pelagianism, the focus will now shift to those writings. First, a brief history lesson will place some people and events in perspective. The first official condemnation of Pelagianism was not directed against Pelagius, but against one of his followers, Caelestius. Augustine met with a group of bishops in Carthage. Then the bishops, in Augustine's absence, issued the condemnation of Pelagius and his teachings in 410. Marcellinus wrote Augustine a letter asking about Pelagianism, which had been so controversial in Africa. Augustine replied in 412 by writing *A Treatise on the Merits and Forgiveness of Sins and On the Baptism of Infants*. In the same year, he wrote *On the Spirit and the Letter*. In 415, Augustine read a copy of Pelagius' *On Human Nature* and quoted it extensively in the work he wrote that year in response, entitled *A Treatise on Nature and Grace*. Also in 415, Pelagius was acquitted of heresy by a group of bishops at Lydda. Augustine wrote in 417 about those events in *On the Proceedings of Pelagius,* and the next year he wrote *On the Grace of Christ and On Original Sin*.[15] That year, Pope Zosimus opposed his predecessor, Pope Innocent, by supporting Pelagius in an encyclical. In 418, a council of bishops met and issued decrees against both the teachings of Pelagius and the letter of Zosimus. Why was Augustine reacting so strongly against Pelagianism?

The British monk Pelagius argued against any defect in human nature by which Christians could excuse their actions.[16] Such a defect, Pelagius taught, must be charged to God, who has already declared his creation to be good.[17] Further, Pelagius wrote, "God has not willed to command anything impossible, for God is righteous; and will not condemn anyone for what they could not help, for God is holy."[18] Augustine, though, cited grace as the gift of God that enabled man to obey God's

---

15. For this chronology of events, see Burnaby, "Introduction," 184–92, and Brown, *Augustine of Hippo,* 280–83.

16. See, for example, the writings of one of his disciples, Julian of Eclanum, in Augustine, *Incomplete Work Against Julian,* in PL 45:1049–1608. This work has not yet been published in English.

17. Hall, *Learning Theology,* 134.

18. Pelagius, *To Demetrias* 16, in PL 33:1109–10. The English translation is from McGrath, *Christian Theology Reader,* 222.

command. Without such a gift of grace, it would be impossible to obey his command.[19]

Augustine wrote that Pelagius "argues against the transmission of sin from Adam to infants."[20] Further Pelagians taught that "actual sin has not been transmitted from the first man to other persons by natural descent, but by imitation. Hence, likewise, they refuse to believe that in infants original sin is remitted through baptism, for they contend that no such original sin exists at all in people by their birth."[21] Augustine opposed the idea that sin is only imitating Adam's bad example. Rather, the Rom 5:12 phrase "all have sinned" means that just as the seed of Abraham are blessed in Abraham, likewise every person sinned in the first man, Adam.[22]

One thing to notice in the passage above and throughout Augustine's writings on sin is that he linked infant guilt with baptismal regeneration. In other words, Augustine condemned infants as guilty of original *sin* but he simultaneously argued for their water baptism in order to cleanse them of that original *guilt*. Consider his letter to Boniface as an illustration of the pairing of infant guilt with baptismal regeneration. In this letter, written in 408, Augustine addressed the following dilemma: Do parents harm their sick, baptized infants when they worship false gods in order to ask for healing? Further, if the ungodliness of the infant's parents does not bring the infant any harm, then how can their faith be any advantage as sponsors at baptism?

Augustine answered Boniface by explaining that once an infant had experienced salvation by the sacrament of baptism, then he cannot be "held under the bond of that sin in another to which he does not with his own will consent."[23] Augustine explained that the reason that the in-

---

19. See, for example, Augustine, *On Grace and Free Will* 8, in NPNF 5:447, "In order, however, that this victory may be gained, grace renders its help; and were not this help given, then the law would be nothing but the strength of sin." This was written in 426 or 427. Recall also this prayer, which later frustrated Pelagius, in Augustine, *Confessions* 10.29.40, in WSA I/1, "Give what you command, and then command whatever you will."

20. Augustine, *On the Grace of Christ and On Original Sin* 2.15, in NPNF 5:241.

21. Augustine, *On the Merits and Forgiveness of Sins and On the Baptism of Infants* 1.9, in NPNF 5:18.

22. Augustine, *On the Merits and Forgiveness of Sins and On the Baptism of Infants* 1.11, in NPNF 5:19.

23. Augustine, *Letter* 98.1, in NPNF 1:406–07.

fant was included in the bond of guilt with Adam was because the infant did not have a "separate life" from Adam; an infant, though, does have a "separate existence" from his parents.

The work of regeneration of the infant is the work of the Holy Spirit rather than the work of the parents. He wrote, "By the water, therefore, which holds forth the sacrament of grace in its outward form, and by the Spirit who bestows the benefit of grace in its inward power, cancelling the bond of guilt, and restoring natural goodness, the man deriving his first birth originally from Adam alone, is regenerated in Christ alone."[24] Later in the letter Augustine wrote, "I would, moreover, wish you not to remain under the mistake of supposing that the bond of guilt which is inherited from Adam cannot be cancelled in any other way than by the parents themselves presenting their little ones to receive the grace of Christ."[25] Augustine intended to be clear in affirming baptismal regeneration. In the same letter, he wrote, "Therefore an infant, although he is not yet a believer in the sense of having that faith which includes the consenting will of those who exercise it, nevertheless becomes a believer through the sacrament of that faith."[26]

If the question for Augustine was how to treat an infant's inherited guilt, then his answer was baptismal regeneration (salvation by grace through water baptism). Augustine reframed the discussion of the spiritual condition of infants. At the same time the church was baptizing infants, Augustine shifted his view on original sin. Instead of infants inheriting only *sin*, they also inherit *guilt*. Keep in mind his assumption that water baptism provided a cleansing from original sin. If one begins with Augustine's assumption of *guilty* (rather than only *sinful*) infants, then one is faced with a dilemma when understanding the eternal destiny of those who die in their infancy. Such an explanation was not difficult for Augustine: a baptized infant would be with God, but an infant who had not been baptized would face his condemnation.[27] How does one remain consistent when adopting his view of inherited guilt but rejecting his answer of baptismal regeneration?

---

24. Augustine, *Letter* 98.2, in NPNF 1:407.

25. Augustine, *Letter* 98.6, in NPNF 1:408–09.

26. Augustine, *Letter* 98.10, in NPNF 1:410.

27. See Augustine, *On the Merits and Forgiveness of Sins and On the Baptism of Infants* 1.15, 21, 28, in NPNF 5:20, 23, 25; also Augustine *Sermon* 294.3, in WSA III/8.

Mark Ellingsen writes, "Augustine did not expressly identify a doctrine of original sin in his thought until the Pelagian controversy."[28] The texts above indicate that in his earlier writings Augustine connected the *sin* of Adam to the sin of humans. But it was not until the later period in which he responded to Pelagianism that Augustine's view crystallized so that Adam's *guilt* was passed on to his posterity. It seems that Augustine developed his view of inherited guilt as a correction (or perhaps an over-correction) against Pelagius' heretical teaching of the possibility of human sinlessness.

Augustine taught that infants had not committed any sinful actions independent of Adam. In that sense, infants had not sinned. However, they were to be counted guilty because of their physical[29] relationship to Adam. Although it is true that Augustine drew upon a poor translation of Rom 5:12 to bolster his view of original sin, he also found support for the doctrine in other passages, such as Rom 3:23. Quoting that verse, Augustine wrote, "'For all have sinned'—whether in Adam or in themselves—'and come short of the glory of God.'"[30]

The debate that continued between Augustine and Pelagius eventually resulted in an ecclesial council in the African city of Carthage in 418. The council, which was heavily influenced by Augustine's many arguments against Pelagianism, made the following declarations: Death, or mortality, is a consequence of sin; infants, who cannot commit any sins, are to be baptized for the remission by the original sin contracted by generation; without baptism one cannot see the kingdom of heaven, and there is no intermediate place for infants who die without baptism.[31]

---

28. Ellingsen, *The Richness of Augustine*, 75.

29. Augustine, *Letter* 143.6, NPNF 1:492, "That infant children, even before they have committed any sin of their own, are partakers of sinful flesh, is, in my opinion, proved by their requiring to have it healed in them also, by the application in their baptism of the remedy provided in Him who came in the likeness of sinful flesh."

30. Augustine, *On Nature and Grace* 4, in NPNF 5:122. For more on his use of a poor translation of *eph' hō* in Rom 5:12, see Weaver, "From Paul to Augustine," 187–206; Weaver, "The Exegesis of Romans 5:12," 133–159; and the chapter on Rom 5:12–19 in this book.

31. *Council of Carthage* 16, Canons 1–3 in Schaff, *History of the Christian Church*, 3:799; see also Rondet, *Original Sin*, 126–27.

CONCLUSION

Augustine's doctrine of original sin, like so many of his other doctrines, matured over time. His earlier view only connected the *sin* of Adam to the sin of humans. His later view, especially in response to the Pelagians, stated that Adam's *guilt* was passed on to his posterity. This emphasis on inherited guilt, rather than on inherited sin and mortality, has influenced both Protestants and Catholics. The former disregard his view of baptismal regeneration and the latter disregard his statements of condemnation for unbaptized infants. But both traditions are influenced by his emphasis to the Pelagians that infants should be viewed not only as sinful but also as guilty. For Augustine, infants are considered guilty not because of their own sinful actions but because of the sinful actions of their first father, Adam.

14

The Magisterial Reformers
(Luther, Zwingli, and Calvin)

MARTIN LUTHER, ULRICH ZWINGLI, and John Calvin are considered together under the heading of Magisterial Reformers not because they held all of the same theological convictions but because they attempted to reform the church with the support of magistrates, or ruling authorities. Also they are known by this phrase because they were magisters (teachers) who shared a commitment to teach the Old and New Testaments as the Word of God and to structure local congregations within their understanding of biblical precepts. In this chapter, I will survey the views of Martin Luther, Ulrich Zwingli, and John Calvin on the spiritual condition of infants.

MARTIN LUTHER

Little needs to be written here about the significance of Martin Luther (1483–1546) in Christian history. Besides the publication of his *Ninety-Five Theses* serving as a catalyst for the Protestant Reformation, he made contributions to the church through his writing of hymns and commentaries, his work as a Bible translator, and his ongoing theological debates.

The views of Martin Luther on the spiritual condition of infants will be culled from some of his writings on Genesis and on baptism. In *Lectures on Genesis*, Luther considered the eternal destiny of infants who died before they were able to receive circumcision, which he equated to New Testament baptism. He also addressed the issue of baptism in light of the circumstances surrounding his debates with the Catholics on one side and the Enthusiasts[1] on the other.

---

1. Nam, "A Comparative Study," 66 n. 7, explains that *Enthusiast* (*Schwärmer*) was a word that Luther used polemically against opponents in order to characterize them

Luther dealt explicitly with the spiritual condition of infants in *Lectures on Genesis*. He noted the command to circumcise and the warnings issued in Gen 17. Any male who had not been circumcised would be cut off from the people of God. Luther then asked about the condition of an infant who died before his eighth day of life. He replied that this was "easy" to answer and that his condition was the same as all infants in his day who die before their baptism. God does not condemn these infants because "they do not sin against the covenant of circumcision or of Baptism." Further, "the souls of those infants must be left to the will of the Heavenly Father, who we know to be merciful." They had not sinned like Adam (Rom 5:14) but were like Jacob and Esau, who had "done nothing either good or bad" (Rom 9:11).[2]

It would be wrong, though, to conclude from the above passage that Luther denied that infants inherit sin. Immediately following the passage above, Luther wrote, "Even though infants bring with them inborn sin, which we call original sin, it is nevertheless important that they have committed no sin against the Law." He explained that just as girls were not excluded from the people of God due to their inability to be circumcised, so the infants who died before their eighth-day circumcision were not excluded. Adults, however, who have rejected circumcision or reject baptism are "surely damned." The result is that a five-day old infant who was born to believing parents is simultaneously included among the people of God and also possesses inborn, or original, sin.

Jane E. Strohl writes that Luther viewed children as infected from birth and damned by sin.[3] She attributes this view to Luther, but the only document she cites to support her claim is the *Apology of the Augsburg Confession*, which was not prepared by Luther but by an associate, Philip Melanchthon. Although Luther understood original sin to be inborn, the passage above demonstrates that Luther did not consider an infant's infection to be damnable. David Smith claims that Luther taught that unbaptized infants "are lost" but cited no primary source as evidence to support his claim.[4]

---

as overemphasizing the role of the Holy Spirit in the life of a believer. He referred to the following people and groups as Enthusiasts: Bodenstein von Karlstadt, the Zwickau Prophets, Thomas Müntzer, and the Anabaptists.

2. Luther, *Lectures on Genesis*, in LW 3:103.

3. Strohl, "The Child in Luther's Theology," 141.

4. Smith, *Willful Intent*, 67, 421 n. 16.

Smith, however, is correct in stating that Luther followed Augustine in his view of infants as sinful *before* they express their will. Infants are sinful due to the sin that was passed on by their parents at the moment of conception.[5] But Luther deviated from Augustine in his understanding of the effect of baptism on infants. Both affirmed that infants can be saved apart from their own confession of faith. But Luther understood baptism to be a sign of the new covenant rather than a sacrament of grace.[6] And he argued that the Scriptures imply that infants *can* possess faith.

The idea that infants can possess faith is significant. How did Luther support such a claim? In *Lectures on Genesis*, he offered the following four arguments. First, circumcision only has value because of faith. Second, since God included infants in his command to circumcise, he has thereby promised to "take care of them and save them." Third, Luther continued, "(T)he command to circumcise either served no purpose or infants, who are without any understanding, also believed and through circumcision obtained by faith the righteousness which Abraham obtained while he was still uncircumcised." Fourth, Luther noted, God made the following promise concerning the infants who were circumcised on their eighth day of life, "I will be their God."[7]

In 1528 Luther wrote in order to distinguish his view of baptism from that of Balthasar Hubmaier and other "advocates of rebaptism." Luther offered the following arguments to support his claim that all baptized children can possess saving faith. First, Christ said that the kingdom of heaven belongs to them (Matt 19:14). Second, John the Baptist in his mother's womb "could have faith." Third, "If it is not contrary to the Scripture to hold that children believe, but rather in accord with Scripture to hold that children believe, then your argument, that children cannot believe, must be unscriptural."[8] Luther did not argue that *all* infants can

---

5. Ibid., 66.

6. Luther, *The Babylonian Captivity of the Church*, in LW 36:92, wrote that "the sign alone cannot be a sacrament." But Luther thought the sign of baptism *became* a sacrament when accompanied by the gospel, or word of promise. For more on Luther's view of baptism as a sign, see Nam, "A Comparative Study," 69–73.

7. Luther, *Lectures on Genesis*, in LW 3:103–04.

8. Luther, *Concerning Rebaptism*, in LW 40:242.

have saving faith. Rather, he argued that *baptized* infants (children of believers) can have saving faith.[9]

The previous chapter established Augustine's view that baptism cleanses infants of their guilt of original sin. It is not clear, though, that Luther considered infants to be guilty of sin. Luther explained in *Lectures on Genesis* that infants have not acted against the Law, the covenant, or Baptism.[10] Luther's view must not be confused with *The Augsburg Confession*. In 1530 Philip Melanchthon authored a document that is now referred to as *The Augsburg Confession*. It was meant to reflect the doctrinal stance of Luther's movement. Article 2 deals with original sin. In response to the confession, the Roman church wrote *Roman Confutation*, in which they agreed with the basic view of original sin expressed in the confession. But the church disagreed with the notion that adults have "guilt" but infants can only have "offense." Further the church disagreed with the confession's view of concupiscence (desire). According to the confession, concupiscence is original sin. Luther taught that concupiscence remains in children after their baptism. The church, though, understood concupiscence to be a penalty of sin but not a sin.

In response to the *Roman Confutation*, Melanchthon wrote *Apology*, in which he argued that he has added nothing to church tradition or the Scripture on the subject of original sin. Further, "deficiency and concupiscence are sin as well as penalty." In other words, Melanchthon maintained his view that concupiscence is sin.[11] Luther is wrongly accused of affirming inherited guilt when he is confused with Melanchthon as the person who was responsible for drafting the confession.[12] Church historian William Estep was clear when he wrote, "Melanchthon was the chief architect of

---

9. Luther, *Werke* 53:205–08, also extended this hope for salvation to unbaptized infants due to the longing of Christian mothers who desired to see their infants baptized before death. Luther based this hope on God's mighty actions in biblical times due to the prayers of other people. Perhaps, Luther speculated, God saves unbaptized infants as he saved other people who died without despising the Law of Moses, such as Job and the kings of Nineveh and Babylon. My thanks to Artenis Islamaj, who helped me translate this German text.

10. Luther, *Lectures on Genesis*, in LW 3:103.

11. Warren, *Original Sin Explained*, 26–27.

12. Estep, *Renaissance & Reformation*, 152, is clear, "Melanchthon was the chief architect of the confession."

the confession." And it is the confession that teaches that infants inherit guilt. Luther, in his writings, does *not* make that claim.[13]

What can be concluded about Luther's view of the spiritual condition of infants? Luther affirmed that every person is born with original sin. However, Luther's affirmation was a radical departure from both Augustine's later expression and the church's doctrinal formulations of the doctrine of original sin. The original sin to which both Augustine and the church referred is sufficient to condemn an unbaptized infant.[14] Luther, because of his presupposition of the covenant of grace, allowed for the possibility that an unbaptized infant of believing parents who had aged less than eight days was born with original sin yet should be counted among the people of God. How did Luther understand that sinful people at any age belong to God? These infants had not actually committed any acts of sin and God's righteousness could be imparted to them by their faith. Luther argued that infants could possess faith, which is a claim that has been made in recent years by Protestant as well as Catholic theologians.[15]

ULRICH ZWINGLI

Ulrich Zwingli (1484–1531) was Zürich's methodological Reformer, whose young protégés rebelled against their mentor over the issue of infant baptism. Conrad Grebel was among this group of young men who finally convinced Zwingli that the Scriptures did not support the church's practice of baptizing infants. Zwingli challenged many other practices of the Roman Catholic Church and even agreed that infant baptism could not be supported from the Scriptures. But he was either unwilling or too slow to challenge the practice at the *Grossmünster* in Zürich. As a

13. Rondet, *Original Sin*, 171–75, demonstrates that the church directed only the condemnation of imputed righteousness of the fifth canon against Luther in response to his teaching of justification by faith alone.

14. See International Theological Commission, "The Hope of Salvation," in which the Roman Catholic Church revised its doctrine of limbo. The church continues to affirm both the doctrine of original sin as well as the need for baptism as a sacrament of grace. The new document only holds out a "hope" that infants who die prior to baptism will be welcomed into "eternal happiness."

15. See Grudem, *Systematic Theology*, 500 n. 19, and International Theological Commission, "The Hope of Salvation," 746 n. 127. Both appeal to an infant's response to a mother's smile to suggest that the infant is responding, or at least can respond, to God himself.

result, these young men (re)instituted the practice of believer's baptism. Their believer's baptism in 1525 was in defiance of Zwingli. More important, Estep writes, it "was clearly the most revolutionary act of the Reformation."[16]

This analysis of Zwingli's view of sin will begin with his 1530 work, *An Exposition of the Faith*. The first four articles deal with Christ, and the fifth deals with sin. It is necessary, he wrote, to describe the sickness in order to better understand the healing that Christ brought. When Adam disobeyed God, he suffered the consequence of death and, as a result, so does the rest of humanity. So far, Zwingli's doctrine of sin aligned with that of both Augustine and Luther. It was Zwingli's development of his doctrine of original sin, though, that set him apart from Augustine and moved him in Luther's direction on the spiritual condition of infants.

The distinction between Zwingli and Luther(anism) becomes apparent when one considers Zwingli's explanation of how and why infants were not under condemnation. Zwingli was unwilling to pronounce condemnation upon infants because "the salvation conferred by Christ is no longer a match for sin." He argued that in addition to the effects of Christ's work on the cross, infants should be considered free from God's judgment due to his work of election, which does not require the exercise of faith on the part of the infant.[17]

Like Luther, Zwingli rejected the Augustinian notion that baptism removed the guilt of original sin. However, he admitted to holding that view at one time. In 1525, he admitted that the controversy with Anabaptists "has shown us that it is not the pouring of water which washes away sin. And that was what we once believed, although without any authority in the word of God. We also believed that the water of baptism cleansed children from a sin that they never had, and that without it they would be damned. All these beliefs were erroneous, as we shall see later."[18] Zwingli still affirmed both Adam's seminal unity with humanity and sin's devastating effects upon humanity. But he stated the effects on infants in new ways. Luther attacked his position as Pelagian because of his use of free will, so Zwingli offered a reply to Urbanus Rhegius in Augsburg.[19]

16. Estep, *Anabaptist Story*, 8–17, quote on p. 11.

17. Zwingli, *An Exposition of the Faith*, in LCC 24.

18. Zwingli, *Of Baptism*, in LCC 24:153.

19. Stephens, *The Theology of Huldrych Zwingli*, 150; see also Stephens, *Zwingli: An Introduction*, 74.

In defending his view of original sin, Zwingli wrote his thesis statement in the form of this question: "For what could be said more briefly and plainly than that original sin is not sin but disease, and that the children of Christians are not condemned to eternal punishment on account of that disease?"[20]

Zwingli continued the defense of his alterations to original sin by distinguishing between the words *disease* and *sin*. *Disease* refers to the "original contamination of man," "defect of humanity," or "the defect of a corrupted nature." Rom 5:14 reveals that Adam's fault brought this to every person. *Sin*, however, "implies guilt, and guilt comes from a transgression or a trespass on the part of one who designedly perpetrates a deed."[21] Rollin Armour suggests a theological motive when he writes that Zwingli "developed a completely revised doctrine of original sin as part of his attempt to undermine Catholic sacramentalism."[22] James Leo Garrett Jr. categorizes Zwingli's view as one of five "Theories Not Teaching the Imputation of Guilt" and labels it "Theory of Uncondemnable Depravity." Garrett identifies Zwingli as the originator of this view and explains, "This theory holds that human depravity always leads to sin but is not sin per se, and hence human beings are not condemned for their depravity but for the sins to which depravity has led."[23]

Zwingli defended himself against the claim that he had previously denied that original sin brought condemnation. Original sin *does* bring condemnation, and God provided the only possible remedy through the cross of Christ. Zwingli clarified, though, that his original claim that brought the objections was that *original sin did not condemn the children of Christians*. His argument is as follows: first, children of Christians today are like the children of Abraham in Old Testament days; second, God spoke of his love for Jacob, Jeremiah, and John the Baptist while they were in the womb, so original sin cannot bring immediate condemnation; third, God confirmed his election of and promise to the covenant people by circumcising the Hebrew children, so they were not considered

---

20. Zwingli, *On Original Sin*, 3.

21. Ibid., 4–10.

22. Armour, *Anabaptist Baptism*, 35.

23. Garrett, *Systematic Theology*, 1:489–91. Garrett also includes under "Theory of Uncondemnable Depravity" Charles G. Finney and New England Congregationalists Samuel Hopkins, Nathanael Emmons, Timothy Dwight, and Nathaniel W. Taylor.

by God to have been under condemnation at their eighth day of life. [24] In an interesting move, Zwingli appealed to circumcision as evidence for the *lack of guilt* among infants while his contemporaries appealed to circumcision as a precursor to baptism in order to argue *for* infant guilt due to original sin.

Zwingli's view of the spiritual condition of infants was similar to Luther's view because they both acknowledged that every person received something as a result of Adam's transgression. Luther was comfortable calling what infants receive "original sin," but Zwingli would not refer to what was present in infants as sin, because that word implies guilt due to a transgression. In this way, he moved even farther away than Luther from Augustine's notion of inherited guilt. Zwingli and Luther both affirmed the need for Christ's work in order to atone for what is present even in infants, but they were explicit about the salvation of infants only in the households of believing parents.

JOHN CALVIN

In a 1542 letter dated only weeks after the tragic event, John Calvin (1509–64) wrote to his friend and fellow minister, Peter Viret, "The Lord has certainly inflicted a severe and bitter wound in the death of our infant son. But he himself is a Father, and knows best what is good for his children."[25] The great Reformer and theologian mentioned only one biological child in his writings, James, who died shortly after his birth.[26] Calvin is probably best known for the theological movement that now bears his name, Calvinism.[27] How did Calvin understand the spiritual condition of infants? Does God judge us to be "totally depraved"[28] because of our sinful *nature* or because of our sinful *actions*, which result from that sinful nature? How did Calvin characterize the relationship between baptism and original sin?

---

24. Zwingli, *On Original Sin*, 15–20.

25. Calvin, *XC—To Viret* in SWJC 4:344.

26. Calvin, *CCIC—To Farel* in SWJC 5:138, mentions the baptism of this son in this 1547 letter to his friend, William Farel.

27. See Trueman, "Calvin and Calvinism," 225–44, for a brief comparison between Calvin and the theology that now bears his name.

28. Calvinism is popularly summarized by the mnemonic, TULIP, which was developed after his death. The "T" stands for total depravity.

Although the present study limits its definition of infant to the age of one year, Calvin followed the classic assumption that people exist as babes or infants until the age of seven years.[29] In commenting on Psalm 8, he argued that even nursing infants, those who are too young to speak, are "proclaimers of the glory of God." God does not need eloquent rhetoricians to praise his name because he ordains praise from people who are unable to speak.[30]

Calvin viewed infants as praising God, but he did not understand them to be innocent. In his commentary on Deut 1:39, he noted that infants do not invoke God's wrath but were affected by original sin.[31] In his sermon on the same passage, though, he noted that God reserved the young children for himself in the judgment due to the Israelites' unbelief and God reserves the young children for himself today.[32] God's work of reserving these children should not be understood as their innocence but their election. Calvin was clear in his earliest edition of *Institutes of the Christian Religion* that it is the inherited sinful *nature* not subsequent sinful *actions* that bring God's condemnation. He wrote,

> As we are vitiated and corrupted in all parts of our nature, we are held rightly condemned on account of such corruption alone and convicted before God, to whom nothing is acceptable but righteousness, innocence, and purity. Even infants bear their condemnation with them from their mother's womb; for though they have not yet brought forth fruits of their own iniquity, they have the seed enclosed within themselves. Indeed, their whole nature is a seed of sin; thus it cannot but be hateful and abominable to God.[33]

Calvin was clear in his view that infants are under God's judgment due to their sinful nature prior to any sinful thoughts, attitudes, or actions they would later perform. Calvin's commitment to an Augustinian view of both inherited sin and guilt can be seen in his frequent appeals in

---

29. Calvin, *Commentary on the Book of Psalms*, 96, "Granting that they are called babes, or infants, even until they arrive at their seventh year." Cf. Aristotle *Politics* 1336b, in LCL 264, who writes of Hippocrates' division of life: *paidion* (birth to seven years), *pais* (seven to fourteen years), and *meirakion* (fourteen to twenty-one years).

30. Calvin, *Commentary on the Book of Psalms*, 95–97.

31. Calvin, *Commentaries on the Last Four Fooks of Moses*, 4:86–87.

32. Calvin, *Sermons on Deuteronomy*, 44.

33. Calvin, *Institutes of the Christian Religion* 4.15.10, in LCC 21.

The Bondage and Liberation of the Will to Augustine's arguments against Pelagius.[34]

Among Calvin's many editions of *Institutes*, chapter 16 of book 4 first appeared in 1539. This chapter is an extended defense of infant baptism written in response to the Anabaptists.[35] Calvin understood baptism to be a sign, or symbol, of the promise of forgiveness through the blood of Christ. Like circumcision, baptism is the sign of mortification, or regeneration.[36] Infants and little children should not be excluded from the sign and benefit of baptism.[37] Calvin responded at length to objections against infant baptism raised by Balthasar Hubmaier. Calvin argued that infants should be considered children of Adam until their regeneration. To this point, Calvin and Hubmaier were in agreement. But Anabaptists differed with Calvin when he taught that infants could experience regeneration (salvation) apart from hearing and understanding the Gospel.

Calvin explained that all die in Adam and an infant's only hope is in Christ (1 Cor 15:22).[38] All people are by nature objects of God's wrath (Eph 2:3) and condemned because they were conceived in sin (Ps 51:5). Hubmaier asked how infants could be regenerated if they have no knowledge of good or evil (Deut 1:39).[39] Calvin responded that "God's work, though beyond our understanding, is still not annulled." All infants bear an "inborn corruption," so any of them who are saved are justified only by the cleansing of rebirth (John 3:3). Calvin pointed to John the Baptist as proof of infant sanctification (Luke 1:15).[40] Although Jesus took on

---

34. Calvin, *The Bondage and Liberation of the Will* 2.259, 3.301–312.

35. The editor, John T. McNeill, documents the addition of this chapter in *Institutes*, 1324 n. 1.

36. Calvin, *Institutes* 4.16.2.

37. Ibid. 4.16.7–9.

38. The following warning on the citation of Scripture in the LCC edition of *Institutes* is provided by Lane, *John Calvin*, xiii: "(N)o distinction is made in the body of the text between Calvin's own biblical and patristic references and those of the editors." It is not important, though, whether Calvin only alluded to a verse or explicitly cited it in his work. His arguments about original sin, infants, and baptism would still be clear without explicit biblical references.

39. Hubmaier, *On the Christian Baptism* in CR 91:612 n.2, in Calvin, *Institutes*, 1340 n. 31.

40. Calvin, *Institutes* 4.16.17.

flesh to impart holiness to the elect, Christ is another example of infant sanctification.[41]

Hubmaier cited Rom 10:17 as evidence that faith comes only after hearing the Gospel.[42] Calvin replied that Paul was only describing "the ordinary arrangement and dispensation of the Lord which he commonly uses in calling his people—not, indeed, prescribing from him an unvarying rule so that he may use no other way."[43] According to Calvin, God usually calls people to himself by the preaching of the Gospel, but he does not limit himself to that method.

Hubmaier argued that infants are not capable of repentance or faith.[44] But Calvin cited Jer 4:4; 9:25; Deut 10:16 and 30:6 to support his claim that circumcision was a "sign of repentance." He added, "Paul calls it the seal of the righteousness of faith (Rom 4:11)." Baptism and circumcision "are in the same case," Calvin explained. So, God's command to baptize infants can be inferred from his command to circumcise them.[45] Calvin rejected the "fiction" that infants should be considered sinful and condemned but prohibited from baptism, which is necessary for salvation.[46] Calvin either had Roman Catholics in mind or he was misrepresenting Anabaptist views, because they never insisted on water baptism for the remission of sins.[47]

Calvin viewed infants as sinful from birth and in need of redemption. But this cleansing has been provided only for the children of believers. This promise is made evident in baptism. God's mercy should lead parents to instruct their children in godliness. Calvin wrote, "For when we consider that immediately from birth God takes and acknowledges them as his children, we feel a strong stimulus to instruct them in an earnest fear of God and observance of the law."[48]

Calvin followed an Augustinian view of infants inheriting guilt but answered the question about their regeneration in a different way than

41. Ibid. 4.16.18.

42. Hubmaier, *On the Christian Baptism* in CR 91:610, 612, in Calvin, *Institutes*, 1342 n. 33.

43. Calvin, *Institutes* 4.16.19.

44. Hubmaier, *On the Christian Baptism* in CR 91:612, in Calvin, *Institutes*, 1342 n. 34.

45. Calvin, *Institutes* 4.16.20.

46. Ibid., 4.16.26.

47. Ibid., 1349 n. 46.

48. Calvin, *Institutes* 4.16.32.

the Western father. Rather than opting for baptismal regeneration, Calvin taught that infants of believing parents could be saved by God through Christ's work at the cross apart from hearing and responding to the Gospel.

CONCLUSION

The Magisterial Reformers, represented by Luther, Zwingli, and Calvin, all understood the spiritual condition of infants in terms of God's covenant with his people, but each of them began with a different presupposition. Luther understood infants to be born with original sin but would not affirm their guilt because they had not sinned against the law. Luther's view is often wrongly confused with the view of Melanchthon, who affirmed inherited guilt. Zwingli viewed original sin as a disease that has infected infants. However, he rejected the idea that infants sinned, because that wrongly implies their guilt. In contrast, Calvin considered infants to be guilty and condemned by God for their sinful nature. All three of them taught that infants who die can be saved. And all three of them limited that hope to the children of believers. The difference among them is that for Zwingli and Calvin, faith is not necessary in order for infants to be saved. Luther, however, held out the possibility that infants with believing parents *can* have saving faith.

There are several points of agreement between the views of the Magisterial Reformers and the thesis of this book. First, all three reformers taught that every infant inherits a corrupted nature from Adam. Second, they rejected the Roman Catholic Church's teaching of baptismal regeneration. Third, Zwingli and Luther acknowledged that infants do not commit sinful actions. Although Luther neither affirmed nor denied infant guilt, Zwingli stated explicitly that guilt only comes after one commits sinful actions. For that reason, he argued, infants should not even be referred to as sinful.

There are two major differences between the views of these reformers and the argument in this book. First, all three men assume a covenantal rather than a confessional view of both salvation and baptism. That means they assume that children of believers are in the covenant and should be considered believers unless the child later proves otherwise. In the confessional view of salvation and baptism, however, children are treated as believers only after they believe. So, the child of believers is treated the same as the child of unbelievers. All children are assumed not to be among the people of God until they confess faith in Christ and profess that faith by identifying with the death, burial, and resurrection of Christ in believer's baptism. The second major difference is only with Calvin. He assumes that infants are guilty because of their inherited sin nature. The argument of this book, though, is that infants inherit sin and later become guilty when they make their first choice to sin after they become morally responsible before God.

15

The Anabaptist Reformers
(Hubmaier and Marpeck)

THE STORY OF THE sixteenth century Anabaptists (rebaptizers) has been told in an even-handed manner only since the 1960s. This was due to a number of factors. Anabaptists were viewed negatively during and after the Reformation period. There was a lack of interest among historians. There was a lack of available primary sources. And because Anabaptists had neither a religious center nor a confessional document, there was some confusion about the movement. The work of historians such as William Estep and George Hunston Williams[1] has begun to reverse that trend.[2] Anabaptist Reformers can be distinguished from their Catholic and Magisterial contemporaries, and even the other Radical Reformers with whom they are often linked, due to the following four particular concerns: the doctrine of regeneration, the covenant of the regenerate, the objective power of baptism, and the baptized life.[3] One of the practices that hindered unity among the Anabaptists, Catholics, and the Magisterial Reformers was infant baptism. So, the writings of two Anabaptists, Balthasar Hubmaier and Pilgram Marpeck, will be surveyed in order to determine their understanding of the spiritual condition of infants.

---

1. See Estep, *The Anabaptist Story*; and Williams, *Radical Reformation*.

2. Caner, "Truth," 2–6.

3. Armour, *Anabaptist Baptism*, 135–42. The following could also be included in that list: the priesthood of the believer, missions, and the importance of the layman in the church.

BALTHASAR HUBMAIER

Balthasar Hubmaier (ca. 1480–1528) claimed ignorance on the issue of the spiritual condition of infants. When asked about the eternal destiny of unbaptized infants, he wrote, "I confess here publicly my ignorance. I am not ashamed not to know what God did not want to reveal to us with a clear and plain word."[4] However, as a Reformer who argued for the baptism of believers rather than infants, his few years of writing on this subject made a significant contribution to the topic. In this section, I will reconstruct Hubmaier's view of infants by surveying his doctrines of original sin, baptism, man, and salvation.

Hubmaier's doctrine of original sin is similar to Augustine's because they considered infants to be both sinful and guilty. Based on 1 Cor 15:22, Hubmaier traced infant sin and guilt to Adam. Based on Eph 2:3, he considered every person by nature to be a child of wrath.[5] In a publication that ended his friendship with Oecolampadius,[6] Hubmaier added the following biblical citations to his case for infant sin and guilt: Job 3:3 and Jer 20:14, in which the prophets cursed the day of their birth; and Ps 51:5, in which David stated that his "mother gave birth to him in evil." Hubmaier then accused Oecolampadius of following Zwingli, whose two errors were endorsing infant baptism and claiming "that original sin is no sin."[7]

Martin Bucer and Ulrich Zwingli attempted to argue for infant baptism from the Scriptures. Their four principal arguments were as follows: household baptisms in Acts, Christ blessing the children and promising the kingdom in Matt 19:14, the holiness statement in 1 Cor 7:14, and the continuity of Old Testament circumcision in New Testament baptism.[8] In addition to countering each of the arguments above, Hubmaier noted that baptism is a pledge, which infants cannot take. He even cited Zwingli's references to baptism as a sign.[9]

Hubmaier argued that infant baptism cannot be a sign of the infant's future faith. One can't know that baptism "will be the will of the child"

---

4. Hubmaier, *On the Christian Baptism*, 140. In this chapter, the citations from this source come only from the Pipkin and Yoder edition.

5. Hubmaier, *On the Christian Baptism*, 139.

6. Pipkin and Yoder, introduction to *On Infant Baptism Against Oecolampad*, 275.

7. Hubmaier, *On Infant Baptism Against Oecolampad*, 285.

8. Armour, *Anabaptist Baptism*, 22.

9. Hubmaier, *Letter to Oecolampad*, 70.

later in life in the same way that one can't guarantee that a barrel of grape juice prepared for fermentation will later turn into wine. For that reason, baptism cannot be regarded as an initiatory sign, the beginning of faith, and the beginning of new life.[10]

For Hubmaier, infants were not proper candidates for baptism because they were unable to exert either their will or their mind. He wrote, "Since every Christian believes and is baptized for himself every one should see and should judge by Scripture, whether he is being rightly fed and watered by his pastor."[11] Hubmaier also asked this tongue-in-cheek question about infants in the pre-baptismal examination, "Look at what your child knows or what it answers when one asks, 'Do you believe in God the Father Almighty, Creator of heaven and earth?' Then it cries or wets its diapers."[12]

Hubmaier thought it was important that candidates for baptism exercise their will because he viewed the participation of the will as necessary in salvation, which should precede baptism. The will is a key to understanding Hubmaier's doctrine of man. He views man in three parts—body, soul and spirit—which were affected in different ways by the fall. Adam willed his flesh and soul to disobey God in the garden, so all of humanity's flesh and souls were subsequently sinful and corrupt. However Adam's spirit did not disobey, so all men maintain their original righteousness. Still man lost his ability to discern between good and evil, so his spirit is unable to guide the other two parts of his being even if they had not been corrupted.[13] For Hubmaier, salvation requires an act of the will. A person is saved by the external calling of God through the preaching of the gospel after he wills himself to respond to the Holy Spirit's inward call and illumination of his soul.[14]

Because salvation requires an act of the will, Hubmaier was unable to state that infants are saved. When asked about the eternal destiny of unbaptized infants, he conceded that "according to the strictness of Scripture," they are sinful and guilty. However, God has mercy on whom he chooses and "can save the infants very well by grace since they know

---

10. Hubmaier, *On the Christian Baptism*, 118–19.

11. Hubmaier, *Eighteen Theses*, 33.

12. Hubmaier, *On the Christian Baptism*, 138.

13. Hubmaier, *Freedom of the Will*, 429–39.

14. Armour, *Anabaptist Baptism*, 33.

neither good nor evil, Deut 1:39." Still, he admitted ignorance since God never explicitly states in Scripture how he will judge unbaptized infants. Hubmaier taught that infants cannot be saved by their parents' faith or any "infused faith which God imparted to them" or by having water poured on them, which he regarded as no baptism at all.[15] After his death, it was reported that Hubmaier made this statement about the eternal destiny of unbaptized infants: "I affirm that they are destined neither to be saved nor damned, but that they ought to be committed to the omnipotent God. Let him do as he wills."[16]

Hubmaier viewed infants as both sinful and guilty. However, he argued against infant baptism out of a concern for faithfulness to the biblical teachings on salvation and the church. First, he understood from the Scriptures that people are to be baptized only after they have freely responded to God's offer of salvation. Second, the church is composed only of baptized believers. So when he was asked about the eternal destiny of unbaptized infants, Hubmaier pleaded ignorance. This view emerged out of his conviction that infants are guilty but unable to exercise their will in order to receive the offer of salvation and then be baptized.

If Hubmaier had incorporated into his view of original sin some of the views of his chief opponent, Zwingli, then he might have found a satisfactory answer to his question about the spiritual condition of infants.[17] Zwingli cited an infant's inability to exert his will as evidence *against* infant guilt. But Zwingli maintained that an infant of believing parents would be saved due to the covenant, apart from his will. Conversely, Hubmaier assumed an infant's guilt prior to the use of his will. But Hubmaier insisted that because an infant could not exert his will, an infant could not be saved and then baptized. For Zwingli, the inability of infants to exert their

---

15. Hubmaier, *On the Christian Baptism*, 140–42.

16. Faber, "Concerning the Baptism of Little Children," 354. Although it is often unwise to rely on quotations from one's opponents, Crimson, "Interview," 39, maintains that the comments attributed to Hubmaier in the interview with Faber reflect the positions in his extant works.

17. Armour, *Anabaptist Baptism*, 35, writes, "From this vantage point one can say that there would seem to have been no reason why Hubmaier could not have successfully and profitably taken Zwingli's views and adapted them to his own framework as, e.g., Pilgram Marpeck would later do—no inherent reason, that is. However, the debate was doubtless sharp enough to keep Hubmaier from looking to the opponent's camp to find the solution to his own problems."

will disqualified them from being guilty of sin; for Hubmaier, however, it disqualified them from salvation and baptism.

PILGRAM MARPECK

Pilgram Marpeck (1495–1556) was born into a Catholic family and served as a civil engineer, city councilman, and pastor. He was "lost to the world" for nearly three hundred years until his major writings were recovered. He is now recognized as one of the greatest leaders among the Anabaptists.[18]

Marpeck held a view of covenant that was different than that of the Magisterial Reformers. He argued that the true succession from the old covenant to the new covenant was from outward circumcision to inward circumcision. For that reason, infant circumcision was not succeeded by infant baptism because both of them are outward signs.[19] Also, he challenged the separation of inner spirit baptism and outer water baptism by the Lutheran and Reformed pastors and the Spiritualists.[20] This section will focus on the defense of his doctrine of original sin in his work entitled *Response to Caspar Schwenckfeld's Judgment*.[21]

In 1542 Marpeck translated and edited a revision of an earlier work by Bernard Rothmann and published it under the title *Admonition*.[22] Caspar Schwenckfeld, a Spiritualist pastor who had followers in Marpeck's city of Augsburg, responded with a publication entitled *Judgment*. Marpeck completed his *Response to Caspar Schwenckfeld's Judgment* in 1546. The fifth section, entitled *On Human Nature*, was a refutation of the charge of Pelagianism and an explanation of his doctrine of original sin.

Marpeck offered two arguments against "everyman's"[23] understanding of the doctrine of original sin and then applied his view of the doctrine

18. Rempel, "Pilgram Marpeck: An Introduction," 10–11, labels leaders such as Hubmaier, Sattler, and Denck who were imprisoned and even killed among the First Wave of Anabaptists. He included Simons and Marpeck among the Second Wave.

19. Armour, *Anabaptist Baptism*, 115.

20. Ibid., 113.

21. Rempel, "Introduction to *Response to Caspar Schwenckfeld's Judgment*," 68.

22. Ibid. Rempel writes, "In comparison with the *Admonition* of 1542, whose substance Marpeck plagiarized from Bernard Rothmann, the *Response* is an original work of sustained argument."

23. Marpeck, *Response to Caspar Schwenckfeld's Judgment*, 87, "Schwenckfeld writes that our view of original sin is not that of the Christian church and Holy Scripture and

specifically to children. First he argued that a child born to a married couple cannot have inherited sin because Jesus blessed marriage. Second, "flesh and blood" cannot be a "partaker of inherited sin" because God created flesh. He supports this notion in the following ways: God created Adam's flesh, which was among his creation that in Gen 1 he called "very good;" God created neither sin nor death, which is a wage of sin; and if flesh and blood were sin, then Mary and even Jesus Christ were sinful.[24]

Next Marpeck made an extended argument that is significant for the present study. Although he wrote specifically about "children," his arguments can certainly be counted for infants, who must be regarded as either the same age or younger than the children to whom he referred. He wrote,

> Our witness is that for children neither inherited nor actual sin counts before God because a child remains in ignorance and in created simplicity until it grows up into understanding and the inheritance is realized in and through it. Before that, sin has no damning effect; neither inherited nor actual sin is counted against a child before God. . . . When children come to a knowledge of good and evil, that is, when they reach understanding, then the inheritance which leads to damnation becomes effective in them. Then inherited sin becomes inheritable.[25]

Marpeck explained that the command of Jesus to become like children was not a command to become ignorant but to "become simple, without falseness or guile." Jesus meant that "children are like Adam and Eve in their created ignorance before they became presumptuous." Sinfulness only leads to condemnation as children grow out of their simplicity into a knowledge of good and evil. When they act out of their fallen nature as Adam's heir, they will be judged by Jesus Christ. However, he wrote, "We excuse young, innocent children from guilt and the remnants of their inheritance through none other than Christ . . . [for] the wrath of

---

accuses us of the Pelagian error. But he has yet to prove his accusation. We readily grant him that we do not hold to what is said to be 'everyman's' understanding in the Christian church. In our judgement, Schwenckfeld and many others need to be shown that not everything the Christian church confesses is in keeping with the ancient teachers of the churches concerning this article on inherited sin."

24. Ibid., 87–89.

25. Ibid., 89.

God is not upon such children until they reach understanding, that is, the common knowledge of good and evil."[26]

As has been demonstrated in this study, it was common throughout the history of Christian thought to make a distinction between inherited and actual sin. Among the Reformation writings we considered, only Zwingli and Marpeck made this distinction. As a result, they did not view infants accountable for the sin, or defect, which they inherited due to their relationship to Adam. Neither Zwingli nor Marpeck declared infants to be innocent, which would have made them guilty of the charge of Pelagianism. Rather, Marpeck noted that infants are ignorant and simple, excused by God of the sinful inheritance through Christ. Their simplicity "dies out" when they grow in that knowledge of good and evil.[27]

Marpeck and Zwingli followed a similar line of reasoning, which is that infants are not held accountable by God for sinful actions because they did not knowingly perform sinful actions. Again, rather than innocence, this simply leaves them uncondemned. Marpeck did, though, end his section on the doctrine of original sin by explaining that the ignorance and simplicity to which he referred is a natural holiness that is always eventually darkened by the emergence of an infant's growing understanding and reason.[28]

In this study, Hubmaier and Marpeck have represented the Anabaptist views on the spiritual condition of infants. Hubmaier presupposed infants as both sinful and guilty but Marpeck presupposed them to be neither sinful nor guilty. Still, both pointed to the work of Christ as necessary for them to be safe with God. For Hubmaier, this was more of a mystery but for Marpeck, the infants were never under God's condemnation because they had not matured in their moral knowledge and reason.

A link between Hubmaier and Marpeck's views on the spiritual condition of infants was their emphasis on willful actions. Hubmaier argued that infants could not be baptized because they could not first respond to the Gospel out of their own will. Similarly Marpeck taught that infants were not under God's condemnation because they did not knowingly will to commit sinful actions. In this way, Anabaptists recognized that an infant is in a different spiritual condition than that of a morally responsible

26. Ibid., 90.
27. Ibid., 91.
28. Ibid., 92.

people because of an infant's inability to commit willful actions, either for good or for evil.

CONCLUSION

The argument of this book is similar to those of the two Anabaptist leaders we have considered. Consistent with Marpeck but against Hubmaier, I have argued that infants do not inherit guilt from Adam. Instead, infants inherit sin, or a sinful nature. In the Scriptures, God does not judge people for their inherited sinful nature. Instead Scripture presents two conditions for God's judgment. First, God judges people who are morally responsible. For example God judged the older generations of Israelites in the desert because they were responsible to him for their ability to make moral choices. Infants, like the younger generation, are spared God's judgment because they are not yet morally responsible people. Infants are not judged as people who know the difference between right and wrong.

The second condition for God's judgment is that God judges people as guilty when they know the difference between right and wrong and still choose to break God's law by committing a sinful thought, attitude, or action. Infants are not innocent. They inherit from Adam a sinful nature. But God does not judge people for their inherited sinful nature. He judges people for acts of sin that they commit as a result of that sinful nature. All morally responsible people know the difference between right and wrong, violate God's law, and are in need of salvation from God's condemnation of and wrath over their acts of sin. But following in the traditions of Hubmaier and Marpeck, I argue that infants lack the knowledge of good or evil (moral discernment). Because infants don't yet know the difference between right and wrong, they cannot exert their will to knowingly choose either for or against God. And because they lack moral knowledge, they are not yet under God's condemnation of and wrath over their sin.

The Anabaptist Reformers Hubmaier and Marpeck began with opposing ideas about the sinfulness of infants but arrived at the same conclusions. Hubmaier began with an Augustinian view of infants as both sinful and guilty. In contrast Marpeck taught that children are guilty of neither inherited nor actual sin. Although admitting ignorance on the issue, Hubmaier concluded that those who die in their infancy will experience God's mercy because they lack a knowledge of good and evil. Marpeck, beginning with infants as not guilty, concluded that this is only their condition until they later come to a knowledge of good and evil. In this way, moral knowledge was the key in the Anabaptists' view of the spiritual condition of infants. For Hubmaier, its absence brought them mercy; for Marpeck, its presence brought them guilt.

16

Nineteenth-Century Baptists
(Boyce, Strong, and Mullins)

If I am going to provide a thorough examination of the spiritual condition of infants, then why in this chapter and the next chapter do I consider only the views of Baptists? I focused my study on Baptist theologians from the contemporary period in order to present a sample of the views held by one large evangelical group. It would benefit the reader to consider books by non-Baptists on the topic of infant salvation such as those by B. B. Warfield, R. A. Webb, and John MacArthur.[1] But in defense of my approach, consider that the covenantal view was examined in previous biblical (Holy Children) and historical (Magisterial Reformers) chapters. The other major view of infant salvation is election, which was held by some of the Baptist theologians who will be considered. So, although I consider only Baptist theologians in these two chapters, I interact in the rest of the book with all of the major evangelical perspectives on infants.

Also, this book focuses on the spiritual condition of *living* infants rather than those who have *died*. The Augustinian-Calvinist tradition assumes that infants from the moment of conception are guilty and under God's condemnation. Because my thesis challenges that viewpoint, I have interacted with its proponents throughout the book. Why did I write an entire book arguing against a view that I do not affirm? Because it's not enough to simply disagree. It's also necessary to articulate a biblically-based alternative. Why? Because the question of exactly *what* an infant inherits from Adam must be settled prior to any discussions of infant salvation.

---

1. Warfield, *The Development of the Doctrine of Infant Salvation*; Webb, *The Theology of Infant Salvation*; MacArthur, *Safe in the Arms of God*.

JAMES P. BOYCE

James P. Boyce (1827–88) was a Southern Baptist pastor, founder and first president of The Southern Baptist Theological Seminary, and served nine terms as the president of the Southern Baptist Convention. His *Abstract of Systematic Theology* was used at the seminary for thirty years.[2] The depth and breadth of his influence on generations of Southern Baptist leaders and their theology and practice was significant. His teachers in both his early life and his academic preparation were Calvinists. In his early life, he sat under the preaching of Basil Manly Sr., at First Baptist Church in Charleston, South Carolina. In his academic preparation at Princeton Theological Seminary, he was trained by Archibald Alexander and Charles Hodge. Boyce maintained this Calvinist viewpoint through-out his later work and writings.[3]

Boyce wrote *Brief Catechism of Bible Doctrine* for use in the spiritual training of ten- to twelve-year-old children. In the book, Boyce asked and answered two questions that shed light on his view of the spiritual condition of infants. First, he asked, "What evil effect followed the sin of Adam?" Boyce answered, "He, with all his posterity, became corrupt and sinful, and fell under the condemnation of the law of God." In that answer, Boyce affirmed the Augustinian-Calvinist tradition by indicting Adam's posterity in not only the sin but also the guilt of Adam. Second, Boyce asked, "Have not all men been willful transgressors of the law in their persons also?" This question was an effort to implicate humanity in not only inherited guilt but actual guilt. His answer was, "Yes; as soon as they have become old enough to know what is right and what is wrong."[4] By his answer, Boyce acknowledged that infants have not yet matured in their ability to distinguish between good and evil. For this reason, they are not implicated as "willful transgressors." But the first passage considered views infants as under the condemnation of God due to their relationship to Adam.

His *Brief Catechism of Bible Doctrine* did not explicitly address in-fants, but he does address the eternal destiny of those who have not heard and responded to the Gospel. He wrote that salvation is "to be offered to every creature." Repentance and faith are necessary for salvation. Still,

2. George, *James Petigru Boyce: Selected Writings*, 5–7.

3. George, "James Petigru Boyce," 74–76.

4. Boyce, *Brief Catechism of Bible Doctrine*, 127.

he acknowledged, some people will be punished who have not had a chance to hear and respond to the Gospel. How is this just? He answered, "Because they, too, are sinners, and have disobeyed the law of God written in their hearts and in nature."[5] At this point, Boyce indicated that people who have not heard and responded to the Gospel will be judged guilty not because of their sinful nature but because of their disobedience, or their sinful actions.

Boyce was inconsistent on this issue of God's judgment. Either God would judge people as guilty and condemn them for their relationship to Adam, or God would judge people guilty and condemn them for their disobedience of the law of God written on their conscience and in creation. In his book, *Brief Catechism*, though, Boyce taught both views.

In 1868 Boyce preached at the funeral of his former pastor, Basil Manly. Boyce began the sermon by saying that God intends life to be a blessing. But, he said, the exception to this truth is found in the death of infants. Boyce continued, "The life of pilgrimage on earth is not essential to the Christian. There are many saved who never live it. In the case of infants, it is enough that they live long enough to die. God gives them life in no other respect as their portion."[6] It is interesting that when he commented on the eternal destiny of those who die in infancy, Boyce made no distinction between children of believers and children of unbelievers. Further he made no distinction between original guilt and transgressions. Also Boyce did not explicitly appeal to the sinfulness and guilt of the infant or the atonement brought about by the work of Christ at the cross.

In his *Abstract*, he presented a more developed view of the spiritual condition of infants, especially as he wrote about infant salvation. Boyce followed Hodge in stating that man fell when he was under the covenant of works.[7] The effects of Adam's sin upon humanity include natural, spiritual, and eternal death. Adam's descendants never had an "innocent nature" but have always had a "corrupt nature." Boyce opined, "God righteously punishes all men, not only for what they do, but for what they are." He then appealed to Rom 1 as evidence that men do not fully express their sinful natures because of the restraints that God places in the world.

5. Ibid., 129.

6. James P. Boyce, *Life and Death the Christian's Portion: A Discourse Occasioned by the Funeral Services of the Rev. Basil Manly, D.D.* (New York: Sheldon & Co., 1869), 6.

7. Boyce, *Abstract of Systematic Theology*, 324–39. On page 235, Boyce cites Hodge's use of Scripture in *Outlines of Theology* for the word *covenant*.

Boyce wrote that "a corrupt nature makes a condition as truly sinful, and guilty, and liable to punishment, as actual transgressions. Consequently, at the very moment of birth, the presence and possession of such a nature shows that even the infant sons of Adam are born under all the penalties which befell their ancestor in the day of his sin."[8]

Boyce argued that humanity's relationship to Adam can be explained by both natural and federal headship but our relationship to Christ's work on the cross can be understood only in light of federal headship.[9] He separated regeneration and conversion. Regeneration is God's work of changing a person's heart; conversion is that person's response to God.[10] This distinction makes for the following unique situation for infants: "Regeneration (as in infants) may exist without faith and repentance, but the latter cannot exist without the former."[11] In other words, Boyce affirmed that an infant may be regenerated but denied that he could be converted.

In his dissertation on Baptist views of infant salvation, Earl Waggoner calls Boyce's view "salvation via strict election" and summarizes it as follows: "By God's sovereign, electing work, infants' corrupt hearts are changed regardless of their depth of guilt or inability to respond to God. If a child dies in infancy, he or she lives eternally in heaven."[12]

A. H. STRONG

August Hopkins Strong (1839–1921) was a theology professor and president of Rochester Theological Seminary for forty years and his *Systematic Theology* was used in seminaries for another half century. He studied under two teachers at Yale University who were both students of New England Congregationalist Nathaniel W. Taylor. Strong and his father were both converted under the ministry of Charles Finney, and the younger Strong studied under and was taught "how to think"[13] by Ezekiel Robinson at

8. Boyce, *Abstract of Systematic Theology*, 240–50.

9. Ibid., 251–55.

10. Ibid., 374–79.

11. Ibid., 381.

12. Waggoner, "Baptist Approaches," 43.

13. Strong, *Autobiography*, 120.

Rochester Theological Seminary.[14] The influence of these theologians can be seen in Strong's view of the spiritual condition of infants.

Strong defined sin as "lack of conformity to the moral law of God, either in act, disposition, or state." He then explained that he attempted to provide a mediating view between the Old School, which located sin in the state of the soul, and the New School (Taylor), which located sin solely in wrongful actions. He then cited Robinson, who argued that sin is not only an act but a "mode of being" and that "God punishes sinners, not sins."[15] He continued his examination of sin by noting that it was "universal" and that humans are born with a "corrupt nature," which "constitutes him a sinner before God." Strong supported his view by citing Ps 51:5 and Eph 2:3 and theologians such as W. T. Shedd and Ezekiel Robinson; he noted that Taylor held an opposing view. Strong understood Rom 5:12–14 to teach that death is a result of sin even upon infants who have not yet "exercised a personal and conscious choice."[16]

Strong summarized and critiqued six views of the imputation of Adam's sin to his posterity. In the first three views, infants do not inherit condemnation, but in the last three views, they do. He called Pelagianism heretical because it denies man's original corruption. He regarded Arminianism as inadequate because it fails to associate inborn evil with guilt. Also, it rejects both election (God's choice of certain people for salvation) and man's organic moral connection with Adam. Strong rejected the third view, called the New School. Held by Taylor, Finney, and others, it was rejected because of its claim that the disposition toward sin is not in itself sinful. Also, the New School views infants as innocent due to a lack of moral consciousness and therefore not in need of Christ's atoning work. Strong rejected these first views of imputation in which infants do not inherit condemnation. In the next three views, infants do inherit condemnation.

Strong rejected the Federal Theory, claiming that it wrongly depends on a poor translation of *adam* in Gen 6:7 ("Adam" rather than "men") to establish its only biblical support for a covenant with Adam. The result is that God treats all of humanity as sinners prior to their sinning. Strong also rejected what he labeled the Theory of Mediate Imputation,

14. Thornbury, "Augustus Hopkins Strong," 141–46.

15. Strong, *Systematic Theology*, 550–51.

16. Ibid., 573–79. For his exposition of Rom 5:12–19, see pages 625–27.

or Condemnation for Depravity. The reason is that it separates inborn sinfulness from Adam's sin. Strong endorsed Augustine's view of Natural Headship because of humanity's organic unity in Adam. The sinful nature that we possess is ours because we all "existed as one moral person" in Adam when he sinned.[17] Strong set up and answered nine objections to Natural Headship, which he explained was "merely a valuable hypothesis." Then he explained the following three consequences of sin to Adam's posterity: depravity, guilt, and penalty.[18]

Strong concluded his chapter on sin with a brief section entitled "The Salvation of Infants." Specifically, he asked whether infants who died before developing in their moral consciousness are saved. He responded with seven statements. First, infants need to be regenerated because of their sin (Job 14:4; Ps 51:5; Eph 2:3) and they can be saved only through Christ. Second, when infants are compared with people who have "personally transgressed," it is recognized that infants have "relative innocence" and "submissiveness and trustfulness" (Deut 1:39; Jonah 4:11; Rom 9:11; Matt 18:3–4). Third, infants are "objects of special divine compassion and care and, through the grace of Christ, are certain of salvation." Strong cited Matt 19:14 and argued that although Jesus was commending adults who acted in childlike faith and obedience, he logically would have received the infants and children who were the subject of his affirming illustration.[19] He acknowledged that infants have not yet attained a moral conscience but stated that they have been assured salvation by Christ himself. Fourth, Rom 5 demonstrates that just as the corruption of Adam was applied to infants apart from their conscious actions, so life in Christ was applied to those infants.

Fifth, adults are saved upon their personal faith, which is something that infants cannot exercise. So, God provides for infants the ability to receive Christ "in some other way." Strong cites Robinson to support his view that infants are passively condemned and passively saved.[20] Strong

17. Ibid., 593–628.

18. Ibid., 625–60.

19. Ibid., 661.

20. "Passive condemnation" and "passive salvation" are my terms not those of Robinson or Strong. To see the influence of Robinson's view of the salvation of infants upon his student, compare Robinson, *Christian Theology*, 164–69, with Strong, *Systematic Theology*, 660–64. Notice:

1) Both men argue for a difference in moral status between infants and adults.

objected to the notion that the guilt of sin is removed upon the death of an infant. Rather, guilt is only removed when a person comes into "vital union with Christ." Sixth, infants will be saved because what is tested at the final judgment is "personal conduct," of which infants are incapable (Matt 25:45–46; Rom 2:5–6).[21] Seventh, Strong articulated a view of post-mortem salvation.[22] Regeneration occurs for the infant when its natural depravity is eradicated at the time of death "through the sight of Christ and union with him" (2 Cor 3:18; 1 John 3:2). Stated another way, "subjective and personal reconciliation depends upon a moral union with Christ which can be accomplished for the infant only by his own appropriation of Christ at death."[23]

Strong affirmed Augustinian Natural Headship and its accompanying guilt for infants due to their sinful nature. But he contradicted this view when he tried to explain how guilty infants could be saved. He excused them from the final judgment based on their inability to commit personal transgressions. Also, he wrote that although "certain and great is the guilt of original sin, no human soul is eternally condemned solely for this sin of nature."[24] In a critique of Strong's views of sin and salvation, Waggoner suggests that when Strong's attempt to maintain infant inherited guilt is combined with his view of infant salvation on the basis of divine compassion and moral and developmental inabilities, the result is a penalty for original sin which "is rendered powerless and ineffective." The logical result of Strong's view, Waggoner writes, is universalism.[25]

2) Both argue from Rom 5 and from reason that infants who die will be saved.

3) Robinson, *Christian Theology*, 168–69, argues that infants might be brought into a love and knowledge of Christ "on their entrance into another life." Similarly, Strong, *Systematic Theology*, 663, wrote that an infant was saved upon "the infant soul's first view of Christ in the other world."

Thanks to James Leo Garrett Jr., for pointing out this possible origin for Strong's view of the postmortem salvation on infants in his teacher, Ezekiel Robinson.

21. Strong, *Systematic Theology*, 662.

22. Waggoner, "Baptist Approaches," 111 n. 66 makes the point that Strong's postmortem *salvation* should not be confused with postmortem *evangelization* when he writes, "Postmortem evangelization is characterized by the opportunity for the unevangelized to hear the gospel and respond to it after they have died. Strong posited no decisions postmortem, only the completion of a process which was begun in eternity."

23. Strong, *Systematic Theology*, 663.

24. Ibid., 662–63.

25. Waggoner, "Baptist Approaches," 112–13.

E. Y. MULLINS

Edgar Young Mullins (1860–1928) was a Southern Baptist pastor, professor of theology, and president of The Southern Baptist Theological Seminary. He served as a president of both the Southern Baptist Convention and the Baptist World Alliance, and was the architect of the Baptist Faith and Message (1925). Mullins provided a moderating and unifying position when Calvinism, Landmarkism, and the Fundamentalist-Modernist Controversy were polarizing Baptists.[26] His articulation of soul competency as a worldview influenced not only twentieth century North American Baptists but evangelicals worldwide.

Mullins viewed soul competency as a "Baptist contribution" to Christian thought and "an underlying assumption in New Testament Christianity." Soul competency is the idea that man, who was made in God's image, has the capacity to relate to God, who communicates to him through both the incarnation of Christ and the Bible.[27] It is the emphasis on the individual's ability and need to respond to God that distinguishes Baptists from Roman Catholics and from "Inconsistent Protestantism," which endorses infant baptism.

Roman Catholics consider the soul incompetent to deal with God apart from an earthly priesthood, the sacraments, and the Church's interpretation of Scripture. Protestants who baptize infants rightly insist on justification by faith but then baptize and admit into the Church people before they are able to exercise personal obedience. Consider Mullins' remark, "Infant baptism takes away from the child its privilege of individual initiative in salvation and lodges in the hands of parents or sponsors the impossible task of performing an act of religious obedience for another."[28] It is this insistence that each person must individually respond to God that clearly sets Mullins apart from the Calvinistic roots of the seminary over which he presided for nearly three decades. How did Mullins' emphasis on the competency of the soul impact his view of sin and the spiritual condition of infants?

In *Baptist Beliefs*, Mullins explained humanity's inheritance as a result of the fall without naming Adam. He appealed to the transmission of hereditary traits as support for the biblical viewpoint that "sin has

26. Humphreys, "Edgar Young Mullins," 181–85.

27. Mullins, *The Axioms of Religion*, 58–59.

28. Ibid., 59–65. Quotation from page 63.

become hereditary." He did not, however, associate this "sinful heredity" with guilt and condemnation. Rather, he wrote, "Condemnation is not for hereditary sin, but only for actual sin."[29] Also, "all men actually sin when they *acquire capacity for sinning*."[30] Infants, he added, possess "the hereditary tendency to sin," which is "before actual sin."[31] In these statements, Mullins clearly distinguished between an infant's inherited *capacity* for sin and *actual* sin (sinful actions).

Further, Mullins distinguished between "infants" and "men." First, he did this by assigning only hereditary sin to infants but both hereditary and actual sin to men. Compare the statements above with the following: "Hereditary *and* actual sin render *men* not only corrupt but also guilty and condemned."[32] Second, he noted that although the Scriptures "say little" on the subject of infant salvation, enough is known to justify the view that the "grace of God deals with them in a special manner." Third, those who die in their infancy will "share in the blessing" of Christ's atonement, which was "for all the race."[33] Thus Mullins' view of unlimited atonement extends the saving effect of Christ's blood to those who die in their infancy *apart* from their repentance and faith. This is not the case for men, for "(h)ereditary and actual sin render men not only corrupt but also guilty and condemned *until they are justified* by faith in Jesus Christ."[34] Infants, though, will be saved by God's grace because they are not "capable of exercising repentance and faith" in order to be saved. Fourth, infants are different from men because infants lack "moral discernment."[35]

Mullins' insistence on soul competency required that he distinguish between infants and men and then allowed him to affirm a view of inherited tendency to sin but to reject the doctrine of inherited guilt. For Mullins, man is not guilty because of his nature (Eph 2:3),[36] because he was represented by Adam in the garden, or because we were semi-

29. Mullins, *The Christian Religion*, 301.
30. Mullins, *Baptist Beliefs*, 24–25. Emphasis mine.
31. Ibid., 25.
32. Ibid. Emphasis mine.
33. Ibid., 25.
34. Ibid. Emphasis mine.
35. Mullins, *The Christian Religion*, 301. See also, 286, in which he referred to "actual sin in all children as they become morally responsible."
36. Mullins, *Studies in Ephesians*, 62–63.

nally present in Adam. Rather, man "is guilty when he does wrong."[37] Mullins explained, "Men are not condemned therefore for hereditary or original sin. They are condemned only for their own sins." In a confusing move, though, Mullins insisted in the same paragraph that men are condemned when they reject the Gospel's call to repentance and faith.[38] The significance of those statements is that Mullins stated on the one hand that men are condemned for their sinful actions but on the other hand for their rejection of the Gospel. In either case, infants are not under condemnation.

CONCLUSION

This examination of nineteenth-century Baptists reveals a variety of views, some of which are internally inconsistent. James P. Boyce affirmed infant sinfulness and guilt even though they had not knowingly sinned. In this way, he taught that God will judge our sinful *nature*. However, when he explained why men would be condemned even if they had not heard the gospel, Boyce wrote that men will be judged according to their sinful *actions*. Similarly A. H. Strong affirmed Augustine's Natural Headship but contradicted it when he taught that infants would *not* be condemned for their sinful nature.

Boyce and Strong contradicted themselves as they attempted to affirm these two truths of Scripture: infants inherit a sinful nature, and God judges sinful actions. E. Y. Mullins better maintained those twin truths. He taught that people inherit sinful *tendencies* rather than sin and guilt. And his view of soul competency forced a distinction between the spiritual condition of men and that of infants.

---

37. Mullins, *The Christian Religion*, 294.

38. Ibid., 302. The problem with Mullins' affirmation of those two views is this: If condemnation follows sinful actions, then all men stand condemned. But if condemnation only follows a rejection of the gospel, then those who have not heard the gospel will not be condemned. The faulty implication is that people are spiritual safe until they hear the gospel. Since they might reject it, the better course is to never share the gospel and therefore not risk that a person might reject the call to repentance and faith. Such a view, of course, is faulty.

17

Twentieth-Century Baptists
(Hendricks and Erickson)

WILLIAM HENDRICKS

WILLIAM HENDRICKS (1929–2002) WAS a professor of theology at three Southern Baptist seminaries before he spent his final years teaching at Brite Divinity School, Texas Christian University. Three of his works provide his thoughts on the spiritual condition of infants.

In his 1970 article entitled "The Age of Accountability," Hendricks wrote that "the image of God means that man is capable of response to God."[1] In 1977 he nuanced this view by writing that it is "the potentiality, ability, and responsibility to respond to God." He included infants and the mentally disabled people as having been made in God's image. Infants have the potential to respond to God because they can do so later in life granted that they have enough time to experience a normal maturing process. Mentally disabled person were also made in the image of God even if their potential for responding to God never fully develops.[2]

Hendricks explained that man's responsibility to respond increased as God's revelation moved from general to special. Man's sense that he is missing something in life and his observation of both good and evil in the world provide an awareness of God's existence, but Jesus Christ is God's "clearest revelation." Although Christians are to share the gospel, some people will come to the end of their life without having heard the message. Like the people of Tyre and Sidon in Jesus' day, they will experience a less-severe judgment than the Pharisees (Matt 11:22).[3] This idea of

1. Hendricks, "The Age of Accountability," 85.
2. Hendricks, *The Doctrine of Man*, 48–49.
3. Hendricks, "The Age of Accountability," 85–87.

a less-severe judgment relates to infants because they have not yet been confronted with the responsibility to respond to God and his gospel.

Hendricks' doctrine of salvation is characterized by man's need to respond to God and his gospel. In 1970 he explained that children in Old Testament times were covered by the covenant until they personally rebelled against God.[4] Hendricks added that in order for a person to be saved, a person—including one who is the age of a child—must be able to fulfill the requirements for faith, which include the ability to understand the message of the gospel, place faith in God, and repent of sin.[5] Hendricks blended what he called Sacramental and Conversionist Theology.[6] In his view, infants are simultaneously *not* in need of salvation because they are already under God's covenant but they *are* in need of salvation. The key to understanding his affirmation of both covenant and the need to respond to God and his gospel is found in his understanding of original sin.

Hendricks rejected what he considered to be classical errors in the doctrine of original sin. In 1970 he rejected the Augustinian view as well as the ideas that children inherit a "bent" toward sin or are born "neutral." He mentioned the inevitability of sin and the need for redemption but did not try to go beyond what he viewed as the Bible's silence on *why* man was a sinner.[7] Eight years later, Hendricks' *Doctrine of Man* was the distributed for the convention-wide annual Baptist Doctrine Study. In a section entitled "Adam Didn't Make Me Do It," he restated his rejection to the Augustinian view, which he described as the "boldest" and the "popular" expression of original sin. He noted the view's foundation in Rom 5:12–21 and 1 Cor 15:20–28 and characterized the wrong interpretation as follows:

> When Adam fell in the Garden, he became a sinner; and every one of his descendants inherits that sin from him. Therefore, everyone who is born has this spiritual taint, gained by being conceived and

---

4. Ibid., 88. See also Hendricks, *The Doctrine of Man*, 48–49, for an explicit statement that God's "covenant mercy" covers infants and the mentally undeveloped.

5. Hendricks, "The Age of Accountability," 91–92.

6. Although Hendricks, *Theology for Children*, 15–17, limited this covenantal view to Sacramental Theology (with its baptismal regeneration), the broader idea is that the child is to be nurtured in the faith that he already possesses. Conversionist Theology, on the other hand, emphasizes man's separation from God and his need to repent and believe in order to be saved.

7. Hendricks, "The Age of Accountability," 88.

born. All who are born are sinners. Sinners who do not repent go to hell. Since we are sinners by birth, we had no choice in the matter. Therefore, Adam is responsible, and God seems unfair.[8]

Original sin referred to Adam's sin as well as a "weakness," or "a sinful inclination which we all possess."[9] In 1986 Hendricks published another rejection of Augustine's view of original sin as well as a statement on the true nature of original sin.

In this brief article, Hendricks attempted to answer whether or not a person is "in one sense condemned from the beginning of its existence." He wrote that Baptists followed Augustine and Calvin by answering that children are condemned even at infancy. He cited Frank Stagg as an example of a Baptist who would raise but not answer the question. In this way, Stagg followed the biblical example of silence on the issue. Hendricks also mentioned the "Arminian answer . . . modernized via Wesley and Finney," which is that infants are sinful but not yet sinners. The Arminian view was closer to the truth but did not satisfy Hendricks. He then announced his "phenomenological version" of the Arminian answer. He admitted that it was not easy to explain but made an attempt when he wrote, "Original sin is a theological construct to foreshadow, but not to explain" people as sinners.[10]

Hendricks affirmed that all *people* are sinful. But he argued against the notion that *infants* are sinful. Each and every person will eventually become a sinner, but each must do so personally. Hendricks explained, "It is appropriate to speak of all persons as sinful. It is correct to say they *become* sinners when they actualize their sinful inclination."[11]

Earl Waggoner provided an excellent summary and critique of Hendricks' view of infant salvation. Although Waggoner's sixteen-page treatment was carefully documented and more comprehensive in its content than the present section, I question his use of the phrase "innocent children" to characterize Hendricks' view for two reasons.[12] First, Hendricks objected to any view of original sin that imputed sin or guilt to infants. Rather, he insisted that infants inherit only a sinful tendency that

8. Hendricks, *The Doctrine of Man*, 29–30.

9. Ibid., 75–76.

10. Hendricks, "Baptists and Children," 50.

11. Hendricks, *The Doctrine of Man*, 30. Emphasis mine.

12. Waggoner, "Baptist Approaches," 159–75.

will eventually result in their becoming, by their own actions, sinners. In this way, Hendricks did not regard infants as innocent but, rather, as not-yet-condemned.

Second, Waggoner claims that Hendricks made a shift in his 1986 article from infant salvation by covenant to infant salvation by cosmic redemption. Redemption, though, still implies that someone or something needs to be redeemed. In this case, infants are in need of redemption. However, innocent infants would not be in need of redemption. This must mean that for Hendricks, infants had not acted in such a way to incur God's judgment but were still in need of God's redemptive work. In this way, Hendricks did not consider infants to be innocent but, rather, they were not-yet-condemned.

MILLARD ERICKSON

Millard Erickson (b. 1925) has been called "one of the most significant and prolific Baptist and conservative Evangelical theologians" of the last fifty years.[13] He has published dozens of theological works, including his popular college and seminary-level theology textbooks entitled *Introducing Christian Doctrine* and *Christian Theology*.[14] Erickson addresses the spiritual condition of infants in the latter work and in a chapter in *How Shall They Be Saved? The Destiny of Those Who Do Not Hear of Jesus*.[15]

In *Christian Theology*, Erickson acknowledges that all people are sinners. Not only do all people sin, but they "all have a depraved or corrupted nature which so inclines us toward sin that it is virtually inevitable." He then asks how this "common factor that is often referred to as original sin" is "derived, and how it is transmitted or communicated."[16] He surveys Pelagianism, Arminianism, and Calvinism (under which he includes both Natural and Federal Headship). Next he constructs a "biblical and contemporary model" of original sin.[17] He identifies Rom 5:12–19 as the key biblical text. Erickson acknowledges that Augustine

13. Green, "Millard J. Erickson," 317.

14. Erickson, *Introducing Christian Doctrine*; and Erickson, *Christian Theology*.

15. Erickson, *How Shall They Be Saved?*

16. Erickson, *Christian Theology*, 648.

17. Ibid., 649–52. In *How Shall They Be Saved?*, 239–48, Erickson considers the approaches to infants' salvation and adds to these three the approaches of Sentimentalism, Probation of the Infant, and Baptismal Regeneration.

used a poor translation of verse 12 ("in whom" rather than "because" all sinned). He also acknowledges that Paul used an aorist verb ("sinned"), which refers to an action that occurred *prior* to Paul's day. If Paul had intended to refer to our sin, then he would have used a present or imperfect verb, which would have indicated that all people die because all people sin (continuing action). Erickson resolves this issue by explaining that we ought to "regard the sin of all human beings and the sin of Adam as the same." So the reason that death came to all people is that when we sinned, we participated in the sin of Adam. Erickson effectively affirms both the Augustinian (Natural Headship) and Calvinist (Federal Headship) views and explains that God is justified in the condemnation and death that follows our sin.[18]

At this point, Erickson raises the "problem" of infants and children. He writes, "If the reasoning that precedes is correct, then all of life begins with both the corrupted nature and the guilt that are the consequences of sin." He asks whether infants and children who die before being able to make a "conscious decision" to receive his gift of salvation will be eternally lost. After noting the "difficulty" of such a question, he answers that the Lord does not regard "infants and those who never reach moral competency" to be under condemnation. Erickson then cites Jesus, who says that infants and children are examples of those who would inherit the kingdom (Matt 19:14). He also notes David's declaration that he would again see his deceased infant (2 Sam 12:23).

Erickson writes that people are "not morally responsible before a certain point, which we sometimes call 'the age of accountability.'" He cites Deut 1:39 and comments, "Even with the Hebrew idea of corporate personality and corporate responsibility, these children were *not held responsible* for the sins of Israel." He also cites Isa 7:15–16, which refers to a time when the person in question "knows enough to reject the wrong and choose the right." Finally, Erickson points to the "less clear" comment in Jonah 4:11 about people not knowing their right hand from their left. He thinks this refers to people who are unable to distinguish between right and wrong.[19]

Erickson then returns to Rom 5 and notes that Paul's parallel of Adam and Christ. He explains that this parallel cannot mean that condemnation

18. Erickson, *Christian Theology*, 653–54.

19. Ibid., 654–55. Emphasis mine. See also Erickson, *How Shall They Be Saved?*, 250–51, for an expanded treatment of these passages.

and guilt come to every person apart from their conscious choice. Why not? Salvation does not come to a person apart from his "conscious and personal acceptance" of Christ's atoning work.[20] In other words, Erickson discerns a need to understand Rom 5 in a way that incorporates human ratification of the actions of both representatives. Just as it is necessary for humans to *ratify* the work of Christ by *appropriating* the salvation offered by Christ, it is likewise necessary to ratify the sin of Adam in order to fall under condemnation and guilt.[21] In *How Shall They Be Saved?*, Erickson explains, "Until the first conscious or responsible moral action or decision by a person, there is no imputation of the Adamic sin, just as there is no imputation of Christ's righteousness until there is a conscious acceptance of that work." Erickson demonstrates this dilemma: In light of the Adam-Christ parallel in Rom 5, how does one affirm that everyone *passively* receives Adam's guilt but they must *actively* appropriate Christ's work on our behalf?

But Erickson does not view this dilemma as a rejection of the Augustinian-Calvinist tradition. He maintains that everyone was involved in Adam's sin as well as the resulting corruption, guilt, and condemnation. Erickson writes in *Christian Theology*,

> With this matter of guilt, however, just as with the imputation of Christ's righteousness, there must be some conscious and voluntary decision on our part. Until this is the case, there is only a conditional imputation of guilt. Thus, there is no condemnation until one reaches the age of responsibility. If a child dies before becoming capable of making genuine moral decisions, then contingent imputation of Adamic sin does not become actual, and the child will experience the same type of future existence with the Lord as will those who have reached the age of moral responsibility and had their sins forgiven as a result of accepting the offer of salvation based upon Christ's atoning death.[22]

Erickson explains that "childish innocence" ends when we become aware of our "tendency toward sin" and ratify Adam's sin. The acceptance, or approval, of our "corrupt nature" is also an approval of Adam and Eve's sin in the garden.[23]

20. Erickson, *Christian Theology*, 655.
21. Erickson, *How Shall They Be Saved?*, 250.
22. Erickson, *Christian Theology*, 656.
23. Ibid.

Erickson's view of the spiritual condition of infants is sensitive to both the church's long-and widely-held Augustinian-Calvinist view of original sin as well as the biblical texts that address the issue. He simultaneously views all of humanity as sinful and guilty while arguing for an exception among infants, children, and people who do not mature mentally.[24] Their conditional guilt is not imputed to them until they personally ratify and appropriate the sinful work of Adam. In this way, he affirms universal sinfulness and even participation in Adam's sin, but he safeguards infants, children, and the mentally incompetent from being called sinners before they knowingly sin. This insistence upon the need to also ratify the sinful work of Adam maintains an individual's responsibility for his own sin. Erickson's insistence on the need to personally ratify and appropriate the work of Christ upholds the evangelical conviction that all people have an individual need to repent of their sin and confess their faith in Christ in order to be saved. Erickson's view of the Adam-Christ parallel in Rom 5 and the imputation of conditional guilt to infants rightly rejects the views of Universalism and infants as guilty but affirms Exclusivism and infants as not guilty.

CONCLUSION

William Hendricks taught that infants are born with sinful inclinations but are not guilty. Rather, people *become* sinners. Millard Erickson taught the Augustinian-Calvinist view of original sin but excluded infants from guilt and condemnation due to their lack of moral competency. Infants are unable to distinguish between good and evil. I agree with the conclusions of both men. Although they began with different assumptions, they arrived at the same conclusion about infants: not guilty.

Hendricks denied that people inherit sin and guilt from Adam, but Erickson claimed to affirm that Augustinian-Calvinist tradition. However, Erickson's exclusion of infants from the imputation of guilt refutes the view that he claims to affirm. Erickson's explanation is that infants receive a conditional imputation of guilt. This means that infants are not presently guilty but will later become guilty of sin. Isn't that an affirmation

24. Erickson, *How Shall They Be Saved?*, 235 n. 1, includes certain adults in the same category as infants and children when he writes in a footnote to his chapter entitled, "The Salvation of Those Incapable of Faith," "While the discussion will refer primarily to infants, it should also be understood as applying to those who may attain physical maturity, but never mentally pass beyond the capability of rather young children."

that infants are *not* presently guilty of sin? If so, then Erickson does *not* affirm the Augustinian-Calvinist position on original sin.

Despite that minor question about Erickson's assumption, I find his argument as a whole to be very helpful. I explained in an earlier chapter that this book grew out of an attempt to respond to Grudem's view of infant guilt and salvation. In an early stage of this project, though, it was Erickson's treatment on infants that provided me direction as well as the assurance that such a view was even possible.

Conclusion

IN THIS CHAPTER, I will try to synthesize all of this book's previous material. Rather than restate, I will assume the findings from the biblical and historical chapters. I will address the following questions:

- What exactly is the spiritual condition of infants?

- How does sin affect infants?

- What are some of the theological implications of inherited guilt?

- What are some of the theological implications of an inherited sinful nature?

- What are the pastoral implications of the present thesis?

WHAT EXACTLY IS THE SPIRITUAL CONDITION
OF INFANTS?

The argument of this book is that infants inherit from Adam a sinful nature but not guilt. The sinful nature that infants inherit will eventually result in their becoming guilty by knowingly committing acts of sin. It is at that point that people immediately fall under God's judgment and condemnation. This view is consistent with the ten biblical passages that were considered and similar to the views of following theologians: Irenaeus, Gregory of Nyssa, Gregory of Nazianzus, Tertullian, Martin Luther, Pilgram Marpeck, E. Y. Mullins, William Hendricks, and Millard Erickson.

Also, the argument of this book is consistent with the 1963 and 2000 editions of the *Baptist Faith and Message*.[1] Article 3 of the 2000 edition explains that Adam's "posterity inherit a nature and an environment in-

---

1. See Stewart, "Article III: Man," 32, who points out that the phrase "as soon as they are capable of moral action" appears in all three editions (1925, 1963, 2000) of the *Baptist Faith and Message*. For this reason, he argues, "all three editions seem to affirm an 'age of accountability.'"

clined toward sin. Therefore, as soon as they are capable of moral action, they become transgressors and are under condemnation." This article does not state that people inherit Adam's *guilt* but a *nature* inclined toward sin. Also, this article does not state that people are under condemnation from the moment of their conception. Instead, they *become* transgressors and fall under God's condemnation. When does this happen? People fall under God's judgment when they are capable of moral action, which implies that there is an earlier period of time in which people are *not* capable of moral action. Surely this includes the period of time known as infancy.

For those readers who have been reading through this book waiting for a declarative statement on the spiritual condition of infants, here it is: Infants are sin-stained, not guilty. Infants are not sinless because they inherit a sinful nature. But infants are not guilty because God judges our thoughts, attitudes, and actions, not our nature. If I were pressed to speculate how God might deal with people who die in their infancy, I would offer this suggestion: All people who die in their infancy will be included in God's restoration of his fallen creation through Christ's work at the cross. Perhaps this is the time Jesus mentioned as "the renewal of all things" (Matt 19:28). Paul said that creation would be set free from its bondage to decay (Rom 8:19–23). Although infants are not guilty of sin, they have been stained by it. Even though they have not knowingly acted in ways that would incur God's judgment, they may be in need of God's redemptive and renewing work. And it is Jesus who promises, "Behold, I make all things new" (Rev 21:5).

HOW DOES SIN AFFECT INFANTS?

All of the biblical texts and historical views presented in this study consider all people at the earliest stages of their life to have been negatively impacted by sin. The sin that impacts infants, though, is not related to their thoughts, attitudes, or actions. Infants are not affected by their own actual sin but by their own sinful nature as well as the fallen nature of the cosmos and the resulting evil. The effects of sin on infants will be considered under the categories of natural evil and moral evil.

Natural evil "does not involve human willing and acting, but is merely an aspect of nature that seems to work against human welfare."[2] Natural evil includes things such as meteorological events and genetic

2. Erickson, *Christian Theology*, 437.

disorders. More specific to infants, natural evil includes sudden infant death syndrome (SIDS), miscarriage, and a range of mental and physical disorders. Any of those natural evils can threaten the health and even the life of an infant in the absence of any malicious action against that infant and in spite of all reasonable precautions to protect the infant. As an example of suffering due to natural evil, consider SIDS.

The American Academy of Pediatrics defines SIDS as follows: "The sudden death of an infant under one year of age, which remains unexplained after a thorough case investigation, including performance of a complete autopsy, examination of the death scene, and review of the clinical history." In 2002 SIDS occurred in .57 of every one thousand live births in the United States. The frequency of SIDS has declined in recent decades due to recommendations against mothers smoking and about the proper position and environment for sleeping infants. The numbers of SIDS deaths in 2002 was nearly half the number that was recorded in the United States in 1992. However, that number seems to have leveled off, so it is doubtful that the disorder will ever be eliminated.[3] This decrease in infant deaths, though, offers little comfort to those parents who have lost an infant to this mysterious disorder.

One might argue that the death of an infant is not an example of natural evil because the infant is not yet conscious of his existence. However, such a person will be hard pressed to sustain the claim that an infant is not conscious of his existence. There is conflicting medical data on whether or not infants are capable of feeling pain in the womb.[4] But even if the death of an infant were not considered natural evil by that infant, his or her death would be considered natural evil by the parents. The suffering that occurs at the death of an infant due to SIDS, even if that suffering

3. Task Force on Sudden Infant Death Syndrome, "The Changing Concept of Sudden Infant Death Syndrome," 1245–46.

4. See Derbyshire, "Can Fetuses Feel Pain?" 909–12, who argues that the neuron anatomical system is mature by twenty-six weeks in the womb, but infants do not experience pain until many months outside the womb because "pain experience requires development of the mind to accommodate the subjectivity of pain." For a contrary view, see Slater, et al., "Cortical Pain Responses in Human Infants," 3662–66. There was not even a medical category for the state of an infant crying in the womb until 2005, when three doctors made the suggestion based upon the incidental capture of such an action in a video recording of an ultrasound. See Gingras, et al., "Fetal Homologue of Infant Crying," 415–18.

is experienced only by the infant's parents, is an example of natural evil because it is suffering that occurs without anyone's willful intent.

Infants do not suffer the effects of natural evil because they have inherited guilt. Rather, infants are susceptible to natural evil for the same reason that animals, older children, and adults are vulnerable. We live in a fallen world. Although God is engaged in a plan of cosmic redemption, in which he will renew the heavens and the earth, the world remains only in labor pains (Rom 8:19–23). This redemption has not been fully delivered.

Infants are also subject to the effects of sin due to moral evil, which has been defined as personal suffering "which is the direct result of human volition."[5] This includes mental or physical abuse, substance abuse, rage, malice, deceit, murder, and suicide. The following are examples of moral evil that are specific to infants: shaken baby syndrome, abortion, and fetal alcohol syndrome.

Fetal alcohol syndrome (FAS) can occur when a mother ingests alcohol during her pregnancy. FAS can cause prenatal and postnatal growth retardation as well as problems in the nervous system. An article in *American Family Physician* reports, "The consequences are lifelong, and the behavioral and learning difficulties are often greater than the degree of neurocognitive impairment." Tragically the spectrum of FAS disorders may affect up to 1 percent of the infants born in the United States.[6] Infants can neither choose nor influence the behaviors of their mother. All infants who are injured by this disorder must be considered free from any guilt or blame. These infants have been negatively impacted by moral evil, which in such cases is due to the mother consuming harmful beverages while the infant is still in her womb.

Infants are *not* innocent because they have inherited a sinful nature. And they can be impacted by the effects of sin through both natural and moral evil. Infants, however, are *not* under God's condemnation. Although infants inherit a sinful nature, they are not under God's condemnation because of their lack of moral knowledge and the character of God's judgment. Lack of moral knowledge refers to an infant's inability to distinguish between good and evil. God's judgment is revealed against sinful *actions* rather than a sinful *nature*. My thesis is that infants inherit a

5. Nelson, "The Work of God: Creation and Providence," 287.
6. Wattendorf and Muenke, "Fetal Alcohol Spectrum Disorders," 279.

sinful nature, not guilt. This view contradicts the traditional Augustinian-Calvinist view of inherited guilt. The next section will consider the theological implications of that traditional view.

WHAT ARE SOME OF THE THEOLOGICAL IMPLICATIONS OF INHERITED GUILT?

Are infants *guilty* before God due solely to the sinful *nature* inherited from Adam? Are infants guilty before God before they have the ability to make moral judgments or to think sinful thoughts? The Augustinian-Calvinist tradition presupposes inherited sin *and guilt* in the case of infants and answers "Yes" to those questions about their guilt before God. But if you think that infants are guilty before God and you hold an exclusivist view of salvation, in which a person must hear and respond in repentance and faith to the gospel, then there are only four possible conclusions about the eternal destiny of those who die as infants:

1. Some, or all, infants who die will enter heaven due to election.[7]

2. Some infants who die will enter heaven due to the covenant, or household sanctification.[8]

3. Some, or all, infants who die will enter heaven due to God's mercy and the sanctifying work of Christ at the cross.[9]

4. Some infants who die will enter hell due to Adamic guilt.[10]

The strength of holding to one of the first three views is that there can be no argument that the work of an infant's salvation would be an

---

7. See MacArthur, *Safe in the Arms of God*; and Nash, *When a Baby Dies*. Consider this explicit treatment in this document originally drafted in 1647 entitled the *Westminster Confession of Faith* 10.3: "Elect infants, dying in infancy, are regenerated, and saved by Christ, through the Spirit, who worketh when, and where, and how He pleaseth: so also are all other elect persons who are uncapable of being outwardly called by the ministry of the Word." Although affirming the salvation of elect infants, the statement is ambiguous on the question of whether every person who dies as an infant is one of the elect.

8. This assurance of heaven, though, only applies to the children of believers. See Wikner, *To You and Your Children*; and Lusk, *Paedofaith*.

9. Cragoe, "An Examination of the Issues of Infant Salvation."

10. Augustine, *A Treatise on the Merits and Forgiveness of Sin* 1.21, in NPNF 5:22–23, "It may therefore be correctly affirmed, that such infants as quit the body without being baptized will be involved in the mildest condemnation of all. That person, therefore, greatly deceives both himself and others, who teaches that they will not be involved in condemnation."

exercise of God's grace rather than God's response to the infant's intellectual assent or some other cooperation on the part of the infant. But there are two issues that are unresolved even among those who affirm infant salvation by election or the covenant. First, are *all* infants who die among the elect? Some Reformed theologians, such as Charles Spurgeon, John MacArthur, and Ronald Nash, answer in the affirmative.[11] Others, such as Loraine Boettner and Wayne Grudem, only affirm a hope for the salvation of infants with *believing* parents.[12] Second, are infants guilty of sin? Reformed theologians, such as John Murray and Wayne Grudem, argue that infants are guilty of sin because of their participation in the sin of Adam.[13] Other Reformed theologians, such as Ronald Nash, Thomas Cragoe, and John MacArthur, argue that infants are not guilty of sin because they are *incapable* of committing acts of sin.[14]

The first three views of salvation for guilty infants (by election, covenant, and mercy) should be regarded by Exclusivists as inadequate explanations. Why? Those infants never heard and responded to the gospel. Those views reject the need for an individual to make an explicit confession of faith in Christ as either a necessity for or as a sign of his salvation. In this way, these views necessarily support an Inclusivist view of salvation, in which people can be saved through Christ without making an explicit confession of faith in Christ. The fourth option, hell, is not viewed by many people as a possibility for those who die in their infancy. However, it is the only conclusion that is *consistent* when affirming both infant guilt and an Exclusivist view of salvation. The problem with the four conclusions above is that infants are assumed to be *guilty* due solely to their inherited sinful *nature*.

If God will save infants who die without having a chance to hear and respond to the gospel, then will he likewise save adults who die without

11. Spurgeon, "Infant Salvation (Sermon 411);" MacArthur, *Safe in the Arms of God*; and Nash, *When A Baby Dies*, 59–60.

12. See Boettner, *The Reformed Doctrine of Predestination*, 146, "(T)he Scriptures seem to teach plainly enough that the children of believers are saved; but they are silent or practically so in regard to those of the heathens." See also Grudem, *Systematic Theology*, 499–501.

13. See Murray, *The Imputation of Adam's Sin*, 15–16; and Grudem, *Systematic Theology*, 494–95.

14. Examples of Reformed theologians who argue both that infants are guilty of sin but excluded from judgment because God judges sinful actions include: Nash, *When a Baby Dies*, 60–61; Cragoe, "Infant Salvation," 77; and MacArthur, *Safe*, 79–90.

having a chance to hear and respond to the gospel? The argument of this book allows you to maintain both an exclusivist view and a consistent doctrine of salvation. God forgives guilty sinners who explicitly call upon him for salvation. God's condemnation does not come only to people for hearing of and rejecting Christ. Rather, people are condemned when they act out of their inherited, sinful nature *after* they become responsible moral agents. The result is that an infant who dies apart from hearing the gospel is safe because he was never under God's condemnation. However the man who has never heard the gospel remains lost because he met the two conditions above for condemnation.

Those who claim that infants inherit sin *and guilt* are faced with the following inconsistencies in their viewpoint: First, it would be inconsistent for God to hold infants guilty of the sin of another person (Adam) because he states that he holds people responsible for their own sin, not for the sin of another person (Ezek 18:20). Each of us will give an account of himself to God (Rom 14:12). We will not give an account to God of our parents or grandparents or even our furthest descendant, Adam. Second, because the Scriptures indicate that God judges people for their sinful thoughts, attitudes, and actions, it would be inconsistent for him to judge infants to be guilty of sin solely based on their sinful nature. Jesus was delivered over to death for our sins (Rom 4:25), not for our sinful nature. Third, if guilty adults must repent of their sin and confess faith in Christ in order to be saved from their sin and guilt (Rom 10:9–13), then why is such a confession not required of guilty infants? The obvious dilemma is that infants are not able to make any kind of confession. But that is not a problem for some people who teach that infants inherit guilt. They state that a confession of faith in Christ is required for the salvation of most guilty people but not of guilty infants.[15] Fourth, many of the people who affirm infant guilt also think that many (or in the cases of those with believing parents, all) of those infants who die will be cleansed of the stain of original guilt and enter heaven.[16] If so, then they don't regard infants to be under condemnation *until* they commit sinful acts. They effectively

15. Some people have taught that everyone must confess faith in Christ in order to be saved, but some guilty infants are saved without an explicit knowledge of or confession of Christ. For examples, see the previous sections in this book on Grudem, Hubmaier, and Boyce.

16. This was the conclusion of Cyprian, Augustine, Boyce, and Strong.

affirm an age of accountability, before which infants are not under God's judgment but after which they will become culpable for their sin.

WHAT ARE SOME OF THE THEOLOGICAL IMPLICATIONS OF AN INHERITED SINFUL NATURE?

I have tried to argue throughout this book that infants do not inherit guilt from Adam. Instead infants inherit a sinful nature. In the Scriptures, God does not judge people for their inherited sinful nature. Instead, God judges people who are morally responsible. Infants, like the younger generation of Israelites in the desert, are spared God's judgment because they are not yet morally responsible people. Infants inherit from Adam a sinful nature. From the moment of conception, every thought, attitude, and action they make flows out of and through that sinful nature. But God does not judge people for their inherited sinful nature. He judges people for acts of sin that they commit as a result of that sinful nature. All morally responsible people know the difference between right and wrong, eventually violate God's law, and are thus in need of salvation from God's condemnation of and wrath over their acts of sin. But infants don't yet know the difference between right and wrong. Because they lack moral knowledge, they are not yet under God's condemnation for sin, unlike morally responsible people who have a need for salvation from God's condemnation of and wrath over their acts of sin.

If you affirm that infants are *not guilty* before God, then you still face the following three questions: First, what does it mean for infants to have been corrupted by sin but not be guilty of sin? Second, how does one account for the universality and inevitability of sin among humans? Third, if infants are not guilty of sin but death is a result of sin, then why do some infants die?

In response to the first question, infants inherit a sinful nature and have been corrupted by sin but are free from guilt and condemnation until they knowingly sin. In response to the second question, sin is universal and inevitable among humans because every person who was born of a woman (with the exception of Jesus) is in Adam. It isn't necessary to choose between Augustine's Natural or Calvin's Federal Headship. Regardless of how we are related to Adam, the result is that everyone has a sinful nature from the beginning of their life. In response to the third question, infants sometimes die but not because they are guilty of either a sinful nature or the sin of Adam. Instead, previous chapters in this book demonstrated that infants sometimes die as the result of the sins of other people. For example there were probably infants swept up in the flood (Gen 6:5–6). Also David and Bathsheba's infant son died through no sinful act of his own but because of the sinful actions of his father (2 Sam 12:23). Additionally infants can suffer even to the point of death due to both moral and natural evil.

The present thesis distinguishes between inheriting a sinful nature and inheriting Adam's guilt. It rejects the Augustinian-Calvinist view of inherited guilt due to either a sinful forefather or representative. Rather, the present thesis affirms our relationship to Adam and the judgment of and personal culpability for actual sins that people are commit after they have mature in their ability to make moral judgments.

The present thesis allows for a consistent, Exclusivist view of salvation based on moral agency. Infants who die without hearing and responding to the gospel are not condemned because they are not yet responsible moral agents. But all responsible moral agents who die without hearing and accepting the gospel will face the condemnation and wrath of God over their sin. It's not true that infants who die will be forgiven of their guilt and condemnation apart from hearing and responding to the gospel of Christ. Rather, infants are free from guilt and condemnation because they have never knowingly committed acts of sin out of their sinful nature.

WHAT ARE THE PASTORAL IMPLICATIONS OF THE PRESENT THESIS?

This view on infants can be used by pastors and counselors to offer comfort to those who have lost infants due to miscarriage, abortion, or death. The present thesis also has implications for Christian parents and leaders on the issue of making disciples, baptizing, and teaching children.

First, remember that the Scriptures do not explicitly address the spiritual condition of infants. I agree with Balthasar Hubmaier, who wrote, "I confess here publicly my ignorance. I am not ashamed not to know what God did not want to reveal to us with a clear and plain word."[17] For this

17. I agree with Hubmaier, *On the Christian Baptism*, 140, who wrote, "I confess here publicly my ignorance. I am not ashamed not to know what God did not want to reveal to us with a clear and plain word."

reason, the issue must be approached with humility and grace toward one another, because one cannot be *certain* of his position. Although there may not be certainty on this issue, it is a good practice in such cases to appeal to what has been clearly revealed in the Scripture of God's character and ways. So, if the finer points of the spiritual condition of infants cannot be known with perfect clarity, believers can have confidence in God, who always acts in ways that reflect his holiness, justice, mercy, grace, and love. Whatever the spiritual condition of infants, it reflects God's revealed character and ways.

Second, use caution when speaking to grieving people in the days and weeks immediately following the death of an infant. Offering detailed explanations of an infant's spiritual condition during that raw time of loss would likely be negatively received. During that period, the best things to offer are the ministry of one's presence, prayers, appropriate expressions of sorrow over their loss, and (if one believes it to be true) assurances that the infant is eternally safe with God. After an extended period of time has passed and at the request of the one who has experienced the loss, it would be appropriate to address any questions that arise from the situation. At that point, you might offer them a book on infant salvation.

Third, my thesis makes no distinction between children of believers and children of unbelievers. Neither the spiritual condition nor the eternal destiny of infants is based upon the spiritual condition of their parents. The arguments for salvation of believing children (through either election or the covenant) can provide comfort and assurance, but only to believing parents. My argument is that all infants have a sinful nature. They are not currently but will later be subject to God's judgment. And all infants who die, whether or not their parents are believers, will be included in God's work of restoring through the cross his fallen creation, and they will live eternally with God in heaven.

Fourth, there are implications for Christian parents and leaders. Although infants are not under God's condemnation, they have a nature that is horribly and irrevocably stained by sin. In a short amount of time, these infants will grow into children who will develop moral knowledge. It is the presence of this moral knowledge when coupled with their sinful actions that brings God's condemnation. Whether you think infants inherit a sinful nature or Adam's guilt, Christians in both camps ought to agree that if an infant matures to adulthood, there will remain no question about his guilt before God. Children need to hear the truth about their sinful and guilty condition. They need to understand that Jesus lived a perfect life, died a horrible death, and rose victorious from the dead for the forgiveness of *their* sin. And they need to be encouraged from the youngest possible age to make a personal decision to repent of and confess their sin to God, follow him by submitting to believer's baptism, and commit to living daily for Jesus Christ.

Bibliography

Aland, Kurt. *Did the Early Church Baptize Infants?* Philadelphia: Westminster Press, 1963.

Aristotle. *Politics.* Translated by H. Rackham. In Loeb Classical Library, vol. 264. Cambridge, MA: Harvard University Press, 1932.

Armour, Rollin S. *Anabaptist Baptism: A Representative Study.* Scottdale, PA: Herald Press, 1966.

Augustine. *Answer to Julian.* In *Answer to the Pelagians II.* I/24. Translated by Roland J. Teske. Edited by John E. Rotelle. The Works of Saint Augustine: A Translation for the 21st Century. Edited by John E. Rotelle, et al., Hyde Park, NY: New City Press, 1998.

————. *The City of God.* Translated by Marcus Dods. In *St. Augustin's City of God and Christian Doctrine.* Edited by Philip Schaff. A Select Library of the Nicene and Post-Nicene Fathers of the Christian Church, vol. 2, first series. New York: Christian Literature Publishing, 1890; reprint, New York: Charles Scribner's Sons, 1899.

————. *The Confessions.* I/1. Translated by Maria Boulding. Edited by John E. Rotelle. The Works of Saint Augustine: A Translation for the 21st Century. Edited by John E. Rotelle, et al., Hyde Park, NY: New City Press, 1997.

————. *On Genesis Against the Manicheans.* Translated by Edmund Hill and Matthew O'Connell. Edited by John E. Rotelle. I/13. The Works of Saint Augustine: A Translation for the 21st Century. Edited by John E. Rotelle, et al., Hyde Park, NY: New City Press, 2002.

————. *Incomplete Work Against Julian.* In Patrologiae latina, ed. J. P. Migne. Vol. 45. Paris: n.p., 1845.

————. *Letters.* Translated by J. G. Cunningham. In *The Confessions and Letters of St. Augustin, With a Sketch of His Life and Work.* Edited by Philip Schaff. A Select Library of the Nicene and Post-Nicene Fathers of the Christian Church, vol. 1, first series. New York: Christian Literature Publishing, 1886; reprint, New York: Charles Scribner's Sons, 1902.

————. *Sermon LXV (CXV).* In *Saint Augustin: Sermon on the Mount, Harmony of the Gospels, Homilies on the Gospels.* Edited by Philip Schaff. A Select Library of the Nicene and Post-Nicene Fathers of the Christian Church, vol. 6, first series. New York: Christian Literature Publishing, 1888.

————. *Sermon 294.* In *Sermons, (273–305A) on the Saints.* III/8. Translated by Edmund Hill. The Works of Saint Augustine: A Translation for the 21st Century. Edited by John E. Rotelle, et al., Hyde Park, NY: New City Press, 1994.

————. *To Simplician—On Various Questions.* Translated and edited by J. H. S. Burleigh. In *Augustine: Earlier Writings.* In vol. 6 of The Library of Christian Classics. Edited by John Baillie, John T. McNeill, and Henry P. van Dusen. Philadelphia: Westminster Press, 1953.

―――. *A Treatise on the Grace of Christ and On Original Sin.* Translated by Peter Holmes. In *St. Augustin: Anti-Pelagian Writings.* Edited by Philip Schaff. A Select Library of the Nicene and Post-Nicene Fathers of the Christian Church, vol. 5, first series. New York: Christian Literature Publishing, 1890; reprint, New York: Charles Scribner's Sons, 1902.

―――. *A Treatise on Grace and Free Will.* Translated by Peter Holmes. In *St. Augustin: Anti-Pelagian Writings.* Edited by Philip Schaff. A Select Library of the Nicene and Post-Nicene Fathers of the Christian Church, vol. 5, first series. New York: Christian Literature Publishing, 1890; reprint, New York: Charles Scribner's Sons, 1902.

―――. *A Treatise on the Merits and Forgiveness of Sin, and On the Baptism of Infants.* Translated by Peter Holmes. In *St. Augustin: Anti-Pelagian Writings.* Edited by Philip Schaff. A Select Library of the Nicene and Post-Nicene Fathers of the Christian Church, vol. 5, first series. New York: Christian Literature Publishing, 1890; reprint, New York: Charles Scribner's Sons, 1902.

―――. *A Treatise on Nature and Grace.* Translated by Peter Holmes. In *St. Augustin: Anti-Pelagian Writings.* Edited by Philip Schaff. A Select Library of the Nicene and Post-Nicene Fathers of the Christian Church, vol. 5, first series. New York: Christian Literature Publishing, 1890; reprint, New York: Charles Scribner's Sons, 1902.

Azkoul, Michael. *St. Gregory of Nyssa and the Tradition of the Fathers.* In vol. 63 of Texts and Studies in Religion. Lewiston, NY: Edwin Mellon Press, 1995.

Bakke, O. M. *When Children Became People: The Birth of Childhood in Early Christianity.* Translated by Brian McNeil. Minneapolis: Fortress, 2005.

Barr, James. *The Garden of Eden and the Hope of Immortality.* Minneapolis: Fortress, 1992.

Barth, Karl. *The Humanity of God.* Richmond: John Knox, 1960.

Barth, Markus. *Ephesians 1–3.* In The Anchor Bible, vol 34. Edited by William Foxwell Albright and David Noel Freedman. Garden City, NY: Doubleday, 1974.

Bauer, Walter, and W. F. Arndt, eds. *A Greek-English Lexicon of the New Testament and Other Early Christian Literature.* 2nd rev. ed. Chicago: University of Chicago, 1979.

Bell, Richard H. *No One Seeks for God: An Exegetical and Theological Study of Romans 1.18—3.20.* Wissenschaftliche Untersuchungen zum Neuen Testament 106. Edited by Martin Hengel and Otfried Hofius. Tübingen: Mohr Siebeck, 1998.

Biddle, Mark E. *Missing the Mark: Sin and Its Consequences in Biblical Theology.* Nashville: Abingdon Press, 2005.

Bloom, Paul. "The Moral Life of Babies." The New York Times Magazine. 5 May 2010. Online at www.nytimes.com/2010/05/09/magazine/09babies-t.html. Accessed 18 December 2010.

Bock, Darrell L. *Luke 1:1–9:50.* In vol. 3A of *Baker Exegetical Commentary on the New Testament.* Edited by Moisés Silva. Grand Rapids: Baker Books, 1994.

Boettner, Loraine. *The Reformed Doctrine of Predestination.* Philadelphia: Presbyterian & Reformed, 1974.

Bonner, Gerald. *Augustine of Hippo: His Life and Controversies.* Norwich: Canterbury Press, 1986.

―――. *God's Decree and Man's Destiny: Studies on the Thought of Augustine of Hippo.* London: Variorum Reprints, 1987.

Boyce, James P. *Abstract of Systematic Theology*. Philadelphia: American Baptist Publication Society, 1887.

———. *Brief Catechism of Bible Doctrine* in *Baptist Catechisms: To Make Thee Wise Unto Salvation*. Edited by Tom Nettles. Fort Worth: Self-Published, 1982.

———. *Life and Death the Christian's Portion: A Discourse Occasioned by the Funeral Services of the Rev. Basil Manly, D.D.* New York: Sheldon & Co., 1869.

Brown, Peter. *Augustine of Hippo: A Biography*. Rev. Ed. Berkeley: University of California Press, 2000.

Brown, Raymond. *The Birth of the Messiah: A Commentary on the Infancy Narratives in Matthew and Luke*. New updated edition in The Anchor Bible Reference Library. Edited by David Noel Freedman. Garden City, NY: Doubleday, 1993.

Browne, Charles Gordon, and James Edward Swallow. "Prolegomena." In *Select Orations of Saint Gregory Nazianzen*. A Select Library of the Nicene and Post-Nicene Fathers of the Christian Church, ed. Philip Schaff and Henry Wace, vol. 7, second series. New York: Christian Literature Company, 1894.

Bruce, F. F. *The Epistles to the Colossians, to Philemon, and to the Ephesians*. Grand Rapids: Eerdmans, 1984.

Bruggemann, Walter. *Genesis*. Interpretation: A Bible Commentary for Teaching and Preaching. Edited by James Luther Mays. Atlanta: John Knox, 1982.

Burnaby, John. "Introduction, *The Spirit and the Letter*." In *Augustine: Later Works*. Edited by John Burnaby. In The Library of Christian Classics: Ichthus Edition. Edited by John Baillie, John T. McNeill and Henry P. van Dusen. Philadelphia: Westminster Press, 1955.

Burns, J. Patout. *The Development of Augustine's Doctrine of Operative Grace*. Paris: Etudes Augustiniennes, 1980.

Calvin, John. *XC—To Viret*. In Vol. 4: Letters, Part 1, 1528–1545. Edited by Jules Bonnet. Translated by David Constable. *Selected Works of John Calvin*. Edited by Henry Beveridge and Jules Bonnet. Grand Rapids: Baker, 1983.

———. *CCIC—To Farel*. In Vol. 5: Letters, Part 2, 1545–1553. Edited by Jules Bonnet. Translated by David Constable. *Selected Works of John Calvin*. Edited by Henry Beveridge and Jules Bonnet. Grand Rapids: Baker, 1983.

———. *The Bondage and Liberation of the Will A Defence of the Orthodox Treatment of Human Choice against Pighius*. Edited by A. N. S. Lane. Translated by G. I. Davies. Grand Rapids: Baker, 1996.

———. *Commentary on the Book of Psalms*. Vol. 1. Translated by James Anderson. Grand Rapids: Eerdmans, 1949.

———. *Commentaries on the Last Four Books of Moses*. Vol. 4. Edited and Translated by Charles William Bingham. Grand Rapids: Eerdmans, 1950.

———. *Institutes of the Christian Religion*. In vol. 21 of The Library of Christian Classics. Edited by John T. McNeill. Translated by Ford Lewis Battles. Philadelphia: Westminster, 1960.

———. *Sermons on Deuteronomy*. Translated by Arthur Golding. London: Middleton, 1583; reprint Carlisle, PA: Banner of Truth, 1987.

Campbell, Antony. *2 Samuel*. In vol. 8 of *The Forms of the Old Testament Literature*. Edited by Rolf P. Knierim, Gene M. Tucker, and Marvin A. Sweeney. Grand Rapids: Eerdmans, 2005.

Caner, Emir Fethi. "Truth is Unkillable." Ph.D Diss. The University of Texas at Arlington, 1999.

Chapman, Stephen B. "Reading the Bible as Witness: Divine Retribution in the Old Testament." *Perspectives in Religious Studies* 31 (2004): 171–90.

Collins, C. John. "A Syntactical Note (Genesis 3:15): Is the Woman's Seed Singular or Plural?" *Tyndale Bulletin* 48 (1997): 139–48.

Collins, Raymond F. *First Corinthians.* In vol. 7 of *Sacra Pagina Series.* Edited by Daniel J. Harrington. Collegeville, MN: Liturgical Press, 1999.

Cragoe, Thomas. "An Examination of the Issues of Infant Salvation." Ph.D Diss. Dallas Theological Seminary, 1987.

Craig, William Lane. "Middle Knowledge: A Calvinist-Arminian Rapprochement?" In *The Grace of God and the Will of Man.* Edited by Clark Pinnock. Minneapolis: Bethany, 1995.

Cranfield, C. E. B. *The Epistle to the Romans. Volume I* in The International Critical Commentary. Edited by J. A. Emerton and C. E. B. Cranfield. Edinburgh: T & T Clark, 1975.

Crimson, Leo T. "The Interview Between John Faber and Balthasar Hubmaier, Vienna, December, 1527–January, 1528," *Review & Expositor* 46 (1949): 38–42.

Cumming, John. *Infant Salvation; or All Saved that Die in Infancy.* Philadelphia: Lindsay and Blakiston, 1855.

Cyprian. *Epistles.* In *Fathers of the Third Century.* Edited by Alexander Roberts and James Donaldson. The Ante-Nicene Fathers, vol. 5. Buffalo: Christian Literature, 1885; reprint, New York: Charles Scribner's Sons, 1907.

———. *Letter 64.* Translated by Rose Bernard Donna. In Vol. 51: St. Cyprian's Letters of *The Fathers of the Church: A New Translation.* Edited by Roy Joseph Deferrari. Washington, D.C.: Catholic University of America, 1964.

———. *On the Lapsed.* In *Fathers of the Third Century.* Edited by Alexander Roberts and James Donaldson. The Ante-Nicene Fathers, vol. 5. Buffalo: Christian Literature, 1885; reprint, New York: Charles Scribner's Sons, 1907.

Dahood, Mitchell. *Psalms II: 51–100.* In vol. 17 of *The Anchor Bible.* Edited by William Foxwell Albright and David Noel Freedman. Garden City, NY: Doubleday, 1968.

Dalglish, Edward R. *Psalm Fifty-One: In the Light of Ancient Near Eastern Patternism.* Leiden: Brill, 1962.

Delitzsch, Franz. *Biblical Commentary on the Psalms.* Vol. 2. Translated by Francis Bolton. Grand Rapids: Eerdmans, 1949.

Derbyshire, Stuart W. G. "Can Fetuses Feel Pain?" *British Medical Journal* 332 (2006): 909–912.

Donahue, John R. and Daniel J. Harrington. *The Gospel of Mark.* In vol. 2 of *Sacra Pagina Series.* Edited by Daniel J. Harrington. Collegeville, MN: Liturgical Press, 2002.

Dunn, James D. G. *The Theology of Paul the Apostle.* Grand Rapids: Eerdmans, 1998.

Dyer, George J. "The Unbaptized Infant in Eternity." *Chicago Studies* 2 (1963): 141–53.

Ellingsen, Mark. *The Richness of Augustine: His Contextual & Pastoral Theology.* Louisville: Westminster John Knox, 2005.

Erickson, Millard. *Christian Theology,* 2nd ed. Grand Rapids: Baker, 1998.

———. *How Shall They Be Saved?* Grand Rapids: Baker, 1996.

———. *Introducing Christian Doctrine.* Edited by L. Arnold Hustad. Grand Rapids: Baker, 1992.

Estep, William R. *The Anabaptist Story.* Grand Rapids: Eerdmans, 1975.

———. *Renaissance & Reformation.* Grand Rapids: Eerdmans, 1986; 1998 reprint.

Faber, John. "Concerning the Baptism of Little Children, A Translation." Translated by Leo T. Crimson. *Review & Expositor* 46 (1949): 353–73.

Fanning, B. M. *Verbal Aspects in New Testament Greek* . Oxford: Clarendon, 1990.

Fee, Gordon D. *The First Epistle to the Corinthians.* The New International Commentary on the New Testament. Ed. Idem. Grand Rapids: Eerdmans, 1987.

Fitzmyer. Joseph A. *Romans: A New Translation with introduction and Commentary.* In vol. 33 of The Anchor Bible. Edited by William Foxwell Albright and David Noel Freedman. Garden City, NY: Doubleday, 1993.

Garland, David E. 1 *Corinthians.* Baker Exegetical Commentary on the New Testament. Edited by Robert W. Yarbrough and Robert H. Stein. Grand Rapids: Baker Books, 2003.

Garrett, James Leo, Jr. *Systematic Theology: Biblical, Historical, and Evangelical.* 2 Vol. Grand Rapids: Eerdmans, 1996.

George, Timothy. "James Petigru Boyce." In *Theologians of the Baptist Tradition,* eds. Timothy George and David S. Dockery. Nashville: Broadman & Holman, 2001.

————. Editor, *James Petigru Boyce: Selected Writings.* Nashville: Broadman Press, 1989.

Gingras, J. L., E. A. Mitchell and K. E. Grattan. "Fetal Homologue of Infant Crying." *Archives of Disease in Childhood—Fetal and Neonatal Edition* 90 (2005): 415–18.

González, Justo. *Volume One: The Early Church to the Dawn of the Reformation.* In *The Story of Christianity: Complete in One Volume, The Early Church to the Present Day.* Peabody, MA: Prince Press, 2004.

Gordis, Robert. "The Knowledge of Good and Evil in the Old Testament and the Qumran Scrolls." *Journal of Biblical Literature* 76 (1957): 123–38.

Goulder, Michael. *The Prayers of David (Psalm 51–72): Studies in the Psalter, II.* Journal for the Study of the Old Testament Supplement Series 102. Edited by David J. A. Clines and Philip R. Davies. Sheffield, England: JSOT Press, 1990.

Grant, Robert M. *Irenaeus of Lyons.* The Early Church Fathers. Edited by Carol Harrison. New York: Routledge, 1997.

Green, Bradley G. "Millard J. Erickson." In *Theologians of the Baptist Tradition,* eds. Timothy George and David S. Dockery. Nashville: Broadman & Holman, 2001.

Gregory of Nazianzus. *Orations.* Translated and edited by Charles Gordon Browne and James Edward Swallow. In *Select Orations of Saint Gregory Nazianzen.* A Select Library of the Nicene and Post-Nicene Fathers of the Christian Church, ed. Philip Schaff and Henry Wace, vol. 7, second series. New York: Christian Literature Company, 1894.

Gregory of Nyssa. *The Great Catechism.* Translated by William Moore. In *Select Writings and Letters of Gregory, Bishop of Nyssa.* Edited by Philip Schaff and Henry Wace. A Select Library of the Nicene and Post-Nicene Fathers of the Christian Church, Second Series, ed. Philip Schaff and Henry Wace, vol. 5, second series. New York: Christian Literature Company, 1893.

————. *On Infants' Early Deaths.* Translated by William Moore. In *Select Writings and Letters of Gregory, Bishop of Nyssa.* Edited by Philip Schaff and Henry Wace. A Select Library of the Nicene and Post-Nicene Fathers of the Christian Church, Second Series, ed. Philip Schaff and Henry Wace, vol. 5, second series. New York: Christian Literature Company, 1893.

Grenz, Stanley J. *Theology for the Community of God.* Nashville: Broadman and Holman, 1994.

Grudem, Wayne. Response to Adam Harwood, "Grudem on Infant Guilt: A Critique of Wayne Grudem's Proposed Solution to the Dilemma of Inherited Guilt for People

Who Die in Infancy." Paper presented at the Southwestern Region's Meeting of the Evangelical Theological Society, 24 March 2006, Southwestern Baptist Theological Seminary, Fort Worth, TX. Audio cassette. In hand.

————. *Systematic Theology*. Grand Rapids: Zondervan, 1994.

Hall, Christopher A. *Learning Theology With the Church Fathers*. Downers Grove: InterVarsity Press, 2002.

Hamilton, Victor P. *The Book of Genesis: Chapters 1–17*. The New International Commentary on the Old Testament. Edited by R. K. Harrison. Grand Rapids: Eerdmans, 1990.

Harmon, Steven R. *Every Knee Should Bow*. Lanham, MD: University Press of America, 2003.

Harris, R. Laird, Archer, Gleason L., and Bruce Waltke. *Theological Wordbook of the Old Testament*. 2 vols. Chicago: Moody, 1980.

Hayford, Jack. *I'll Hold You In Heaven*. Ventura, CA: Regal, 2003.

Hendricks, William. *A Theology for Children*. Nashville: Broadman, 1980.

————. "Baptists and Children: The Beginnings of Grace." *Southwestern Journal of Theology* 28 (1986): 49–53.

————. "The Age of Accountability." In *Children and Conversion*. Edited by Clifford Ingle. Nashville: Broadman Press, 1970.

————. *The Doctrine of Man*. Nashville: Convention Press, 1977.

Hoehner, Harold W. *Ephesians: An Exegetical Commentary*. Grand Rapids: Baker, 2002.

Holeton, David. *Infant Communion—Then and Now*. Grove Liturgical Study 27. Bramcote: Grove, 1981.

Holladay, William Lee, ed. *A Concise Hebrew and Aramaic Lexicon of the Old Testament: Based upon the Lexical Work of Ludwig Koehler and Walter Baumgartner*. Leiden: Brill, 1988.

Hopkins, Samuel. *The Works of Samuel Hopkins*, vol. 1. Boston: Doctrinal Tract and Book Society, 1865; reprint, New York: Garland, 1987.

Hubmaier, Balthasar. *Eighteen Theses Concerning the Christian Life*. In *Balthasar Hubmaier: Theologian of Anabaptism*. Translated and edited by H. Wayne Pipkin and John H. Yoder. In vol. 5 of Classics of the Radical Reformation. Scottdale, PA: Herald Press, 1989.

————. *Freedom of the Will, I*. In *Balthasar Hubmaier: Theologian of Anabaptism*. Translated and Edited by H. Wayne Pipkin and John H. Yoder. In vol. 5 of Classics of the Radical Reformation. Scottdale, PA: Herald Press, 1989.

————. *Letter to Oecolampad*. In *Balthasar Hubmaier: Theologian of Anabaptism*. Translated and edited by H. Wayne Pipkin and John H. Yoder. In vol. 5 of Classics of the Radical Reformation. Scottdale, PA: Herald Press, 1989.

————. *On the Christian Baptism of Believers*. In *Balthasar Hubmaier: Theologian of Anabaptism*. Translated and edited by H. Wayne Pipkin and John H. Yoder. In vol. 5 of Classics of the Radical Reformation. Scottdale, PA: Herald Press, 1989.

————. *On the Christian Baptism of Believers*. In vol. 4 of *Huldreich Zwinglis Samtliche Werke*, ed. Emil Egli and Georg Finsler. Corpus Reformatorum, vol. 91. Leipzig: Heinsius, 1905.

————. *On Infant Baptism Against Oecolampad*. In *Balthasar Hubmaier: Theologian of Anabaptism*. Translated and edited by H. Wayne Pipkin and John H. Yoder. In vol. 5 of Classics of the Radical Reformation. Scottdale, PA: Herald Press, 1989.

Humphreys, Fisher. "Edgar Young Mullins." In *Theologians of the Baptist Tradition*, eds. Timothy George and David S. Dockery. Nashville: Broadman & Holman, 2001.

International Theological Commission. "The Hope of Salvation." *Origins* 36 (2007): 725–46.

Irenaeus. *Against Heresies*. Translated by Alexander Roberts and W. H. Rambut. In *The Apostolic Fathers with Justin Martyr and Irenaeus*. Edited by Alexander Roberts and James Donaldson. The Ante-Nicene Fathers, vol. 1. Buffalo: Christian Literature, 1885; reprint, New York: Charles Scribner's Sons, 1903.

———. *Proof of the Apostolic Preaching*. Translated by Joseph Smith. In Ancient Christian Writers 16. Westminster, MD: Newman, 1952.

Jeremias, Joachim. *Die Kindertaufe in den ersten vier Jahrhunderten*. Göttingen: Vandenhoeck & Ruprecht, 1958.

———. *Infant Baptism in the First Four Centuries*. Translated by David Cairns. Philadelphia: Westminster Press, 1960.

———. *The Origins of Infant Baptism*. London: SCM Press, 1963.

Jewett, Paul K. *Infant Baptism and the Covenant of Grace: An Appraisal of the Argument That as Infants Were Once Circumcised, So They Should Now be Baptized*. Grand Rapids: Eerdmans, 1978.

John Chrysostom. *On Infants*. Edited and translated by Henry Bettenson. In The Later Christian Fathers. New York: Oxford University Press, 1970.

Keck, Leander. *Romans*. In Abingdon New Testament Commentaries. Edited by Victor Paul Furnish. Nashville: Abingdon Press, 2005.

Kelly, J. N. D. *Early Christian Doctrines*. Rev. ed. New York: Harper & Row, 1978.

Koch, Klaus. "Is There a Doctrine of Retribution in the Old Testament?" In *Theodicy in the Old Testament*. IRT 4. Edited by James L. Crenshaw. 57–87. Philadelphia: Fortress, 1983.

Kraus, Hans-Joachim. *Psalms 1–59: A Continental Commentary*. Translated by Hilton C. Oswald. Minneapolis: Fortress Press, 1993.

Lane, Anthony N. S. *John Calvin: Student of the Church Fathers*. Grand Rapids: Baker, 1999.

Lightner, Robert P. *Safe in the Arms of Jesus*. Grand Rapids: Kregel, 2000.

Lohfink, Norbert. "Canonical Signals in the Additions in Deuteronomy 1.39." In *Seeing Signals, Reading Signs: The Art of Exegesis, Studies in Honour of Anthony F. Campbell, SJ for his Seventieth Birthday*. Edited by Mark A. O'Brien and Howard N. Wallace, Journal for the Study of the Old Testament Supplement Series 415. Edited by Claudia V. Camp and Andrew Mein. London: T&T Clark, 2004.

Louw, Johannes P., and Eugene A. Nida, eds. *Greek-English Lexicon of the New Testament based on Semantic Domains*. 2nd ed. New York: United Bible Society, 1989.

Lusk, Rich. *Paedofaith: A Primer on the Mystery of Infant Salvation and a Handbook for Covenant Parents*. Monore, LA: Athanasius Press, 2005.

Luther, Martin. *The Babylonian Captivity of the Church*. Translated by A. T. W. Steinhäuser and revised by Fredrick C. Ahrens and Abdel Ross Wentz. In vol. 36 of *Luther's Works*. Edited by Helmut T. Lehmann. Philadelphia: Muhlenberg Press, 1959.

———. *Concerning Rebaptism*. Translated by Conrad Bergendoff. In vol. 40 of *Luther's Works*. Edited by Helmut T. Lehmann. Philadelphia: Muhlenberg Press, 1958.

———. *D. Martin Luthers Werke* 53. Weimar: Hermann Böhlaus Nachfolger, 1920; reprinted 1968.

———. *Lectures on Genesis: Chapters* 15–20. Translated by George V. Schick. In vol. 3 of *Luther's Works*. Edited by Jaroslav Pelikan. St. Louis: Concordia, 1961.

MacArthur, John. *Safe in the Arms of God*. Nashville: Thomas Nelson, 2003.

Malone, Fred. *The Baptism of Disciples Alone: A Covenantal Argument for Credobaptism Versus Paedobaptism*. Cape Coral, FL: Founders Press, 2003.

Marpeck, Pilgram. *Response to Caspar Schwenckfeld's Judgment*. In *The Writings of Pilgram Marpeck*. Edited by Walter Klaassen and William Klaassen. In vol. 2 of Classics of the Radical Reformation. Scottsdale, PA: Herald Press, 1978.

Marshall, I. Howard. *The Gospel of Luke: A Commentary on the Greek Testament*. The New International Greek Testament Commentary. Edited by I. Howard Marshall and W. Ward Gasque. Grand Rapids: Eerdmans, 1978.

Mathews, Kenneth. *Genesis 1–11:26*. New American Commentary, vol. 1A. Edited by E. Ray Clendenen. Nashville: Broadman & Holman, 2002.

McCarter, P. Kyle. *II Samuel*. In vol. 9 of *The Anchor Bible*. Edited by William Foxwell Albright and David Noel Freedman. Garden City, NY: Doubleday, 1984.

McClear, Ernest V. "The Fall of Man and Original Sin in the Theology of Gregory of Nyssa." *Theological Studies* 9 (1948): 175–212.

McConville, J. G. *Deuteronomy*. Apollos Old Testament Commentary, vol. 5. Edited by David W. Baker and Gordon J. Wenham. Downers Grove, IL: InterVarsity Press, 2002.

McDavid, Edmund R., III., *Infant Salvation and The Age of Accountability*. Birmingham, AL: Hope, 2003.

McGrath, Alister. Editor. *The Christian Theology Reader*. Oxford: Blackwell, 1995.

McIlhenney, Charles. "Will My Child Go To Heaven?" In *To You and Your Children*, ed. Benjamin K. Wikner, 173–89. Moscow, ID: Canon Press, 2005.

McKinion, Steven A. "Baptism in the Patristic Writings." In *Believer's Baptism: Sign of the New Covenant in Christ*, eds. Thomas R. Schreiner and Shawn D. Wright. NAC Studies in Bible & Theology, ed. E. Ray Clendenen. Nashville: B & H Academic, 2006.

———. *Life and Practice in the Early Church: A Documentary Reader*. New York: New York University Press, 2001.

Meilaender, Gilbert. *Bioethics: A Primer for Christians*. Grand Rapids: Eerdmans, 1996.

Moo, Douglas. *Romans 1–8*. The Wycliffe Exegetical Commentary. Edited by Kenneth Barker. Chicago: Moody Press, 1991.

Moody, Dale. *The Word of Truth: A Summary of Christian Doctrine Based on Biblical Revelation*. Grand Rapids: Eerdmans, 1981.

Mullins, E. Y. *The Axioms of Religion*. Philadelphia: Judson Press, 1908.

———. *Baptist Beliefs*. Louisville: Baptist World Publishing, 1912.

———. *The Christian Religion in its Doctrinal Expression*. Valley Forge, PA: Judson Press, 1917; Reprinted 1974.

———. *Studies in Ephesians*. Nashville: Sunday School Board, 1935.

Murray, John. *The Imputation of Adam's Sin*. Grand Rapids: Eerdmans, 1959.

Nam, Samuel Byung-doo. "A Comparative Study of the Baptismal Understanding of Augustine, Luther, Zwingli, and Hubmaier." Ph.D Diss. Southwestern Baptist Theological Seminary, 2002.

Nash, Ronald. *When a Baby Dies*. Grand Rapids: Zondervan, 1999.

Nelson, David P. "The Work of God: Creation and Providence." In *A Theology for the Church*. Edited by Daniel L. Akin. Nashville: B & H Academic, 2007.

Newman, Albert Henry. *A History of Anti-Pedobaptism: From the Rise of Pedobaptism to A. D.* 1609. Eugene, OR: Wipf & Stock, 2004.

Nutkowicsz, Hélène. "Propos Autour De La Mort D'Un Enfant: 2 Samuel XI, 2-XII, 24." *Vetus Testamentum* 54 (2004): 104–18.

Origen. *Commentary on Romans*. In Idem, *Commentary on the Epistle to the Romans, Books* 1–5. In Fathers of the Church. Vol. 103. Translated by T. P. Scheck. Washington, D.C.: Catholic University Press of America, 2001.

———. *Homilies on Leviticus*. In Fathers of the Church. Vol. 83. Translated by G. W. Barkley. Washington, D.C.: Catholic University Press of America, 1992.

Osborn, Eric. *Tertullian, First Theologian of the West*. Cambridge: Cambridge University Press, 1997.

Pagels, Elaine. *Adam, Eve, and the Serpent*. New York: Random House, 1988.

Patterson, Paige. *The Troubled, Triumphant Church: An Exposition of First Corinthians*. Eugene, OR: Wipf and Stock, 2002.

Pelagius. *To Demetrias*. In *Patrologiae Cursus Completus: Series Latina*, ed. Jacques Paul Migne, 33:1099–1120. Paris: n.p., 1845.

Pelikan, Jaroslav. *The Christian Tradition: A History of the Development of Doctrine*. Vol. 1: The Emergence of the Catholic Tradition 100–600. Chicago: University of Chicago Press, 1971.

Philbeck, Ben F. Jr., "1–2 Samuel." In vol. 3: "1 Samuel–Nehemiah" of *The Broadman Bible Commentary*. Edited by Clifton J. Allen, et. al. Nashville: Broadman Press, 1970.

Pinnock, Clark H. "An Inclusivist View." In *Four Views on Salvation in a Pluralistic World*. Edited by Dennis L. Okholm and Timothy R. Phillips. Grand Rapids: Zondervan Publishing House, 1996.

———. *A Wideness in God's Mercy: The Finality of Jesus Christ in a World of Religions*. Grand Rapids: Zondervan, 1992.

Pipkin, H. Wayne and John H. Yoder. Introduction to *Balthasar Hubmaier: Theologian of Anabaptism*. Translated and Edited by H. Wayne Pipkin and John H. Yoder. In vol. 5 of Classics of the Radical Reformation. Scottdale, PA: Herald Press, 1989.

Quasten, Johannes. *Patrology*. Vol. II: The Ante-Nicene Literature After Irenaeus. Westminster, MD: Newman Press, 1953.

Rayburn, Robert. "Parental Conditions and the Promise of Grace to the Children of Believers." In *To You and Your Children: Examining the Biblical Doctrine of Covenant Succession*, ed. Benjamin K. Wikner, 3–27. Moscow, ID: Canon Press, 2005.

Rempel, John. "Introduction to *Response to Caspar Schwenckfeld's Judgment*." In *Later Writings by Pilgram Marpeck and his Circle, Vol 1: The Exposé, A Dialogue, and Marpeck's Response to Caspar Schwenckfeld*. Translated by Walter Klaassen, Werner Packull, and John Rempel. Anabaptist Texts in Translation. Kitchner, Ontario: Pandora Press, 1999.

———. "Pilgram Marpeck: An Introduction to his Theology and Place in the Reformation." In *Later Writings by Pilgram Marpeck and his Circle, Vol 1: The Exposé, A Dialogue, and Marpeck's Response to Caspar Schwenckfeld*. Translated by Walter Klaassen, Werner Packull, and John Rempel. Anabaptist Texts in Translation. Kitchner, Ontario: Pandora Press, 1999.

Robinson, Ezekiel Gilman. *Christian Theology*. Rochester, NY: Andrews, 1894.

Rondet, Henri. *Original Sin: The Patristic and Theological Background*. Translated by Cajetan Finegan. Staten Island, NY: Alba House, 1972.

Rowe, Robert D. *God's Kingdom and God's Son: The Background to Mark's Christology from Concepts of Kingship in the Psalms*. In Geschichte des Antiken Judentums und des Urchristentums 50. Edited by Martin Hengel, et. al. Leiden: Brill, 2002.

Russell, David. *Infant Salvation; Or, An Attempt to Prove That All Who Die in Infancy Are Saved*, 3rd ed. Glasgow: James Maclehose, 1844.

Sage, Athanase. "Le péché originel dans la pensée de saint Augustin, de 412 á 430." *Revue des études augustiniennes* 15 (1969): 75–112.

Sanders, John. *No Other Name*. Grand Rapids: Eerdmans, 1992.

Schaff, Philip. *History of the Christian Church*. Vol. 3: Nicene and Post-Nicene Christianity from Constantine the Great to Gregory the Great A.D. 311–590. 5th ed. Peabody, MA: Hendrickson, 1996.

Schreiner, Thomas R. "Baptism in the Epistles." In *Believer's Baptism: Sign of the New Covenant in Christ*, eds. Thomas R. Schreiner and Shawn D. Wright. NAC Studies in Bible & Theology, ed. E. Ray Clendenen. Nashville: B & H Academic, 2006.

Slater, Rebeccah, et. al. "Cortical Pain Responses in Human Infants." *The Journal of Neuroscience* 26 (2006): 3662–66.

Smith, David L. *With Willful Intent: A Theology of Sin*. Wheaton: BridgePoint, 1994.

Spurgeon, Charles. "Infant Salvation (Sermon 411)." Online at www.spurgeon.org/sermons/0411.html. Accessed 18 December 2010.

Stagg, Frank. "The Abused Aorist." *Journal of Biblical Literature* 91.2 (1972): 222–32.

Stephens, Peter. *The Theology of Huldrych Zwingli*. Oxford: Clarendon Press, 1986.

———. *Zwingli: An Introduction to His Thought*. Oxford: Clarendon Press, 1992.

Stern, Herold S. "The Knowledge of Good and Evil." *Vetus Testamentum* 8 (1958): 405–18.

Stewart, Robert B. "Article III: Man." Pages 25–35 in *The Baptist Faith and Message: Critical Issues in America's Largest Protestant Denomination*. Edited by Douglas K. Blount and Joseph P. Woodell. Lanham, MD: Rowman & Littlefield, 2007.

Stordalen, Terje. *Echoes of Eden: Genesis 2–3 and Symbolism of the Eden Garden in Biblical Hebrew Literature*. Contributions to Biblical Exegesis and Theology 25. Leuven: Peeters, 2000.

Stortz, Martha Ellen. "'Where or When Was Your Servant Innocent?'" In *The Child in Christian Thought*, ed. Marcia J. Bunge. Grand Rapids: Eerdmans, 2001.

Strange, William A. *Children in the Early Church: Children in the Ancient World, the New Testament, and the Early Church*. Carlisle: Paternoster, 1996.

Strohl, Jane E. "The Child in Luther's Theology: 'For What Purpose Do We Older Folks Exist, Other Than to Care for…. the Young?'" In *The Child in Christian Thought*, ed. Marcia J. Bunge. Grand Rapids: Eerdmans, 2001.

Strong, A. H. *Autobiography of August Hopkins Strong*. Philadelphia: Judson Press, 1981.

———. *Systematic Theology*. 8th ed. Philadelphia: Judson, 1907; Reprinted 1972.

Talbert, Charles H. *Romans*. Smyth & Helwys Bible Commentary. Macon, GA: Smyth & Helwys, 2002.

Task Force on Sudden Infant Death Syndrome. "The Changing Concept of Sudden Infant Death Syndrome: Diagnostic Coding Shifts, Controversies Regarding the Sleep Environment, and New Variables to Consider in Reducing Risk." *Pediatrics* 116:5 (2005): 1245–55.

Tertullian. *On Baptism*. Translated by S. Thelwall. In *Latin Christianity: Its Founder, Tertullian*. Edited by Alexander Roberts and James Donaldson. The Ante-Nicene

Fathers, vol. 3. Buffalo: Christian Literature, 1885; reprint, New York: Charles Scribner's Sons, 1905.

———. *The Five Books Against Marcion.* Translated by Peter Holmes. In *Latin Christianity: Its Founder, Tertullian.* Edited by Alexander Roberts and James Donaldson. The Ante-Nicene Fathers, vol. 3. Buffalo: Christian Literature, 1885; reprint, New York: Charles Scribner's Sons, 1905.

———. *A Treatise on the Soul.* Translated by Peter Holmes. In *Latin Christianity: Its Founder, Tertullian.* Edited by Alexander Roberts and James Donaldson. The Ante-Nicene Fathers, vol. 3. Buffalo: Christian Literature, 1885; reprint, New York: Charles Scribner's Sons, 1905.

Thornbury, Gregory Alan. "Augustus Hopkins Strong." In *Theologians of the Baptist Tradition,* eds. Timothy George and David S. Dockery. Nashville: Broadman & Holman, 2001.

Tiessen, Terrance L. *Irenaeus on the Salvation of the Unevangelized.* ATLA Monograph Series. No. 31. Edited by Kenneth E. Rowe. Metuchen, NJ: Scarecrow Press, 1993.

———. *Who Can Be Saved? Reassessing Salvation in Christ and World Religions.* Downers Grove: InterVarsity Press, 2004.

Trouwborst, Thomas. "From Covenant to Chaos: The Reformers and Their Heirs on Covenant Succession." In *To You and Your Children: Examining the Biblical Doctrine of Covenant Succession,* ed. Benjamin K. Wikner, 59–103. Moscow, ID: Canon Press, 2005.

Trueman, Carl R. "Calvin and Calvinism." In *The Cambridge Companion to John Calvin.* Edited by Donald K. McKim. Cambridge: Cambridge University Press, 2004.

Venema, Cornelis. "The Doctrine of the Sacraments and Baptism According to the Reformed Confessions." *Mid-America Journal of Theology* 11 (2000): 21–86.

Waggoner, Earl. "Baptist Approaches to the Question of Infant Salvation." Ph.D Diss. New Orleans Baptist Theological Seminary, 1999.

Wallace, Howard N. *The Eden Narrative.* Harvard Semitic Monographs 32. Atlanta: Scholars Press, 1985.

Waltke, Bruce. *Genesis: A Commentary.* Grand Rapids: Zondervan, 2001.

———. "Reflections from the Old Testament on Abortion." *Journal of the Evangelical Theological Society* 19 (1976): 3–13.

Warfield, B. B. *Two Studies in the History of Doctrine: Augustine and the Pelagian Controversy, The Development of the Doctrine of Infant Salvation.* New York: CLC, 1897.

Warren, Charles E. *Original Sin Explained?: Revelations from Human Genetic Science.* Lanham, MD: University Press of America, 2002.

Wattendorf, Daniel J., and Maximillian Muenke. "Fetal Alcohol Spectrum Disorders." *American Family Physician* 72 (2005): 279–85.

Weaver, David. "The Exegesis of Romans 5:12 Among the Greek Fathers and Its Implications for the Doctrine of Original Sin: The 5th-12th Centuries, Part II." *St. Vladimir's Theological Quarterly* 29 (1985): 133–159.

———. "From Paul to Augustine: Romans 5:12 in Early Christian Exegesis." *St. Vladimir's Theological Quarterly* 27 (1983): 187–206.

Webb, R. A. *The Theology of Infant Salvation.* Richmond: Presbyterian Committee of Publication, 1907. Reprint, Harrisonburg, VA: Sprinkle Publications, 1981.

Weinfeld, Moshe. *Deuteronomy 1–11: A New Translation with Introduction and Commentary.* In vol. 5 of *The Anchor Bible.* Edited by William Foxwell Albright and David Noel Freedman. New York: Doubleday, 1991.

Wellum, Stephen. "Baptism and the Relationship Between the Covenants." In *Believer's Baptism: Sign of the New Covenant in Christ,* eds. Thomas R. Schreiner and Shawn D. Wright. NAC Studies in Bible & Theology, ed. E. Ray Clendenen. Nashville: B&H Academic, 2006.

Wenham, Gordon. "The Coherence of the Flood Narrative." Vetus Testamentum 28 (1878): 336–48.

———. *Genesis 1–15.* Word Biblical Commentary, vol. 1. Edited by David A. Hubbard and Glenn W. Barker. Waco: Word Books, 1987.

Westermann, Claus. *Genesis 1–11: A Commentary.* Translated by John J. Scullion. Minneapolis: Augsburg, 1990.

Wikner, Benjamin K. "Introduction." In *To You and Your Children: Examining the Biblical Doctrine of Covenant Succession,* ed. Benjamin K. Wikner, 3–27. Moscow, ID: Canon Press, 2005.

Wiley, Tatha. *Origins, Developments, Contemporary Meanings.* New York: Paulist Press, 2002.

Williams, George Hunston. *Radical Reformation.* 3rd ed. Kirksville, MO: Sixteenth Century Publishers, 1992.

Wilson, Doug. "Baptism and Children: Their Place in the Old and New Testaments." In *The Case for Covenantal Infant Baptism,* ed. Gregg Strawbridge, 286–302. Phillipsburg, NJ: P & R Publishing, 2003.

Wright, David F. "How Controversial Was the Development of Infant Baptism in the Early Church?" In *Church, Word, and Spirit.* Edited by James E. Bradley and Richard A. Muller. Grand Rapids: Eerdmans, 1987.

———. "The Origins of Infant Baptism—Child Believers' Baptism?" *Scottish Journal of Theology* 40 (1987): 1–23.

———. "Recovering Baptism for a New Age of Mission." In *Doing Theology for the People of God.* Edited by D. Lewis and Alister McGrath. Downers Grove: Inter Varsity, 1996.

Zuck, Roy. *Precious in His Sight: Childhood & Children in the Bible.* Grand Rapids: Baker, 1996.

Zwingli, Ulrich. *An Exposition of the Faith.* Translated by Geoffrey Bromiley. In The Library of Christian Classics. Vol. XXIV: Zwingli and Bullinger. Philadelphia: Westminster Press, 1953.

———. *Of Baptism.* Translated by Geoffrey Bromiley. In The Library of Christian Classics. Vol. XXIV: Zwingli and Bullinger. Philadelphia: Westminster Press, 1953.

———. *On Original Sin.* In *On Providence and Other Essays.* Translated by Samuel Jackson. Durham, NC: Labyrinth Press, 1983.

Name & Subject Index

abortion, 8, 26, 156, 161
age of accountability, 20, 26, 86, 145, 149, 160
age of responsibility, 20, 150
Aland, Kurt, 72, 87
Ambrose, 107
apokatastasis, 10
Arianism, 88
Arminian/ism, 19, 139, 147–48
Armour, Rollin, 119
Augustine, 9, 17, 34, 37, 92, 101, 104–12, 115–18, 120, 122, 127, 140, 144, 147–48, 160
Augustinian view, 14, 19, 97–98, 118, 121, 123, 133, 141, 146, 149
   see Natural Headship, seminalism
Augustinian-Calvinist view, 14–17, 21, 33–35, 38, 40, 45–46, 50, 58, 64, 135–36, 150–52, 157, 161
Bakke, O. M. , 85, 93, 99, 103
baptismal regeneration, 86, 105, 109–10, 112, 124
Barr, James, 59
Barth, Karl, 10
Barth, Markus, 48
Basil of Caesarea, 88
Biddle, Mark, 54
Bloom, Paul, 56
Boettner, Loraine, 158
Boniface, 109
Bonner, Gerald, 106
Boyce, James P., 136–38, 144
Brown, Raymond, 67
Bruce, F. F. , 45
Bock, Darrell, 67
Bruggemann, Walter, 58

Bucer, Martin, 127
Bullinger, Henry, 75
Caelestius, 108
Calvin, John , 37, 75, 113, 120–25, 147, 160
Calvinism, 120, 142, 148
Calvinist view, 14, 37, 136, 142, 149
   see Federal Headship, federalism
Campbell, Antony, 53–54
Chapman, Stephen B., 54
circumcision, 90, 103, 113–15, 120, 122–23, 127, 130
Collins, C. John, 59
Collins, Raymond, 78
Council of Carthage, sixteenth, 9, 32, 105, 111
Council of Constantinople, 88, 92
Council of Nicea, second, 92
Council of Orange, second, 32
Council of Trent, 105
covenant succession, 74–77
Cragoe, Thomas , 20, 44–46, 158
Cranfield, C. E. B., 35–36
Cumming, John , 6
Cyprian, 96, 101–04
Dahood, Mitchell, 43
Dalglish, Edward, 43
Decian persecution, 101–02
Delitzsch, Franz, 42–43
Dunn, James D. G. , 34, 39–40
Dwight, Timothy, 37–38
Edwards, Jonathan, 37
Ellingsen, Mark, 111
Erickson, Millard, 11, 18–21, 148–53
Estep, William, 116, 118, 126
Exclusivism/ist, 19, 151, 157–59, 161

Fanning, Buist, 16
Federal Headship, 138, 148–49, 160
    see Calvinist view
federalism, 14–15, 37
    see Calvinist view
Fee, Gordon, 77
Felicissimus, 101
fetal alcohol syndrome, 156
Fidus, 103
Finney, Charles, 138–39, 147
Fitzmyer, Joseph, 32, 39–40
Garland, David, 78
Garrett, James Leo Jr., 119
Gnosticism, 84
Goulder, Michael, 44
Grant, Robert M., 84
Grebel, Conrad, 117
Gregory of Nazianzus, 83, 88–91, 153
Gregory of Nyssa, 83, 88, 91–95, 153
Grenz, Stanley, 19
Grudem, Wayne, 12–27, 44–45, 55, 65, 67,
    152, 158
heaven , 3–5, 7, 9, 11, 24–26, 47, 55, 75–
    76, 111, 115, 138, 157, 159, 162
hell, 4–5, 23, 26, 147, 157–58
Hamilton, Victor, 57–58
Hendricks, William, 145–48, 151, 153
Hodge, Archibald Alexander, 136–37
Hodge, Charles, 136
Hoehner, Harold, 47–48
Hopkins, Samuel, 37–38
household sanctification, 24–27, 157
Hubmaier, Balthasar, 5, 115, 122–23,
    126–30, 132–34, 161
image of God, God's image, 8, 93, 145
imputation,
    immediate, 33–34, 37
    see also Augustinian-Calvinist view
    mediate, 33–35, 37, 139
    see also inherited sinful nature
inclusivist, 22, 25, 158
infant baptism, 24, 70–72, 77, 79, 86–87,
    90, 99, 117, 122, 126–27, 129–30, 142
infant salvation, 3, 5, 10, 68, 87, 135, 137–
    38, 141, 143, 147–48, 158, 162
inherited guilt, 9, 13–14, 17–19, 23, 33,
    36, 38, 40, 45–46, 59, 64, 83, 89, 94, 98,

101, 104, 106–07, 110–12, 116, 120,
    124, 136, 141, 143, 153, 156–57, 161
    see also Augustinian-Calvinist view
inherited sinful nature, 8, 20, 33–34, 36–
    38, 40, 60, 64, 121, 133, 153, 158–60
Innocent, Pope, 108
Irenaeus, 83–87, 153
Jeremias, Joachim, 71–72, 87
John Chrysostom, 17, 84
Justin, 71, 84
Keck, Leander, 58
knowledge of good and evil, 56–58, 63–64,
    93, 131–34
Koch, Klaus, 54
Kraus, Hans-Joachim, 44
Landmarkism, 142
Lord's Supper, 102
Luther, Martin, 113–18, 120, 124, 153
MacArthur, John, 63, 135, 158
Malone, Fred, 70, 72, 77–78
Manly, Basil Sr., 136–37
Marcellinus, 108
Marcion, 100
Marpeck, Pilgram, 126, 130–34, 153
Marshall, I. Howard, 67
Mathews, Kenneth, 58
McCarter, Kyle, 54
McConville, J. G. , 62
McIlhenney, Charles A., 76–77
McKinion, Steven, 90
Melanchthon, Philip, 114, 116, 124
mentally disabled, 145
mentally incompetent, 9, 151
miscarriage, 8, 26, 155, 161
Molina, Luis, 95
Molinism, 95
Montanists, 96
Moo, Douglas, 39–40
Moody, Dale, 96
moral evil , 154, 156
Morris, Leon, 39–40
Mullins, E. Y. , 142–44, 153
Murray, John, 16, 21, 34–38, 50, 60, 158
Nash, Ronald, 6, 11, 20, 48–49, 158
natural evil, 154–56, 161
Natural Headship, 138, 140–41, 144,
    148–49, 160

see Augustinian view
New England Theology, 37
Nona, 88
Nutkowicsz, Hélène, 54
Oecolampadius, 127
Old Latin version, 34
Olevianus, Caspar, 75
Origen, 10, 84, 86
original sin, 14, 32, 46, 87, 89, 91–92, 96–98, 101, 104–12, 114, 116–21, 124, 127, 129–30, 132, 141, 144, 146–48, 151–52
Osborne, Eric, 101
palingenesia , 46
Pagels, Elaine, 17
Patterson, Paige, 77–78
Pelagian/ism, 8–9, 34–35, 106, 108–09, 111–12, 118, 130, 132, 139, 148
Pelagius, 8–9, 108–09, 111, 122
Philbeck, Ben F. Jr., 53–55
Pinnock, Clark, 10–11
Polycarp, 84
postmortem opportunity, 10–11
postmortem salvation, 94
recapitulation, 85
Rhegius, Urbanus, 118
Roberts, Alexander, 86
Robinson, Ezekiel, 138–40
Rondet, Henri, 85
Rothmann, Bernard, 130
Rousseau, Adelin, 86
Russell, David, 6
Schreiner, Thomas, 77
Schwenckfeld, Caspar, 130
seminalism, 14–15, 37
    see Augustinian view
Shedd, W. T. , 139
Simplician, 107
Smith, David L., 91, 114–15
soul, 8, 10, 18, 84, 93–95, 97, 99–101, 104, 114, 128, 139, 141
soul competency, 142–44
Spurgeon, Charles, 158
Stagg, Frank, 16, 147
Stern, Herold, 59
Stordalen, Terje, 58
Strohl, Jane E., 114
Strong, A. H. , 10–11, 138–41, 144

sudden infant death syndrome, 8, 155
Synod of Dort, 75
Talbert, Charles, 39–40
Tatian, 84
Taylor, Nathaniel W., 138–39
Tertullian, 86, 96–101, 103–04, 153
theodicy, 94
Theophilus, 84
Tiessen, Terrance, 11, 86
Tridentine Council, 32
Trinity, 88
Trouwborst, Thomas, 75
unevangelized adults, 9
Universalism/ist, 10, 18–19, 88, 141, 151
Viret, Peter, 120
Vulgate, 34
Waggoner, Earl, 138, 141, 147–48
Waltke, Bruce, 43, 59
Warfield, B. B. , 135
Webb, Robert, 47–48, 135
Westermann, Claus, 51
Wikner, Benjamin, 74
Williams, George Hunston, 126
Williamson, G. I. , 77
Wright, David F., 87
Zosimus, Pope, 108
Zwingli, Ulrich, 75, 113, 117–20, 124, 127, 129, 132

Scripture Index

Gen 1	131	Deut 1	61	Jer 1:15	68
Gen 1–2	50	Deut 1:39		Jer 4:4	123
Gen 1–11	56	56–57, 61–64, 121–22,		Jer 9:25	123
Gen 2–3	56–59	129, 140, 149		Jer 20:14	127
Gen 2:24	78	Deut 2:1	61	Jer 31:29	98
Gen 3	4, 50	Deut 5:9	53	Jer 31:30	43
Gen 3:15	59	Deut 10:16	123	Ezek 3:18–19	43
Gen 3:19	58	Deut 24:16	53	Ezek 18:1–4	54
Gen 3:22–24	58	Deut 29:29	27	Ezek 18:20	
Gen 4	50	Deut 30:6	123	18, 54, 63, 159	
Gen 5	50	Josh 22:20	43	Ezek 33:8–9	43
Gen 6	50	1 Sam 4:3	54	Jonah 4:11	140, 149
Gen 6:5	36	1 Sam 15:29	51	Matt 7:13	4
Gen 6:5–6	50–51, 161	1 Sam 25:38	54	Matt 11:22	145
Gen 6:7	139	2 Sam 11	52	Matt 18:3–4	140
Gen 6:14	50	2 Sam 11:27b	52	Matt 19:13–15	69, 72
Gen 7:1	24	2 Sam 12:10–23	52	Matt 19:14	
Gen 17	114	2 Sam 12:23		115, 127, 140, 149	
Gen 17:7	76	24, 52–53, 55, 149, 161		Matt 19:28	46, 154
Gen 48:14–18	71	1 Kings 3:9	58	Matt 22:37	11
Exod 2:15–21	100	2 Chr 13:20	54	Matt 25:45–46	141
Exod 20:5	53	2 Chr 21:18	54	Mark 5:23	71
Exod 20:5–6	54	Ezra 10:2–3	78	Mark 5:28	71
Exod 29:37	78	Job 3:3	127	Mark 5:39–42	70
Exod 30:14	62	Job 14:4	140	Mark 10:13–16	
Exod 30:29	78	Ps 8	121	69, 71–73	
Exod 32:35	54	Ps 22:10	21, 65	Luke 1:7–17	66
Exod 34:7	53	Ps 23:6	24, 55	Luke 1:15 21, 65–68, 122	
Lev 6:18	78	Ps 51	42–43	Luke 7:26	67
Num 14:3	61–62	Ps 51:5 19–20, 42–44,		Luke 12:5	4
Num 14:18	53	49, 101, 122, 127,		Luke 16:19–31	11
Num 14:29	62	139–40		Luke 18:15–17	69–70
Num 14:31	61–62	Isa 7:15	62–63	John 1:12–13	25
Num 23:19	51	Isa 7:15–16	149	John 3:3	122

John 3:5   71–72, 97
John 3:16   26
John 3:36   4, 47
John 16:21   70
Acts 2   67, 76
Acts 2:38   26
Acts 2:39   76
Acts 10:28   103
Acts 11:17   71
Rom 1   6, 137
Rom 1:16   12
Rom 1:18–32   48, 59
Rom 1:18–3:20   47
Rom 2:5–6   141
Rom 3:10–18   40
Rom 3:23   111
Rom 3:24–25   18
Rom 4:11   123
Rom 4:25   159
Rom 5
      4, 18, 32–33, 58–59,
            140, 149–51
Rom 5:8   11
Rom 5:12
      15–17, 21, 33–36, 109,
                   111, 149
Rom 5:12–14   36, 139
Rom 5:12–19   35,
            38–39, 101, 148
Rom 5:12–21
                   31–34, 146
Rom 5:14   114, 119
Rom 5:15–19   37
Rom 7:7–25   107
Rom 8:18–25   36
Rom 8:19–23   154, 156
Rom 9:10–29   107
Rom 9:11   114, 140
Rom 10:9–10   26
Rom 10:9–13   159
Rom 10:13   11
Rom 10:17   123
Rom 11:16   77
Rom 14:12   159

1 Cor 1:18   12
1 Cor 1:30   77
1 Cor 3:16–17   78
1 Cor 6:9–10   6, 48
1 Cor 6:11   77
1 Cor 6:16   78
1 Cor 6:19   78
1 Cor 7:1–11   74
1 Cor 7:10–11   79
1 Cor 7:14
            24, 74–79, 127
1 Cor 15   58
1 Cor 15:1–4   4
1 Cor 15:20–28   146
1 Cor 15:22   122, 127
2 Cor 3:18   141
2 Cor 5:21   11
Eph 2:1–3   47
Eph 2:3
      19–20, 42, 44–49, 122,
            127, 139–40, 143
Eph 2:8–10   11
1 Tim 2:5–6   4
1 Tim 6   41
Titus 3:4–5   11
Heb 9:27   11
Heb 11:7   24
1 Peter 2:24   11
1 Peter 3:15   78
1 John 3:2   141
Rev 20:11–13   11
Rev 21:5   154